EUROPEAN FOREIGN POLICY

European
Foreign Policy

SIMON J. NUTTALL

OXFORD

UNIVERSITY PRESS

OXFORD

UNIVERSITY PRESS

Great Clarendon Street, Oxford OX2 6DP

Oxford University Press is a department of the University of Oxford.
It furthers the University's objective of excellence in research, scholarship,
and education by publishing worldwide in

Oxford New York

Athens Auckland Bangkok Bogotá Buenos Aires Cape Town
Chennai Dar es Salaam Delhi Florence Hong Kong Istanbul Karachi
Kolkata Kuala Lumpur Madrid Melbourne Mexico City Mumbai Nairobi
Paris São Paulo Shanghai Singapore Taipei Tokyo Toronto Warsaw

with associated companies in Berlin Ibadan

Published in the United States
by Oxford University Press Inc., New York

British Library Cataloguing in Publication Data

Data available

Library of Congress Cataloging in Publication Data

Data available

ISBN 0–19–829336–4

3 5 7 9 10 8 6 4 2

Typeset by Best-set Typesetter Ltd., Hong Kong
Printed in Great Britain
on acid-free paper by
Biddles Ltd
Guildford and King's Lynn

Dedicated to
the students at the College of Europe, Promotion Ramon Llull
especially
Alex, David, Lie, Thomas, and Valerie

ACKNOWLEDGEMENTS

The author is grateful to the many friends who encouraged him in the writing of this book, and to the Centre for International Studies at the London School of Economics and Political Science, which provided hospitality for two crucial years during its gestation.

CONTENTS

LIST OF ABBREVIATIONS

ANC	African National Congress
ASEAN	Association of South-East Asian Nations
BiH	Bosnia and Herzegovina
CEECs	Central and Eastern European countries
CFE	Conventional Armed Forces in Europe
CFSP	common foreign and security policy
CINCSOUTH	Allied Forces in Southern Europe
CIS	Commonwealth of Independent States
CMEA	Council for Mutual Economic Assistance
Comecon	Council for Mutual Economic Assistance
Coreper	Committee of Permanent Representatives
COSAC	Conférence des organes spécialisés des Assemblées de la Communauté
CPSU	Communist Party of the Soviet Union
CSCE	Conference on Security and Co-operation in Europe
DG	Directorate General
EBRD	European Bank for Reconstruction and Development
EC	European Community
ECMM	European Community Monitoring Mission
Ecofin	Council of the Union (Economy and Finance)
ECOMSA	European Community Observer Mission to South Africa
EFTA	European Free Trade Association
EIB	European Investment Bank
EMU	European Monetary Union
EPC	European Political Co-operation
ERTA	European Road Transport Agreement
ESDI	European Security and Defence Identity
Euratom	European Atomic Energy Community
G7	Group of Seven (Canada, France, Germany, Italy, Japan, UK, US)
IGC	Intergovernmental Conference
IISS	International Institute for Strategic Studies
JNA	Yugoslav People's Army
KEDO	Korean Peninsula Energy Development Organization
MOU	Memorandum of Understanding

NAC	North Atlantic Council
NATO	North Atlantic Treaty Organization
NGO	non-governmental organization
OECD	Organization for Economic Co-operation and Development
PECO	Pays de l'Europe centrale et orientale
PVDALA	Pays en voie de développement de l'Amérique latine et d'Asie
PVD-NA	Pays en voie de développement non-associés
RPR	Rassemblement pour la République
SEA	Single European Act
SHAPE	Supreme Headquarters Allied Powers in Europe
TEMPUS	Trans-European Mobility Scheme for University Studies
TEU	Treaty on European Union
TFGU	Task Force for German Unification
UDF	Union des Français
UN	United Nations
UNHCR	United Nations High Commissioner for Refugees
UNPROFOR	United Nations Protection Force
WEU	Western European Union

1

Argument

Die Geschichte darf man nicht vergessen. Denn wer die Geschichte nicht kennt, kann die Gegenwart nicht begreifen und die Zukunft nicht gestalten.

(Helmut Kohl)[1]

It is the duty of an historian to paint a picture of the past in order to make it comprehensible. To do this, it is necessary to be selective. Facts must be chosen and presented in such a way as to pick out a pattern which enables the reader to retain an image of events. The picture is inevitably partial and personal. Other pictures, other images, could be presented with equal conviction and truth.

The purpose of this book is, by following this rule, to paint a picture of recent events surrounding the development of the common foreign and security policy of the European Union.[2] It starts with the situation after the entry into force of the Single European Act in 1987, continues through the upheaval of the fall of the Communist régimes in 1989–90, describes the negotiation and adoption of the Maastricht Treaty, and ends with attempts to implement the new foreign policy provisions in the year following the entry into force of the Treaty on 1 November 1993. The focus is not on the Union's foreign policy, but on the forces which brought that policy into being, and indeed prevented it from being other than what it was. This approach leads to emphases which may well be considered off-balance. For example, the Gulf War and the conflict in Yugoslavia are dealt with, not as the great international crises they were, but in so far as they

[1] 'History should never be forgotten, for ignorance of history makes it impossible to understand the present or shape the future'. From the record of a conversation between Bush and Kohl: *Deutsche Einheit*, no. 353, 1354.

[2] The current denomination 'European Union' will be used throughout the book, unless the context requires otherwise. Furthermore, the author is well aware of, and shares, the view that EU foreign policy is about more than the narrow focus of the CFSP. However, like it or not the fact is that EU foreign policy as a whole is constructed through two different processes. The pretensions of this book are limited to explaining the origins of one of them.

did or did not influence the development of the Union's foreign and security policy. Again, the concentration on the details of procedure will seem excessive to some. Yet the details were significant enough for the negotiators of the Treaty to spend many hours in debate over them, and they affected the outcome. To explain why that should have been so, and to place the debate in a wider political context, are the aims of this book.

At the time the Single European Act came into force in 1987, the Member States of the European Community had been co-ordinating their foreign policies for seventeen years. This was the process known as European Political Co-operation (EPC). It enabled them, big and small, to exercise collectively more influence than any would have been able to separately. The policies and positions it produced were rarely if ever bold and exciting, but they provided a reasonable middle way which many other countries found it convenient to follow. On the whole, the product was less interesting than the procedure. EPC worked through an intensive network of meetings, contacts, and relationships. The EPC establishment was an élite, all of whose members knew each other well. For the first time, foreign ministry officials felt that they were part of the European Community adventure, with toys of their own to play with. There was an EPC culture and sense of solidarity which only worked so long as decisions were restricted to the charmed circle, with interference neither from the EC Institutions nor from other ministries at home. This, in that now vanished age of diplomacy, was most of the time.

And yet, for many participants, the co-ordination of national policies through the assemblage of a corpus of positions held in common was not enough. They wanted action, deeds instead of words; in other words, a common foreign and security policy. The movement to create a single market, which culminated in the Single European Act, was ably exploited by those who wished to bring EPC and the Community closer together. The Single Act was not originally designed to deal with foreign policy questions, but it ended up devoting a whole section to them (Title III). The substance of foreign-policy making was not significantly changed, but the fact that EPC and EC procedures were handled in a single legal instrument was considered to be an important step towards bringing the two together. In fact it inaugurated the 'pillars' structure which was consecrated in the Maastricht Treaty.

The co-existence of the two pillars gave rise to the problem which came to be known as 'consistency'. For the previous decade EPC had increasingly had recourse to EC instruments in order to further its policies. This raised the question of the procedure to be followed in such cases. Was the 'political' wing of the Community to determine—by consensus, and with no proposal from the Commission—the policies to follow, which would then be implemented by the 'technical' wing? Or were EC decisions to be taken by EC procedures, involving a Commission proposal and, as like as not, qualified majority voting? In other words, who was in charge? The Single Act put the question, but did not answer it.

A pragmatic answer might have been worked out through experience, but time was lacking. The collapse of the Communist system in Central and Eastern Europe, which began the year after the Single Act came into force, caused new questions to be asked about the future shape of Europe and the role the European Community could be expected to play. These issues went well beyond the closed circle of EPC, and called into question the basis on which EPC had been built.

The origins of the collapse must be sought as far back as the 'new thinking' inaugurated by Gorbachev on his appointment as General Secretary in 1985. This included recognition of the existence of universal human values, including freedom of choice. Only gradually did it become apparent that this included freedom for the Soviet Union's satellites to choose the system of government they preferred. The Western foreign policy establishment was slow to catch on to the significance of what was going on. It was difficult for them to transcend the attitudes which had been shaped by decades of the Cold War. They temporized by adopting a policy of 'wait and see'.

EPC followed the same approach, not only because it reflected the views of a majority of Member States but also because it was structurally incapable of being innovative. Its attitude towards the Soviet Union had been defined as recently as December 1987, after long and difficult negotiations to reconcile fundamentally conflicting points of view. It was not going to resume this exercise so soon, even though the emergence throughout 1988 of genuinely democratic forms of government, especially in Poland and Hungary, might have been thought reason enough to review the position. EPC suffered from the absence of an objective mechanism for bringing issues forward for discussion.

Another reason for EPC's relative quiescence was that some work was going on, but in the EC framework. Agreement between the Community and Comecon was reached in June 1988, and negotiations for trade and co-operation agreements with Comecon members were put in hand. This was the business of the Community; EPC was not interested and did not interfere. The Community was beginning to respond to events in the East, but it did so through its economic, not its political, branch.

By the middle of 1989, as freedom of movement was established and the move towards democratic government began to take hold, the 'acceleration of history' could no longer be ignored, and the contest to define a 'new European architecture' began. The discussion was launched by Gorbachev, who promoted his idea of a 'common European home'. This was a call for pan-European institutions, which would replace the structure of rival military blocs. The Soviet Union's preference was ultimately revealed as being for a transformed CSCE. Was there a role in this for the European Community? Not, in the view of many at the time, if this meant precipitate enlargement of the EC. The Community had to be deepened before it could be widened.

The debate in Western Europe on the different forms which the structure of the new Europe might take was intensive and took a high political profile. For that very reason, it tended to be conducted separately by Heads of Government, not collectively by their Foreign Ministers. The 'new European architecture' was essentially about security in the broadest sense, and might therefore have been expected to be debated in EPC. That it was not was because of the personal involvement of Heads of Government and their staffs, less conditioned by personal experience than the Foreign Ministers and their officials to thinking in EPC terms. Nor was the wider EC forum used for the debate, for two reasons: the Americans decided that they had to be closely involved in the discussions, which would have been difficult had they taken place in the EC; and the reunification of Germany took place in conditions which precluded the EC as a forum. And it was the outcome of the debate on the unification of Germany which determined for the time being the future shape of Europe.

The decisive initiative for a common foreign and security policy for the European Union emanated from two men: Mitterrand and Kohl. But it seemed to be almost a by-product of their drive towards a wider objective: political union to set alongside the economic and monetary union of Western Europe. Mitterrand himself recognized at an early stage that German unification was inevitable, if undesirable, but hesitated long before opting for the strategy of 'embedding' united Germany even more tightly in a political and economic union, in order to minimize the risk of a stronger Germany taking an independent line as a Central European power—the nightmare of the French political élite throughout the life of the European Community. Kohl, who saw himself as the political heir of Adenauer and thus committed to reassuring Germany's partners through unflinching support for the Community, was also keenly aware of the need to keep in front of his domestic adversaries—whether or not they were partners in the ruling coalition. But in order to make economic and monetary union more palatable to German public opinion—which in this case could practically be reduced to the Bundesbank—he put forward as a requirement the parallel achievement of political union. At the same time, the prospects for unification which were opening up made both economic and political union indispensable for Kohl if he was to persuade his allies and neighbours to acquiesce. In this context, political union meant essentially strengthening the powers of the European Parliament. The idea of a common foreign and security policy was mysteriously included at a late stage of the Franco-German discussions which led to the joint launch by Kohl and Mitterrand in April 1990 of the initiative to add political union to the agenda of the Intergovernmental Conference which was to be called on economic and monetary union.

The Americans took a keen interest in the discussion on the new European architecture as it developed in Western Europe. Indeed, they appeared to be in advance of the Europeans in their reflections on this subject. In a series of speeches made in the spring and summer of 1989, the newly elected President Bush set out the US position. This was resumed at the end of the year in a speech made by Secretary Baker in Berlin. In essence, the new Europe of free nations would rely on the triple structure of NATO, the EC, and the CSCE, each refurbished to suit it to the new situation. But the important point was that the US would have its say in each of these three organizations. In NATO and the CSCE, it would participate as of right; in the EC, its voice would be heard through strengthened links—'it makes sense for us to fashion our responses together as a matter of common course'.

The European Community as such was strangely absent from these deliberations. It did of course pronounce itself on numerous occasions on the developments in Europe, and its role as co-ordinator of Western aid to the CEECs and negotiator of a series of path-breaking agreements with them should not be neglected. But it was not the forum chosen by the Member States to reach a common position on events, still less the place where decisions about the future shape of Europe were taken. In the words of Jacques Delors, the Community was a subject of history, not an actor. It was an important building block in the new structure which was being created, but it was not itself the architect.

The main reason for this, as has already been suggested, was that the shape of Europe was determined by the outcome of the negotiations on the unification of Germany, and those negotiations, in order to succeed, had to be conducted among an extremely small number of interested parties. In particular, it was in the Federal Republic's interest to keep as low as possible the number of countries which had to be squared through political or even cash payments. That reduced the number of players to six—the two Germanies and the four Allied powers (the United States, the Soviet Union, the United Kingdom, and France) who were guarantors of the post-war régime. These six formed the so-called Two Plus Four, the formula invented in the State Department for the conduct of the negotiations. No more than the West Germans did the Americans want the CSCE, still less the EC, to be involved. The other EC members did not like this, but they had no choice. 'You are not part of the game,' said Genscher to Italian Foreign Minister De Michelis. The Community was excluded from this crucial phase of the discussions on the new European architecture because Kohl wanted it that way.

The Community was nevertheless an important part of the new settlement. Its co-ordination of international assistance to first Poland and Hungary, then the rest of the Central and East European countries (through the G24); its conclusion of agreements with those countries, giving expression to their wish to be linked once again with their Western neighbours; and its smooth absorption of the new German *Länder*, all contributed to this. What was significant for the future development of EU foreign policy was that all these activities were carried out in the EC framework. EPC was barely involved. This was the result, not of political choice, but of a combination of circumstance, neat diplomatic footwork, and institutional responsibility.

The Western Economic Summit at the Arche in July 1989 entrusted the European Commission with the task of co-ordinating international assistance to Poland and Hungary. This was surprising; the EC Council had not been informed, let alone consulted. What had happened was that President Bush was under pressure to provide concrete assistance to the countries casting off their Communist régimes, but was having difficulty in finding the money. He therefore looked to the Europeans for help. Kohl suggested that the Summit should set up a mechanism to co-ordinate aid, and Delors was quick to seize the opportunity of securing this task for the Commission. For the first time the Community, represented by the Commission, found itself in the driver's seat for the hottest international issue of the day. Nor was the co-ordination operation a purely technical one. The Commission found itself called upon to play a leading part in deciding some sensitive political issues, particularly regarding the application of the principle of conditionality. It was important to know at what point a potential beneficiary should be admitted to the aid programme, and this was in effect decided by the Commission on the basis of the evaluation missions it carried out in the countries concerned. The Member States were consulted, but not in the EPC framework.

At the same time, the Community was engaged in negotiating a series of agreements with the CEECs. At first these were normal non-preferential trade and co-operation agreements. They were not in principle subject to conditionality rules, but a degree of *de facto* conditionality was inevitably introduced through the rhythm of negotiation and the precise type of agreement offered. The Commission's institutional position as EC negotiator gave it a good deal of leeway here. The same applied to the second-generation agreements, which took the form of association agreements, with conditionality as well as a political dialogue (now for the first time involving EPC) formally incorporated.

The Community had not been allowed to take part in the negotiations on German unification, but its assistance was called for to enable the new *Länder* to be integrated into the EC. Arrangements had to be made almost overnight to accommodate the situation in East Germany to the economic and regulatory régime of the Community. This involved work on an impressive mass of technical detail, which had to be carried out to deadlines which were progressively shortened as the date of unification was advanced. The nature of the work was such that it could only be done by the Commission; the deadlines were such that the job could only be completed on time by an alliance between Commission and Parliament to cut through procedure. The successful achievement of this task earned Commission and Parliament the respect and gratitude of Germany and showed that the Community was capable of handling successfully a task with sensitive political overtones.

The three contributions the Community made to the new structure of Europe all came from the EC side. The Commission found itself, mainly by virtue of its institutional position, carrying out sensitive foreign policy functions but in accordance with normal EC procedures, and that on the headline topic of the day. This was thought by some, and feared by others, to be the model for the future. It explains why attempts were confidently made in the Intergovernmental Conference debate leading to the Maastricht Treaty to introduce a form of foreign-policy making on EC lines which the experience of nearly two decades of EPC might have been thought to condemn to failure in advance.

The European Council at Strasbourg in December 1989 agreed that an Intergovernmental Conference (IGC) on economic and monetary union should be convened before the end of the following year. The question of whether this should be extended to cover political union as well now became of immediate interest. The European Parliament had given its support for the idea the previous November, but it was not until March that it called for political union to include common foreign and security policies achieved through the full integration of EPC into the Community framework. This was followed by a memorandum from the Belgian government proposing a different methodological approach; the Belgian idea was to avoid for the time being a formal review of the Single Act, and instead build on the practical experience that EPC and the EC had gained in working together to deal with Central and Eastern Europe. If a comprehensive framework could be produced covering all aspects of the question, in which all the Member States had important interests in common, then the circumstances might be more propitious for amending rules which were rapidly becoming out of date.

In the event, neither the Belgian initiative nor that of the European Parliament determined the course of discussion. Instead, President Mitterrand and Chancellor Kohl, for the domestic reasons which have been explained above, put their names the following month to a joint letter which confined itself to calling for an IGC on political union, to include a common foreign and security policy (CFSP). Further details were deliberately avoided, to discourage the sort of niggling discussion which would have sabotaged the initiative from the start. In fact, the CFSP was a late addition to the concept of political union, which at the beginning was mainly about increasing the powers of the European Parliament. The drafters of the letter may have been influenced by the moves made by Belgium and the Parliament.

The Franco-German approach was nevertheless totally different from the Belgian one. Whereas the Belgians had called for a pragmatic, incremental approach limited to one area and avoiding the philosophical debate which would inevitably result from an attempt to amend legal texts, Mitterrand and Kohl advanced a global vision of a new brand of foreign policy, to be included in the Treaty negotiations. They prevailed because the pragmatic, almost bureaucratic, approach was in the circumstances politically unattractive; it did not tally with the political rhetoric of the day. The problem was that neither the Germans nor the French had very clear ideas on what a common foreign and security policy might look like. Their silence on that subject until the end of the year puzzled their partners and allowed free rein for all sorts of competing and not necessarily coherent ideas to be put on the table. The result was that by the end of 1990 there was a shopping-list of procedural reforms on which the

Member States more or less agreed, but the individual proposals reflected the different Member States' philosophical ideas about how the European Community should look, rather than forming an interlocking body of measures to produce an effective foreign-policy making structure.

Until Saddam Hussein invaded Kuwait in August 1990 little attention had been paid to the security dimension of European foreign-policy making. The Community's experiences before and during the Gulf War changed all that. The CFSP took on greater prominence in the IGC agenda, and within the CFSP debate was concentrated on the security and defence aspects. By the time the IGC formally convened, at the beginning of 1991, there were only two major issues concerning foreign-policy making which remained to be resolved: security and defence, and whether or not EPC should be incorporated into the Community. The risk, as it seemed at one time, that the Community might move towards setting up an independent defence capability aroused the interest of the Americans, who effectively intervened to prevent it.

The effect of the Gulf War was to convince many of those involved in the IGC that the Community's ambition to count for something in the world could not be achieved as long as it did not have the means of projecting power. Previous experience in Central and Eastern Europe had pointed in a different direction. There, it seemed that the Community's strength lay in being a civilian power, and the same approach was followed in the early months of the Gulf crisis. But the imposition of economic sanctions and economic aid to the front-line states soon proved to be an inadequate response, and Community solidarity began to crumble as different approaches to the recovery of hostages appeared and the Member States could no longer agree on diplomatic moves to fend off conflict. When the fighting began, the Community was powerless; Member States had to take individual decisions about participation.

The fighting coincided with the stage in the IGC at which the crucial first drafts of the Maastricht Treaty were being discussed. Member States drew different conclusions from their experiences. The British had had a good war, and were pleased to be able to recover their position as the Americans' best friend in Europe, which they had ceded to the Germans under the pressures of unification. They were strong allies of the Americans in arguing in the IGC against any moves which would have undermined NATO. The Germans, inhibited by their interpretation of the Federal Constitution from taking part in the fighting but looking for ways of overcoming this handicap, kept a low profile and supported the French when it was safe to do so. The French learnt that they were equipped to fight the wrong wars, and disagreeably dependent on the Americans for fighting the right ones. They therefore turned to the WEU, which had shown itself to be effective in surveillance operations in the Persian Gulf and the Red Sea, as the potential security and defence arm of the Community. The Gulf War had put security and defence at the top of the CFSP agenda; the positions of these three Member States, behind which the others more or less lined up depending on their national preferences, ensured that the outcome of the debate was inconclusive.

Apart from security and defence, the main question which remained open until the end of the IGC was the relationship between the CFSP and the EC, and the extent to which the CFSP should be subsumed into EC procedures. The Commission, the Benelux countries, Germany, and Italy were in favour of going quite far down this road; France, the United Kingdom, Denmark, Greece, and Portugal were not. The argument was not about what a common foreign and security policy ought to be, and how it could be made effective, but about the extent to which Member States were prepared to make further transfers of sovereignty to the Union. This was a domestic issue, not a foreign policy one. The draft produced by the Luxembourg Presidency in April 1991 was on French lines, not out of conviction but because the Luxemburgers reasoned that, where consensus was the rule, it was better to be politically realistic. The debate resolved itself into one between a 'pillar' structure, in which the three facets of the Union—the old Community, the CFSP, and justice and home affairs— retained their separate identities and procedures, and the 'tree' structure, in which they did not. It came to a head at the Foreign Ministers' meeting at Dresden in June, at which the Member States remained divided on the issue. The Presidency proposed as a compromise formula a single institutional framework to cover all three pillars, and held out the prospect of subsequent evolution.

No decision was reached at the Luxembourg European Council at the end of June, and the torch passed to the incoming Netherlands Presidency. The Dutch were encouraged by the line-up of Member States at Dresden to believe that a political forcing might produce a more integrationist result than the Luxembourg Presidency had thought possible, and set about producing a new draft. But when this was made available in September, it became clear that it did not even command enough support to be an alternative basis of discussion. The Dutch were particularly aggrieved that Germany had withdrawn its support at the last minute, presumably under pressure from France. The CFSP was simply not a sufficiently important part of the IGC for it to become a make-or-break issue.

The effect of the failure of the Dutch paper was that the CFSP 'Pillar II' had to be finalized with very little time left. The Luxembourg paper was therefore taken up again as it stood, without any further attempts to impart a rational structure in foreign policy terms. The three-pillar structure and the single institutional framework were agreed, and the procedural reforms were adopted more or less as they had stood a year earlier. There remained the question of qualified majority voting, on which the integrationists were fighting a rearguard action, and the area of security and defence. Both issues were settled by forms of words which imperfectly concealed the failure to agree on substance. The possibility of majority voting was included in the Treaty, but in conditions which effectively prevented its use, and, with the assistance of the NATO Summit at Rome at the beginning of November, which recognized the European vocation to a security and defence identity, agreement was reached on a formula which, while sweeping away the remaining taboos on the discussion of security issues, did nothing to answer the question of whether the Union should rely on NATO for its defence dimension or whether it should have an independent capacity of its own.

The CFSP provisions of the Maastricht Treaty were sedimentary, in the sense that they were all that was left when everything else had been washed away by the objections of one or the other Member State. This made them difficult to understand, and even more difficult to present to public opinion in the ratification process. They played, however, only a minor part in increasing the climate of disaffection in which the Community increasingly found itself, and which almost caused the Treaty not to be ratified. The first referendum in Denmark was negative, that which followed in France was positive by a whisker; the ruling of the German Constitutional Court went in a direction contrary to that country's traditional support for the integrationist approach. Only in Denmark were the CFSP provisions a significant factor, and even there they were not the only one. Throughout the Community, however, the failure of the foreign policy machinery to deliver policy successes to attract the attention of the public contributed to the general disenchantment. The Community's failure to prevent civil war in former Yugoslavia was particularly damaging.

The outbreak of the conflict in Yugoslavia in June 1991 did not have the direct impact on the discussions leading to the Maastricht Treaty which the invasion of Kuwait and the Gulf War had had in the previous year. By the time fighting broke out, negotiations in the IGC were too far advanced for positions to change. Indeed, the reverse was the case: the IGC prevented the Community from taking the type of action over Yugoslavia which might have been effective. To begin with, the Community reacted imaginatively. The diplomatic efforts of the Troika resulting in the Brioni Agreement marked the first time that EPC had engaged in representative, as opposed to collective, diplomacy, and the deployment of the EC Monitoring Mission in support of it was also a first. The theory has been put forward that these activities were only undertaken to distract attention from the Luxembourg European Council's failure to come to an agreement on the Treaty, and to demonstrate that a common foreign and security policy was a realistic possibility. The reality is likely to have been more complex: the European Council's action can best be seen as the logical continuation of policies pursued previously, triggered by an Italian move to defend its national interests, especially in Slovenia.

As the situation worsened, however, and successive cease-fires lasted only a matter of days or even hours, the view gained ground that armed intervention was required in order to halt the slide to chaos. On two occasions in the summer and autumn of 1991 France proposed the deployment of armed forces in support of the Monitoring Mission. Faithful to the approach they were then vigorously defending in the IGC, the French suggested making use of the WEU for the purpose. By doing so, they wished to make a point in the IGC debate; for the same reason, the United Kingdom was bitterly opposed. The British had other reasons for opposing armed intervention, but the intransigence of their stand can be explained by their determination not to give ground in the IGC. The upshot was that the route of armed intervention was closed to the Community.

The Community nevertheless came through the first few months of the Yugoslav crisis with its credit more or less intact. It was to suffer severe damage, however, as a result of the highly publicized quarrel between Germany and the majority of the Member States over the recognition of Slovenia and Croatia. The majority wished to keep recognition in their pockets for use at the appropriate moment in the diplomatic negotiations; the Germans, under very heavy pressure from public opinion, were in favour of immediate recognition. It is sometimes argued that there was a deal at the Maastricht European Council: Germany made concessions in the final negotiations, and the others, especially France and the United Kingdom, gave in on recognition. This seems not to have been the case. The deal had been made earlier, between Mitterrand and Kohl, and it was to put the question of recognition to one side until the Maastricht Treaty was safely in the bag. After Maastricht, Germany was able to trade on its partners' fears of being seen to split so soon after the CFSP had been agreed.

The Community's handling of the conflict in Yugoslavia did not tip the balance against the Maastricht Treaty in the ratification debate. Indeed, it was used as an argument on both sides of the case, some saying that it showed that EPC needed strengthening, while others maintained that there was no hope of an effective CFSP. But it did contribute to the general lack of confidence in the new Union. As a German politician said: 'How can I tell people at home we should abandon the D-mark for a currency union, when Europe is not in a position to stop a war?'

The new lack of confidence in the Union inevitably had an effect on the implementation of the CFSP. On the defence and security side, the new sector opened up by the Maastricht Treaty, the WEU, far from becoming the defence arm of the Union, strengthened its relationship with NATO, and the proliferation of categories of WEU membership to include countries outside the EU made the link with the Union more difficult to achieve. The new forms of action at the disposal of the Union, common positions and joint actions, proved complicated to define and put to work, not helped by the institutional rivalries between Council and Commission and Council and Parliament. Even within the Council, there was a struggle for influence between Permanent Representatives and Political Directors, together with their respective apparatuses, with the Permanent Representatives appearing to come out on top. Not surprisingly in the circumstances, the Member States did not feel unduly bound by the intended disciplines of the CFSP, and did not hesitate to set up rival fora like the Contact Group on Former Yugoslavia when it suited their book. This was resented by those who felt they were being excluded.

The CFSP has disappointed expectations because it has never had a clearly defined objective and purpose, agreed to by consensus. But contrary to the popular view, it is more than a grandiose version of the intergovernmental EPC. There has been a sea-change in the ambience, which has been gradually moving towards the EC side of the Union. Only time will tell whether bureaucratic, incremental change will succeed in transforming EU foreign-policy making where the direct, institutional approach has hitherto failed.

2

'Consistency' and the Single Act

The Single European Act, which came into force on 1 July 1987, gave European Political Co-operation (EPC) for the first time a foundation in an instrument of international law. EPC, founded in 1970, was the name given to the informal arrangement by which the Member States of the European Community co-ordinated their national foreign policies. For the seventeen years of its existence, it had been based on nothing more than a set of understandings among the foreign ministries laying down certain collective procedures and, in a series of largely rhetorical formulas, announcing commitment to common policy-making. This was not to deny the effectiveness of the procedures within their limits: the vigour with which the Six, then the Nine (EPC was most often referred to by the number of states making up the Community at the time) presented a common position in the preparation and implementation of the Conference on Security and Co-operation in Europe (CSCE) surprised the Americans and contributed decisively to the success of the Conference. The successive positions taken over the conflict in the Middle East revealed more clearly the divisions among the Member States, but nevertheless were sufficiently cohesive for EPC to be courted by the Arabs, reviled by Israel, and the object of a muscular intervention by the United States when for a moment it seemed as though European policy in the area might threaten US interests.[1]

The two examples given show some of the advantages afforded by EPC. In the preparations for the CSCE and in their subsequent participation in it, the Six, later Nine, were able to exercise collective influence beyond the capabilities of any one of them acting separately. For some of them, it was a means of projecting national positions which might otherwise have had little resonance. In the Middle East, however inadequate their policies might seem to themselves as well as to others, the Nine could not be ignored as an actor on the international political stage. Left to themselves, they might have produced policies which inconvenienced the other

---

[1] For the history of EPC see Nuttall, *European Political Co-operation.*

actors—the Arabs, the Israelis, and the Americans. And so they were not left to themselves—attempts were made to influence them, both collectively and as individual participants in EPC. As a result, the way diplomacy was habitually conducted had to be modified. This was not all: some participants proffered their international obligation to achieve convergent polices as cover for effecting a change in national policy which otherwise might have met with too much domestic opposition. Furthermore, other countries sometimes found it convenient to wait until EPC had taken a view before committing themselves. The way EPC procedures worked habitually led to uncontroversial, middle-of-the-road positions. To take them as a model might not be exciting, but at least it was safe.

EPC began with the CSCE and the Middle East, but its activities soon came to extend to other regions, such as Asia and Latin America, and later to topics like non-proliferation. Its ambitions were global, the only exception being security questions, and even then co-operation on issues like non-proliferation, just mentioned, and participation in the UN Disarmament Committee showed that some exceptions to the exception were allowed. EPC's global ambition was the reason why what was seen as an attempt by Secretary Kissinger to confine the Europeans to a regional role during the 'Year of Europe' in 1973 was strongly resented.

Although EPC produced policies of greater or lesser success and resonance on any subject under the sun, for many participants the value of EPC was less in this than in the process itself. The system worked through a network of ever more frequent meetings at all levels from the Heads of State and Government, through Ministers and Political Directors right down to the working desk level in the Foreign Ministry Departments. All these people were also able to communicate with each other at their different levels, if need be on a daily basis, through the Coreu network of cypher telex communications, frequently supplemented, in defiance of all security regulations, by the telephone. There grew up an EPC community of Foreign Ministry officials, confined to those who took part in the process, but who nevertheless were frequently the officials with a decisive influence on the formation of national policy. Their views were inevitably conditioned by the contacts they had with their European colleagues, sometimes closer than with colleagues in other ministries at home. The evolution over time of an EPC policy community gave rise to a distinctive EPC culture, which, in different ways, became part of the national foreign policy ethos. There are striking examples of occasions when national policies failed to converge with EPC policies; examples of convergence are less easy to document, but are significant and real.

The active participation in the EPC process of national officials from Foreign Ministries, and of them alone, was the distinguishing feature, and the great advantage, of European Political Co-operation. It derived from the historical origins of EPC. Designed to give a political dimension to the European Community at a time of uncertainty about where the *Ostpolitik* was leading Germany, and Europe with her, it could only be established on French terms. This meant that the arrangements for foreign policy co-ordination set up at the time of the Fouchet negotiations[2] were revived and transmuted into a new order under the Luxembourg Report. General de Gaulle had wanted foreign policy co-ordination to be serviced by a secretariat based in Paris; this proved to be unacceptable to the other members of the EC, so the system was run by the Political Directors (senior policy officials in the Foreign Ministries) themselves. This was important because the Political Directors, unlike the Permanent Representatives in Brussels, were not diplomats 'sent to lie abroad for their countries' but officials in the home ministry with direct responsibility for the conception and implementation of policy.

Add to the do-it-yourself feature of EPC the iron rule of consensus, another part of the Gaullist inheritance, and the barring of supranational officials from any significant part in the process, and it is not difficult to see why EPC was so popular with diplomats. It gave them a European shop of their own to run, and it did so in a way which both enhanced national influence in international affairs and yet could be represented as maintaining national sovereignty intact. As a bonus, the Foreign Ministry officials were able to recover ground lost to colleagues from other ministries who had, in spite of the Foreign Ministry's co-ordinating role, inevitably been more closely involved than they in the frequently technical transactions of the European Community. The drawback was that the magic of EPC did not work outside the charmed circle; one had to participate to fall under its spell. But this was a minor inconvenience at a time when there was by and large a national and indeed European and Western consensus on foreign policy issues, by favour of the Cold War. Foreign policy decisions were rarely taken outside the magic circle anyway.

And yet, Political Co-operation failed to satisfy. It was not just that it had its ups and downs. The latter half of the 1970s was a noted down, culminating in the bungled responses to the seizing of US hostages in

---

[2] Nuttall, *European Political Co-operation*, 39–40; Cattani, 'Essai de coopération politique entre les Six'.

Tehran and the Soviet invasion of Afghanistan, but the new resolve symbolized by the London Report of October 1981 and successful actions thereafter, beginning with the response to the Argentinian occupation of the Falkland Islands, seemed to point the way to the recovery of the system. It was rather that too many people were not content with a cosy process moving at its own pace. In the place of declaratory diplomacy, they wanted action; rather than reacting to events, they wanted to take the initiative. In other words, they wanted, not the co-ordination of national policies, but a Common Foreign and Security Policy.

The Single European Act (SEA) was not designed to provide such a policy. Indeed, it was not originally designed to deal with foreign policy questions at all. The original purpose of the SEA had been to make such changes in the Treaty of Rome setting up the European Economic Community as were necessary in order to make the Single Market a reality. Inevitably the opportunity was taken to make other changes in the Treaty of Rome, but these did not at first include anything to do with foreign policy. Title III of the SEA, containing 'Treaty provisions on European co-operation in the sphere of foreign policy', was included, if not quite by accident, then by a concatenation of circumstances ably exploited by those who wished to bring the procedures of EPC more closely into the EC fold.

The first step was taken by the Netherlands, which in May 1985 proposed that a protocol should be added to the revised EEC Treaty consolidating and institutionalizing political co-operation.[3] To counter this move, the United Kingdom circulated a separate draft agreement on Political Co-operation which had the form of a treaty but not its title. Unlike in other countries, such an instrument would not have had to be ratified by the United Kingdom Parliament. The United Kingdom was not opposed to improving EPC procedures—indeed it had played an important part in making the system more efficient following the Afghanistan débâcle—but it did not want to be involved in a Treaty revision for this purpose, or for the time being any other. France and Germany, on the other hand, trumped the British card by presenting, a few days before the Milan European Council in June 1985 which was to decide on the calling of an Intergovernmental Conference to revise the Treaty, a document boldly entitled 'Draft Treaty on European Union'.

The institutional approach of the French and the Germans did not differ from that of the British, since EPC was to operate alongside the EC rather than be incorporated in it, but the tabling of the document was a striking

---

[3] On the foreign policy aspects of the SEA see especially Nuttall, *European Political Co-operation*, 244–59, and De Ruyt, *L'Acte unique européen*, 219–51.

gesture which gave its authors the initiative at the European Council. The Heads of State and Government decided, against opposition from the United Kingdom, Denmark, and Greece, to call a conference 'to work out with a view to achieving concrete progress on European Union: (i) a Treaty on a common foreign and security policy on the basis of the Franco-German and United Kingdom drafts' and (ii) amendments to the Rome Treaty to bring about the Single Market and to extend the Community's activities to other areas. The General Affairs Council, which had been asked to put the European Council's decision into legal form, took the opportunity at its meeting the following month to introduce a subtle change into the wording concerning the foreign policy part of the conference's mandate: the Political Committee was 'to draw up . . . the text of a draft Treaty on the basis *in particular* of the Franco-German and United Kingdom drafts concerning political co-operation *with a view to* a common foreign and security policy'.[4] The nuance thus introduced was a foretaste of the trench warfare to come between those who wished to strengthen the commitment to a common foreign policy and those who did not.

In the event, the engagement was of short duration. The requirement of unanimity in the Intergovernmental Conference meant that the Community was held back to the pace of the most reluctant member. Title III of the Act, dealing with 'European co-operation in the sphere of foreign policy', was to a large extent a rehash of existing EPC texts. Attempts were made to go further, but there was always at least one partner to block any initiative, and no incentive to make concessions except the fear of being seen to fail, which resulted in purely verbal agreement. The British were interested in more co-operation on security issues, but ran up against opposition from the Greeks and the Irish, with the result that no advance could be made on the language agreed in the Stuttgart Declaration of 1983. Foreshadowing the debate on 'flexibility' in the 1996 Intergovernmental Conference, there was even difficulty about referring to security co-operation outside the EPC framework, by which was meant NATO and the WEU.

Attempts to align the procedures of EPC more closely with those of the Community were no more successful. Belgium tried to effect a breach in the principle of consensus, on the lines of the recommendation in the Dooge Committee report[5] to 'seek a consensus in keeping with the major-

---

[4] Emphasis added.
[5] The report of the committee chaired by the Irish senator Dooge to prepare the ground for the Intergovernmental Conference.

ity opinion', but the other Member States were not prepared to go further than 'as far as possible, [to] refrain from impeding the formation of a consensus and the joint action which this could produce'—the device which later became known as 'constructive abstention'. Italy sought to merge the meetings of the General Affairs Council and the EPC Ministerial Meetings, which even if they now as often as not took place on the same day and in the same place were still formally separate, but ran up against opposition from almost all the Member States except Benelux. The SEA merely states that 'the Ministers . . . may also discuss foreign policy matters within the framework of Political Co-operation on the occasion of the meetings of the Council', something they had been entitled to do since 1974, and had in fact increasingly done. A substantive change would only have come about if the agendas of the two bodies had been merged, as occurred in practice in the early part of 1990 but not in law until the Maastricht Treaty.

In spite of these failures—or what were regarded as failures by the would-be innovators—the Single European Act marked a significant stage in the development of European Political Co-operation in its progression towards a common European foreign policy. This was not only because the obligations of the Member States to observe a certain foreign policy discipline, together with the rules and procedures by which this was to be achieved, were for the first time set out in a legal document binding (although not enforceable)[6] in international law, but also because the document in question was a single document (hence the title 'Single European Act'), in which EPC provisions featured alongside provisions for amending the Treaty of Rome. This had originally been neither the intention nor the expectation of the Member States. It will be recalled that both the European Council in Milan and the subsequent General Affairs Council which put the Intergovernmental Conference's mandate into legal form had been thinking in terms of a separate Treaty on foreign policy. The move towards a single legal instrument covering both EC and EPC questions was begun by the Commission, which in its formal opinion of 22 July 1985 stated that 'it is necessary, in the general context of transition to European Union, to make fresh progress not only on economic and social integration but also on foreign policy. Indeed, the fact that the two form an indivisible whole should be recognized by incorporating the proposed new provisions in a single framework.' The Commission pursued its reflections on the need to integrate the Community's external relations

---

[6] The jurisdiction of the International Court of Justice was excluded by the fact that the SEA had not been registered with the United Nations, and that of the European Court of Justice by the terms of the SEA itself.

and the foreign policies resulting from EPC by declaring that 'Efforts to consolidate, strengthen and widen cooperation between the Member States on common foreign and security policy . . . must draw on the experience of fifteen years of political cooperation. If there is a genuine desire to move towards European Union, it is imperative that the two areas of activity be combined . . . Realistic conditions for osmosis between economic, social, financial, and monetary affairs on the one hand and foreign policy on the other must be established. At the end of the day only unified institutions—one Council, one Parliament, one Commission—will prove effective and speed progress towards European Union.'

To illustrate the institutional approach it favoured, the Commission then tabled a paper on the structure of the texts it believed the Conference should produce—a single Act with a preamble and a short common section affirming the common goal, followed by two separate Titles, one dealing with amendments to the EEC Treaty, the other with EPC under traditional public international law. The Commission stressed that it did not propose that the intrinsic nature of EPC should be altered—there was to be no change in the principle of consensus, nor were the Community institutions to be given an enhanced role. However, the Act was to contain final provisions for an ultimate *rapprochement* between the Community and EPC. Ironically in view of the position it was later to take in the Inter-governmental Conference which led to the Maastricht Treaty, it was the Commission which proposed the 'pillar' structure which integrationists subsequently found so objectionable. In 1985 the situation was of course different: the choice then was between a system in which EPC and the EC coexisted, albeit with their separate procedures and philosophy, and one in which the two were psychologically as well as legally divorced.

The question was too delicate to be handled by the officials to whom the drafting of the foreign policy provisions of the SEA had been entrusted, and was left to the very end of the negotiations and handled at Ministerial level. The turning point came in November 1985 when France tabled a draft 'Act of European Union', based on the structure proposed by the Commission but without the final provisions for ultimate *rapproche-ment* and with a secretariat to service a revamped European Council.[7] The proposals for a strengthened European Council with its own secretariat were not accepted, but for the rest the French paper passed, and the following month the Single Act—single because it dealt with both EC and EPC in the same legal instrument—came into being.

[7] The idea of a permanent secretariat directly responsible to the Heads of State and Government was a constant of French policy across the generations.

This crucial decision determined the future structure of European foreign-policy making. It ensured that institutional reform would henceforth concentrate on ways to bring the two competing systems more closely together. Indeed, a provision was included to review Title III of the Act in five years' time,[8] the unspoken purpose being to see then how to advance *rapprochement*. The question was left open as to which of the two systems—the intergovernmental and the integrationist, which henceforward had equally valid bases in international law—was to predominate over the other.

Apart from determining its future structure, the SEA brought few changes to either the substance or the procedures of European foreign-policy making. The scope of EPC was not affected, discussion of security matters still being limited to the political and economic aspects, and the commitments into which Member States entered were not significantly different from before. In any event, they could not be enforced.[9] The Commission's full association with EPC was reaffirmed, but this had been admitted since the London Report of 1981. One innovation was the setting up of a permanent Secretariat for EPC.

This was not the powerful secretariat deriving its authority from the European Council which the French had proposed, but a low-key body reporting to the Presidency in effect at the level of Political Director. It replaced the peripatetic 'Troika' secretariat[10] which had serviced the Presidency since 1981, was composed of seconded diplomats from the five Member States of the 'enlarged' Troika, and was headed by a senior but not too senior diplomat, of a rank roughly equivalent, but certainly not superior, to that of Political Director. Unlike its predecessor, which had followed the Presidency round from one capital to the next, shifting every six months accompanied by the EPC archives, the new Secretariat was permanently established in Brussels. The conditions of its establishment gave considerable scope for subtle diplomatic manoeuvring on the part of the rival intergovernmentalist and integrationist schools of thought. The former were reconciled to the Secretariat's being permanently in Brussels (the French had convinced their partners that Gaullist ambitions to house it in Paris were a thing of the past), but there was still room for argument as to whether it should be provided with premises of its own, albeit rented from the Secretariat General of the EC Council, or should be allocated a wing of the Charlemagne Building in which

---

[8] Art. 30.12.   [9] See n. 6.

[10] One young diplomat from each of the preceding and succeeding Presidencies was seconded to the current Presidency for its duration.

most Council business was transacted. The more intergovernmentalist Member States were gently manoeuvred into accepting the Charlemagne solution—the alternative premises were singularly unattractive, being liberally provided with large plate glass windows at ground floor level, affording the passer-by unrivalled views of the workings of European foreign policy. The political aim of these manœuvres was to facilitate subsequent integration into the Council Secretariat, as indeed was done by the Maastricht Treaty.

A more serious question than office space was the problem of finance. Was the new Secretariat to be funded by the Presidency, the Member States collectively, or the Community budget? The running costs of EPC had almost without exception[11] been met by successive Presidencies. This was more convenient than sharing the costs among partners, since in many countries the Foreign Ministry was able to extract a special contribution from the Ministry of Finance for the once-in-a-blue-moon responsibility of the Presidency, but would have had to find the more modest amounts of an annual charge from existing budgetary provision. Furthermore, it avoided what would certainly have been a difficult debate about whether contributions from partners should be equal shares of the expense or calculated according to a key—and if so, what key. An obvious solution would have been to charge the running costs of the new Secretariat to the Community budget, but this ran up against objections of principle from the Member States, particularly Denmark, which were opposed to closer links with the Community. The solution finally adopted was a mixed one: the Presidency continued to meet its traditional costs, such capital costs as were involved in setting up the Secretariat were met by the Member States collectively in a one-off payment calculated using the Community budget key, and recurrent administrative costs were charged to the budget of the Secretariat General of the Council against payment of a symbolic ecu by each Presidency. The salaries of the seconded diplomats who made up the Secretariat continued to be paid by their home administrations. The solution adopted was the least troublesome of those on offer, and face was saved all round.

The solution did, however, mean that the Secretariat did not dispose of any budgetary line of its own, which would have had to be funded by contributions from the Member States, some of whom, especially Belgium, would have preferred it to have some financial autonomy. The

---

[11] The running costs of the Coreu network (the cypher telex communications system) had been met equally by all partners, including the Commission.

Commission saw danger in such a move and engaged in quiet diplomacy to counter it. It reasoned that EPC's reliance on the Community budget for implementing any policies which required expenditure was a powerful factor in bringing it closer to the Community system, and that to give the Secretariat financial autonomy, however modest the sums in question, would have acted against this trend and ultimately perpetuated the division between the two systems. The difficult discussions on financing CFSP joint actions which took place after the entry into force of the Maastricht Treaty showed that the Commission had been right in singling out the financing capability as a crucial procedural issue.

Member States had taken great care in drafting the SEA to ensure that the Secretariat had no powers of its own. It was placed under the authority of the Presidency, and could neither prepare papers on its own initiative nor represent EPC to the outside world. Nevertheless, the existence of a permanent secretariat in Brussels and the changes in practice which were associated with it began imperceptibly to have an effect on the nature of the process. The fact that the meetings of the Working Groups (although not of the Political Committee, which continued to be held for the most part in capitals) took place henceforth in Brussels, either in the meeting room on the premises of the EPC Secretariat or elsewhere in the Charlemagne Building, and no longer in the capital of the Presidency, began to bring about a subtle change of ambience. Presidencies no longer vied to impress the Working Group participants from other countries with the cultural, gastronomic, or scenic splendours of their own, and the uniform surroundings of the Charlemagne began to impart a drab and unexciting flavour to day-to-day business. For the ordinary participant, EPC was definitely less fun.

Moreover, in spite of its subordinate status, the Secretariat inevitably began to take on a more significant role than had been intended. Merely by its existence in one place and its relative continuity, the Secretariat became the 'keeper of the books', the guardian of the frequently arcane principles and procedures of EPC, a role which had formerly been played by the European Correspondents or simply by the longest-serving participant in the process. This had the effect of limiting the inventiveness of EPC. Whereas EPC had been noted for its ability to innovate in times of need, now innovation was more difficult because the Secretariat was in a position to demonstrate that the proposed new procedure was contrary to precedent.

Finally, and mainly thanks to the supreme tact and diplomacy of the first Head of the Secretariat, Ambassador Jannuzzi,[12] the Secretariat started to become a useful point of contact for those outside seeking information about the EPC position on any given subject. In particular, the Head of the Secretariat became a familiar and respected figure at the Political Committee of the European Parliament, where he was frequently able to provide information and, in effect, represent the Presidency given that the latter had no representative permanently in Brussels for EPC matters. The Secretariat was slowly moving towards a position in which the French model of a high-level secretariat for EPC no longer seemed inconceivable.

For its part, the Commission began to reorganize the way in which it managed its association with EPC, following the entry into force of the SEA.[13] This was partly coincidental, partly designed to gear the Commission up for a more active role. The Commission had previously been represented in the Political Committee by the Deputy Secretary General, whose main task was to speak for his Institution in Coreper. This kept him busy for at least three weeks out of four, which was manageable since the Political Committee met monthly. The day-to-day association of the Commission with EPC was co-ordinated by the European Corre-spondent at the head of a small Division in the Secretariat General. The duties of this unit were to attend all EPC meetings and report on the results to the Commissioners and Directorates General concerned, to make sure that Commission officials were duly made aware of EPC positions rele-vant to the policies they were conducting, and to be vigilant for opportu-nities to make EC external relations policy instruments available for the implementation of EPC policies—the practice of 'interaction', by which it was hoped to bring the two machines discreetly together.

This highly flexible arrangement, which relied on the Secretariat General's authority as co-ordinator and on the extensive personal net-works of the officials concerned, had the advantage that the Deputy Secretary General was the embodiment of 'interaction', since he was the only official to sit on both the Political Committee and Coreper. He was thus able to maximize the Commission's bridging role between EPC and the Community. On the other hand, as the volume of EPC business rapidly increased and with it the number of cases of 'interaction',[14] the need was

---

[12] Previously Deputy Political Director in the Italian Foreign Ministry.
[13] Nuttall, 'The Commission and Foreign Policy-making', 299–300; Nuttall, 'The Commission: The Struggle for Legitimacy', 143–4.
[14] For the development of 'interaction', see Nuttall, *European Political Co-operation*, Ch. 8.

felt to have a more senior official devote himself full time to EPC, and for this official to be given increased resources. A new post of Political Director was created,[15] at the level of Director, and a new Directorate was formed in the Secretariat General out of the existing Division and two other units (a small planning staff and a unit dealing with human rights). The new Directorate was able to increase output, but lost the personal link with Coreper.

Cases of 'interaction', which had for institutional reasons been the exception when EPC began, gathered momentum throughout the 1980s until they became, if not the rule, then at least a more frequent and familiar event. Economic sanctions taken against the Soviet Union by the European Community as such following the imposition of martial law in Poland provided the precedent for similar sanctions against Argentina following the invasion of the Falkland Islands, and against South Africa as pressure on the apartheid regime was stepped up. Furthermore, recourse was increasingly had to the EC's financial resources to reinforce policies adopted in EPC. Examples of this are the aid given to Central America and the positive measures in favour of the victims of apartheid.

This convergence of the EPC and EC machines gave rise to the question known as 'consistency',[16] a term of art which, like 'subsidiarity' in the Maastricht Treaty and 'reinforced co-operation' ('flexibility') in its successor, acquired overtones going well beyond its dictionary meaning.[17] It was used in EPC circles to refer to at least three different things. The first meaning was the obvious one: that EPC and the EC should not adopt policies which cut across each other, or were inconsistent with each other in the generally accepted sense of the word. This was the superficial use of the concept, and if it had been the only one the importance attached to it would have seemed incomprehensible, since actual cases of inconsistency in this sense had rarely if ever occurred. The second meaning of the term was to give expression to the practice of 'interaction': in this sense 'consistency' meant that, instead of EPC and EC policies pursuing their separate ways, they should be harnessed together in the service of an overriding purpose. This might be described as a 'benign' or 'positive' deeper layer of

[15] The first occupant of this post was Mr Günter Burghardt, President Delors' Deputy Chef de Cabinet. Although appointed in the autumn of 1987, he was not released by the President to carry out his duties full-time until spring 1988.

[16] 'Cohérence' in French.

[17] For discussions of 'consistency', see Neuwahl, 'Foreign and Security Policy'; Nuttall, 'External Political Relations'; Krenzler and Schneider, 'The Question of Consistency'; and Müller-Graff, 'Europäische Politische Zusammenarbeit'.

meaning. The third ('malign' and 'negative') layer of meaning was about power and responsibility. In this signification, 'consistency' meant that EC external policies were to be subordinated to the political control of that part of the Community which had political legitimacy, namely the Member States. At its most noble, it was a crucial debate about the limits to power of a supranational authority whose origins had been economic; at its most base, it was an undignified bureaucratic jockeying for position.[18]

The need for adequate mechanisms to co-ordinate the policy activities of EPC and the EC had of course been recognized right from the beginning of Political Co-operation, and provisions for the involvement of the Community Institutions may be found in the Luxembourg and Copenhagen Reports. The principle was given expression at the Paris Summit of 1972, when Heads of State and Government declared that 'on matters which have a direct bearing on Community activities, close contact will be maintained with the Institutions of the Community'. EPC was still young: the implication was that the EC institutions might be allowed to intervene in EPC discussions when it was strictly necessary. The idea that the Member States might intervene in the reverse direction had not yet taken hold. This is shown by the language used in the Copenhagen Report: 'The Political Cooperation machinery, which is responsible for dealing with questions of current interest and where possible for formulating common medium-and long-term positions, must do this keeping in mind, *inter alia*, the implications for and the effects of, in the field of international politics, Community policies under construction'.

A more specific reference to interaction can be found in the London Report of 1981, which stated that 'the Foreign Ministers agree that further European integration, and the maintenance and development of Community policies in accordance with the Treaties, will be beneficial to a more effective coordination in the field of foreign policy, and will expand the range of instruments at the disposal of the Ten'. The word 'consistency' itself was not, however, used until the Single European Act. The preparatory work done in the Dooge Committee[19] had preferred to use the word

---

[18] A fourth meaning, to ensure consistency between European policies and those of the Member States, was not covered by the concept of 'consistency' in the foreign policy context, although the word figured in that sense in the TEU with regard to research and technological development (Art. 130h.1). A similar concept applies to development co-operation (Art. 130x.1), although the word 'consistency' is not used. 'Consistency' in this sense with regard to the CFSP is dealt with under other provisions of Title V of the TEU.

[19] Nuttall, *European Political Co-operation*, 243.

'interaction'.[20] Article 30.5 of the SEA stated, however, that 'the external policies of the European Community and the policies agreed in European Political Co-operation must be consistent. The Presidency and the Commission, each within its own sphere of competence, shall have special responsibility for ensuring that such consistency is sought and maintained'.

The text in itself does not shed any light on which of the three meanings of 'consistency' is primarily intended. Some exegesis of what was by no means an innocent text may however be instructive. Its origin lies in the British and Franco-German drafts on which the Intergovernmental Conference was directed to base its work. Both placed responsibility for ensuring consistency on the Member States, which can be seen as an indication that the emphasis was on political control of the external policy of the EC. The proposed arrangement was however thought to be insufficiently operational: the Member States acting collectively would not be in a position to exercise effective practical control. The SEA therefore placed special responsibility on the Presidency and the Commission, which as identifiable bodies were thought to be better able to assume it. The proviso that the two institutions should each act within its own sphere of competence was added at the request of the Danish delegation, which feared that the Commission might otherwise be thought to acquire a role in the management of EPC, which would have been unacceptable to parliamentary opinion in Denmark. The addition made it plain that the Commission acquired no new powers; it was warmly welcomed by the Commission because it also worked in the reverse direction, preventing the Presidency on behalf of EPC from intervening in the proper operation of the Community system. As it ended up, the SEA favoured the 'benign' theory of interaction.[21]

This is not to say that the Member States were not keenly interested in the way the Commission carried out policies which had clear political implications, especially when these had been discussed or raised in EPC. No Member State, not even the most Community-minded, was prepared to allow the Commission a completely free hand in the implementation of policy, even when the instruments used were of a purely Community

---

[20] 'Europe's external identity can be achieved only gradually within the framework of common action and European political cooperation (EPC) in accordance with the rules applicable to each of these. It is increasingly evident that interaction between these two frameworks is both necessary and useful. They must therefore be more closely aligned.'

[21] The arrangement was modified in the TEU, which transferred responsibility from the Presidency to the Council: TEU Art. C and J.8.2.

nature. Indeed, the argument was advanced that the Commission should be more open to advice from Member States on these matters, as a counterpart to acceptance of its full association with EPC. There were three reasons for this. The most politically important was the continued influence of the Cold War: depending on the degree of its commitment to active détente, a Member State might seek to influence the way in which the Commission handled policies which affected relations with Marxist governments. This explains the battle which took place within the Council machine over whether Nicaragua should benefit from EC aid in the framework of assistance to Central America,[22] the criticism directed against the Commission with regard to its support for agricultural restructuring in Ethiopia, which was thought to provide undue support for the Marxist Ethiopian government's attempts to collectivize farming, and the dislike of emergency and humanitarian aid to Vietnam and opposition to any attempts by the Commission to strengthen the EC's relations with that country.[23]

This reason for the Member States' wish to have their say in the way the Commission implemented EC policies naturally did not survive the end of the Cold War. But there were two more reasons which were not so affected. The first was the general feeling, not confined to EPC, that the Commission could not be trusted to take all Member States' interests into account, which was scarcely surprising since these frequently diverged. The effect of this can be seen, on the Community side, in the increasingly bitter debate on 'comitology'.[24] The second was the conviction on the part of the Member States that, when it came to foreign policy, they had greater expertise on the ground than did the Commission. This conviction was reinforced by sustained pressure from Member States' Ambassadors outside the Community, who resented the Commission's failure to involve them satisfactorily in the implementation of EC policies, the success of which was becoming increasingly important for the image of the countries they represented. These various factors led to increasing tension between the Commission and the Member States, and to a series of procedural innovations which significantly increased the extent to which Member States supervised the implementation of policy.

---

[22] Nuttall, *European Political Co-operation*, 223; Smith, *European Union Foreign Policy and Central America*, 67.

[23] Nuttall, *European Political Co-operation*, 268–9.

[24] Docksey and Williams, 'The Commission and the Execution of Community Policy', 121–31.

The problem was particularly acute in the case of the management of EC aid programmes. The way in which the Commission's relative autonomy was progressively curtailed can be traced over the years. On the first occasion on which EC financial assistance was deployed with the specific object of implementing EPC policy, the aid programme for Central America, the usual procedures for PVDALA,[25] as yet unreformed, were applied. The relevant group in the Council pronounced a blessing on the programme as a whole, but did not go into individual projects. Matters were different when it came to the aid programme for the victims of apartheid, for which, since it was a new type of programme, no procedures existed. The Commission claimed sole responsibility for the execution of the budget, while the Member States, prodded by their Ambassadors in Pretoria, insisted on having the opportunity to vet individual projects. There was more to this than an institutional quarrel: one of the groups of beneficiaries was the Kagiso Trust, a body assembled at the instigation of the Commission to serve as a channel to those who were not covered by either the trade unions or the churches. It was widely suspected of being a way of allowing ANC circles to benefit from EC funds, a policy with which not all Member States were in agreement. Furthermore, in order to be able to continue to use this channel, the Commission had to refrain from giving money to Inkatha, a grouping which enjoyed the strong support of the United Kingdom. The Commission maintained, with some justice, that unless absolute secrecy on individual grants was maintained, the recipients would be likely to meet with disagreeable consequences on the part of the South African authorities. The implication was that the Member States would be either unable or unwilling to maintain such secrecy. The Member States, with equal justice, demanded the right to know what was being done in their name and to express their views as appropriate. A compromise was struck in Coreper (not the Political Committee), whereby an *ad hoc* consultative group of national officials under the chairmanship of the Commission was set up to give advice, but not take decisions, on projects submitted. The *ad hoc* group forwarded its reports to EPC, but the latter was not involved in the management of the programme. The recipients could therefore be assured, the Commission claimed, that there was no political interference in the choice of beneficiaries and of projects.[26]

A similar situation arose when the Council approved in October 1986

---

[25] Pays en voie de développement de l'Amérique latine et d'Asie.
[26] Holland, *The European Community and South Africa*, 116–21.

the grant of financial assistance to Palestinians in the Occupied Territories. The Consuls General in Jerusalem, even more than the Ambassadors in Pretoria, were conscious of their special status and responsibilities, and voiced continual complaints about the Commission's lack of readiness to consult them on individual projects, let alone hand over to them responsibility for their selection. An *ad hoc* procedure was adopted, modelled on the PVDALA Regulation, whereby the projects were discussed with Member States in the Council framework, in a group chaired by the Council Presidency (and not by the Commission, as in the South African case).

A further procedural development concerning the provision of aid for the return of refugees and for long-term reconstruction occurred when the Soviet withdrawal from Afghanistan began in April 1988. Both the Commission and EPC set up *ad hoc* groups, the EPC group's task being to look after the political aspects of aid. Inevitably this involved a measure of supervision of the projects, and the shift in Member State involvement from EC to EPC was significant.[27]

These were minor institutional skirmishes which, with the exception of South Africa, probably did not even register with the countries which benefited from the Community's aid. The substance of European policies was scarcely, if at all, affected. These policies for the most part continued as before, substantially unchanged as a result of the Single European Act. Judging by the mass of declarations issued by EPC, throughout 1987 and 1988 Afghanistan, Angola and Namibia, Chile, Cyprus, Iran/Iraq, the Middle East, Central America, and the CSCE continued to be the countries and areas which most attracted the attention of EPC. South Africa was at the head of the list of preoccupations.[28]

There was no reason to expect any changes in the EPC system in the immediate future. The closed circle of participants would continue to build, brick by slow brick, a body of positions and policies which would all go to make up a more defined international profile. Internal procedural difficulties would be resolved without attracting public attention. When, five years after the entry into force of the Single Act, the time came in the middle of 1992 to review the workings of EPC, there would have been

[27] For a fuller discussion of all these cases, see Nuttall, *European Political Co-operation*, 270–3, and Nuttall, 'The Institutional Network and the Instruments of Action', 76–8.

[28] See the useful cumulative and analytical indexes in successive volumes of the *European Political Cooperation Bulletin*; also the survey by Renaud Dehousse, 'European Political Cooperation, 1 July 1987–31 December 1988', *EJIL* (1990), 378–99, and the annual survey of European Political Co-operation by the author in the *Yearbook of European Law 1987*, 269–84.

some modest improvements which would have added to the incremental development of the process without fundamentally changing its nature. It was not to be. Within a very short time these modest expectations were blown away by the collapse of the Communist system in Central and Eastern Europe. Beginning in 1988, this not only revolutionized the agenda of EPC, but also destroyed the basis on which it had been built and led to calls to replace it with a new way of making foreign policy in Europe. The story of how this came about will be told in the following chapters.

3

The 'new European architecture'

'New thinking' and the Western response

The most immediately striking sign of the collapse of the Communist system of government in Central and Eastern Europe was the dismantling of the Iron Curtain in the late summer and autumn of 1989, culminating in the breach of the Berlin Wall in November of that year. This was, however, but a stage, and an advanced one at that, in a process which had been set in train several years earlier by the 'new thinking' introduced into Soviet domestic and foreign policy by Mikhail Gorbachev.

When precisely this 'new thinking' began to influence relations between the Soviet Union and its Central and East European allies is a matter for debate.[1] Probably the potential was there right from the appointment of Gorbachev as General Secretary in 1985, even though the countries concerned, and the Kremlin itself, may not have realized it at the time. Certainly the implications for Soviet foreign policy in general were being spelt out at the Twenty-Seventh Party Congress in February 1986:[2] doubts about the Soviet presence in Afghanistan, reliance on 'mutual security' with regard to the United States, a shift to a multipolar foreign policy, and attachment to 'humanistic universalism'—belief in the existence of universal human values.[3] Gorbachev himself ascribes the beginning of full-scale implementation of the 'new thinking' to a conference in May 1986 on the new role of Soviet diplomacy, to which all the Ambassadors in Moscow were invited.[4] How many of them reported to their capitals that an earth-shaking transformation of Soviet foreign policy was at hand?[5]

---

[1] For the most detailed study so far, see Lévesque, *The Enigma of 1989*. For a comprehensive short account of the development of Soviet thinking regarding relations with the East European countries, see Garton Ash, *In Europe's Name*, 118–25.

[2] Gates, *From the Shadows*, 344.

[3] Brown, *The Gorbachev Factor*, 220 ff; Garton Ash, *In Europe's Name*, 122.

[4] Gorbachev, *Memoirs*, 402. For a memorandum on the subject submitted to the Politburo in the autumn of that year, see Garton Ash, *In Europe's Name*, 123.

[5] Shultz began to realize the implications as early as Nov. 1987: *Turmoil and Triumph*, 1003.

One of the universal human values was freedom of choice. Did this apply also to the Soviet satellites? According to the Gorbachevian logic, it did; but it took some time for this conclusion to be drawn, and still longer for those principally concerned to come to full realization of their new-found freedom. The reversal of the Brezhnev doctrine, according to which the Soviet Union was pledged to intervene in support of the 'leading role' of the Communist parties of its European allies, was slow to sink in, in spite of the fact that the Central and East European leaders were so informed as early as 1985, and again at a Comecon meeting in Moscow in November 1986.[6] The crucial steps to turn these warnings into practical policy seem to have been taken in the summer of 1988, in connection with the Nineteenth Party Conference. The Socialist Countries Department of the Central Committee was incorporated in a reorganized International Department, with Falin at its head in place of Dobrynin.[7] Gorbachev made his policy clear to the world community in a speech to the United Nations in December of that year. He himself describes his speech as a watershed, and selects as one of its main ideas the axiom that 'freedom of choice is a *sine qua non* for preserving diversity in the social development of nations'. He said: 'For us the necessity of the principle of freedom of choice is clear. Denying that right of peoples, no matter what the pretext for doing so, no matter what words are used to conceal it, means infringing even that unstable balance that it has been possible to achieve. Freedom of choice is a universal principle and there should be no exceptions'. The message was repeated on 6 July 1989 before that quintessentially European organization, the Council of Europe.[8] But it was not apparently until later that year that the Foreign Ministry spokesman, Gennady Gerasimov, to the mystification of his authorities, invented the formula of genius—the 'Sinatra doctrine' ('I did it my way').[9] The Brezhnev doctrine was not formally abandoned until the Bucharest meeting of the Warsaw Pact on 7–8 July 1989. For many of the participants, that was the end of the Warsaw Pact.[10]

---

[6] Brown, *The Gorbachev Factor*, 249–50.   [7] Ibid. 185.

[8] Fritsch-Bournazel, *Europe and German Unification*, 31; Lévesque, *The Enigma of 1989*, 118; Mayhew, *Recreating Europe*, 9–10.

[9] Oct. 1989, at Helsinki: Beschloss and Talbott, *At the Highest Levels*, 134; Garton Ash, *In Europe's Name*, 4, 431; Sep.–Oct. 1989, on the occasion of Gorbachev's visit to Finland: Torreblanca, *The European Community and Central Eastern Europe*, 86 n. 31; Dec. 1989, around the time of the Malta Summit: Brown, *The Gorbachev Factor*, 240. Mr Gerasimov no doubt deployed this pearl on numerous occasions.

[10] *Deutsche Einheit*, no. 101, 570; Brown, *The Gorbachev Factor*, 247–51. The common decision to terminate the Treaty was announced at the last meeting of the Political

The Western foreign policy establishment was slow to pick up the signals which Gorbachev was sending out—or rather was reluctant to interpret them generously. It was too soon for policy makers and analysts to make the intellectual leap required to transcend the modes of thought endemic to the Cold War. How could they, indeed, when their opposite numbers in Central and Eastern Europe, let alone in the Soviet Union, were imprisoned in the same structure? Even Westerners who saw that changes were in the making were not sure that a self-confident, principled, and efficient Soviet foreign policy would necessarily be in their interest. George Shultz, at the time US Secretary of State, thought in early 1986 that 'the Soviets were managing their foreign policy in an entirely new way'. It was not clear, however, whether this was to be welcomed or not.[11] Moreover, it was not unreasonable to demand results from the new rhetoric. Pending these, an attitude of wait and see was adopted. The conditions were scarcely right for adventurous thinking about new policy worlds.[12]

European Political Co-operation certainly engaged in no such adventures. The statement issued in June 1988 was a prize specimen of the 'wait and see' school.[13] At their meeting on 13 June, the Foreign Ministers declared that 'the Twelve are paying close attention to the developments currently taking place in the Soviet Union and Eastern Europe. They welcome them, and hope that these changes will contribute to openings in the political systems of these countries. . . . They are hopeful that such policies will contribute to a lasting improvement in East–West relations'.

The reasons for this unadventurous stance are partly to be found in the structure of EPC. It was only the previous December that the Member States had been able, after long and painful negotiations, to reach a consensus position on the attitude to be taken towards the Soviet Union in the light of the apparent relaxation of Soviet policy, especially on disarmament and the decision to withdraw from Afghanistan.[14] There was a

Consultative Committee at Prague on 1 July 1990: Körmendy, 'View from Hungary', 249–50. For Gorbachev's disgust with the conservatism of the Communist leaders in Central and Eastern Europe, see Gorbachev, *Memoirs*, 464–86.

    [11] Brown, *The Gorbachev Factor*, 217; Védrine, *Mitterrand*, 273–5; Shultz, *Turmoil and Triumph*, 702–4.

    [12] Cradock, *In Pursuit of British Interests*, 91–101, 104–6; Shultz, *Turmoil and Triumph*, 864; Bush and Scowcroft, *A World Transformed*, 12–14.

    [13] *Bull. EC*, June 1988, 2.4.2. In March the following year, the EPC Working Group still considered Gorbachev's initiative a ploy to divide the allies: Torreblanca, *The European Community and Central Eastern Europe*, 83, n. 24.

    [14] *Bull. EC*, Dec. 1987, 2.4.1.

clear difference of opinion between those, led by Germany, who wanted to make the best of these signs, and those, led by the United Kingdom, who remained cautious and reserved. The Member States had no taste for reopening such difficult discussions so soon, especially since there had apparently been no developments to cause them to change their national positions. Not that Germany's enthusiasm for developing relations with the East argued particular perceptiveness about the future course of events; it was little more than a continuation of the *Ostpolitik* with a more congenial opposite number in Moscow.

EPC was the less likely to detect changes in the situation and to respond imaginatively to them because it lacked an instance of initiative. In the Community framework the Commission would have been able to table a paper without axe-grinding *arrière-pensées*, which would have allowed discussion to be engaged on a moderately objective basis. In EPC, the initiative would have had to come from one or the other Member State, which would naturally table proposals reflecting its national point of view.[15] This would immediately attract opposition from those who did not share that point of view, and there would be no basis for discussion.

Another reason for the apparent immobilism of EPC was that some work was indeed going forward, but in the framework of the Community. The long-standing log-jam in the discussions between the Commission and the Council for Mutual Economic Assistance (CMEA), vulgarly known as Comecon, had been broken in September 1985 by Comecon's acceptance that an agreement between it and the Community could be asymmetrical—in other words that the two bodies did not have to be placed on an equal footing with regard to their legal powers—and that consequently there was no objection to the Community's also concluding individual agreements with the CMEA members as part of the same process. Negotiations with Comecon began in February 1986, and agreement was reached a year later on all points except the so-called 'Berlin clause'.[16] Even this difficulty was cleared away by a formula satisfactory to the Community, and the 'Joint Declaration on the Establishment of Official Relations between the European Economic

---

[15] Initiatives from the Commission were not welcome. In Mar. 1987 President Delors suggested, in response to the proliferation of disarmament proposals from the Soviet Union, that the European Council should hold a special meeting on security issues, adopt a common position, and lay the foundations for a common security policy. Nothing came of this initiative: De Gucht and Keukeleire, 'The European Security Architecture', 33–4.

[16] The standard clause in EC agreements whereby it was recognized that West Berlin formed part of the territory to which Community law applies.

Community and the Council for Mutual Economic Assistance' was issued on 25 June 1988.[17]

The negotiations were conducted on behalf of the Community by the Commission, in the Community framework and in accordance with normal EC procedures, in spite of the heavily political overtones. The EPC Eastern Europe Working Group was kept informed, but did not intervene in the proceedings. The EC's only concrete response so far to the changes in Moscow had therefore been a workmanlike handling of a specific issue of an economic nature, dealt with as such by the Community. The joint declaration remained, however, a child of the Cold War age, embodying the bloc-to-bloc approach which the Europeans had resisted for so long, and which was to disappear, within a year or two, with Comecon itself. The bilateral approach whereby general trade and co-operation agreements were concluded individually with the CMEA members—that with Hungary was signed in July 1988—proved, on the other hand, to be the main policy vehicle for the Community's future *Ostpolitik*.

This development coincided with the first incontrovertible signs to the outside world that something out of the ordinary was afoot in Eastern Europe. In both Poland and Hungary, there were moves towards broadening the political representativeness of the government, leading to fair elections in which parties other than the ruling Communist parties were allowed to take part. In Poland, the talks between the government and Solidarity led to the signature in April 1989 of the Roundtable agreements, which set out the conditions for elections. When these were held on 4 June, Solidarity won by as close to a landslide as the conditions allowed. In Hungary, the principle of a multiparty system was endorsed in February, designed to lead to elections the following year. In both cases, the Soviet Union declined to intervene in the internal affairs of third countries, which amounted to intervening heavily on the reformist side.[18]

Both the Western Europeans and the Americans remained cautious in their attitude to these events. They certainly did not foresee—who did?— the imminent sweeping away of the strategic certainties of a generation. President Bush, who had taken office at the beginning of 1989, is reported to have authorized an approach to the Soviet leaders whereby the United States would undertake not to exploit the Soviet Union's position if the

[17] van Ham, *The EC, Eastern Europe and European Unity*, 139–43; Nuttall, *European Political Co-operation*, 274–5; de la Serre, 'A la recherche d'une Ostpolitik', 17; *Bull. EC*, June 1988, 1.5.1–1.5.5.

[18] Indeed, Gorbachev encouraged the Polish Communists to take part in the Mazowiecki government: Treverton, *America, Germany, and the Future of Europe*, 149.

latter refrained from repressing reform movements in Eastern Europe by force.[19] Even though the initiative was not followed through, the Soviet authorities continued to think they had an unspoken understanding on these lines.[20]

The Soviet Union extended its new policy of non-interference in the affairs of Eastern Europe as far as declining to continue to provide economic and financial support. It was not surprising, therefore, that Eastern Europe turned to the rich countries of the Western world to fill the gap. When President Bush visited Poland and Hungary in June 1989 (just before the Western Economic Summit at the Arche in Paris) to furnish the reformers with moral encouragement and sympathy, he found himself also expected to provide support of a more concrete nature. This is the background to the startling decision by the Paris Summit to ask the European Commission to co-ordinate the Western response to this plea. At the same time, the European Community was engaged in negotiating trade or trade and co-operation agreements with the Central and East European countries in the framework of the Joint Declaration with Comecon. In both cases, *de facto* conditionality was observed. It would have seemed absurd to treat all the Central and East European countries alike, regardless of the differing rates of reform. The EC did therefore have a policy towards Eastern Europe, and it had the political overtones conferred by conditionality, but it was an economic policy and did not originate from within the organs of EPC.

The acceleration of history

When the Hungarians cut the wire on their frontier with Austria in May 1989, opening the way to a flood of visitors, and indeed immigrants, to the West, and setting in train an unstoppable chain of events which was to culminate in the breach of the Berlin Wall on 9 November, it can be said that the policy of wait and see had succeeded. The West had waited; now it saw. The process characterized by Jacques Delors as the 'acceleration of history' had begun.[21] The collapse of the Soviet intellectual as well as physical domination of Eastern Europe required the West to review in short order not only its short-term policies but also its vision of how the world

[19] Beschloss and Talbott, *At the Highest Levels*, 13. Bush's own account is more hesitant: Bush and Scowcroft, *A World Transformed*, 26–8.
[20] Lévesque, *The Enigma of 1989*, 102.
[21] Delors, *Le Nouveau concert européen*, 195, 207.

was constructed. The dismantling of the Iron Curtain, and especially of the Berlin Wall, was immediately followed by a plethora of speeches setting out blueprints for the 'new European architecture'.[22] The scene was not unnaturally one of some confusion. National leaders each had their own ideas to put across, corresponding to personal preference, national interest, domestic political requirements, or a mixture of all three. But the thinking was being done in national forums; the European Community frequently figured as a 'building block' in the 'new European architecture', but, not having an institutional brain, it did not think for itself. To use an expression employed by Delors at the time, it was a subject, and not an actor, in contemporary history ('Nous devons démontrer que la Communauté . . . est un acteur et non simplement un sujet de l'histoire contemporaine'[23]).

It was Gorbachev, who had the advantage of a head start in knowing what the 'new thinking' was about, who initially set the terms of the debate. The Soviet Union's new foreign policy was not just, nor even principally, about the application of universal human values to Eastern Europe; it was about a new way of coexisting with the United States which would make militarily alliances redundant. This was to be achieved through a new grouping of European states in what the Soviet leader called the 'common European home'.[24] The expression seems to have been first called into service abroad on the occasion of Gorbachev's speech to the British Parliament on 18 December 1984. Still only the head of a parliamentary delegation, Gorbachev said: 'Whatever is dividing us, we live on the same planet and Europe is our common home—a home, not a theatre of military operations'. Gorbachev himself claimed spontaneity for a second use of the expression in reply to questions at a press conference in Paris in October 1985—'Europe is our common home'. The avowed aim was to get rid of the notion that Europe was a potential theatre of war, by promoting pan-European integration. That, indeed, was stated to be his motive in choosing France for his first official visit abroad as General Secretary. Pressed to elaborate the concept, Gorbachev threw out the idea of a European Summit on the lines of the Soviet–US Summit which had taken place

---

[22] For an overview of the architecture debate, see Allen, 'West European Responses'.

[23] Speech to the European Parliament, 17 Jan. 1989: Delors, *Le Nouveau concert européen*, 116.

[24] The concept of a 'common home' had a long history in Soviet thought, and was an evolutive one. This historical baggage was one of the reasons why Gorbachev's initiatives were taken with a pinch of salt. See Malcolm, 'The "Common European Home"', 662–6; van Ham, *The EC, Eastern Europe and European Unity*, 155–8; de la Serre 'A la recherche d'une Ostpolitik', 13.

in Reykjavik; it remained unclear, nevertheless, what role would remain for the United States and Canada, and whether the 'common home' presupposed the dissolution of the military alliances.[25] The Soviet position on this latter point became clearer as negotiations on the unification of Germany progressed; their preference was for European security to be assured by a renewed and strengthened Conference on Security and Co-operation in Europe (CSCE).[26]

The Soviet vision of a united Europe, free to choose its own destiny, was a logical consequence of the abandonment by Moscow of tight control over its allies. It was, indeed, the only way the Soviet Union could hope to maintain its influence in Europe and its very security. The vision was tempting to some in the West, and policies directed towards creating and strengthening pan-European institutions, although not necessarily on the lines originally conceived by Gorbachev, were followed by many European governments. It was this line of thinking that led, among other things, to the renewal and transformation of the Conference on Security and Co-operation in Europe in the Paris Charter of November 1990 and the decision, in December 1989, to set up a European Bank for Reconstruction and Development (originally intended to be a purely European organization, excluding the United States, with a political mandate to bring together all the democratic and free market countries of Europe). The European Community was seen by many as part of this pan-European structure, but not itself the universal vehicle for it. Many of the existing EC members feared that the over-hasty extension to their Eastern neighbours of their familiar and on the whole comfortable arrangements would endanger the *acquis communautaire*. This was the origin of the otherwise artificial 'deepening versus widening' debate— should the Community be institutionally strengthened before it was enlarged, or should it just be enlarged? Several ideas were floated to provide devices for attaching the Central and East European countries to the Community family, without incurring the political and economic costs of actual accession.[27] President Mitterrand's vision of a European Confederation fell into this category, as did Jacques Delors' proposals

---

[25] Gorbachev, *Memoirs*, 161, 427–9, 431–3.

[26] Gorbachev, *Memoirs*, 529, 534; Beschloss and Talbott, *At the Highest Levels*, 148; Wallander and Prokop, 'Soviet Security Strategies towards Europe', 78. The Soviet leadership realized the dangers of the common political synecdoche whereby 'European integration', meaning the EC, was confounded with 'pan-European integration', meaning a wider forum like the CSCE: *Deutsche Einheit*, no. 112A, 618.

[27] Accession was not agreed in principle until the Copenhagen European Council of June 1993.

for a system of 'concentric circles', including the contentious but short-lived European Economic Area.

In spite of reluctance to see the Community as the all-embracing vehicle for pan-European integration, the EC might yet have been the preferred and dynamic forum for discussion of the 'new European architecture' had it not been for two complicating factors, which proved exceptionally potent when combined. These were the decision of the United States to remain a power in Europe, and the headlong rush to reunification of Germany. For reasons explained below, no country which mattered was prepared to locate the German unification debate in the Community forum; the United States in particular naturally preferred the discussions on the future shape of Europe to take place in bodies where it was present. The two factors came together in the NATO Council in London in June 1990, which was crucial for both the continued American presence and for Soviet acquiescence in German unification.

Until the summer of 1989, it had seemed that the Community might be capable of dealing with events to the east in its accustomed way. Traditional trade and co-operation agreements with the Central and East European countries were being negotiated, and succour was being provided in cash and in kind. If questions about the future shape of the continent were being raised, there seemed to be no immediate compulsion to provide answers; a routine EC response was adequate. This changed almost overnight, as a result of the decision by large numbers of citizens of the German Democratic Republic to take advantage of new loopholes to move to West Germany, and of massive demonstrations by those who were left that they were no longer prepared to tolerate the existing government. Although German unification was still believed by almost everyone to be a remote possibility for the distant future, answers to questions now had to be given without delay. It is certainly the case that Community procedures would not have allowed common positions to be worked out on anything like an acceptable timescale, but it is more significant that the debate had now gone beyond the closed circle of EPC policy makers. The issues at stake were of national importance for several of the EC Member States; it was therefore not surprising that statements on them came direct from Presidents and Prime Ministers. The monopoly of Foreign Ministers on foreign policy issues was broken, and with it the role of EPC as a forum.[28] And the Presidents and Prime Ministers had their own policy staffs to

---

[28] For the disjunction between the Elysée and the Quai d'Orsay at this time, see Cohen, 'L'Imprévision et l'imprévisible', 370–2. For similar developments in Germany, see Mazzucelli, *France and Germany at Maastricht*, 50.

prepare their statements, and their own political persona to ensure an audience for them. EPC had neither.

As President of the French Republic, with a constitutional responsibility for security and foreign affairs, François Mitterrand might have been expected to give an early lead. In fact he took some time before making up his mind, his indecisiveness being concealed by the opacity of his public declarations. As François Heisbourg has remarked in another context, 'the Mitterrand method of government: in dealing with a problem, never become a prisoner of a single conduit or a single angle of approach; keep as many channels and perspectives open as you can, until you are forced to choose.'[29] Mitterrand's response to the rapidly developing situation in Europe was made up of a number of strands, which without being entirely inconsistent nevertheless derived from different logics. The move towards European political union was one of those strands, but only became predominant with time.[30]

Especially during the latter part of his two terms in office, Mitterrand staked out a claim as a European of long standing. His attendance at the Congress of the European Movements at The Hague in 1948 became, together with his experiences as a prisoner of war in Germany, a *locus communis* of his later speeches. In fact, he had concerned himself very little with the building of Europe during his time as a Minister and the long years in opposition.[31] It was not until the winter of 1983, on the threshold of the French Presidency of the EC, that Mitterrand decided to make Europe—meaning the European Community—his great priority.[32] This was in part because the President's position in the European Council gave him the opportunity to conduct EC policy to greater political effect than domestic affairs—and this at a time when his domestic record was under attack after the fiasco of the Socialist measures of 1981–3.[33] His vision of

[29] Heisbourg, 'France and the Gulf Crisis', 25–6; Moravcsik, *The Choice for Europe*, 405–8.
[30] For an overall view of the Mitterrand foreign policy at this period, see Cohen (ed.), *Mitterrand et la sortie de la guerre froide*, esp. the contributions by Françoise de la Serre, Christian Lequesne, and Samy Cohen.
[31] Cole, *François Mitterrand*, 116–19; Lacouture, *Mitterrand*, i. 189–90. Mitterrand's silence on European issues may be explained by his overriding need to draw together the various strands of the Socialist movement, which had widely differing views on the matter: Mazzucelli, *France and Germany at Maastricht*, 47.
[32] Védrine, *Les Mondes de François Mitterrand*, 295–6; Moravcsik, *The Choice for Europe*, 332–5. Védrine makes the point that the initiative was the President's own: Cohen, *Mitterrand et la sortie de la guerre froide*, 463–4.
[33] Védrine, *Les Mondes de François Mitterrand*, 393; Lequesne, 'Une lecture décisionelle', 127–8; Lequesne, *Paris–Bruxelles*, 166 ('François Mitterrand a retrouvé dans la construction européenne un projet politique de substitution après l'abandon de la politique

Europe was, however, more that of de Gaulle than of Schuman or Monnet.[34] He seems not to have been naturally attuned to the integrationist discourse of the Monnet school, although he was not averse to deploying it when the need arose. The mainsprings of his eventual commitment to the building of Europe were to be found elsewhere. He resented American hegemony, and saw the Community as potentially a bulwark against it;[35] he was determined to uphold the influence of France, and saw the Community as a means of doing this in an age in which no European country was more than a medium-sized power;[36] he gave passionate expression to the belief that nationalism led to war,[37] and yet believed that the intergovernmental parts of the Community—the European Council and EPC—were better channels for the furtherance of national interests than the institutions of the founding Treaties.[38] All these concerns had to be accommodated in Mitterrand's response to the events in Eastern Europe, and especially East Germany.

In July 1989 Mitterrand had declared that it was legitimate to aspire to the unification of Germany, provided this was done peacefully and democratically.[39] As the likelihood increased of precisely that coming about, the situation became more complicated. There was still a current of opinion in France which feared the power of a united Germany, although this was stronger among the political élite than in the population at large.[40] Mit-

---

économique socialiste.'). The spurt of Presidential policy-making on Europe coincided in both 1984 (according to some interpretations) and 1988 not only with French EC Presidencies but also with periods of 'domestic cohabitation' with Socialist Prime Ministers: Cole, *François Mitterrand*, 88–9; see also, but with due caution, 119–24.

[34] Mitterrand's parting advice to John Major at the Franco–British Summit at Chartres in Nov. 1994 was worthy of de Gaulle: 'Après moi, la Commission et le Parlement européens risquent de se coaliser pour marginaliser le Conseil européen, qui est la seule autorité véritable. Après moi, ce sera à vous et aux autres d'y veiller.' ('When I am gone, the European Commission and Parliament are likely to get together to marginalise the European Council, which is the only genuine authority. When I am gone, it will be up to you and the others to watch out': Favier and Martin-Roland, *La Décennie Mitterrand*, iv. 612).

[35] This did not stop Mitterrand from valuing the US military presence in Europe as a curb on Germany: Zelikow and Rice, *Germany Unified and Europe Transformed*, 171.

[36] Cohen, *Mitterrand et la sortie de la guerre froide*, 286–7 (testimony of Hubert Védrine).

[37] 'Le nationalisme, c'est la guerre!', farewell speech to the European Parliament, 17 Jan. 1995: Mitterrand, *Onze discours*, 162; Mitterrand, *Les Forces de l'esprit*, 86; Cohen, *Mitterrand et la sortie de la guerre froide*, 456.

[38] For the 'posting of a great European design' in general, see de la Serre, 'France: The Impact of François Mitterrand', 25–6.

[39] Mitterrand, *De l'Allemagne, de la France*, 32–3; Lacouture, *Mitterrand*, ii. 363–4.

[40] A poll conducted in France immediately after the opening of the Berlin Wall found that two-thirds had feelings of good will toward the Germans and only 17% expressed either fear or hostility: Szabo, *The Diplomacy of German Unification*, 144 n. 101; see also 48. Seventy per cent thought that unification presented no obstacles to European union,

terrand was under attack from his political opponents for inactivity. What was to be done? One of the reasons for Mitterrand's reluctance to take an initiative was his belief that unification would be prevented by the United States and the Soviet Union. One move was therefore to verify this impression directly. The visit he paid to Gorbachev in Kiev on 6 December 1989 achieved precisely that; Gorbachev begged Mitterrand to help him prevent the reunification of Germany, failing which he (Gorbachev) would fall victim to a military coup.[41] Mitterrand denied that he had visited Kiev (and later Prime Minister Modrow in Berlin) to encourage Gorbachev in his resistance,[42] and the available records of the discussions confirm that view.[43] What he did do was to set out what he daringly claimed to be a common European position, namely that many questions, including the CSCE, had to be dealt with before the German question; that for the sake of balance in Europe and of peace, he had told the Germans that the German question would come up only when progress had been made in the West in building the Community and there had been evolution in the East, including evolution in Comecon, with the CSCE providing the framework of a peaceful settlement among all European countries, together with the United States and Canada. Gorbachev drew the conclusion that he could not count on France to slow down the process of German unification.

Support for a strengthened CSCE was designed to encourage Gorbachev, who shortly before Mitterrand's visit to Kiev had called for the CSCE Summit planned for 1992 to be brought forward to the end of 1990.[44] With the backing of Mitterrand and Kohl, and indeed of the European Community, negotiations for the transformation of the CSCE from a process for the non-conflictual management of the relationship between East and West into a new institution based on a community of values, principles, and norms culminated in the signing of the Charter of Paris in November 1990.

But this was not enough for Mitterrand, or rather it was too much: a body which included the United States and Canada could not be a complete answer to the question of how to organize pan-European

and 60% thought that it would be a good thing for France. Support had declined sharply a year later: Fritsch-Bournazel, 'Die Einigung Deutschlands', 75. See also Lippert, 'Die EG als Mitgestalter', 53 and n. 70.

[41] Attali, *Verbatim III*, 322–3; 297, 335, 337; 366.

[42] Mitterrand, *De l'Allemagne, de la France*, 93–4.

[43] Favier and Martin-Roland, *La Décennie Mitterrand*, iii. 196–9; Attali, *Verbatim III*, 360–7.

[44] 30 Nov. 1989: Remacle, *La Charte de Paris*, 5; Védrine, *Les Mondes de François Mitterrand*, 446.

relations. Towards the end of 1989 Mitterrand was exploring the idea of a pan-European confederation. This idea was to be expounded in the President's New Year address to the nation on 31 December 1989. The concept was based on a structure of concentric circles, of which the innermost was to be the European Community with its budget and binding norms; the next, those European countries which already had close economic ties with the Community, including members of EFTA such as the Scandinavian countries, Austria, and Switzerland; and the outermost, the Central and East European countries and the Soviet Union. This last circle would be joined together in a European Confederation, a political structure with an economic, cultural, and technological base, in which heads of government would meet three or four times a year to acquire the habit of working together, their discussions to be prepared by a permanent secretariat.[45] After discussion with President Havel in March 1990, the idea was formally launched by Mitterrand during his visit to Prague on 13–14 September 1990.[46]

The idea had been ill prepared and was not favourably received. It did not survive the 'Assises' held in Prague in June 1991, at which Mitterrand put up a half-hearted defence of his own project.[47] The very word 'confederation' rang warning bells in the ears of federalists like Delors, for whom it had disagreeable intergovernmental connotations,[48] while the Central and East European countries, already nervous at the proposed inclusion of the Soviet Union, saw the initiative as a ploy to defer their accession to the Community, which indeed it was.[49] More important, however, was the opposition of the US administration, which was bound to give preference to European structures like the CSCE in which it was itself present.[50]

[45] Mitterrand, De l'Allemagne, de la France, 222–9; Deutsche Einheit, no. 135, 687 and 689, and no. 187, 849–50; Favier and Martin-Roland, La Décennie Mitterrand, iii. 223–6.

[46] Rupnik, 'La France de Mitterrand', 200–1.

[47] Cohen, 'L'Imprévision et l'imprévisible', 376; Mitterrand, Onze discours, 49–61; Favier and Martin-Roland, La Décennie Mitterrand, iv. 174–7.

[48] Delors supported the idea in public, but later admitted that the Commission had been opposed for bureaucratic reasons: Favier and Martin-Roland, La Décennie Mitterrand, iii. 225 and iv. 174.

[49] Doutriaux, Le Traité sur l'Union européenne, 30–1; Védrine, Les Mondes de François Mitterrand, 448; Smith, The Making of EU Foreign Policy, 110. The most authoritative account of the rationale and fate of the Confederation initiative is that by Jean Musitelli, to whom Mitterrand had entrusted the organization of the Prague 'Assises', in Cohen, Mitterrand et la sortie de la guerre froide, 216–19.

[50] Delors, L'Unité d'un homme, 267; Hoffmann, 'French Dilemmas and Strategies', 141; Nicolaïdis, 'East European Trade', 431 n. 18.

The third strand in Mitterrand's policy was the embedding of Germany more closely in the European Community. Although surely never absent from Mitterrand's thinking,[51] this did not take a central place until after the European Council in Strasbourg in December 1989. Only then did Mitterrand determine to make 'political union' the centrepiece of his approach[52] and to launch with Kohl, the following April, the initiative to advance towards political union at the same time as economic and monetary union. The original idea had come from Bonn, and was adopted by Mitterrand as a riposte to a rapidly evolving political situation rather than from deeply held conviction. It did not displace his other strategies, but came to assume the predominant role in both policy and rhetoric. Although originally conceived in terms of the institutional development of the Community, it was to prove decisive in the transformation of European Political Co-operation into the Common Foreign and Security Policy.

The President of the European Commission, Jacques Delors, had his own version of the 'concentric circles' theory, but was less enthusistic to begin with about early moves towards political union. His thinking had begun further back, before the collapse of Communism, and was inspired by the new interest shown in the Community by other European countries as a result of the move towards a Single Market. The Community had since 1984 been conducting a desultory dialogue with the EFTA countries (the 'Luxembourg process') which was satisfactory to neither side. The Community was prepared to do more, but only if certain principles were

---

[51] Mitterrand's immediate reaction to the fall of the Berlin Wall had been to see it as an opportunity to be directed towards the development of Europe: *Deutsche Einheit*, no. 85, 512. See also his speech to the European Parliament on 25 Oct. 1989, reflecting a remark made a week earlier in the French Council of Ministers: 'Au nom de quoi accuserait-on le peuple allemand de désirer se retrouver, dès lors qu'il s'agit strictement d'un appel qui monte vers nous, qui vient de l'Est et qui en appelle aux valeurs qui sont les nôtres? Il faut tirer cette leçon qui consistera à renforcer et à accélerer la construction politique de l'Europe, seule réponse au problème qui nous est posé': Favier and Martin-Roland, *La Décennie Mitterrand*, iii. 177.

[52] The timing suggested here relies on Védrine, *Les Mondes de François Mitterrand*, 433, but could be even later. Christian Lequesne dates it to after the CDU's victory in the East German elections on 18 Mar. 1990: Lequesne, *Paris–Bruxelles*, 176–8. Favier and Martin-Rolland associate Mitterrand's final decision with the Irish Presidency's decision on 16 [sic] Feb. 1990 to call a special European Council in Dublin. Mitterrand, it is claimed, then decided to seize the opportunity of NATO's apparent decline to give the Community a security and defence dimension: Favier and Martin-Rolland, *La Décennie Mitterrand*, iii. 244–5. They admit, however, that backstage discussions were meanwhile taking place between the respective advisers, Élisabeth Guigou and Joachim Bitterlich. Guigou proposed an initiative to the President, who is reported to have reacted favourably to it, on 6 Feb. 1990: Attali, *Verbatim III*, 412.

accepted by its partners—priority for EC internal integration, preservation of the EC's autonomous powers of decision, and a fair balance between benefits and obligations.[53] Now that things were moving in Eastern Europe, it became even more urgent to set out a structure adaptable to all eventualities. This was done by Delors in his speech to the European Parliament, looking forward over the four-year period of office of the new Commission, on 17 January 1989.[54]

Delors began by setting out the achievements of the Community over the previous four years, in particular the Single European Act and its accompanying budget settlement. For him, the priority was to 'réussir l'Acte unique': not only to implement the Single Market, but to exploit the new potential with which the Single Act had endowed the Community, beginning with economic and monetary union. The Community needed breathing space to make progress in its internal integration; what response was it to make to those other Europeans who were knocking at the door? 'As for the "other Europes", the question is simple: how to make a success of integration without rejecting those who have as much right as we to call themselves Europeans? As you know, the Commission has already taken up a position of principle: priority must be given to deepening over enlargement. Nothing must distract us from our duty of making the Single Act a reality.' For Delors, this meant primarily inventing a new form of relationship with the EFTA countries, the initiative which later turned into the European Economic Area. Depending on the degree of institutional development within EFTA, this would either be a twin-pillar arrangement or acceptance of EC rules.[55] Delors did not conceal the difficulties of the operation, which indeed turned out to be just as great as he had predicted.

Delors was aware that the EFTA countries were not the only ones knocking at the Community's door. He made a special reference to Gorbachev's 'common home', in disparaging terms. 'We should be wary of lyrical outbursts or publicity effects. To speak very clearly, our ideal is a "European village", in which peace reigns and economic and cultural activities go forward in mutual trust. But if I had to sketch that village today, I would put in a house called "the European Community", of which we would be the sole architects and whose keys we would carefully keep for ourselves, opening our doors only for contacts with our neighbours.' No more than

---

[53] The Interlaken principles: *Bull. EC*, June 1987, 2.2.14; Pedersen, *European Union and the EFTA Countries*, 35.   [54] Delors, *Le Nouveau concert européen*, 116–48.

[55] Pedersen, *European Union and the EFTA Countries*, 33–6; Hayes, 'The Internal Market and EFTA', 58–60; Krenzler, 'Der Europäische Wirtschaftsraum', 62; Luif, *On the Road to Brussels*, 149–52.

the members of EFTA were the Central and East European countries welcome to walk inside and make themselves at home, just when the proprietors had spent so much time redecorating and were preparing to rearrange the furniture.

Delors recalled this image when he spoke to the European Parliament exactly a year later.[56] But, as he himself said, a lot had happened in the meanwhile; the acceleration of history had begun.[57] The strategic objective, however, remained the same: to ensure that nothing came in the way of the Community's further integration. It was recognized that a response had to be made to those countries which were moving towards pluralist democracy and a market economy. A new co-operative framework (not accession) was called for, which could take the shape of revised 'association contracts' providing a forum for political and economic dialogue covering a range of topics from the technical and scientific to financial co-operation.[58] Running through what had already been done—trade and co-operation agreements, G24, European Investment Bank loans—Delors made the point that henceforth the Community's economic and political roles could no longer be kept separate.

This did not mean that he was in favour of moving straightaway to an integrated Community foreign policy as part of a political union. Delors maintained a reserved attitude towards the Kohl–Mitterrand initiative of April 1990 for political union, on the grounds that it was premature; the Community had to be strengthened first.[59] For the same reason, his support for Mitterrand's newly launched concept of a Confederation was ambiguous: 'What will the end result of this process be? Will it, as President François Mitterrand has suggested, be a grand European confederation? What an invigorating prospect for all who believe in a European identity and a common store of ideas and traditions! My firm belief is that such a confederation can only come about when the Community has achieved political union. We shall each make up our own mind when the time is ripe [Chacun se décidera le moment venu]'. For Delors, the Community would only retain its magnetic attraction if it persevered in the work of integration. This meant progress in two directions: EMU and political co-operation. The style and rhythm of EPC had to change, abandoning the habit of reacting to events for a determined effort to define the

[56] 17 Jan. 1990: Delors, *Le Nouveau concert européen*, 194–219.
[57] See also Delors' address at the College of Europe, 17 Oct. 1989: *Bull. EC*, Oct. 1989, 3.2.1, esp. pp. 116–17.
[58] The Commission was shortly to be authorized to negotiate 'Association Agreements' with the Eastern and Central European countries.
[59] Doutriaux, *Le Traité sur l'Union européenne*, 89.

essential interests in common of the Member States. This would open the way, not to an external policy which was fully common, but to actions corresponding to the essential interests so defined. Delors suggested the CSCE as the most suitable area in which to test this new approach—no longer the CSCE in which EPC had been such a success in the early years, but the revised and reinvigorated CSCE which Gorbachev was promoting as the basis for his new pan-European security system.

Delors' proposals for EPC were not earth-shaking. His boldness was reserved for his institutional suggestions: the Commission should be transformed into a genuine executive answerable to a democratic European Parliament with increased powers, as well as to national parliaments. This aroused the wrath of Mitterrand: 'But it's stupid! Why can't he mind his own business! No one in Europe will ever agree! By going too far, he will scupper what can be achieved'.[60] As far as foreign policy was concerned, the Commission's aim at this stage was still to make EPC more effective and to narrow the gap between it and the Community. In June 1990 Delors felt that 'it was too early to create a single EC foreign policy, or even to make foreign policy questions the subject of weighted majority voting in the Council of Ministers'.[61] But foreign-policy making was to be considered as part of the *acquis communautaire* and thus protected along with the rest. This meant that it was perfectly proper, and even desirable, to offer political dialogue to countries seeking a closer relationship with the Community, so long as there was no suggestion that the partners thereby acquired any right to intervene in the decision-making process.

A different approach was taken a year later by Vice-President Andriessen, then responsible for external relations. In a speech in April 1991, Andriessen proposed a new kind of affiliate membership whereby especially the Central and East European countries could have EC membership, including representation in the Council and the European Parliament, for some areas but not others. The areas suggested were political co-operation and, bizarrely, monetary affairs.[62] Similar views were expressed by Volker Rühe, then Secretary General of the CDU, but the idea did not catch on.[63] It was, of course, at odds with the Commission ortho-

---

[60] Attali, *Verbatim III*, 401.

[61] Hamlet, 'The Core of Decision-making', 102 and 97 n. 33.

[62] Pedersen, *European Union and the EFTA Countries*, 141–2; Smith, *The Making of EU Foreign Policy*, 111; Torreblanca, *The European Community and Central Eastern Europe*, 249–50.

[63] Körmendy, 'View from Hungary', 252–3; Rummel, 'Beyond Maastricht', 312 n. 33. The idea aroused some interest among the CEECs at the time: Mayhew, *Recreating Europe*, 372. Mayhew dates the original idea to 1990.

doxy of narrowing the gap between EPC and the Community. To set up two decision-making bodies, one for foreign policy questions (and monetary affairs) and one for the rest, one with a wider membership than the other, would tend to drive the two apart, not bring them closer together— or promote consistency, as the jargon went. Consistency was a good thing for the Commission as long as the movement went in the direction of the Community. When the movement was reversed, the lack of interest in the Andriessen plan might well have been regretted.

Chancellor Kohl's view of the 'new European architecture' was superficially similar to those of President Mitterrand and President Delors, but sprang from very different origins. He had been brought up to believe that the Federal Republic's destiny lay in the twin pillars of NATO and the European Community. He was a fervent admirer of Chancellor Adenauer, who had laid the foundations for this policy.[64] This did not mean that he was always a true disciple of the Monnet method, any more than Adenauer had been, nor did it mean that Germany was not entitled to a foreign policy of its own. Rather, German foreign and security policy was best channelled through NATO and the EC, to forestall any fears on the part of its allies that the old Germany might one day be reborn, and indeed to prevent just such an eventuality.[65] In general, a settlement in Europe, and more particularly the unification of Germany, could only come about through a more integrated Europe. This was a point the Chancellor rarely failed to make to his visitors throughout 1989.[66]

Hans-Dietrich Genscher, the Federal Foreign Minister, had a more developed and personal view of how Europe should look. As long ago as 1966 he had clearly set out the parallelism between German unification and the development of a Europe-wide security system—and the unification of Germany was for him the objective which transcended all others.[67] Germany's *Ostpolitik*, launched by Brandt but supported by Scheel, Genscher's predecessor both as Foreign Minister and FDP party leader, was for

---

[64] Paterson, 'Helmut Kohl', 26–30.

[65] Kohl described NATO and the EC as the 'twin roofs' of Germany: *Deutsche Einheit*, no. 297, 1173.

[66] *Deutsche Einheit*, nos. 58, 62, 64, 70, 89, 106, 109. Kohl made the point in a particularly stark way in a conversation with Prime Minister Németh of Hungary on 16 Dec. 1989: 'Je mehr man die Deutschen einbinde, je mehr Deutsche Kompetenzen an die Europäische Gemeinschaft übertragen würden, desto weniger Angst brauche man vor ihnen zu haben' ('The more the Germans are drawn in, the more German sovereignty is transferred to the European Community, the less need there is to be afraid of them': *Deutsche Einheit*, no. 124, 656). The principle held good even when its application in specific cases, like EMU, ran counter to German interests: *Deutsche Einheit*, no. 120, 638.

[67] Genscher, *Erinnerungen*, 93–5.

Genscher a means of reuniting Germans of both East and West. This led to charges of *Genscherismus*[68]—incipient neutralism—and to tensions with the Chancellor's office. Like Kohl, however, Genscher was a strong supporter of the European Community as the indispensable vehicle for asserting Germany's international existence, although no more than the Chancellor was he intimately attached to the Monnet method. Indeed, the Genscher–Colombo initiative of 1981, the purpose of which was to give the Community a security and legal affairs dimension, was purely inter-governmental in its original Genscher version, any emphasis on the Community as such being at the insistence of Colombo.[69]

Although the competition between Genscher and Kohl was to lead to important policy developments, its significance should not be overemphasized. German foreign policy had been stable since the launching of the *Ostpolitik*. It was natural that Germany should be among the first to take an optimistic view of Gorbachev's new approach, and it was in Germany that 'Gorbymania' reached its apogee.[70] It was to be expected, therefore, that Germany should take the lead in urging support for Gorbachev, should encourage his vision of a pan-European security system based on the CSCE, and should go slowly in encouraging reform, if that meant separatism, in the Soviet Union's satellites. Germany nevertheless found itself in a dilemma. Support for a pan-European security system had to be reconciled with the continued effectiveness of NATO and the wishes of the United States, and after the summer of 1989 due gratitude had to be shown in particular to Hungary and Czechoslovakia for their help in solving the problem of the East German immigrants.[71] This ambivalence may explain Germany's relative silence regarding the new order in Europe in the period before the fall of the Berlin Wall.

The question in particular of the future shape of the EC gave Kohl some difficulties. In principle, he was in favour of everything which strengthened the Community, and Germany had been a strong supporter of the

[68] Genscher denied that this was the aim of his policies: see for example Genscher, *Erinnerungen*, 382. But his persistent support for some form of attenuation of NATO's presence in East Germany (Zelikow and Rice, *Germany Unified and Europe Transformed*, 232–3), at a time when Kohl was supporting a united Germany's full membership of NATO, continued to nourish suspicions.

[69] Nuttall, *European Political Co-operation*, 184–5. For an overview of Kohl's and Genscher's thinking, see Moravcsik, *The Choice for Europe*, 389–91.

[70] Gorbachev, *Memoirs*, 520; Kohl, *Ich wollte Deutschlands Einheit*, 47–8; Garton Ash, *In Europe's Name*, 112–14.

[71] Already in 1989 Kohl had promised Hungary Germany's support in its application to become a member of the EC, distant prospect though that was: Kohl, *Ich wollte Deutschlands Einheit*, 74; Teltschik, *329 Tage*, 82–3.

Single European Act. But the debate in 1988 and 1989 on EMU was not an easy one for the Chancellor. France, no longer content to have its monetary policies and the rate of exchange of the franc determined, as it believed, by the Bundesbank in Frankfurt, had secured at the European Council at Hanover in June 1988 agreement on a committee chaired by Delors to work out the basic requirements for economic and monetary union. This committee reported to the European Council at Madrid a year later, and there was agreement that preparation for an intergovernmental conference should begin. The Chancellor had agreed to both these decisions, but it was proving difficult to pin him down on a date for the conference. He knew that, without some balancing provisions on democratic control of the EC, the abandonment of the Deutschmark would be difficult to sell.[72] The events of the latter part of 1989 gave him the opportunity of taking a leading position in the debate.

These events were largely unanticipated by the Federal Government, at least as regards the speed of developments. In August and September 1989 the immediate problem facing the government was how to secure the onward journey to West Germany of thousands of immigrants from the East arriving in Hungary and Czechoslovakia, then to organize their reception and housing; by October, the question was what attitude to take towards the mass demonstrations in the East calling for changes in the régime; by November, with movement now free between the two Germanies, the question of unification finally had to be faced.

Chancellor Kohl acted in typically decisive fashion. In a speech to the Bundestag on 28 November, he announced a 'ten-point programme to overcome the division of Germany and of Europe', which set out the stages leading to unity.[73] He did so without consulting any of Germany's friends and allies. This caused great offence, and seriously damaged in particular the relationship with France.[74] The affront was felt the more as, without saying a word about his intentions, Kohl had just sounded out Mitterrand about a timetable for EMU, precisely to demonstrate his continued commitment to European integration.[75] More generally, Germany was seen to be throwing its weight about. Was this the shape of things to come? Even the Americans were disconcerted; the Chancellor had intended Bush to be

[72] Günther, 'Makroökonomische Implikationen der Deutschen Einheit', 142. For a full account of Kohl's EMU strategy, see Dyson, 'Chancellor Kohl as Strategic Leader'.

[73] Fritsch-Bournazel, *Europe and German Unification*, 18–20.

[74] Mitterrand: 'Mais il ne m'a rien dit! Rien dit! Je ne l'oublierai jamais! . . . Mais il ne parle pas de modification du statut politique des Allemagnes. Il n'obtiendra rien de moi là-dessus avant que l'unité de l'Europe n'ait beaucoup progressé': Attali, *Verbatim III*, 350.

[75] Attali, *Verbatim III*, 348, 350; Teltschik, *329 Tage*, 54.

given advance notice, but because of the time difference and delays in transmission the message did not arrive in time.[76]

The decision to keep advance information about the Chancellor's speech to a minimum was intentional, but not primarily directed at the outside world. The purpose of the speech was to seize the political initiative, thus cutting the ground from under the feet of both the SPD and the FDP, and to restore the Chancellor's flagging political fortunes. It brilliantly succeeded in achieving this aim.[77] More significant in the longer term than either domestic victories or bilious reactions abroad, however, was the concept which Kohl developed to provide moves towards unification with an intellectual infrastructure.

This was firmly embedded in a pan-European structure, described in points 6 to 8 of the Programme. They are worth quoting extensively.[78]

Sixth: The development of German internal relationships remains embedded in the overall European process and in East–West relationships. The future architecture of Germany must be fitted into the future architecture of Europe as a whole. For this the West, with its concept of a lasting and just European system of peace, has rendered yeoman service.

Seventh: The European Community's power of attraction and influence is and remains a constant factor in overall European development. We wish to strengthen it further. The European Community is now being called on to approach the reform-oriented States of Central, Eastern and South-Eastern Europe with openness and flexibility.

We see the process of regaining German unity as a European matter. It must therefore also be seen in combination with European integration. In this sense, the European Community must keep itself open for a democratic GDR and for other democratic States of Central and South-Eastern Europe. The Community must not end at the Elbe, but must maintain openness eastward too . . .

[76] Beschloss and Talbott, *At the Highest Levels*, 139; Teltschik, *329 Tage*, 52; Kohl, *Ich wollte Deutschlands Einheit*, 168–70; Zelikow and Rice, *Germany Unified and Europe Transformed*, 408 n. 56; Bush and Scowcroft, *A World Transformed*, 194–5.

[77] Teltschik, *329 Tage*, 49, 58; Kiessler and Elbe, *Der diplomatische Weg zur Deutschen Einheit*, 49–55. Kohl himself emphasizes the need to act before the ideas of the East German government took hold (Kohl, *Ich wollte Deutschlands Einheit*, 159): Modrow had launched the idea of a 'treaty community' (*Vertragsgemeinschaft*). Kohl also claimed the need to forestall any similar initiative by Gorbachev: *Deutsche Einheit*, no. 112, 616, and no. 120, 639. The Chancellor had been in difficulties even within his own party, and, in an attempt to cut out an individual line, declared at the CDU party conference in Bremen in September that the idea of one Germany was closer than ever: Zelikow and Rice, *Germany Unified and Europe Transformed*, 79–80; Kohl, *Ich wollte Deutschlands Einheit*, 75–6; *Deutsche Einheit*, no. 50, 426, n. 4. The SDP, meanwhile, was struggling to adapt its own version of the *Ostpolitik* to the rapidly changing situation: Garton Ash, *In Europe's Name*, 327–30.

[78] Ttranslation by Renate Fritsch-Bournazel.

Eighth: The CSCE process is and remains the core of this architecture of Europe as a whole, and must be pushed energetically forward. For this the existing CSCE forums must be taken advantage of . . .

Germany now had for the time being a view on the new European architecture, and it was the property of Chancellor Kohl. Three things stand out. First, the European Community played a crucial role in Kohl's vision of the future, but neither its institutions nor its members had been consulted.[79] The Community was indeed the subject of history, not an actor. This was to continue; on a number of occasions, Kohl was actively to oppose using the Community as a forum in which to forward the process of unifying Germany. Second, there was no explicit mention of NATO, thus casting doubt on whether Kohl saw a place for the United States in his new European order. He was later to claim that the omission was deliberate, so as not to frighten the Kremlin, and that there was no question of German withdrawal from NATO as the price of unification.[80] Certainly, the Americans made sure that that was the case.[81] Third, Kohl felt the need to mend his fences with Mitterrand, and launched the process which led to the Kohl–Mitterrand initiative of April 1990 calling for political union.

Mrs Thatcher had views similar to President Mitterrand's on the prospect of German unification, and was both disappointed and scornful when he failed, in her eyes, to hold fast to them. Unlike Mitterrand, however, Mrs Thatcher did not have a strategy to deal with the situation. Just saying 'no' was not enough, especially as she came under pressure from a US President considerably more sympathetic than she to the German cause. The option of 'binding Germany more tightly into an integrated Europe' was repugnant to her for gut reasons of national sovereignty. The result was that although the United Kingdom, as an Allied Power, was closely involved in the details of German unification, it did not have a determining influence on the outcome of the negotiations. Still less did it play a significant role, at this stage, in the debate on the new European architecture.

[79] When asked whether the Chancellor's proposals had been discussed with the Western powers, the Soviet Union, and the GDR, Teltschik replied that the 10 points were the distilled result of a large number of recent bilateral and multilateral contacts: Teltschik, *329 Tage*, 56–7. In other words, they had not. For a summary of international reactions to the 10-point plan as brought to the attention of the Chancellor, see *Deutsche Einheit*, no. 102, 574–7, and no. 109, 606.

[80] Kohl, *Ich wollte Deutschlands Einheit*, 166.

[81] 'Baker had in mind a straightforward quid pro quo: the United States would help make unification happen, *if* the West Germans stood with the Americans on the issue of NATO': Zelikow and Rice, *Germany Unified and Europe Transformed*, 173.

Chancellor Kohl believed that Mrs Thatcher was living in the past, obsessed with the idea of countering German domination of Europe by a 'balance of power' approach which belonged more properly to the nineteenth century.[82] She had lived through the collapse of the British Empire in the Second World War, and now here were the Germans popping up again.[83] Her private secretary, Charles Powell, spent three hours trying to explain to Teltschik in the Chancellor's office what the British Prime Minister felt about Germany: she belonged to an older generation, her views had been formed at a time when there had been a 'cultural gap' between Britain and Germany, she was 'uneasy' at the thought of a large, strong Germany.[84] The Chequers seminar on Germany attended by a number of distinguished academics has become infamous because of Powell's titillating account of the German character embedded in the record of the meeting and subsequently leaked to the press. The most likely explanation of this event, however, is that it had been organized at a time when the Prime Minister was ready to admit that she had to bow to the inevitable, and the pill was sugared by a modicum of pandering to her personal views—a technique well known to private secretaries endowed with forceful masters or mistresses.[85]

Mrs Thatcher's policy to deal with the perceived threat from German reunification was to 'encourage democracy in East Germany while slowing down the country's unification with West Germany'. She herself admitted that it was an unambiguous failure.[86] She attempted to persuade both Gorbachev and Mitterrand of the virtues of this approach, ultimately without success. Both were inclined to listen, but both in the end found greater advantage in extracting a price for their consent to the inevitable. Mitterrand pointed out to her that the Franco-British alliance, which she wished to strengthen in order to counterbalance the power of Germany, was devoid of substance and that the United Kingdom was to blame for it.[87]

Combined with these Fabian tactics were support for a Great Power

[82] Kohl, *Ich wollte Deutschlands Einheit*, 196; *Deutsche Einheit*, no. 109, 607, and no. 148, 719–20.   [83] *Deutsche Einheit*, no. 266, 1083, and no. 291, 1157.

[84] Teltschik, *329 Tage*, 134; Cradock, *In Pursuit of British Interests*, 110; Kiessler and Elbe, *Der diplomatische Weg zur Deutschen Einheit*, 63–5.

[85] Urban, *Diplomacy and Disillusion at the Court of Margaret Thatcher*, 118–50; Zelikow and Rice, *Germany Unified and Europe Transformed*, 236 and 441 n. 89.

[86] Thatcher, *The Downing Street Years*, 813.

[87] Thatcher, *The Downing Street Years*, 792, 795; Mitterrand, *De l'Allemagne, de la France*, 43. President Mitterrand's remarks to Mrs Thatcher may have been more emollient than he chose to recall: Attali, *Verbatim III*, 400–1.

conference for a peace settlement (Gorbachev's favoured option, but one never tolerated for a moment by Kohl or Bush) and moderate enthusiasm for a revived CSCE. Mrs Thatcher had begun by being sceptical about the Helsinki process, but had come round to the view that it 'provided a useful framework within which at least some of the problems arising in the new democratic Europe might be tackled'. It involved the Americans and the Soviet Union in Europe's future, it was a good forum for discussions of border disputes, and the principles of private property and free markets could be built on the human rights content of Helsinki.[88]

Mrs Thatcher was in no circumstances prepared to countenance the idea that a more powerful Germany might be contained within a strengthened European framework. This was not just because of her antipathy to the European Community as such, or at least to those parts of it which did not directly serve the cause of free trade; the very concept of multilateral security was foreign to her ideas about the way the world worked. Chancellor Kohl was right in concluding that she was wedded to nineteenth-century ideas of balance of power which the post-war history of Western Europe had been moving away from. Mrs Thatcher's own words express her position best:

As I have already argued, that[89] is one reason why so many Germans genuinely— I believe wrongly—want to see Germany locked in to a federal Europe. In fact, Germany is more rather than less likely to dominate within that framework; for a reunited Germany is simply too big and powerful to be just another player within Europe. Moreover, Germany has always looked east as well as west, though it is economic expansion rather than territorial aggression which is the modern manifestation of this tendency. Germany is thus by its very nature a destabilizing rather than a stabilizing force in Europe. Only the military and political engagement of the United States in Europe and close relations between the other two strongest sovereign states in Europe—Britain and France—are sufficient to balance German power: and nothing of the sort would be possible within a European super-state.[90]

If Mrs Thatcher was finally obliged to moderate her position on German unification, it was because of pressure from precisely that country which she saw as the main contributor to security in Europe—the United States. Indeed, it is ironic that the United States seemed to be more aware of the changes taking place in Europe, and more agile in adapting to them, than the Europeans themselves. This, combined with the ability to define the

---

[88] Teltschik, *329 Tage*, 134; Thatcher, *The Downing Street Years*, 799–800.
[89] The fact that 'the true origin of German *angst* is the agony of self-knowledge'.
[90] Thatcher, *The Downing Street Years*, 791; Cradock, *In Pursuit of British Interests*, 135.

national interest, explains why it was the US administration which appeared to play the leading role in drafting the new European architecture.

The Reagan Administration, it will be recalled, had been in no hurry to revise its attitude towards the Soviet Union and Eastern Europe, even though Secretary Shultz sensed that important changes were under way and towards the end of his time in office engineered a warmer tone in the relationship.[91] The wait and see policy had been followed by many European governments, and, almost by definition, by EPC. When George Bush took office in January 1989, there followed the lengthy reappraisal of policy which the United States' partners had come to expect at every changeover, even when the new incumbent had been Vice-President. The cautious President was anxious not to make a mistake, but in their concern to grind exceeding small the mills of the Washington policy machine ground so slowly that a wave of criticism mounted, both domestic and foreign. Something was needed to demonstrate American leadership.[92] Finally, the results began to emerge in a series of speeches between April and June 1989. The first, given on 17 April in the unlikely setting of Hamtramck, Michigan, an enclave of Detroit with a population of predominantly Polish origin, was focused on developments in Poland but by extension held out the prospect of Western support for all East European countries which engaged in political and economic liberalization. It passed practically unnoticed in the United States. The second was at Texas A & M University on 12 May, and was devoted to American policy towards the Soviet Union. This speech did not catch the public's imagination either, but it did lay the basis for the idea of 'moving beyond containment, to seek to integrate the Soviets into the community of nations, to help them share the rewards of international cooperation'. It was followed up by a new initiative focused on conventional arms control in Europe, enthusiastically welcomed at the NATO Summit on 29–30 May.[93] It was reputedly Mitterrand, when he visited Bush at Kennebunkport, Maine in May 1989, who convinced the US President to do more in the field of arms control in order to defuse the increasingly venomous debate within NATO about the proposed deployment of Lance missiles in Germany.[94] Be that as it may, the major concern of American policy at the time was the relationship with

[91] Shultz, *Turmoil and Triumph*, 1003.

[92] For the Bush policy review, see Bush and Scowcroft, *A World Transformed*, 37–48.

[93] Zelikow and Rice, *Germany Unified and Europe Transformed*, 24–32; Beschloss and Talbott, *At the Highest Levels*, 69–72; Bush and Scowcroft, *A World Transformed*, 46–56.

[94] Beschloss and Talbott, *At the Highest Levels*, 77. By his own account, Bush was already determined on this policy: Bush and Scowcroft, *A World Transformed*, 73–8.

the Soviet Union and the military aspects of the transatlantic relationship, rather than a rethinking of the political landscape in Europe.

The US CFE initiative had nevertheless been developed together with policies towards Europe East and West. The US Administration would promote reform in the East: Bush was to visit Poland and Hungary in June 1989, and launch the international effort to help these countries transform their economic systems. As for the West, the new American approach to the European Community, now on track for the Single Market scheduled for January 1993, was set out by Bush, in the presence of President Mitterrand, in the third of his series of speeches at Boston University on 21 May.[95]

Bush began by reaffirming America's traditional ties with Europe: 'The changes that are occurring in Western Europe are less dramatic than those taking place in the East, but they are no less fundamental. The postwar order that began in 1945 is transforming into something very different . . . Our alliance . . . is based on far more than the perception of a common enemy. It is a tie of culture, kinship and shared values.' He went on to offer unequivocal support for a united Europe: 'Now a new century holds the promise of a united Europe . . . The nations of Europe are already moving towards greater economic integration, with the ambitious goal of a single European market in 1992. The United States has often declared it seeks a healing of old enmities, an integration of Europe. At the same time, there has been an historical ambivalence on the part of some Americans toward a more united Europe. To this ambivalence has been added apprehension at the prospect of 1992. But whatever others may think, this Administration is of one mind. We believe a strong, united Europe means a strong America.'

Bush drew the conclusion that a united Europe should be a partner of the United States: 'The United States welcomes the emergence of Europe as a partner in world leadership. We are ready to develop—with the European Community and its member States—new mechanisms of consultation and co-operation on political and global issues, from strengthening the forces of democracy in the third world, to managing regional tensions, to putting an end to the division of Europe. A resurgent Western Europe is an economic magnet, drawing Eastern Europe closer, toward the commonwealth of free nations.' There were bound to be 'clashes and controversies' over economic issues, but these paled in comparison with keeping the peace in Europe. This had been done for forty years by the NATO

---

[95] Unclassified telegram USINFO 21 1846Z May 89/01/04.

shield. 'With a Western Europe that is now coming together, we recognize that new forms of co-operation must be developed. We applaud the defense co-operation developing in the revitalized Western European Union, whose members worked with the US to keep open the sea lanes of the Persian Gulf.[96] We applaud the growing military co-operation between West Germany and France. We welcome British and French programs to modernize their deterrent capability, and their moves toward cooperation in this [area]. It is perfectly right and proper that Europeans increasingly see their defense co-operation as an investment in a secure future.'

Nevertheless, Bush warned against complacency: 'There is a great irony here. While an ideological earthquake is shaking asunder the very foundation of Communist societies, the West is being tested by complacency.' America remained committed to the Alliance and to NATO's policy of flexible response which kept the United States linked to Europe: 'The history of this century teaches Americans and Europeans to remain prepared.' The steps being taken by Gorbachev were welcome: 'we should give credit where credit is due'. But 'we have an obligation to temper optimism with prudence.'

This surprising speech expressed both a commitment to a process, going beyond economic to political union, which had barely begun in Europe itself, and the determination of the US Administration to retain its transatlantic responsibilities. True, the continuing importance of NATO was recalled, but Bush expressed readiness to negotiate new mechanisms with the evolving European Community, which was to be a partner of the United States in world leadership,[97] and specifically mentioned the WEU as a desirable forum for defence co-operation. The initiative was not given the attention it merited, either at the time or later. This was perhaps because the support expressed for European union became less clear-cut under the pressure of events, as the Americans began to think through the implications of their generous stance, perhaps because the Europeans themselves, regardless of their views on the United States and NATO, were unable to envisage a relationship with the Americans which was not one of inferiority.

Bush extended his vision from the European Community to the whole of Europe in a speech he gave at Mainz on 31 May, immediately after the NATO Summit meeting at which the CFE initiative was

[96] During the Iran–Iraq war.

[97] The idea of a US-EC partnership covering both economic and political questions had been launched in Feb. 1989 by Delors, but had not been taken up at the time by the US Administration: Grant, *Delors*, 165.

launched.[98] The theme had already been announced at a press conference after the Summit: 'Our overall aim is to overcome the division of Europe and to forge a unity based on Western values'. At Mainz, Bush proclaimed the goal of the West to be to 'let Europe be whole and free'—the 'new mission of NATO'. 'The Cold War . . . can only end when Europe is whole. Today it is this very concept of a divided Europe that is under siege.' So far, Gorbachev might have agreed, recalling his idea of a common European home. But Bush went on to say that 'there cannot be a common European home until all within it are free to move from room to room'. Noting the Hungarian decision to begin dismantling the Iron Curtain, Bush exclaimed, six months ahead of events, 'Let Berlin be next! Let Berlin be next!' Self-determination was sought for all of Germany and all of Eastern Europe. How was this pan-Europeanism to be given institutional expression? The CSCE (of which the United States was of course a member) could do more to promote pluralism and set guidelines for holding free elections in Eastern Europe. Finally, the West Germans were welcomed not only as 'friends and allies', but also as America's 'partners in leadership'.

There was a 'vision' to be discovered here, had more attention been paid to what Bush had to say. He himself ruefully admitted that the series of speeches intended to set out a view on the changes in Europe (Boston University, Mainz, and a third in Leiden on 17 July) had been little noted at the time.[99] While it would be going too far to say that the new European architecture had already been laid out, the Bush speeches certainly contained what were to be its main features: a Europe of free nations, each at liberty to decide its own destiny, the continuance of the US security role in Europe in a posture which did not threaten the Soviet Union, an autonomous but not independent security role for Europe itself, and a European Community gaining in strength and power of attraction, recognized as a partner of the United States in world leadership. Particularly noteworthy was the emphasis on the future of Germany, which had been under close study by the White House staff since the beginning of the Bush Presidency. An earlier draft of the Mainz speech had contained more direct references to German unification, but these had been omitted so as not to get ahead of Kohl's own stance on the question.[100] The offer of 'partnership in leadership' to the Federal Republic, noted wryly in

---

[98] The following account is based on Zelikow and Rice, *Germany Unified and Europe Transformed*, 31–2. See also Beschloss and Talbott, *At the Highest Levels*, 81; Bush and Scowcroft, *A World Transformed*, 83–4.

[99] Zelikow and Rice, *Germany Unified and Europe Transformed*, 123–4 and 409 n. 62.

[100] Zelikow and Rice, *Germany Unified and Europe Transformed*, 31.

London,[101] reflected accurately not only the Bush Administration's attitude towards the 'special relationship' but also the reality of the evolving situation. The partnership between the United States and Germany over German unification was to have an important influence on the way European foreign-policy making developed.

Why was it that, at a time when his European counterparts seemed content to wait on events and manage them as they occurred, George Bush was able to seize on an as yet uncertain trend and turn it into a strategic opportunity?[102] Admittedly, Bush had just taken up office as President and was looking for an initiative to make his mark, while the European leaders had been in government for many years and presumably suffered from the disinclination to think afresh consequent upon long familiarity with power.[103] But beyond this, the American President had the advantage of a numerous and highly effective staff in the White House, renewed at least every four years, and devoted to considering foreign policy options from the viewpoint of the President's political requirements as well as from that of the national interest. From the admittedly partisan viewpoint of Zelikow and Rice, both White House staffers, there would have been no daring 'vision' on Europe if matters had been left to the State Department.[104] This advantage was denied to the Europeans. Even Mitterrand,

---

[101] Mrs Thatcher read the Mainz speech with close attention, although she attributed the decline in the United Kingdom's standing in Washington to the malign influence of Secretary Baker: Beschloss and Talbott, *At the Highest Levels*, 81; Thatcher, *The Downing Street Years*, 783, 789. According to Scowcroft, the offer was for 'flourish and encouragement' only: Bush and Scowcroft, *A World Transformed*, 84. The discrepancy between the offer of partnership to the European Community in Boston and to the Federal Republic in Mainz can be explained in part by courtesy to the audience (President Mitterrand on the first occasion and Chancellor Kohl on the second). It also reflects, however, the perception that Germany's economic strength made it weigh heavily within the EC's councils. The tendency to give preference to the bilateral relationship was confirmed by the operational requirements of German unification.

[102] It must be recognized that as early as Oct. 1988 Mrs Thatcher had in her famous Bruges speech called for recognition of a wider Europe as an entity which made historical and cultural sense. But the message was overlaid by the neo-Gaullist notes which the Prime Minister gleefully incorporated in a text which the Foreign Office did its best to emulsify: Thatcher, *The Downing Street Years*, 744–5; Cradock, *In Pursuit of British Interests*, 130; Young, *This Blessed Plot*, 348–50; Nelsen and Stubb, *The European Union*, 45–50.

[103] Thatcher had been in power since 1979, Mitterrand since 1981, and Kohl since 1982. It was Kohl's astonishing ability, in his turn, to perceive the political opportunities afforded by the fall of the Berlin Wall that ensured his political survival.

[104] Zelikow and Rice, *Germany Unified and Europe Transformed*, 24–6. Was Bush himself aware of the full import of what he was saying? By his own account, his thinking on the specific question of the 'new European architecture' came later and was a more rushed affair: Bush and Scowcroft, *A World Transformed*, 231–2. But the staffers knew what they were doing.

whose constitutional position most nearly resembled that of the American President, had a very small personal staff—and he was by nature inclined to work up his own initiatives.[105] It goes without saying that EPC had neither National Security Council nor State Department, which in itself was enough to disqualify institutional Europe from innovating in foreign policy questions.

Although Bush's Mainz speech had invited the people of all Germany to decide their own destiny, it certainly did not foresee that they would be called upon to do so quite so soon. The events from the summer of 1989 on—the stream of immigrants from East Germany, the mass demonstrations in the country, the breaching of the Berlin Wall—required the United States, like all other countries, to review its approach towards the future shape of Europe. While the Europeans, with the exception of Kohl, were still in several minds on the question, the results of the American review were seen in a speech given by Secretary of State James Baker in Berlin on 12 December 1989.[106] The speech was significantly entitled 'A New Europe, a New Atlanticism: Architecture for a New Era'.

Avoiding triumphalism, but with a controlled rhetoric which rose to the occasion, Baker built his argument on the premise that the peoples of Eastern Europe had freed themselves: 'From the Baltic to the Adriatic, an irresistible movement has gathered force—a movement of, by, and for the people. In their peaceful urgent multitude, the peoples of Eastern Europe have held up a mirror to the West and have reflected the enduring power of our own best values.' The task now was to provide the architecture for continued peaceful change. The first step was for free men and women to create free governments. These were the building blocks 'of a Europe whole and free'. However, a Europe undivided might not necessarily be a Europe peaceful and prosperous:

As Europe changes, the instruments for Western cooperation must adapt. Working together, we must design and gradually put into place a new architecture for a new era.

This new architecture must have a place for old foundations and structures that remain valuable—like NATO—while recognizing that they can also serve new collective purposes. The new architecture must continue the construction of institutions—like the EC—that can help draw together the West while also serving as an open door to the East. And the new architecture must build up frameworks— like the CSCE process—that can overcome the division of Europe and bridge the Atlantic Ocean.

[105] Cole, *François Mitterrand*, 94–5.
[106] Department of State press release, 12 Dec. 1989.

This new structure must also accomplish two special purposes. First, as a part of overcoming the division of Europe there must be an opportunity to overcome through peace and freedom the division of Berlin and of Germany. The United States and NATO have stood for unification for 40 years, and we will not waver from that goal.

Second, the architecture should reflect that America's security—politically, militarily, and economically—remains linked to Europe's security. The United States and Canada share Europe's neighbourhood.

As President Bush stated in May, 'The United States is and will remain a European power'. And as he added last week, 'The US will maintain significant military forces in Europe as long as our allies desire our presence as part of a common security effort'. This is our commitment to a common future, a recognition of a need for an active United States role in Europe, a need even acknowledged by President Gorbachev.

The charge for us all, then, is to work together toward the New Europe and the New Atlanticism.'

The task for NATO was to construct a new security architecture that maintained the common defence. At the same time, the non-military component of European security would grow. 'NATO will become the forum where Western nations co-operate to negotiate, implement, verify and extend agreements between East and West.' Intensified NATO consultations on regional conflicts would play an important role. NATO should consider initiatives, in particular through the CSCE process, 'to build economic and political ties with the East, to promote respect for human rights, to help build democratic institutions, and to fashion, consistent with Western security interests, a more open environment for East–West trade and investment'. Finally, NATO could be a model for the benefits of collective security.

The Secretary of State then launched into a startling encomium of the achievements and future role of the European Community:

The future development of the European Community will play a central role in shaping the New Europe.

The example of Western co-operation through the European Community has already had a dramatic effect on Eastern attitudes toward economic liberty. The success of this great European experiment, perhaps more than any other factor, has caused Eastern Europeans to recognize that people as well as nations cooperate more productively when they are free to choose. The ballot box and the free market are the fundamental instruments of choice.

But the European experiment has succeeded not just because it has appealed to the enlightened self-interest of European producers and consumers. This experiment has succeeded because the vision of its founders encompassed and yet transcended this material. This experiment has succeeded because it also held out the higher goal of political as well as economic barriers overcome, of a Europe united.

This was the goal of Monnet and Schumann. This was the goal of the United States of Marshall and Acheson. This was the goal contained in the Treaty of Rome and more recently in the European Single Act. The United States supports this goal today with the same energy it did 40 years ago.

This support came at a price. The single market should become ever more open, and the link with the United States should be strengthened. Baker proposed that 'the United States and the European Community work together to achieve, whether in treaty or some other form, a significantly strengthened set of institutional and constitutional links. Working from shared ideals and common values, we face a set of mutual challenges—in economics, foreign policy, the environment, science, and a host of other fields. So it makes sense for us to fashion our responses together as a matter of common course.' Furthermore, the United States recognized the Community's leading role in promoting reform in Eastern Europe, centred on the Commission in the G24. A new role was also foreseen for the CSCE, by giving new content to each of the three baskets. Its highest priority would be to encourage free elections and political pluralism.

Baker ended his survey of the New Architecture by reaffirming the United States' support for German unification, on the four conditions Bush had laid down at the NATO Summit the previous week.[107] Among these was that 'unification should occur in the context of Germany's continued commitment to NATO and an increasingly integrated European Community'.

The vision put forward by Baker was therefore of a rapidly changing Europe, held together by the institutions which already existed but which would have to adapt to change. In all these institutions, the United States would be to a greater or lesser degree involved:

. . . we will create a New Europe on the basis of a New Atlanticism.

NATO will remain North America's primary link with Europe. As arms control and political arrangements increasingly supplement the still vital military component of European security, NATO will take on new roles.

The European Community is already an economic pillar of the transatlantic relationship. It will also take on, perhaps in concert with other European

---

[107] In fact, these conditions had been supplied to the President by Baker: Zelikow and Rice, *Germany Unified and Europe Transformed*, 132; *Deutsche Einheit*, no. 102, 574 n. 1. For extracts from the President's speech, see Fritsch-Bournazel, *Europe and German Unification*, 81–2.

institutions, increasingly important political roles. Indeed, it has already done so, as evidenced by the Community's co-ordination of a Western effort to support reform in Eastern Europe. And as it continues to do so, the link between the United States and the European Community should become stronger, the issues we discuss more diversified, and our common endeavours more important.

At the same time, the substantive overlap between NATO and European institutions will grow. This overlap must lead to synergy, not friction. Better communication among European and transatlantic institutions will become more urgent.

The CSCE process could become the most important forum of East–West co-operation. Its mandate will grow as this cooperation takes root.

By this speech, the United States confirmed the position it had been working out over the previous months and in three respects imparted a new turn to the debate on the new European architecture.[108] First, the Americans had realized, sooner than the Europeans, that the unification of Germany was the key to 'The Big Game',[109] and were not hampered by history from drawing the logical conclusion. Henceforward, and coinciding with the tide of events in East Germany, discussions on the architecture had to take unification as a given; other scenarios were no longer credible. This had the important procedural consequence of excluding the Community from the most important decisions shaping Europe's future. Second, the Bush Administration confirmed its choice to stay in Europe, both militarily and politically. The United States was and would remain a 'European power'.[110] No scenario for the future of Europe which did not include the United States—whether Gorbachev's 'common home' or the independent power dreamed of by some Western idealists—would be a practical possibility. Third, while the European Community was assigned a prominent role in the American vision, the United States assumed that adequate consultative procedures would be set up between the transatlantic partners to ensure unity of purpose and approach. This was made clear not only by the language used by Baker in his speech ('it makes sense for us to seek to fashion our responses together as a matter of common course'), but also by subsequent diplomatic action.[111] The American line was not so very different from that taken by Dr Kissinger in the Year of Europe.[112] Then, too, the Americans had wanted a place behind the scenes

---

[108] For the thinking leading up to the NATO Summit and the Berlin speech, see Zelikow and Rice, *Germany Unified and Europe Transformed*, 404–5 n. 32, and 132. For comments on the Berlin speech, see ibid. 142–4 and Teltschik, *329 Tage*, 77–8.

[109] Zelikow and Rice, *Germany Unified and Europe Transformed*, 179.

[110] Ibid. 169.

[111] Teltschik, *329 Tage*, 218; Attali, *Verbatim III*, 457, 616, 618.

[112] Nuttall, *European Political Co-operation*, 82–93.

from where they could intervene before a final decision was taken, if they felt their interests were at risk. Transatlantic political consultations had made great strides since the Gymnich agreement of 1974, beginning with the British Presidency of 1986 and being extended by the Irish Presidency of 1990.[113] Even the French, traditionally most resistant to transatlantic influence, no longer made any objections to meetings at working-group level. The primacy subsequently claimed for NATO nevertheless set the Member States against each other, embittering the IGC discussions on the security dimension and ensuring that they would result in a stalemate.

The sidelining of the Community

Amid all these blueprints for the future of Europe put forward by eminent statesmen and women, where was the Community itself, and in particular EPC? It has been argued above that the 'acceleration of history', beginning in the summer of 1989, removed the monopoly of Foreign Ministries in European foreign-policy making by bringing Heads of Government centre stage, with their generally keener sense of domestic pressures and sharper eye for domestic effect. Prime Ministers were less inclined, and had fewer opportunities, than Foreign Ministers to engage in an exercise of collective reflection with their European colleagues, and EPC was the weaker for it. This did not mean, however, that the Community had taken a vow of silence. Especially at the level of the European Council, declaration succeeded declaration, but they followed the trend rather than set it, and when it came to hard negotiations on the status of unified Germany, the Community was no more than a bystander.

The European Council first set out a comprehensive position on the international role of the Community at its meeting at Rhodes on 2–3 December 1988.[114] The purpose of this text, drafted jointly by the Political Committee and Coreper, was primarily to allay widespread fears that the post-1992 Community of the Single Market would be isolationist and protectionist. It therefore stressed the EC's attachment to free trade and to a continued relationship with its traditional partners. Following the suggestion made by Mr Tindemans at the informal meeting of Foreign Ministers at Ioannina earlier in the Greek Presidency, the text included a passage on the Community's policy 'against the background of improving East–West relations'. This concentrated on readiness for further

[113] Ibid. 285–6; Murray, 'View from the United States', 214–15.
[114] *Bull. EC*, Dec. 1988, 1.1.10; Smith, *The Making of EU Foreign Policy*, 45–6.

co-operation with the European members of the CMEA (the Joint Declaration with the CMEA had been issued in June of that year), but also
included commitments to further progress in the CSCE, the establishment
of a secure and stable balance of conventional forces in Europe, promotion of human rights, and the development of political dialogue. The
Community was still operating in the mindset of détente.

On internal procedures, however, and foreshadowing the Belgian memorandum of March 1990, the European Council declared:

The European Community and the Twelve are determined to make full use of the
provisions of the Single European Act in order to strengthen solidarity among
them, co-ordination on the political and economic aspects of security, and
consistency between the external policies of the European Community and the
policies agreed in the framework of European political co-operation. They will
strive to reach swift adoption of common positions and implementation of joint
action.

The General Affairs Council continued to focus on developments in
Eastern Europe at its meeting on 24 April 1989.[115] It emphasized the need
'to ensure a more comprehensive, concerted and dynamic approach to
[the] countries [of Eastern Europe]', but betrayed the essentially internal,
procedural nature of its concerns by stipulating that 'the co-operation
which the Community is in the process of establishing with those countries must be complementary to that of the Member States, and greater
consistency should be sought between Community policies and those
agreed in the framework of European political co-operation'. 'Consistency'
was on a fair way to becoming a mantra. The European Council at Madrid
on 26–7 June 1989 vigorously rotated the prayer-wheel, intoning, in a text
prepared by EPC, 'satisfactory progress has been made in establishing an
appropriate policy towards the East European countries ensuring consistency between Community policies and those agreed within political co-
operation, in accordance with Article 30(5) of the Single Act'.[116]

One might have expected an immediate reaction from EPC to the
breach of the Berlin Wall. The Statement concerning the German Democratic Republic issued on 10 November 1989 is breathtaking in its concision and simplicity, and deserves quoting in full: 'The Twelve welcome
the decision taken by the authorities of the German Democratic Republic

[115] *Bull. EC*, Apr. 1989, 2.2.11; Smith, *The Making of EU Foreign Policy*, 47–8.
[116] *Bull. EC*, June 1989, 1.1.13. A report on the Community's economic and political
relations with Eastern Europe, submitted to the European Council, had been jointly prepared by Coreper and the Political Committee: Smith, *The Making of EU Foreign Policy*,
48.

to authorize East German citizens to leave the country freely. They hope that the practical arrangements that have been established will permit the real exercise of this freedom. The Twelve hope that this represents a stage in a process of far-reaching reforms that will allow the people of the GDR to define their future and to enjoy their democratic rights in full freedom'.[117] However, no special meeting was held until the informal dinner of the European Council in Paris on 18 November 1989. For this France, which held the Presidency in the second half of 1989, was in part responsible. Mitterrand was too uncertain of his own position to wish to take the risk of co-ordinating that of others, and resisted calls to bring forward the December European Council in Strasbourg. Kohl attributed to Mrs Thatcher the idea of calling a special meeting of the Heads of State and Government, but the British Prime Minister makes no mention in her memoirs of an initiative on her part, and ascribes the meeting to a French desire to clear the decks in order to allow the Strasbourg European Council to concentrate on EMU and the Social Charter—a justification advanced *après coup* by the French. In fact, Mitterrand was obliged to cede to domestic pressure, particularly from Giscard d'Estaing, who, in the words of the President, 'jumped on every idea that came along'.[118] In any event, none of the participants seemed anxious to talk about unification, or to engage in a discussion on the future shape of Europe.

President Mitterrand launched the proceedings by asking four practical questions: Should assistance be given to the East European countries immediately, or not until the democratization process is more advanced? Should the question of frontiers be raised? What attitude should be taken towards Gorbachev? What could the Community do? The first to reply was Chancellor Kohl. We have Mrs Thatcher's word for it that he said people wanted to hear Europe's voice, and then obliged by speaking for forty minutes. Mrs Thatcher herself was in favour of as little change as possible, as slowly as possible. Both NATO and the Warsaw Pact must be kept intact to create a background of stability. The only practical contribution was made by Jacques Delors, who described the different types of agreement

---

[117] *EPC Bulletin*, Doc. 89/262.

[118] Attali, *Verbatim III*, 339, 340; Kohl, *Ich wollte Deutschlands Einheit*, 138; Thatcher, *The Downing Street Years*, 759, 793; van Eekelen, *Debating European Security*, 28; *Deutsche Einheit*, no. 94A, 541–2; Favier and Martin-Roland, *La Décennie Mitterrand*, iii. 183. Chancellor Kohl appears to have misunderstood a proposal made to him by Mrs Thatcher on the telephone for a bilateral UK–German summit meeting before the European Council in Strasbourg: *Deutsche Einheit*, no. 81, 507. Giscard's idea was that Mitterrand should bear a common European position to the Bush–Gorbachev summit at Malta in December. This did not happen: Favier and Martin-Roland, *La Décennie Mitterrand*, iii. 183.

the Community could conclude with Poland, Hungary, and East Germany. The unification of Germany was not mentioned at all.[119] This was a deliberate tactic on the part of the Chancellor, and explained his extensive speech. Kohl did not want to give EC partners, who had no responsibility 'in and for Germany', the opportunity to narrow through discussion his room for manoeuvre. There were other reasons, as will be explained, why the Community did not take part in the discussion on German unification, but the most important was that the German Chancellor wanted it that way.[120]

The informal meeting in Paris did, however, produce one concrete decision: the Troika was asked to explore the possibilities of setting up a bank for the development and modernization of Eastern Europe; of establishing a Training Foundation, and of opening up some of the EC's existing education, training, and technological programmes. The bank was the brainchild of Jacques Attali, President Mitterrand's adviser. The idea was to create a pan-European institution in which all European countries (and only European countries) would take part, disposing of its own financial resources. It followed on from the Western Economic Summit at the Arche, and reflected Attali's dismay both at the American-inspired move towards a G7 aid consortium for the Central and East European countries (CEECs) and the decision to entrust the co-ordination of Western aid to the European Commission. Here were a right-thinking Frenchman's two *bêtes noires*—the United States and European supranational institutions. The European Bank For Reconstruction and Development (EBRD) was a way of circumventing them both, just like France's 'Eureka' initiative in response to 'Star Wars' a few years earlier.[121] Furthermore, it provided President Mitterrand with an eye-catching scheme which put some content into Gorbachev's 'common european home'. It will be recalled that at this stage, and at least until the end of 1989, Mitterrand had by no means

[119] Except by Mrs Thatcher, who 'put her foot in it' when the pudding was reached, and was reminded by Chancellor Kohl of a supportive NATO declaration dating from 1970: Attali, *Verbatim III*, 343. See also Mitterrand, *De l'Allemagne, de la France*, 76. Mrs Thatcher went away with the conviction that it had been agreed to maintain the status quo: Kohl, *Ich wollte Deutschlands Einheit*, 184. Genscher later remarked with some bitterness that while the Heads of State and Government may have kept clear of the subject of unification, the Foreign Ministers, who met separately, did not: Genscher, *Erinnerungen*, 663. This is an example of the way in which control of the situation was passing to the higher level.

[120] Favier and Martin-Roland, *La Décennie Mitterrand*, iii. 185–6; Attali, *Verbatim III*, 342–4; Mitterrand, *De l'Allemagne, de la France*, 74–7; Thatcher, *The Downing Street Years*, 793–4; Teltschik, *329 Tage*, 38.

[121] Haggard and Moravcsik, 'The Political Economy of Financial Assistance to Eastern Europe', 271.

rejected the Gorbachevian architecture. By dint of perseverance, Attali persuaded the President to adopt the idea, and Mitterrand forced through a study of it at the 18 November dinner of Heads of State and Government. No one was enthusiastic, but only Mrs Thatcher was strongly opposed, and her objections were overridden in the haste to depart.[122]

The study was entrusted to the Troika, and according to Mitterrand at the level of Heads of Government.[123] Report was to be made in December to the European Council at Strasbourg. There was thus a presumption of intergovernmentalism, which was not conducive to accommodating the functions of a Bank in the Community framework. Most Member States thought that the Bank would unnecessarily duplicate the work already being done by the European Investment Bank. This point of view, for whatever reasons of its own, was defended especially strongly by the Commission. Others, including Mrs Thatcher, thought that the job would be better left to the international financial institutions. The proponents of this view opposed the inclusion of the Soviet Union and the exclusion of the United States.[124] In the end, it was Mrs Thatcher herself who made a decision possible at Strasbourg. She proposed that the Bank should be open to all OECD members, including therefore the United States, and a compromise was agreed on that basis.[125]

One of the major objections to the Bank, the absence of the Americans, had been resolved (although several months' wrangling was still to come before the statutes of the EBRD were finally agreed); the other, the setting up outside the Community framework of a new institution to assist the process of political and economic change in the countries of Eastern Europe, was not of sufficient concern to prevent the decision from being taken. The European Community was not, for its Member States, the exclusive framework for the new European architecture.

The European Council which met at Strasbourg on 8–9 December 1989 was a chilly affair. Germany's partners had not forgotten, still less forgiven, Chancellor Kohl's ten-point speech the previous month.[126] Yet Kohl and Genscher were able to wring from their colleagues a reference (in a statement prepared in the EPC framework) to the unity of the German people, drawing on the language used in the letter on German unity attached to the Moscow Treaty in 1970, and approved

---

[122] Attali, *Verbatim III*, 298, 315, 318, 321, 324, 325, 328, 344.
[123] President Mitterrand's press conference, 18 Nov. 1989.
[124] Védrine, *Les Mondes de François Mitterrand*, 449–50; Thatcher, *The Downing Street Years*, 759.   [125] *Bull EC*, Dec. 1989, 1.1.14; Attali, *Verbatim III*, 370.
[126] Kohl, *Ich wollte Deutschlands Einheit*, 195–201.

by NATO at the time.[127] This diplomatic success was facilitated by the welcome given to President Bush's support for German unification at the NATO Summit in Brussels just four days before. Indeed, the wording of the European Council's Declaration corresponded closely with the four conditions Bush had set out.[128]

Apart from the section on Germany, the Declaration did not contain any new strategic thinking.[129] True, there was a section which proclaimed, 'At this time of profound and rapid change, the Community is and must remain a point of reference and influence. It remains the cornerstone of a new European architecture and, in its will to openness, a mooring for a future European equilibrium. This equilibrium will be still better ensured by a parallel development of the role of the Council of Europe, EFTA and the CSCE process'. Amidst the welter of mixed metaphor, however, there was nothing to make the assertion true. That was reserved for the conclusions of the European Council itself, drafted on the EC as opposed to the EPC network. (Unlike at Rhodes one year previously, the two had failed to combine.) The European Council referred to the agreements concluded or under negotiation with the CEECs and the USSR, and the aid being given to the CEECs, and gave the process a push forward. As described above, it decided in principle to set up a European Bank for Reconstruction and Development.

This was practical and significant, and demonstrated that the Community depended on its economic powers to give substance to its claim to be a cornerstone. Developments over the unification of Germany, however, disqualified the Community from playing an active role in developing the new structure of Europe.

At the beginning of 1990, the conundrum which faced Chancellor Kohl was the following. In a rapidly deteriorating situation in the GDR, how was German unification to be achieved in conditions which secured the assent of all interested parties, at the lowest political and economic cost, and preferably in a way which maximized political advantage for his own

---

[127] 'We seek the strengthening of the state of peace in Europe in which the German people will regain its unity through free self-determination. This process should take place peacefully and democratically . . . It also has to be placed in the perspective of European integration': *Bull. EC*, Dec. 1989, 1.1.20; Kohl, *Ich wollte Deutschlands Einheit*, 200; Teltschik, *329 Tage*, 73; Zelikow and Rice, *Germany Unified and Europe Transformed*, 137–8; Mitterrand, *De l'Allemagne, de la France*, 97–9; Favier and Martin-Roland, *La Décennie Mitterrand*, iii. 205–11.

[128] Zelikow and Rice, *Germany Unified and Europe Transformed*, 132–3, 138.

[129] A half-hearted attempt to discuss the security implications of unification is reported to have foundered on Irish opposition: van Eekelen, *Debating European Security*, 29.

party? The interested parties which had to be squared were the United States, which had made plain its determination to maintain its influence in Europe through a continued military presence;[130] the Soviet Union, which still entertained real fears about German irredentism in Europe; the Four Powers as a whole, because of their responsibilities under international law; and Germany's other European neighbours, in particular France and Poland, whose memories of past German behaviour remained particularly strong. These categories overlapped, but there was good reason in each case to pay attention to the countries which composed them. *Ex contrario*, there was equally good reason not to enlarge the categories. Kohl did not want to have to square more than the absolute minimum of interested parties.

The solution to the conundrum lay in the choice of forum in which to take negotiations forward. This could not be confined to the two Germanys, as Genscher had suggested in a speech at Tutzing on 31 January, because of the political concerns of the United States and the Soviet Union as well as the legal responsibilities of the Four Powers, and yet it was obviously inappropriate for Germany to have its fate settled by others, as though it had only just emerged from defeat. Furthermore, the forum had to be one in which military questions could be dealt with, since so many of the questions at issue—continued US involvement in NATO, Soviet fears about security, neighbours' memories of invasion—needed military responses. Genscher had seen this clearly when in the same Tutzing speech, while rejecting the neutralization of a united Germany, he proposed that NATO's military structures should not be extended to the territory of what would by then be the former DDR. This was the crux of the matter.[131]

The solution to the riddle was found, not in Bonn, but in Washington. By late January 1990, officials in the State Department had worked out, as part of a package which also included reductions in the levels of US forces in Europe, an approach whereby the external aspects of early German unification would be negotiated in a 'Two Plus Four' framework, in which the Two were the two German States and the Four the Four Powers.[132] At a crucial meeting in Washington on 2 February, this formula was accepted by Genscher, who was anxious to regain the initiative from

---

[130] Zelikow and Rice, *Germany Unified and Europe Transformed*, 169.
[131] Ibid. 174–5; Genscher, *Erinnerungen*, 713–15; Kiessler and Elbe, *Der diplomatische Weg zur deutschen Einheit*, 79–85.
[132] Zelikow and Rice, *Germany Unified and Europe Transformed*, 167–72; Kiessler and Elbe, *Der diplomatische Weg zur deutschen Einheit*, 86–9.

Kohl.[133] Baker then went to Moscow to sell the idea to Shevardnadze and Gorbachev (stopping on the way at Shannon to brief Dumas, who was in Ireland for an EC meeting—there was no suggestion that Dumas should pass the news on to his European colleagues). Gorbachev was interested in the idea he put forward, and endorsed it at a subsequent meeting with Kohl on 10 February.[134]

It remained to secure general endorsement for the formula in the Western camp. The British and French Foreign Ministers had been sounded out,[135] but the news had yet to be broken to the United States' other partners in NATO and the EC. The opportunity presented itself at the 'Open Skies' conference held in Ottawa on 12–14 February 1990—a long-scheduled meeting attended by the Foreign Ministers of all the NATO and Warsaw Pact countries. Once the final details of the formula had been worked out by the Four Powers and the Federal Republic, the result was announced to the NATO Foreign Ministers. The response was extremely hostile. The problem was not so much disagreement with the conceptual approach—although the Community had been inclining towards using the CSCE Summit to be held in Paris in the autumn as a forum to discuss the future shape of Europe—as a feeling that the negotiations had been done behind the backs of the Allies, who would be excluded from discussions on a subject—the future status of a united Germany—which was of vital importance to them. The Netherlands' Foreign Minister, Hans van den Broek, complained that the whole thing was illegal, objecting in particular to the language used on 'the security of neighbouring States', of which the Netherlands was one. It was explained that 'this was a matter for the Allied powers with legal rights in Germany and nobody else. That is why the deal was cut this way, and if you don't like it, I'm sorry but you have no legal rights.' Gianni De Michelis, the Italian Foreign Minister, supported van den Broek, demanding that Germany agree to discuss unification in NATO, the unity of which would otherwise be impaired. He was brutally told by Genscher to shut up: 'You are not part of the game'.[136]

---

[133] Zelikow and Rice, *Germany Unified and Europe Transformed*, 176–7; Genscher, *Erinnerungen*, 716–19.

[134] *Deutsche Einheit*, no. 174, 805; Zelikow and Rice, *Germany Unified and Europe Transformed*, 179–91; Kohl, *Ich wollte Deutschlands Einheit*, 264–77; Teltschik, *329 Tage*, 137–43.

[135] Zelikow and Rice, *Germany Unified and Europe Transformed*, 173–4, 179; Attali, *Verbatim III*, 412.

[136] Zelikow and Rice, *Germany Unified and Europe Transformed*, 191–5; Szabo, *The Diplomacy of German Unification*, 64–5; Attali, *Verbatim III*, 420; Genscher, *Erinnerungen*, 728–9. Even Bush thought that Genscher had been tactless: Kohl, *Ich wollte Deutschlands Einheit*, 306; *Deutsche Einheit*, no. 192, 866. Genscher later claimed that his remarks, although addressed to De Michelis, were really aimed at van den Broek: Kiessler and Elbe,

NATO nevertheless had an important part to play in convincing Gorbachev that by remaining in existence it did not represent a Cold War-type threat to the Soviet Union, but on the contrary was a guarantee of stability on the European continent. This it did at the Summit meeting in London on 5–6 July 1990. The declaration adopted on that occasion showed that the Alliance was committed to transforming the East–West relationship to one of co-operation, and announced a corresponding military reorganization, including setting a ceiling on the number of German forces. It proved crucial in inducing Gorbachev to strike a bargain with Kohl over the status of Germany when they met in the Caucasus on 15–16 July.[137]

In a nutshell, the deal was the following:

- a united Germany, consisting of the FRG, the GDR, and Berlin, was to remain a member of NATO;
- NATO was not to expand eastwards as a result;
- Germany would stand the Soviet Union's friend, giving moral as well as financial support.

This set the parameters for the new shape of Europe—at least until the collapse of the Soviet Union the following year. The architects had been Bush and Baker, Kohl and Genscher, Gorbachev and Shevardnadze. The building site had been the unification of Germany, and the partnership had been the Two Plus Four. NATO, the European Community, and the CSCE had played essentially passive or at most supporting roles.

Why was the Community sidelined? It has been suggested above that Bush had been able to seize the initiative in strategic thinking on Europe because he was equipped with the necessary staff—the US Administration had a brain, but the European Community did not. Furthermore, the United Kingdom and France had legal justification in the case of German unification for seeking a solution separately from their EC partners. These are not sufficient explanations, however. So long as post-Cold War thinking could continue to reflect Cold War hypotheses, the Community could hope to remain active in making policy. It might, for example, have plumped for a revived and transformed CSCE, for which its historical record would have fitted it to play a leading role. This indeed was the line beginning to emerge at the special informal meeting of Foreign Ministers

Der diplomatische Weg zur deutschen Einheit, 103–5. The incident did nothing for subsequent Dutch–German relations.

[137] Zelikow and Rice, *Germany Unified and Europe Transformed*, 321–4; Szabo, *The Diplomacy of German Unification*, 91–2.

at Dublin on 20 January 1990.[138] The CSCE Summit in Paris in November 1990 might thus have been an event of determining significance. The fact that German unification became the arena in which the battle over the future shape of Europe was fought changed all that. The Community was sidelined because the German Chancellor did not want it involved, because the United States had decided to be involved, and because the debate shifted to military ground where the Community could not follow.

Kohl had throughout been determined to keep the negotiations in as small a circle as possible, both to preserve his room for manœuvre and to avoid facing demands for reparations fifty years after the event. This was why he had been adamantly opposed to a peace conference: too many countries might think they had a claim to be paid off.[139] Similarly, he wanted to get the Two Plus Four negotiations over as quickly as possible, to head off any risk that the CSCE countries might be tempted to meddle.[140] The EC was to be informed, but not involved.[141] And when Delors, at the time of the first European Council at Dublin (April 1990), pressed on Kohl the idea of a special EC fund to help pay for the modernization of East Germany, the Chancellor politely declined on the grounds that Germany could not risk courting further unpopularity. In fact, Kohl was determined not to give Germany's EC partners a handle to intervene in the unification process.[142] Delors' instinct had been a good one as far as strengthening the Community's foreign policy capability was concerned: a Community which even in part financed the restructuring of East Germany would be a Community with something to say about how Germany conducted itself.[143] Kohl's reaction was also comprehensible in

---

[138] *Deutsche Einheit*, no. 144, 706 n. 8, and no. 181, 829.

[139] Yugoslavia and Romania had already made applications by the beginning of 1990: Szabo, *The Diplomacy of German Unification*, 68; Kiessler and Elbe, *Der diplomatische Weg zur deutschen Einheit*, 110.

[140] Kohl, *Ich wollte Deutschlands Einheit*, 369; *Deutsche Einheit*, no. 175, 810.

[141] *Deutsche Einheit*, no. 189, 854.

[142] Grant, *Delors*, 139; Teltschik, *329 Tage*, 349; *Deutsche Einheit*, no. 188, 853; no. 215, 936; and no. 238, 1000; Favier and Martin-Roland, *La Décennie Mitterrand*, iii. 246; Anderson and Goodman, 'Mars or Minerva?', 32; Kohl, *Ich wollte Deutschlands Einheit*, 359. The memorandum of 29 Jan. 1990 by Peter Hartmann of the Chancellor's staff is instructive: *Deutsche Einheit*, no. 151, 730. Hartmann advised against giving EC Member States the opportunity in EPC of taking any part in what was exclusively a German process, although this had been requested by the Netherlands and Italy. Even EPC co-ordination for that autumn's CSCE summit meeting, as suggested by Delors, carried with it the danger of the EC partners meddling with the 'German question'.

[143] The extension of the Structural Funds to the new *Länder* after unification was of a different order, and did not give the same leverage. Kohl was nevertheless determined that the absorption of the GDR should not be used as a pretext to raise the EC budget ceiling,

the circumstances, but showed that the initiative on political union, which Germany and France were promoting at the time, was more a political gesture than a well-thought-out attempt to move towards a common foreign policy.

Furthermore, from the moment that the United States decided to remain a 'European power' and determined to press for the early unification of Germany as a means of achieving that end, it was inevitable that, whatever the forum chosen for negotiations, it had to be one in which the United States was present. This therefore excluded the European Community. And the fact that so much of the discussion turned on military questions, like overall force levels and the position of Germany within NATO, was a further barrier to Community participation. It will be recalled that at the time EPC, by the terms of the Single Act, could discuss no more than the political and economic aspects of security. The European Community, to adapt Genscher's retort to De Michelis, was not 'part of the game'.

nor to diminish the share of other Member States in the structural funds: *Deutsche Einheit*, nos. 362, 363, and 364, 1402–3; no. 376, 1448; no. 388, 1481. On the other hand, the Chancellor had no qualms about pressing the EC (to which he assigned a central role) and the G7 to share the burden of providing financial support to the Soviet Union in return for an easing of the Soviet position on unification: *Deutsche Einheit*, no. 284, 1137; no. 312, 1211–2; no. 353, 1362–3; and no. 356, 1376.

4

The role of the Community

The conclusion reached at the end of the last chapter is of course exaggerated. It is true that, once the new European architecture came to depend on the way in which Germany was unified, the European Community had no role to play in actively shaping the outcome. But the Community by its very existence was an essential component of the new settlement, and itself engaged in some important activities on which the master-builders relied. By co-ordinating international assistance to the countries emerging from Communism, by providing a large part of that assistance itself, by concluding agreements with those countries, and not least by facilitating the absorption of the new *Länder* into the EC, the Community made an indispensable contribution. The fact that that contribution relied entirely on EC machinery and instruments caused EPC to recede into the background, and led some to hope, others to fear, that this was to be the future shape of the Community's foreign policy. This explains in good part the course of the debate on the future common foreign and security policy.

G24 and PHARE

The economic situation of the Central and East European countries at the end of the 1980s was poor and worsening. Moves towards market reform did not produce economic benefits in the short term; indeed, as the process gathered pace in subsequent years, their economies took a downturn.[1] Poland in particular was in trouble, its policy of promoting investment through foreign loans having left the country deep in debt. The Soviet Union was not prepared to bail out its former satellites; indeed it was itself in a parlous situation, which had made perestroika inevitable without as yet providing the benefits of reform. This was the counterpart of the abandonment of the Brezhnev doctrine: if the Warsaw Pact countries were free

---

[1] Miall, *Shaping the new Europe*, 39–47.

to run themselves, they were also free to run their own economies. In the circumstances, it was not surprising that they turned to the West for help.

Before attending the Western Economic Summit at l'Arche de la Défense in Paris on 14–16 July 1989, President Bush visited Poland and Hungary as a mark of recognition of the progress those countries had made in introducing market reforms and in moving towards a multiparty system. He was under pressure to make it plain during his visit that the United States was prepared to combine encouragement with material aid. The Bush Administration had previously been hesitant to support very markedly developments in Central and Eastern Europe, the outcome of which was still uncertain. It had only just taken office and was still working out its foreign policy approach. A fixed point was Bush's determination to avoid destabilizing Gorbachev's reform efforts. He was anxious not to rock the boat,[2] but at the same time wanted to make a mark on events in Europe. Encouraged by the recognition of Solidarity, he had been won over by his staff to the idea of linking economic aid with democratic reform.[3] But the US Treasury had been opposed to this, and international financial support would clearly be welcome.[4] The subject was bound to be raised both in Warsaw and at the Paris Summit; indeed General Jaruzelski launched an appeal to President Mitterrand, a fortnight before the event, to support Poland's cause, and Chancellor Kohl, in a private letter to Bush, had suggested that the Summit should set up a 'mechanism' to co-ordinate aid to Poland, with something similar envisaged for Hungary.[5]

Before leaving on his European tour, President Bush launched the idea of a consortium of the members of the Western Economic Summit to co-ordinate economic aid to Poland and the handling of the Polish debt, as well as to set up a business foundation with a public endowment of US$100 million.[6] Jacques Attali, who was President Mitterrand's Sherpa for the preparation of the Summit, was radically opposed to the idea because the consortium would have been under American control. The reality was, for Attali, much worse: the Summit gave the job of co-ordinating an international aid effort to the European Commission.[7]

[2] Beschloss and Talbott, *At the Highest Levels*, 88–92; Bush and Scowcroft, *A World Transformed*, 115–16.

[3] Zelikow and Rice, *Germany Unified and Europe Transformed*, 25.

[4] Bush and Scowcroft, *A World Transformed*, 44, 48–9, 113, 128; *Deutsche Einheit*, no. 10, 314–15.

[5] Attali, *Verbatim III*, 271; *Deutsche Einheit*, no. 12, 320–3.

[6] Attali, *Verbatim III*, 277–8; Bush and Scowcroft, *A World Transformed*, 113–14.

[7] '. . . We welcome the process of reform under way in Poland and Hungary. We

The decision was institutionally startling. The European Commission, the executive organ of the European Community, was being charged by an external body, without the benefit of a decision by the appropriate EC authorities, to take on a high-profile political role managing one of the most sensitive issues then facing the Western world. It is small wonder that some feathers were ruffled; small wonder, too, that Jacques Delors saw this moment as the high point of the Commission's foreign policy ambitions.[8]

The decision should not, however, have come as a complete surprise. Already the previous month, after a meeting with President Delors in Washington, President Bush had come up with the idea that Delors would be well placed by virtue of his contacts with Solidarity and with the Catholic Church to take in hand an aid effort by the Group of Seven in favour of Poland.[9] This was later rationalized by Robert Zoellick, at the time a senior advisor to Baker in the State Department, as an attempt to make EC officials broaden their horizons.[10] In addition, the work done by the Commission in negotiating agreements with Hungary, Poland, and the Soviet Union was recognized.[11] There certainly seems to have been some smart diplomatic footwork at the Summit itself. The necessary amendment to the previously prepared text was worked out on the eve of the Summit, while the participants were engaged with the lavish spectacle

recognise that the political changes taking place in these countries will be difficult to sustain without economic progress. Each of us is prepared to support this process . . .

. . . We agreed to work along with other interested countries and multilateral institutions to concert support for the process of reform . . . in order to make our measures of support more effective and mutually reinforcing . . .

. . . we call for a meeting with all interested countries which will take place within the next few weeks. We underline, for Poland, the urgent need for food in present circumstances.

To these ends, we ask the Commission of the European Communities to take the necessary initiatives in agreement with the other Member States of the Community, and to associate, besides the Summit participants, all interested countries': *Bull. EC*, July–Aug. 1989, 3.2.3.

[8] Delors, *L'Unité d'un homme*, 307.

[9] Delors himself proposed in May 1989 an initiative for action by the EC and the G7 on the Polish debt: Haggard and Moravcsik, 'The Political Economy of Financial Assistance to Eastern Europe', 440 n. 31.

[10] Attali, *Verbatim III*, 261; Grant, *Delors*, 166.

[11] Progress in this area was noted in para. 5 of the Summit Declaration, *Bull. EC*, July/Aug. 1989, 3.2.3. The then Director General of DG I suggested as reasons for the decision geographical proximity and the EC's sympathy with political sensitivities in Eastern Europe, as well as the Commission's experience in mastering problems of economic structure in the structural funds and development and food aid: Krenzler, 'Die Europäische Gemeinschaft und der Wandel', 93.

celebrating the Bicentenary of the French Revolution. A form of words, seeming to link the Commission with food aid to Poland but in fact having a wider significance, was sold by Delors to other leaders, including most importantly Kohl,[12] and by Kohl to Bush. Deaf to Attali's protests, Mitterrand refused to intervene, saying 'You can't have everything'. The amendment duly passed in the formal session the next morning. According to his own account, Attali persuaded Mitterrand to limit the scope of the action to Poland and Hungary, rather than Eastern Europe as a whole, while Mrs Thatcher failed to have the Commission's role limited to food aid.[13]

Having been given the job, the Commission had to organize itself to carry it out. This was not easy. Although it knew how to mobilize food aid, and had a well-oiled machine for that purpose, its experience in development assistance was confined to developing countries, where conditions were very different from those in Central and Eastern Europe. Acting as midwife to the transition from planned to market economies was a new experience, and the necessary skills had to be learnt on the job. In this the Commission differed in no way from the countries also engaged in the exercise. The need for co-ordination and the sharing of experiences was patent, and probably more easily met by the Commission than by any individual country. This did not prevent jealousies and unseemly competition for the rare projects which were available, and ultimately suspicion on the part of the Community's partners that the EC was hogging the best projects and exploiting its position with regard to the beneficiary countries.

The Commission had to engage in two operations simultaneously: the co-ordination of the international aid effort as requested by the Arche Summit, and the organization of the Community's own aid effort.[14] It acted with commendable speed, especially since in mid-July the thoughts

[12] Kohl wanted to help Poland for reasons of specifically German foreign policy, without giving the impression of German domination in Central Europe: Küsters, 'Entscheidung für die deutsche Einheit', 39; *Deutsche Einheit*, no. 15, 343. See also Smith, *The Making of EU Foreign Policy*, 204 n. 2.

[13] Attali, *Verbatim III*, 284–5; Favier and Martin-Roland, *La Décennie Mitterrand*, iii. 152; personal information.

[14] These paragraphs draw principally on Maslen, 'The European Community and Eastern Europe in the Post-1989 Era'; de Largentaye, 'The European Community, the PHARE Programme, and the East–West European Partnership'; Kramer, 'The European Community's Response to the "new Eastern Europe"'; and Mayhew, 'L'Assistance financière à l'Europe centrale et orientale'. All except Kramer have been Commission officials directly involved with the aid programme. See also Mayhew, *Recreating Europe*, 132–58, for an account of the EC programme as it developed over the years.

of many officials, not only in the Commission, were turning to the summer closure. It secured the agreement of the Council on 17–18 July to the substance of measures to be envisaged (food supplies to Poland, the development of commercial co-operation and trade, and the development of economic co-operation, the last two with both countries) and to the definition of the Commission's role (co-ordinating operations in support of the reform process initiated by the various countries concerned in order to put together a consistent overall programme in line with the specific needs of each of the two countries). Food aid to Poland was approved by the Council on 24 July, at a cost to the Community budget of more than 110 million ECU, and the first supplies began to arrive in September. Meanwhile, preparations for the co-ordination meeting went ahead. The Commission conducted missions to establish the economic situation and requirements in Poland and Hungary, both in the countries concerned and to organizations like the IMF, the World Bank and the Paris Club. The first co-ordination meeting took place in Brussels on 1 August, attended by the 24 members of the OECD. The operation thus acquired the name by which it was subsequently known, the 'G24'.[15]

The original aims of the G24 programme were agriculture and emergency food aid, the environment, training,[16] investment and joint ventures, and market access. Energy was later added under the environment heading. Under 'market access', the G24 extended 'most-favoured-nation' treatment, abolished quantitative restrictions, and extended the benefit of the system of generalized preferences which was designed to provide developing countries with tariff-free access. Over the period 1990–5, the assistance provided by the G24 amounted to more than 86 billion ECU (including export credits). The Community and its Member States provided 53 per cent of the total.[17]

At the same time, the Commission was preparing the Community's own aid effort, which came to be known as 'PHARE'.[18] This took a little longer

---

[15] *Bull. EC*, July–Aug. 1989, 1.1.3–1.1.6.

[16] Training included TEMPUS (the Trans-European Mobility Scheme for University Studies) and a European Training Foundation, whose establishment was delayed by disagreement about where it should be set up.

[17] Mayhew, 'L'Assistance financière à l'Europe centrale et orientale', 156–7; Mayhew, *Recreating Europe*, 157.

[18] 'Pologne, Hongrie—Assistance à la Restructuration des Économies', meaning 'lighthouse' in French, a monument to the addiction of Commission officials to catchy acronyms. Technically, PHARE referred to the G24 aid effort as a whole, while the Community's programme should more properly be called 'Community PHARE', but the distinction tends to be blurred: see Mayhew, *Recreating Europe*, 15 n. 11.

to get under way than the G24 co-ordination. The legal basis[19] was in place by December 1989, and the first 'action plan'—financial provisions for grant aid, also addressed to the G24—was produced in May 1990. The financial resources made available in the first six years of PHARE grew from just under 500 million ECU in 1990 to more than double that in 1995. In addition, the Community provided balance of payments loans in co-operation with the IMF, which in 1995 amounted cumulatively to 2.9 billion ECU. To this should be added project-based loans from the European Investment Bank, which for the period 1992–6 totalled 4.28 billion ECU.[20]

To be able to take on these new tasks of co-ordination and the construction and management of an aid programme, the Commission had to put rapidly into place a new administrative structure. The Division of DG I (External Relations) which had previously dealt with the East European countries was small to the point of exiguity. Practically overnight, it had to be transformed into two new services: the PHARE Task Force, in charge of the G24 operation and of co-ordinating the activities of other Commission departments, and the PHOS (Poland Hungary Operational Service), which dealt with the management of the PHARE programmes. Not surprisingly, the Commission was assigned no new staff to carry out these new responsibilities; it was expected to make do with existing resources. In practice this meant that, with the assistance of the President's Cabinet, press-gang raids were carried out on other Commission departments, especially DG VIII (Development).

For the institutional management of its own PHARE programme, the Community resorted to the type of arrangement in force for aid to the Non-Associated Developing Countries (PVD-NA)—those developing countries which were not parties to the Lomé Convention.[21] A Committee of Member States' representatives—the PHARE Committee—was set up within the Council to assist the Commission in the management of the programme. The procedure was cumbersome. Each project above a certain financial threshold had to be approved individually, in the beginning at any rate, which meant that the voluminous documentation had to be translated into all the official languages, causing serious delays. Furthermore, the impression was gained that the Member States were less concerned with efficient management of the programme than with ensuring that their nationals secured an appropriate share of the consultancy cake.

---

[19] Council Regulation (EEC) no. 3906/89 of 18 Dec. 1989, OJ L 375, 23 Dec. 1989.
[20] Mayhew, *Recreating Europe*, 154–5.   [21] Ibid. 148.

The process was further retarded by the Commission's procedures for financial control, which, if they provided some protection against fraud, nevertheless were not conducive to snappy management. The excessive reliance on Western consultants and the delays in disbursing monies were indeed the main targets of criticism of the PHARE programme's management.

For the management of the G24 co-ordination, the Commission set up a three-tier structure which proved remarkably effective. The first level was a permanent network (the 'Brussels network') of officials from the respective countries' embassies in Brussels; the second was the so-called 'high-level' meeting of senior officials from the capitals concerned; and the third was the ministerial level, which met every year or so to give the process some political impetus and profile. The system worked, in that a good flow of information was assured, thus averting the danger that foreign donors might unbeknown to each other find themselves financing the same project. It was, however, beyond the powers of the Commission in the chair to secure agreement on a division of labour; participants were too attached to their own programmes for that. Indeed, some resentment was provoked by the Commission's active role in laying before the G24 the Community's own action plan in a way which appeared to preclude discussion or amendment, giving the appearance that the coordination exercise had become a vehicle for EC foreign policy.[22] Further jealousies were created by the perception that some partners were more favoured than others. The habit grew up of private meetings between the Commission and the United States in advance of formal meetings of the full group. This caused Japan to demand, in rather shrill tones, parity of treatment. The beneficiary countries, too, found it difficult to adapt to the Commission's role; they were slow to accept the need to deal with a supranational agency.[23]

The resentment, combined with a realization that perhaps the European Community was taking on too much of a leading role, led the Western Economic Summit in Houston in July 1990 to entrust the task of evaluating the criteria for assistance to the Soviet Union, not this time to the Commission, but to the 'IMF, the World Bank, the OECD and the designated President of the EBRD . . . in close consultation with the Commission . . .

---

[22] The plan was intended as a 'framework for action by the Community and as an incentive for the other members of the G24 to take similar and coordinated initiatives': *Bull. EC*, Oct. 1989, 1.1.1; Sedelmaier and Wallace, 'Policies towards Central and Eastern Europe', 359.

[23] *Deutsche Einheit*, no. 58, 444, and no. 92, 532.

Th[e] work should be . . . convened by the IMF'.[24] An additional factor was that the Houston Summit was immediately preceded by the meeting of the European Council at Dublin, at which, encountering strong opposition from Mrs Thatcher, President Mitterrand and Chancellor Kohl had failed to secure agreement on a significant aid effort for Gorbachev. The conditions for a lightning strike of the kind which had been so successful at the Arche were no longer present.

The programme was originally designed to benefit Poland and Hungary only, in recognition of those countries' progress towards a multiparty system and a market economy, and to encourage them (and others) to continue down this road. There was therefore an element of discrimination and, as a consequence, of conditionality in the exercise right from the start. PHARE has been criticized[25] for its absence of conditionality. This is true in the sense that, once in place, the country programmes could not be modulated in accordance with an ongoing evaluation of progress towards plural democracy and the free market. However, it should be recalled that the IMF had been applying for some time a strong measure of conditionality in the economic field, which inevitably also affected the political one.[26] This had a knock-on effect on the G24 process (the IMF was represented at G24 meetings), especially since in practice the Community would not envisage G24 macroeconomic assistance for a country in the absence of an agreement with the IMF.[27]

Apart from that, conditionality was exercised in the admission of other Central and East European countries to G24 and PHARE, and the Commission, in its capacity as G24 co-ordinator, was thus led to take an eminently political role.[28] At the G24 ministerial meeting in December 1989, Ministers 'indicated their willingness to respond positively to requests for assistance from other countries in Central and Eastern Europe when the latter put into place the necessary political and economic reforms.'[29] Fol-

[24] *Bull. EC*, July–Aug. 1990, 2.2.2, para. 45. There was also disagreement on substance, the Europeans believing that the conditions set by the Americans were too restrictive: Védrine, *Les Mondes de François Mitterrand*, 496; Teltschik, *329 Tage*, 309–10. See also, for US irritation with the Community and the Commission at the time (the Houston Summit was devoted to an acrimonious discussion about the Uruguay Round), Attali, *Verbatim III*, 537–8, 543.

[25] Mayhew, 'L'Assistance financière à l'Europe centrale et orientale', 151.

[26] Garton Ash, *In Europe's Name*, 257. The United States had been applying a policy of 'differentiation' towards the countries of Eastern Europe since the early 1960s: ibid. 178; Shultz, *Turmoil and Triumph*, 873–5.

[27] Mayhew, *Recreating Europe*, 150–2.

[28] For a different view, see Haggard and Moravcsik, 'The Political Economy of Financial Assistance to Eastern Europe', 260–1.   [29] *Bull. EC*, Dec. 1989, 2.2.23.

lowing a series of evaluation missions to the 'candidate' countries,[30] the Commission stated in its action plan submitted to the G24 in May 1990 its view that 'the implementation of political and economic reform programmes has now reached a stage at which the conditions placed on the granting of co-ordinated aid by the Group in December 1989 have now largely been met.'[31] The evaluation may well have been summary, the political criteria necessarily crude, and co-operation with the IMF essential on the economic side, but the fact remains that it was the Commission which decided when the Western world was ready to begin assistance to countries emerging from the collapse of the Communist system in Eastern Europe. This was in mid-1990 for Romania, Bulgaria, and Czechoslovakia; Albania was not included until December 1991.

Doubts have been cast on the effectiveness of the G24 and PHARE exercises in making a significant impact on the transition of the Central and East European countries to market economies. The sums were too small; the microeconomic approach was misguided; the execution was dilatory. Whatever the truth of that, the fact remains that the European Community was seen politically to be leading the only policy in town on the hottest area of international relations at the time. Of particular significance for the development of the Community's foreign policy was the fact that this operation, including the politically sensitive issue of conditionality, was being managed by the Commission from its position within the Community framework, without benefit of advice from European Political Co-operation.[32] The Commission's role might be diversely appreciated, but it was a fact which influenced the development of attitudes on how to manage an EC foreign policy.

The Agreements with the Central and East European countries: the first generation

The Joint EC–CMEA Declaration of June 1988 was part of the deal on future relations between the EC and the Soviet bloc. Another part was the

---

[30] David Buchan, 'Flying Dutchman Rounds Up Aid for Eastern Europe', *Financial Times*, 16 Jan. 1990.

[31] *Bull. EC*, May 1990, 1.3.3. The Commission's evaluation was contested by some Member States—It is significant that the concerns were raised in Coreper rather than EPC: Torreblanca, *The European Community and Central Eastern Europe*, 194 n. 75.

[32] Such political advice as Member States gave to the Commission was proffered, not through EPC, but through the Groupe des Conseillers, which was a Council body: Smith, *The Making of EU Foreign Policy*, 68.

new series of bilateral Agreements negotiated with individual members of Comecon. Previously, because of the Soviet Union's reluctance to recognize the Community, only sectoral agreements, for example on textiles or steel, had been concluded. Exceptions to this were the agreements with Romania, ever anxious to display its reluctance to toe the Soviet line, and Yugoslavia, which for some time had been considered to be outside the Soviet world. A preferential trade agreement with Yugoslavia had been concluded in 1975, and an agreement covering trade in manufactured goods across the board with Romania in 1980.

Once the Joint Declaration had raised the remaining barriers, the negotiation of non-sectoral Agreements with the countries of Central and Eastern Europe went rapidly ahead. Between September 1988 and October 1990 bilateral agreements were concluded with seven countries, including the Soviet Union. There was nothing special about these Agreements; they were the sort of agreement which the Community would have concluded with any third country which requested one, and were modelled on existing texts.[33] This did not mean that the Agreements were identical. On the contrary, the negotiations were pragmatic, flexible, and tailored to the conditions in the countries concerned. This led to the *de facto* adoption of a policy of differentiation.

A Trade and Co-operation Agreement was concluded with Hungary on 26 September 1988. The Agreement with Czechoslovakia, concluded in December 1988, covered trade only,[34] since it was felt that the steps taken in that country towards a market economy were less convincing than in Hungary. Trade and Co-operation Agreements with Poland and the Soviet Union were concluded in September and December 1989 respectively, and Bulgaria and Romania followed in May and October 1990.

These 'first-generation' Agreements, as they were called, were non-preferential. They included commitments to the progressive dismantling of quantitative restrictions[35] in all sectors except steel, textiles, and agriculture, accompanied by a safeguard clause; provisions for commercial co-operation, to ensure the non-discriminatory treatment of EC products and economic operators; and a section on economic co-operation (without

---

[33] Kramer, 'The European Community's Response to the "New Eastern Europe"', 226–7.

[34] Torreblanca, *The European Community and Central Eastern Europe*, 81. A full Trade and Cooperation Agreement was concluded in May 1990.

[35] For full details of the EC's trade concessions, including those launched or accelerated in the G24 setting, see Pelkmans and Murphy, 'Catapulted into Leadership', 136–42.

corresponding financial support, however). Joint Committees were set up to manage each of the Agreements.[36]

A number of consequences, important for the development of EC foreign policy, flowed from this approach.

First, the approach was a response, not a strategy. Faced with a new situation—the availability of the Central and East European countries to conclude contractual relations with the EC—the Community responded in the only way it knew, namely the negotiation of classic trade and in most cases co-operation agreements.

Second, the response was a Community response. The agreements were negotiated in accordance with classic EC procedures, by the Commission following directives issued by the Council. EPC followed what was going on, but did not seek at this stage to direct the process or to inject a political dimension. True, the Council insisted on the use of Article 235 of the EC Treaty alongside Article 113,[37] and the retention of the 'Canada clause',[38] but these devices were designed respectively to maximize the Member States' control over Community procedures and to preserve some leeway for national activities, not to shift the debate from the economic to the political forum. That forum remained firmly the European Community of the Treaty of Rome.

Third, this was in spite of the strong elements of political appreciation which were in play, both in the contents of the Agreements, because of the differentiation among the partner countries, and in the timing of the negotiations. 'Conditionality' was only specifically agreed with partners in the 'second-generation' Agreements (see below), but it existed *de facto* from the start. Hungary, which was deemed to have made significant progress towards a market economy, was awarded a full Trade and Co-operation Agreement. Czechoslovakia, where the situation was judged to be less satisfactory, had to make do with a Trade Agreement only. The negotiations with Romania were suspended in April 1989 because of concerns about human rights,[39] and with Bulgaria the following month because of its

[36] For a concise but full description of the 'first-generation' agreements see Lequesne, 'Commerce et aide économique', 44–50.

[37] Art. 113 governed trade policy, on which decisions could be taken by qualified majority vote. Art. 235 was the 'catch-all' article, which required unanimity. Member States were in the habit of using Art. 235 in order to limit the scope of Art. 113.

[38] Lequesne, 'Commerce et aide économique', 45. The 'Canada clause' reserved the right of Member States to conclude economic co-operation agreements with third countries.

[39] By joint decision of the Council and the Commission: Krenzler, 'Die Europäische Gemeinschaft und der Wandel', 91; 'the Community and its Member States repeated their deep concern at the Romanian Government's continued failure to meet its commitments

treatment of the Turkish minority. Conversely, the negotiations with the Soviet Union were accelerated in November 1989, to lend support to Gorbachev's reform efforts and possibly in order to ease the situation over the German Democratic Republic.[40] All these judgements were initiated by the Commission, playing its usual role in the Community system.

Fourth, the principle of differentiation not only carried the seeds of conditionality, it inexorably led to the abandonment of region-to-region dialogue as a serious policy option. If the Central and European partners were to be treated individually on their merits, they could not be encouraged by being treated as a whole to strengthen regional ties among themselves. This renunciation of previous Community orthodoxy, as exemplified in the dialogues with ASEAN and Central America, subsequently proved difficult to rectify. It made necessary the Stability Pact,[41] the political dialogue with the Visegrad countries from October 1992,[42] the Structured Dialogue, and the European Conference,[43] none of which has so far successfully provided an institutional answer to the problems to which differentiation has given rise. It has to be said that the greatest difficulties were made not by the Community but by the Central and East European countries, whose recent experience of life as a group under Soviet hegemony had made them disinclined to renew the experience, and whose newly released national energies found expression in national rivalry.[44]

The Agreements with the Central and East European countries: the second generation

The classic approach of non-preferential Trade and Economic Co-operation Agreements, devoid of political and financial content, was not destined to survive the whirlwind which swept through Central and Eastern Europe beginning in the second half of 1989. Everywhere the pace

under the Helsinki process, in particular in the field of human rights . . . Any resumption of the negotiations would take place only should clear evidence emerge of a significant improvement in Romania's respect for human rights': Council and Commission Statement, 24 Apr. 1989, Council Press Release 6000/89 (Presse 66), 4.

[40] de la Serre, 'A la recherche d'une Ostpolitik', 21.

[41] A CFSP Joint Action to encourage the CEECs to settle their bilateral problems in a multilateral framework.   [42] de la Serre, 'A la recherche d'une Ostpolitik', 40.

[43] Whereby the EU and the CEECs meet collectively, rather than bilaterally, to discuss certain subjects.

[44] Delors' proposal to set up a European Payments Union was rebuffed by the CEECs: Delors, *L'Unité d'un homme*, 259.

of economic and political reform was increasing, as governments and peoples realized that the years of Marxist and Soviet domination had come to an end. The ink was barely dry on some Agreements, and others had not even been concluded, when there was pressure, both in Western Europe and in the Central and East European countries themselves, to replace them with something more in keeping with the new situation.

The Commission both responded to and stimulated this intellectual movement.[45] Following the statement of the European Council at Strasbourg in December 1989 that the Community 'has taken and will take the necessary decision to strengthen its co-operation with peoples aspiring to freedom, democracy and progress and with States which intend their founding principles to be democracy, pluralism and the rule of law', and that it would 'continue its examination of the appropriate forms of association with the countries which are pursuing the path of economic and political reforms',[46] and the informal discussions by Foreign Ministers in Dublin on 20 January 1990,[47] the Commission secured from the Council on 5 February an expression of encouragement for its views and suggestions 'regarding the possibility of association agreements, which should provide a flexible and constructive framework, allowing solutions appropriate to the circumstances of each country, and which would succeed the present co-operation agreements'.[48] The Commission thereupon prepared a strategy for relations with the countries of Central and Eastern Europe based on

[45] The idea of offering Association Agreements had been put forward by Mrs Thatcher in her Mansion House speech on 13 Nov. 1989: Sedelmaier and Wallace, *Policies towards Eastern and Central Europe*, 367, 384 n. 4; Lippert, 'Die EG als Mitgestalter der Erfolgsgeschichte', 46; Torreblanca, *The European Community and Central Eastern Europe*, 101–2. The idea had previously been floated by Giscard d'Estaing in a Trilateral Commission report launched the same month: Torreblanca, *The European Community and Central Eastern Europe*, 96, n. 53. The significance of the EC system was that it fell to the Commission to expound and formally present the proposal, thus throwing the political limelight on that institution. See also Mayhew, *Recreating Europe*, 21, for continued British interest and prior contacts between the Commission and Poland.

[46] *Bull. EC*, Dec. 1989, 1.1.14. This section of the European Council's conclusions was drafted in the Community framework. A less operational draft, prepared in EPC, was also adopted by the European Council: *Bull. EC*, Dec. 1989, 1.1.20. The existence of two rival texts did nothing for consistency.

[47] *Bull. EC*, Jan.–Feb. 1990, 1.2.3. The Presidency conclusions presented to the press stated: 'We wish to promote the process of liberalisation in Central and Eastern Europe. We support the movement towards pluralistic democracy, in accordance with the rule of law, fully respecting human rights and offering equal electoral opportunities to all. We also support the intentions of the countries of Central and Eastern Europe to change towards more market-oriented economies', but no direct link was established with the bilateral agreements with the CEECs.   [48] *Bull. EC*, Jan.–Feb. 1990, 1.2.5.

prompt completion of the Community's network of first-generation trade and co-operation agreements: as soon as the necessary political and economic conditions are in place, negotiation of a new generation of association agreements providing an institutional framework for political dialogue, without in any way adversely affecting the quite separate right of accession of the countries concerned; at multilateral level, in addition to active Community participation in the work of the Conference on Security and Co-operation in Europe and the Council of Europe, the extension to other countries of co-ordinated G-24 assistance, reinforced by the activities of the European Bank for Reconstruction and Development, by the European Training Foundation and by the Tempus student mobility scheme.[49]

Following the Commission's proposal, the extraordinary meeting of the European Council held in Dublin on 28 April 1990 authorized discussions on the Association Agreements, including an institutional framework for political dialogue,[50] the negotiations to be completed as soon as possible.[51] The Commission elaborated its strategy in a communication to Council and Parliament the following August.[52]

These apparently classic procedures for the preparation of negotiating directives in fact concealed some significant innovations. Unimpressed by the failure of the EC and EPC channels to present a common text on relations with Central and Eastern Europe to the European Council at Strasbourg in December 1989, President Delors persuaded the incoming Irish Presidency to break with precedent and call special meetings of Ministers in Dublin in a joint EC–EPC framework, in order to facilitate a 'consistent' approach to the main foreign policy challenge facing the Community.[53] The range of subjects dealt with by the Ministers at their meeting on 20 January—change in Europe, integration in the Community, agreements with the CEECs, emergency aid, G24, budget resources[54]—shows the extent to which the EPC and EC strands of the discussion had become involved. Both the Political Committee and Coreper were present at the meeting. The Irish Presidency was sufficiently emboldened by the success of this initiative to consolidate Council business, including both EC and

---

[49] *Bull. EC*, Apr. 1990, 1.1.
[50] Contrast the refusal of the Council to agree in 1985 to the formal incorporation of political dialogue in the Agreement with the Central American countries: Nuttall, *European Political Co-operation*, 228–9. The Commission was conscious that by including the 'volet politique' of the relationship into the actual Agreement, it was committing itself to sharing management of the agreement with the Member States.
[51] *Bull. EC*, Apr. 1990, 1.8.
[52] *Bull. EC*, July–Aug. 1990, 1.4.5; *EUROPE/Documents*, no. 1646/47, 7 Sept. 1990.
[53] Nuttall, *European Political Co-operation*, 278–9.
[54] *Bull. EC*, Jan.–Feb. 1990, 1.2.3.

EPC items on a single agenda. They thus effectively brought about by administrative means the very reforms—abolition of a separate format for EPC ministerial meetings and meetings of the Council —which Italy had sought in vain in the negotiation of the Single European Act.[55] Furthermore, Belgium was led by these developments to put forward proposals for the general institutional development of EPC.

The negotiations with the Central and East European countries (CEECs)[56] were not easy, since the Community proved reluctant to make the trade concessions, particularly in the sensitive steel, textiles, and agricultural sectors, which its partners (and many in the Community) thought to be necessary. Agreements were not concluded with Poland, Hungary, and Czechoslovakia until December 1991, and not with Romania and Bulgaria until November and December of the following year. Twice, in the summer of 1991 with the Central European countries, and in autumn 1992 with Bulgaria, negotiations came close to breaking down because of the effective opposition of organized interests within the EC.[57] The day was saved by the classic internal negotiating procedures of the Council. EPC deplored the reluctance to make trade concessions, but was powerless to intervene. Although a breakdown in negotiations was thus avoided, the coherent strategy advanced by the Commission was tarnished by what was generally seen as petty commercial squabbles. Special credence was given to this view by the vocal attacks of West European economic experts, whose devotion to the tenets of free trade was unsullied by the need to comply with domestic political reality.[58]

The Association Agreement was a recognized form of relationship between the Community and third countries, foreseen in Article 238 of the EC Treaty. Such agreements had in the past been concluded with Greece and Turkey as well as with other countries of the Eastern and Southern Mediterranean. The Association Agreements with the CEECs came to be known as Europe Agreements, in order to distinguish them from the existing Association Agreements, and to give them a flavour of

---

[55] Nuttall, *European Political Co-operation*, 249.

[56] The French acronym PECOs (Pays de l'Europe Centrale et Orientale) was in common use at the time. The English equivalent (CEECs) only came into use later. Before 1989, the Commission had followed the common usage of 'Eastern European countries' ('pays de l'Est'); the expanded form 'Eastern *and Central* European countries' was of German inspiration: Garton Ash, *In Europe's Name*, 381.

[57] Kramer, 'The European Community's Response', 228. For a survey of the negotiation and contents of the Association Agreements, see Smith, *The Making of EU Foreign Policy*, 91–102.

[58] Sedelmaier and Wallace, 'Policies towards Central and Eastern Europe', 371.

exclusivity.[59] They were preferential, 'mixed'[60] agreements, providing for free trade in industrial goods after a transitional period which varied from five to ten years, based on asymmetrical tariff reductions (i.e. the CEECs got better access than the EC). There were special arrangements for agriculture, textiles, and steel. An exceptionally important provision was the approximation of legislation within three to five years, whereby the CEECs were to make their legislation compatible with that of the EC as regards competition policy and state aids. CEEC firms enjoyed national treatment as regards the right of establishment in the Community, but there was no generalized freedom of movement for workers, because of fears of a flood of migration from the East. Nor would this have been usual in an Association Agreement. Economic, cultural, and financial co-operation was confirmed.[61] However, contrary to the CEECs' expectation, there was no Financial Protocol, financial assistance being made through existing instruments.[62]

A political (i.e. EPC) dialogue was instituted.[63] This took place at ministerial level at the meetings of the bilateral Association Councils set up to

[59] On the Europe Agreements, see for preference Kramer, 'The European Community's Response', 227–30, and Lequesne, 'Commerce et aide économique', 64–71.

[60] Covering matters of both EC and Member State competence (the latter particularly as regards political and cultural questions), and therefore requiring separate ratification according to national constitutional procedures. This led to considerable delays in the entry into force of the agreements and the consequent need for Interim Agreements applying the trade provisions only.

[61] For a conspectus of the typical Europe Agreement, see the table in Sedelmaier and Wallace, 'Policies towards Central and Eastern Europe', 368–9. For a full description of the Agreements in their most developed form (1997), see Mayhew, *Recreating Europe*, 41–59.

[62] Mayhew, *Recreating Europe*, 51.

[63] Art. 2 of the Agreements reads: 'A regular political dialogue shall be established between the Parties. It shall accompany and consolidate the rapprochement between the Parties, support the new political order in [country] and contribute to the establishment of lasting links of solidarity and new forms of cooperation. The political dialogue and cooperation, based on shared values and aspirations,

— will facilitate [country's] full integration into the community of democratic nations and progressive rapprochement with the Community. Political convergence and economic rapprochement provided for in this Agreement are closely related and mutually complementary parts of the association.
— will bring about better mutual understanding and increasing convergence of positions on international issues, and in particular on those matters likely to have substantial effects on one or the other Party.
— will enable each Party to consider the position and interests of the other Party in their respective decision making process.
— will contribute to the rapprochement of the Parties' position on security issues and will enhance security and stability in the whole of Europe.'

manage each of the Association Agreements. Additional meetings took place at the level of Political Directors between the country concerned, on the one hand, and the Presidency and the Commission, on the other.[64] A political dialogue at parliamentary level was foreseen, to take place within the Parliamentary Association Committee.[65]

The fact that the same political agenda had to be gone through with each of the associate partners made heavy calls on the time of the EPC representatives, and led to boring results for both sides. The experiment did not survive the test of time, and was replaced at the Copenhagen European Council (June 1993) by the 'structured dialogue', a multilateral forum in which all the associate partners participated. Even this did not prove entirely satisfactory, being described by the partners, disobligingly but accurately, as the 'structured monologue'.

Two further features of the Association Agreements deserve comment. The first is that the tenacious attempts of the EC's partners to have their long-term aim of becoming a member of the Community not only recognized but formally shared were firmly rejected. The most that the CEECs could achieve was recognition that accession was the final objective *of the country concerned*, and that 'this association, in the view of the Parties, will help to achieve this objective'.

The second was the question of conditionality. It will be recalled that, although *de facto* conditionality certainly existed, the 'first-generation' Agreements of 1988–9 did not themselves contain provisions making the relationship between the Community and the CEECs dependent on the respect of certain conditions. In this they followed the hitherto traditional pattern of Trade and Cooperation Agreements of the Community. This was to change for the 'second-generation' Agreements, the very concept of which was to reward those countries which had made significant progress towards multiparty democracy and the free market system, and to provide an incentive to those which had not. The Dublin European Council in April 1990, which gave the green light for the negotiation of the Association Agreements, stated that 'the Community will work to complete association negotiations with these countries as soon as possible on the understanding that the basic conditions with regard to democratic principles and transition towards a market economy are fulfilled'.[66] The Com-

---

[64] Arts. 3 and 4 of the Agreements. It will be noted that the Community chose a bicephalous representation (Presidency and Commission), rather than the Troika. For an account of the first political dialogue meetings, see Torreblanca, *The European Community and Central Eastern Europe*, 449–50.   [65] Art. 5 of the Agreements.

[66] *Bull. EC*, Apr. 1990, 1.8. For the interesting antecedents of this decision, in which the

mission's September 1990 general framework for the Europe Agreements announced the intention of beginning exploratory conversations with those countries 'giving practical evidence of their commitment to the rule of law, respect for human rights, the establishment of multi-party systems, free and fair elections and economic liberalisation with a view to introducing market economies'. Czechoslovakia, Hungary, and Poland were deemed to have met those conditions; in Bulgaria and Romania, the necessary conditions had not been established.[67]

Furthermore, there was a concern on the part of the Community that it should have the legal possibility of resiling from the agreements in the case of marked abuse of human rights. This concern had been growing for some years with regard to relations with all the Community's treaty partners, but was particularly acute in the case of the CEECs, where the durability of reform was not yet assured. It was therefore felt necessary to insert henceforth special clauses, which took different forms, into the agreements being negotiated. The first formula was the 'essential element' clause, which was included in the ('first-generation') Agreements negotiated with the Baltic States and Albania. This clause, which stated that certain principles were an 'essential element' of the agreement, had the effect of making a recourse to restrictive measures possible and of suspending or ending the agreement with abridged periods for giving notice, by virtue of the Vienna Convention. The second formula, applied since May 1992 following a Council Declaration of that date, is known as the 'additional clause', and took two forms. The first (the 'Baltic clause') allows for the immediate suspension of application of the agreement in the event of a serious breach of the essential elements, and was used in the agreements with the Baltic States, Albania, and Slovenia. The second (the 'Bulgarian clause') was a general clause of non-execution allowing appropriate measures to be taken, with prior consultation, if the parties fail to meet their obligations.

The specific arrangements for ensuring respect for conditionality belong to the post-Maastricht period and therefore run ahead of our story. They are nevertheless important, not only because of the role they played in the relationship between the EC and the CEECs, but because they were subsequently adopted as a model for all the Community's agreements with

Council proved more attached than the Commission—or at any rate the responsible Commissioner, Andriessen—to the principle that the criteria were conditions, not objectives, of the Agreements, see Torreblanca, *The European Community and Central Eastern Europe*, 117–19; 151 n. 19.

[67] Torreblanca, *The European Community and Central Eastern Europe*, 179; *EUROPE/Documents*, no. 1646/47, 7 Sept. 1990.

third countries. It was no longer possible for the Community to turn a blind eye to human rights considerations, the more so as the European Parliament had been, since the Single European Act, called upon to give its assent to all agreements based on Article 238 of the EC Treaty, including therefore the Europe Agreements.

This second phase of policy making in relation to East and Central Europe in turn led to a number of consequences.

First, the move to a series of Europe Agreements, so named and structured to imply a special relationship with the Community, was in domestic terms a foreign policy success. It has not been recognized as such because of the attacks made on it by the free-traders and those who wanted early enlargement of the Community, but given that the majority of Member States were not prepared to endanger the Community's achievements so far by precipitate enlargement, the move was an imaginative and realistic response to a given situation. It can be debated whether a commitment to enlargement at this stage would have made a greater contribution to European and world security; at any rate, the Community was not capable of producing such a move.

Second, just as previously with the Trade and Co-operation Agreements and the G24, the Commission found itself in the driving seat. Its institutional position within the Community, and the fact that the Europe Agreements, although mixed, were based on Article 238 of the EC Treaty, made the Commission the focus of political attention and the fixer of the terms of the debate. Within the Commission, the Directorate General for External Relations (DGI) in particular formulated the European interest and could be said to be acting as a European Foreign Ministry.[68] The Commission itself chose to promote institutional convergence between the EC and EPC frameworks, renouncing the alternative strategy of insisting on the primacy of the Community way. Convergence was to lead to conflict in the IGC.

Third, the elements of conditionality which were incorporated into the Europe Agreements confirmed a trend in the Community's dealings with foreign countries and set a precedent for other agreements.

German unification

The President of the European Commission, Jacques Delors, was among the first to see not only that the unification of Germany was inevitable,

---

[68] Torreblanca, *The European Community and Central Eastern Europe*, 212–3.

but that it presented the European Community with opportunities as well as challenges. He robustly denied any need to be fearful of Germany.[69] In his speech at the College of Europe in Bruges on 17 October 1989, Delors said that the only acceptable and satisfactory solution to the German question lay in strengthening the federalist features of the Community.[70] At one of its 'retreats', on 10–11 November, the Commission came to the conclusion that the German Democratic Republic would have to be a 'special case'. It could join the EC as a thirteenth member, or by special procedure as part of the Federal Republic, but accession in some form was inevitable. Some Commission Members were already speaking in favour of the latter.[71] This approach had been cleared by Delors with Genscher.[72] But the Community as a whole was not so far advanced in its thinking: the European Council at Strasbourg in December 1989 limited itself to accepting that the German people could regain its unity through free self-determination, 'in the perspective of European integration'. In his speech to the European Parliament on 17 January 1990, Delors was firm in his support for the position that German unification was as much the business of the Community as of the German people itself, in the terms of the German Basic Law as well as of the Treaty of Rome. East Germany was therefore a special case (in comparison with other countries emerging from the years of Communist domination).[73]

The 'special case' approach could at this stage still imply merely preferential treatment for the GDR, and indeed the negotiations for a Trade and Co-operation Agreement were expedited with exceptional brio.[74] But as it became clearer that the question of how to integrate the GDR into the Community would have to be handled sooner rather than later, the Commission's preference for avoiding a time-consuming accession negotiation strengthened. The fact that in his January speech Delors had set out three possible ways for the GDR to be associated with the Community—by Association Agreement, by accession as a state in its own right, or by absorption as a consequence of unification with the FRG—attracted

---

[69] Delors, *L'Unité d'un homme*, 256; Grant, *Delors*, 139–40; Teltschik, *329 Tage*, 102; Heisenberg, 'Europäische Sicherheit', 102; Lippert, 'Die EG als Mitgestalter der Erfolgs-geschichte', 45; Ross, *Jacques Delors and European Integration*, 49–50 and 264 n. 107; Endo, *The Presidency of the European Commission under Jacques Delors*, 93, 108.

[70] *Bull. EC*, Oct. 1989, 117.

[71] Lippert, 'Die EG als Mitgestalter der Erfolgsgeschichte', 45; Smith, *The Making of EU Foreign Policy*, 85.   [72] Genscher, *Erinnerungen*, 392, 647.

[73] Delors, *Le Nouveau concert européen*, 201; *Deutsche Einheit*, no. 144, 706.

[74] The negotiations began on 29 Jan. and the Agreement was initialled on 13 Mar.: Lippert, 'Die EG als Mitgestalter der Erfolgsgeschichte', 46 n. 50.

adverse comment as both untimely in itself and unacceptable as far as the second option, accession as a separate state, was concerned.[75] At the special informal meeting of Foreign Ministers on 20 January, France, Belgium, the United Kingdom, and the Netherlands in particular criticized this aspect, being still of the view that the GDR should be treated no differently from the other CEECs.[76] It was not until the following month that the Commission was given the task of compiling a paper on the EC and German unification in preparation for the special European Council to be held in April.[77] In that paper the Commission defined what it saw as the three stages involved in the integration of the GDR into a unified Germany, and hence into the Community: an interim adjustment stage, beginning with the introduction of inter-German monetary union; a second transitional stage, beginning with the formal unification of the two Germanies; and a final stage, corresponding to full application of Community legislation.[78] The paper was welcomed by the European Council, which after a surprisingly uncontentious discussion, given the difficulties which had preceded it, undertook that the Community would ensure that the 'integration of the territory of the German Democratic Republic into the Community' would be accomplished in a smooth and harmonious way; that the integration would 'become effective as soon as unification is legally established, subject to the necessary transitional arrangements'; and that it would be carried out 'without revision of the Treaties'.[79]

The European Council's decision meant that it had accepted the view of the German government that the absorption of the GDR into the Community should be regarded as the result of the extension of the territory of the Federal Republic of Germany, requiring no Treaty revision. (The German government thereby accepted that there would be no change for the time being in the Community institutions, including the number of seats for Germany in the European Parliament.) This approach depended

[75] *Deutsche Einheit*, no. 144, 706; no. 151, 730; and no. 187, 849; Védrine, *Les Mondes de François Mitterrand*, 439.

[76] Smith, *The Making of EU Foreign Policy*, 86. The Belgian, French, and British Foreign Ministers made their critical remarks to the press, not at the meeting itself: *Deutsche Einheit*, no. 144, 706. Mitterrand was also critical of Delors: *Deutsche Einheit*, no. 187, 849. For an account of the meeting based on contemporary records, see Torreblanca, *The European Community and Central Eastern Europe*, 112–16.

[77] Spence, *Enlargement without Accession*, 53; Lippert, 'Die EG als Mitgestalter der Erfolgsgeschichte', 46–7. Kohl claims that the mandate had already been given by the European Council at Strasbourg: Kohl, *Ich wollte Deutschlands Einheit*, 200.

[78] *Bull. EC*, Apr. 1990, 1.1; Küsters, 'Entscheidung für die deutsche Einheit', 157.

[79] *Bull. EC*, Apr. 1990, 1.5.

on the outcome of the political debate in Germany over whether unification should be brought about under Article 23 or Article 146 of the Basic
Law. Article 23 provided that the Basic Law would enter into force in 'other
parts of Germany' when these acceded to the Federal Republic, and had
been used for the reincorporation of the Sarre in the 1950s.[80] Article 146
provided for the expiry of the Basic Law when a new constitution, freely
adopted by the German people, entered into force. This would have
required long-drawn-out negotiations, in which the very nature of a
united Germany would have been up for debate, and would have implied
corresponding accession negotiations at Community level. The Christian
Democratic family preferred the former; the Social Democrats, seeing the
chance for a neutral Germany outside NATO, preferred the latter.[81] This
view was shared by many in the GDR. Kohl himself, as he said to Douglas
Hurd, did not want to give the opposition the chance, by a simple majority, to introduce social-democratic features into the federal constitution.[82]
The question was still bitterly contentious in February 1990.[83] The federal
cabinet itself did not finally come down in favour of Article 23 until 6
March.[84] The question was not settled until the elections in East Germany
on 18 March unexpectedly opened the way to a CDU-led coalition government. Thereafter it was accepted that the Article 23 route would prevail,
both in Germany and the Community.

Following the Dublin meeting of the European Council, the Community was faced with two separate requirements: to ensure that developments in the 'interim adjustment' stage, after the entry into force of
monetary, economic, and social union between the Federal Republic of
Germany and the German Democratic Republic (the *Staatsvertrag*), were
consistent with EC law, and to adopt any 'transitional arrangements'
deemed necessary as a result of the unification of Germany (the

[80] The Sarre therefore automatically became part of the European Coal and Steel Community: Morgan, 'Das neue Deutschland in der Europäischen Gemeinschaft', 85. The Legal
Service of the Commission was at first inclined to contest this view, but the College appears
not to have followed this advice: Lippert, 'Die EG als Mitgestalter der Erfolgsgeschichte',
42. For the pros and cons of the alternatives, see Küsters, 'Entscheidung für die deutsche
Einheit', 78. The legal position and the advantages and disadvantages of each solution are
summarized in a note by the Interior Ministry of 27 Feb. 1990: *Deutsche Einheit*, no. 196,
879–86.

[81] Zelikow and Rice, *Germany Unified and Europe Transformed*, 202–3, 229.

[82] *Deutsche Einheit*, no. 214, 933.

[83] Kohl, *Ich wollte Deutschlands Einheit*, 290–3; Küsters, 'Entschciding für die deustche
Einheit' 106; *Deutsche Einheit*, no. 182, 830–1.

[84] The decision was announced to the Bundestag on 8 Mar.: Zelikow and Rice, *Germany
Unified and Europe Transformed*, 218; Teltschik, *329 Tage*, 168–9.

Einigungsvertrag).[85] An important institutional result of the decision to go for 'enlargement without accession' was that the process fell predominantly into the hands of the Commission. Had there been accession negotiations under Article 237 of the Treaty, they would have been conducted by the Member States. As it was, it was the responsibility of the Commission to verify conformity with Community law and to make proposals for transitional arrangements under the Treaty. It was for this reason that the European Council in Dublin stipulated that the Commission would be fully involved with discussions between the authorities of the two Germanies 'for the purpose of aligning their policies and their legislation', and that the Commission should, in the context of an overall report, submit to the Council such proposals as were deemed necessary with regard to transitional arrangements. The Community thus found itself in the ironic situation of being excluded from the negotiations on the external aspects of German unification,[86] but included in the internal negotiations through the intermediary of the Commission.[87]

The Commission set up some rather sophisticated and flexible internal structures in order to be able to carry out these tasks efficiently. Responsibility for the Commission's overall strategy lay with a group of Commissioners comprising Delors, Bangemann, Christophersen, and Andriessen. This was supplemented, from February 1990, with a special group of Commissioners chaired by Vice-President Bangemann, which met weekly until July 1990. Following the Dublin European Council, additional structures were set up at the level of officials. A traditional inter-service group composed of all Directors General was chaired by the Secretary General, but only met twice. The bulk of the work was done by a 'Task Force for German Unification' (TFGU) headed by Carlo Trojan, the Deputy Secretary General.

The combination of structures proved remarkably effective. Close political contact was maintained with the authorities in Bonn, not only through Vice-President Bangemann's personal connections, but also through the President's Cabinet and the German Permanent Representation. The 'Group of Commissioners' was a well-tried device in the

---

[85] The following paragraphs draw heavily on Spence, *Enlargement without Accession*. David Spence was the Secretary of the Commission Task Force for German Unification.   [86] See Ch. 3 above.

[87] The EC had been kept informed of the progress of negotiations since mid-February: *Deutsche Einheit*, no. 185A, 838; Küsters, 'Entscheidung für die deutsche Einheit', 114–15, 144, 157.

Commission, having been used with success on a number of occasions. The Task Force, in the words of its Secretary,

did not involve permanent secondment from directorates general and, unlike previous Commission task forces which became directorates or divisions in their own right, the TFGU had a short-term remit. The only supernumerary staff member was the secretary of the task force, recruited from a national administration specifically for the purpose. Otherwise, the members of the TFGU were officials delegated by their directors-general. The formula was to prove extremely efficient. Its hallmarks were strong leadership and highly committed representatives of the directorates-general with decision-making authority on behalf of their 'hierarchies'.

Negotiations between the two Germanies over the *Staatsvertrag* began after the formation of the coalition government in East Germany;[88] the treaty was signed on 18 May, and came into force on 1 July. The implications of the *Staatsvertrag* were, if anything, more important for the Community order, and the effective implementation of the Single Market at the beginning of 1993, than were those of the *Einigungsvertrag*. Already at this stage questions of competition and state aids arose, and the GDR was well on the way to being part of the EC, without any decisions on transitional measures having been taken by the Community. It was the Commission's responsibility, confirmed by the European Council, to follow events and make any necessary proposals to the Council.

On 13 June this phase of the Commission's work came to an end with the adoption of a communication to the Council on the Community and German unification: implications of the *Staatsvertrag*. The communication contained a detailed economic analysis of the situation—probably the most detailed information available to the Member States, although reflecting the euphoria of the time—and an assessment of the policy implications. The Commission proposed setting up a *de facto* customs union between the GDR and the EC, with special provisions for agriculture, industrial products, and coal and steel products. EIB and Euratom loans were also to be made available.[89]

Commission officials had had several meetings with the German authorities in Bonn during the *Staatsvertrag* negotiations, and claimed that they had been kept fully informed,[90] but the situation had been shaky, and

---

[88] The Federal Government handed over a working paper as the basis for negotiations on 24 Apr. The negotiations themselves lasted barely a month: Lippert, 'Die EG als Mitgestalter der Erfolgsgeschichte', 70.

[89] *Bull. EC*, June 1990, 1.2.1–10.

[90] Lippert, 'Die EG als Mitgestalter der Erfolgsgeschichte', 72.

led to the Commission's seeking and being given an official role in the _Eini-gungsvertrag_ negotiations which followed.[91] Either the Deputy Secretary General or a senior member of the Legal Service attended all sessions, to ensure that the implications of EC law were correctly assessed.

It was to these negotiations that the Task Force now bent its efforts. It assumed that it would have the autumn to make a more detailed assessment of the implications of unification, and make proposals for transitional measures in the New Year, leaving the Council time for leisurely discussions in the spring. This timetable had to be continually revised, as the date for unification was successively brought forward. At the end of July, the Commission assumed that it would make its proposals by September, so that the Community would have finished its work by the new date for unification, which it was assumed would coincide with all-German elections on 2 December. Then, in early August, the Commission was told that unification would take place on 3 October.

These successive foreshortenings gave rise to a number of serious difficulties, which it was imperative should be solved.[92] The German people could not be invited to put off unification because the Community had not been able to pass the necessary laws in time, and indeed the Commission exploited the political situation to sweep the other EC participants along with the tide. The first difficulty was purely physical: the holiday season was in full swing, in Germany as well as in Brussels, and arrangements had to be made to ensure that the machine continued to function at full speed. The College was recalled for a special meeting on 21 August in order to adopt the proposals which had been prepared.

A more serious difficulty was that there was no longer enough time left to complete the Community procedure for the adoption of the proposals by 3 October. Apart from anything else, two readings in Parliament would be necessary, and only one plenary session was scheduled. The Commission therefore proposed special interim measures, which would give it broad powers to implement the proposals pending their formal adoption. This required the agreement of all three EC institutions involved, Council, Commission, and Parliament.

The European Parliament had not until now been closely involved in the Community procedure for the integration of the GDR, and resented the fact. It would, after all, have had to give its assent if the GDR had

---

[91] _Deutsche Einheit_, no. 290, 1153; no. 345, 1324; no. 328, 1266. Curiously, the Commission representatives appeared as part of the Federal German Delegation: _Deutsche Einheit_, no. 345, 1324.

[92] Ibid. no. 378, 1455.

requested accession under Article 237; the choice of the Article 23 route largely deprived it of that right. The Parliament complained that it had not been kept properly informed by the German authorities about the progress of the *Staatsvertrag* negotiations, and that it had had to rely on the Commission for information.[93] A Temporary Committee had been set up in February to consider the impact of the process of unification on the Community, and under the guidance of its energetic rapporteur, Alan Donnelly MEP, had managed to keep pretty well abreast of developments. Parliament now held the key to the Community's successful completion of its work with regard to German unification, and—like the other institutions, under the political pressure of events—was minded to be co-operative. Co-operation nevertheless had its price.[94]

The Inter-institutional Agreement was concluded on 6 September. Under the proviso that the emergency interim measures should be valid only until the end of 1990, Parliament agreed to hold two readings in the September plenary session. The Council also agreed to hasten its procedures. In return, the Council agreed not to stand on legal niceties and to allow the Parliament to give its opinion on the subsequent package of transitional measures as a whole, regardless of whether Parliament's view was strictly required or not. It undertook not to take a final decision itself on the package until after the Parliament's second reading in November.

Parliament achieved a further procedural success on the vexed question of 'comitology'. Most EC legislation contains provisions for the adaptation of legislation as required, by the Commission under the supervision of the Member States. The degree of strictness of the supervision is determined by the type of committee which is established to carry it out. In the case of the emergency interim measures, the Commission had originally proposed that the most binding of the different options, a regulatory committee, should apply. By arguing strongly in favour of the least binding, an advisory committee, Parliament at least achieved, as a compromise, a management committee, which was somewhere between the two. The battle was fought again when it came to the transitional measures, but this time Parliament lost.

The emergency interim measures were duly adopted in September, and the negotiations on the transitional measures were completed in accordance with the agreed timetable, enabling the Council to adopt them on

---

[93] Lippert, 'Die EG als Mitgestalter der Erfolgsgeschichte', 71.
[94] For a complete account of the European Parliament's role in the passage of the emergency interim measures, see Westlake, *The Passage through the Community's Legislative System*.

6 December. The negotiations were, of course, difficult, since real economic interests were at stake. A contributory factor to some Member States' hesitations about German unification was fear that a united Germany would exploit East Germany's supposed industrial efficiency and low wage levels to alter the competitive balance, and this fear showed itself in the negotiations. Particularly difficult areas were environmental policy, the structural funds, and external relations. The last was complicated by the fact that the negotiations were divided into two parts, agriculture and everything else, and that at one stage a link was established with the Community's negotiating position in the Uruguay Round. The agricultural question came close to wrecking the entire package.

Apart from that, the only serious threat to the package came from procedural questions reflecting the economic concerns mentioned above, in particular the related questions of the 'flexibility clause' and 'comitology'. The Commission, suspecting that unforeseen needs for derogations from the Community legal order would arise, proposed a simplified procedure for dealing with this eventuality. This was the 'flexibility clause'. The Council did not like it, the national delegations wishing to retain the closest possible control over any changes. Linked with this was the question of 'comitology'. Precisely in order to allay Member States' fears, the Commission had proposed the most binding form of committee, a regulatory committee. The Parliament maintained its view that an advisory committee should be preferred, but the Council would not budge. In the final compromise, a regulatory committee was retained for the adaptation of derogations, but new derogations were to fall outside the flexibility clause, requiring new proposals on which Parliament would be consulted. As David Spence remarks, 'as extraordinary as it may seem to the uninitiated, comitology and flexibility are the two issues around which the process of legal integration of the former GDR into the Community might have come unstuck'.

The way in which the Community responded to the demands made upon it by German unification had a number of consequences relevant to the forthcoming debate on European foreign-policy making.

First, the 'political' authorities of the Community, and in particular EPC, were not part of the action. It was crucial for the success of unification that a united Germany should be embedded in the European Community, and it was therefore an overriding concern of the Federal Government to ensure that the process of absorption of the new *Länder* into the EC should be swift and problem-free. That result could only be delivered by the economic, not the political, part of the Community.

Second, the Community showed that, when there was a pressing need, it could jettison procedures to procure the desired results. This applied equally to Commission, Council, and Parliament. All who were connected with the operation rightly congratulated themselves on its efficiency and effectiveness.

Third, it fell to the Commission to stage-manage the whole affair. It was the Commission which by its contacts with Bonn and its attendance at the *Einigungsvertrag* negotiations, together with its analysis of Community legislation in the light of unification, a mammoth task, provided the material without which the Community measures would not have been possible. Moreover, it was the Commission which orchestrated the timetable and made important contributions towards finding compromises. The Commission came out of the affair particularly well.

Perhaps as a result, *fourth*, the difficult debate over procedural questions showed that national delegations were not prepared to trust the Commission to manage their affairs for them in the interests of the Community. It was a part of the debate on consistency, and an indication of the underlying difference of opinion on the distribution of responsibility between the national and supranational levels which was to run through the Intergovernmental Conference preceding the Maastricht Treaty.

Finally, Delors personally won the undying gratitude of Chancellor Kohl for the part he had played in the unification process. He had been among the first to realize the inevitability of unification and its implications for the Community, and had ensured that he carried the Commission with him. The success of the operation was in no small part due to the impetus he had imparted to it. It was little wonder that, together with the President of Parliament, Enrique Baron, he was the only foreign statesman to attend the unification celebrations in Berlin on 3 October.[95]

[95] Grant, *Delors*, 140; Küsters, 'Entscheidung für die deutsche Einheit', 195; *Deutsche Einheit*, no. 429, 1552. It is true that Kohl had raised with Gorbachev the possibility of inviting all the Four-Power Heads of State, but the idea seems to have come to nothing: *Deutsche Einheit*, no. 415, 1530.

5

Preparing for the Treaty negotiations

Preliminary moves

The decision was taken at the Strasbourg European Council in December 1989 to fix a date for the start of negotiations on Economic and Monetary Union (EMU). The approach had been slow: authorization of preparatory work at Hanover in 1988, production of the Delors Committee Report over the following year, approval of the broad lines of the Report at Madrid in June 1989, and now agreement to convene an Intergovernmental Conference (IGC), as required for Treaty amendment, before the end of 1990.[1] The decision was an indirect result of the new prospects for the unification of Germany. Although the renewed push for EMU predated the collapse of Communism, and was independent of it, Chancellor Kohl's commitment to a date for the start of negotiations was a concession to President Mitterrand, in order to smooth the latter's acceptance of unification.

The possibility of extending the IGC to allow for the strengthening of the Community had been under discussion for some time. If, in the discussion about widening and deepening, the preference was to be given to deepening, reform of the Community through treaty amendment was essential. In its resolution of 23 November 1989 the European Parliament had called for the IGC's mandate to cover more efficient and more democratic decision-making as well as the social dimension. It did not, however, make any reference to foreign policy. It was not until the Parliament's resolution of 14 March 1990 (following on the first Martin Report on the IGC, so named after its rapporteur, David Martin MEP) that the changes in Europe were cited as one of the reasons for holding a conference ('whereas the rapid changes on the international and European political scene require the Community to speed up its institutional development and the construction of the European Union'), and that the Parliament pressed for the inclusion on the Conference agenda of 'a ration-

[1] *Bull. EC*, Dec. 1989, 1.1.11.

alisation of the Community's instruments for external relations, notably the full integration of EPC into the Community framework including the granting to the Commission of powers akin to those it possesses in other areas of Community policy in view of ultimately achieving common foreign and security policies in the service of peace.' This wholeheartedly integrationist approach to foreign policy was echoed a week later in a resolution adopted by the Italian Chamber of Deputies on 21 March 1990, in language identical to that used by the European Parliament.[2]

This approach was a tribute to the extent to which Community procedures had dominated the European foreign policy agenda over the previous months, but it was scarcely likely to form the agreed basis for discussion at the level of governments. It was an initiative by Belgium which set the ball rolling.

Forestalling any move by France, as had become a tradition, and anxious to avoid the undermining of EC integration by pan-European co-operative structures linked to the CSCE,[3] the Belgian government tabled on 20 March 1990 a Memorandum[4] on reform of the Community, comprising what proved to be the essential points of political union—institutional machinery, democratic shortfall, subsidiarity, and political co-operation.[5] Foreign policy was extensively covered, and indeed foreign policy considerations provided the major part of the rationale for reform. The Memorandum began with a telling exposition of these:

Several considerations combine to suggest that the European Community be given a new stimulus towards political union.

(a)   Firstly, the transformation of the political scene in Europe is creating a climate of uncertainty and giving rise to speculation. It is time to point out that:

— the European Community has shown an example of reconciliation and prosperity to the whole continent;

[2] Corbett, *The Treaty of Maastricht*, 104–5, 106, 125.
[3] Franck, 'Belgium', 156. De Schoutheete, 'The Creation of the CFSP', 43, makes the point that the Memorandum showed that political initiative does not necessarily originate in the larger Member States. Compare Foreign Minister Tindemans' move to revive the WEU after the Stuttgart Solemn Declaration: Franck, 'Belgium', 154.
[4] *EUROPE/Documents*, No. 1608, 29 Mar. 1990; Corbett, *The Treaty of Maastricht*, 121–4; Laursen and Vanhoonacker (eds.), *The Intergovernmental Conference on Political Union*, 269–75; Gerbet, de la Serre, and Nafilyan, *L'Union politique de l'Europe*, 285–9.
[5] See de Schoutheete, 'The Creation of the CFSP', 43–4, and de Schoutheete, 'Gemeinsame Außen- und Sicherheitspolitik'. As Belgium's Permanent Representative to the EC at the time, and a former Political Director, Ambassador de Schoutheete was closely involved in the production of the Belgian Memorandum.

— this anchor-point, far from disintegrating must, in a changing continent, be strengthened and developed in the interests of all Europeans;

— the Community's political purpose, which has always been present in the European Treaties, now becomes essential for guaranteeing its credibility as a major actor on the European stage.

(b) Secondly, the internal development of the Community . . .

(c) Thirdly, the special responsibility which the Community is generally thought to have for seeking solutions to the problems of Central and Eastern Europe requires a capacity to take effective and consistent external action, at least in that part of the world.

The aims which the Community had already set itself regarding the completion of the internal market, the introduction of EMU, and the development of the social dimension were to be

accompanied by a corresponding effort in the institutional and political fields. The aim of the proposals which follow is to:

— strengthen the existing institutional machinery in order to make it more effective;

— increase the democratic component of the institutional machinery by reinforcing the powers of Parliament and developing the Community's social dimension;

— developing convergence between political cooperation and Community policy; here, the policy towards Central and Eastern Europe could be the first opportunity to put this into practice.

On Political Co-operation, the Memorandum stated:

The political challenge constituted by developments in Eastern Europe has shown up more clearly the limitations of the existing machinery of political cooperation. The new international context calls more than ever for truly joint foreign policy. If it is true that the Twelve regard themselves as a focal point for future pan-European integration, the only logical course of action is for them to take part in the discussions as a political entity. This applies not only to a common 'Ostpolitik', but also to new relations with the great powers and also when taking up a position in international bodies such as the Council of Europe or the CSCE. We will be taken seriously only insofar as we assert ourselves. A share in the major decisions of the time has to be earned.

In practical terms, the Memorandum advised against a hasty revision of Article 30[6] of the Single Act. Instead, a series of practical measures was put forward, adapted to the immediate requirements of the situation brought about by liberalization in the East:

------

[6] In which the EPC provisions were to be found.

1. The Ministers for Foreign Affairs should work together to define and organize a set of principles and guidelines for political cooperation and cooperation by the Member States in relation to Eastern and Central European countries which would serve as a common framework for the activities of the Communities. To be consistent, the framework must cover all aspects: economic and political, bilateral and multilateral (CSCE). For this purpose the Ministers should adopt the custom of meeting regularly, both in the Council and in political cooperation. The General Affairs Council should once again become the Community's political decision-making centre. It must endeavour to pursue a policy rather than produce endless declarations. Similarly, it is conceivable that COREPER and the Political Directors (Political Cooperation) might together prepare the decisions on which would be based a global approach to the questions arising out of developments in Central and Eastern Europe and that the role of the Commission should be better defined, so as to secure the desired consistency.

2. It might also be desirable to obtain a better mix between expertise and diplomatic information from the Member States and the Commission's experience. Without changing the institutional framework and with due regard for the respective powers of each party, it would be possible to conduct an initial experiment in synergy by setting up a 'specialized task force' made up of some diplomats specializing in Eastern European countries, who would be seconded by the Member States, and by some Commission officials. This nucleus would serve as a centre for analysis, study and coordination on Eastern Europe to the benefit of both Council and the Commission.

3. With a view to political union and, more particularly, to actual participation in the discussions which are about to take place in the CSCE, it is both desirable and necessary that it should be possible to discuss security issues in the broadest sense without restriction in political cooperation. Without prejudice to the powers of other institutions, which are themselves destined to change, the Member States have no cause to deprive themselves everlastingly of the opportunity to discuss this essential aspect among themselves.

The Belgian Memorandum was a masterpiece of lucid analysis and practical statecraft. Had the Community followed the approach it recommended, the results would almost certainly have been better in every way than those actually achieved. Its most important element, as far as political co-operation was concerned, was the perception that a hasty revision of Article 30 would lead to unsatisfactory results, and that a better course would be to introduce new working practices attuned to practical requirements. These might in due course make it possible to change the rules of EPC, on the basis of successful experience ('It must be hoped . . . that the constraints forced upon us by events will encourage us in the not too

distant future to amend rules which no longer meet the requirements of
the action which it is our ambition and duty to take.'). In other words, the
classic method of EPC was to be adopted: practical innovations in
response to circumstances, later officially incorporated in the body of EPC
procedures. This ensured that change was seen to be necessary, and therefore was accepted, and that the participants did not become bogged down
in arguments of principle far removed from reality.

The practical suggestions were based on experience. The idea that
the Foreign Ministers should define guidelines for policy towards Central
and Eastern Europe was a matter of political common sense, given the
way in which the political and economic aspects of the question were
interwoven.[7] That common sense was nevertheless not always the guiding
rule had recently been indicated by the fact that the European Council
in Strasbourg had been invited to adopt two texts on Central and Eastern
Europe, one prepared in the Community framework and one in Political
Co-operation. Furthermore, Delors had in his speech to the European
Parliament in January 1990 recommended the definition of essential
common interests, leading to common actions, on foreign policy
questions.[8]

The proposal that Ministers should meet regularly both in the Council
and in Political Co-operation was a resurrection of the Italian proposal
which had failed to be adopted in the Single European Act. It had now
acquired the sanction of successful experience in the joint meetings which
had taken place in the first two months of the year under the Irish Presidency and at the instigation of Delors.[9] It was no longer contested and
was incorporated without difficulty in the Maastricht Treaty. The proposal
that Coreper and the Political Committee should jointly prepare the Ministers' decisions was also based on experience under the Irish Presidency,
but it proved harder to bring officials together than Ministers—the Ministers were the same, but the officials were different. This problem has still
not been resolved.

The Belgian Memorandum was ambiguous about the role of the Commission, which 'should be better defined, so as to secure the desired consistency'. This could be taken to mean that the Commission's role should
be strengthened, or the reverse. The latter is marginally the more probable, given that Belgium, like many other Member States, disliked the way

---

[7] The Belgian ideas in this respect were not new. A prescient Mr Tindemans had already
launched similar proposals at the informal meeting of Foreign Ministers at Ioannina on
15–16 Oct. 1988.　　　　　[8] Delors, *Le Nouveau concert européen*, 209.
　[9] Nuttall, *European Political Co-operation*, 249, 278–9.

in which the Commission had, since the London Report, insisted on punctilious respect for its 'full association' with EPC, but nevertheless maintained its autonomy under the EC Treaty. Belgium felt that full association carried with it the obligation to respect EPC discipline, like the Member States, to which the Commission's reply was that, unlike the Member States, it did not have a veto. Belgium's concern for consistency in this area antedated the events of autumn 1989. Already in the spring of that year the Council had, at the instigation of the Belgian Foreign Minister Leo Tindemans, emphasized 'the aim of greater consistency between Community policies and those agreed in the framework of Political Co-operation as being particularly desirable in the context of relations with the East European countries'.[10]

The suggestion to conduct an 'experiment in synergy' by setting up a specialized task force bringing together some diplomats with special knowledge of Eastern Europe and some Commission officials to serve as a 'centre for analysis, study and coordination' was designed partly to meet criticisms that the Commission was diplomatically ill equipped to carry out its new tasks in Eastern and Central Europe,[11] and partly to facilitate a partnership in foreign-policy making between Member States and the Commission without asking difficult questions of principle. It was a prescient move, foreshadowing later calls for a planning unit which finally materialized in the Treaty of Amsterdam. If the suggestion had been adopted, the experience gained might have led to a more satisfactory outcome. It was not. Instead, the Commission recruited national experts into its East European departments, which increased the available expertise but did not provide the requisite structural link with national administrations.

Finally, the almost throwaway reference to the need to be able to discuss security issues without restriction is a reminder that at this stage the debate about a European defence personality, which was later to play an important part in the IGC, had not yet begun to take shape. That development had to await the experiences of the Gulf War.

In spite of its many merits, it was not the Belgian Memorandum which determined the future shape of political union. That honour was reserved for the initiative taken jointly by President Mitterrand and Chancellor Kohl a month later, on 19 April. Although the timing, in a typical

---

[10] *Bull. EC*, Apr. 1989, 2.2.11; Council Secretariat Press Release 6000/89 (Presse 66) of 24 Apr. 1989, 7; *Agence Europe* no. 5002 of 24–5 Apr. 1989, 5.

[11] Ludlow, 'The European Commission', 107; Froment-Meurice and Ludlow, 'Towards a European Foreign Policy', 17–18.

move,[12] was designed to anticipate by a few days the extraordinary meeting of the European Council at Dublin (28 April), the origins of the initiative in fact reach back to the previous autumn. It was of course a common-place of discussion throughout the latter part of 1989 that the Commun-ity needed to make progress towards political union, but the question was what this meant in concrete terms, and what the timetable should be. At a meeting on 24 October, Kohl told Mitterrand that, in his view, there should be progression towards political union once economic union had been achieved;[13] for his part, Mitterrand thought progress should be more rapid, a view he came to hold more strongly the closer German unifica-tion approached.[14] Kohl was still attached to a progressive view of events when he wrote to Mitterrand on 27 November in preparation for the Euro-pean Council shortly to be held at Strasbourg. He proposed an intergov-ernmental conference in three stages, the first beginning at the end of 1990 and devoted to EMU, the second before December 1991 on other ques-tions of institutional reform, and the third, in 1992, to allow the European Council to make a firm commitment to economic and political union.[15] He did not, however, inform the French President that he intended to set out to the Bundestag the next day a step-by-step approach towards uni-fication. This omission was resented. In order to make unification more acceptable to Mitterrand, and to atone somewhat for the affront of the Bundestag speech, Kohl sent a further letter on 5 December, this time proposing that the European Council should send out a 'clear signal' on political union, and that the IGC should finish its work in time for the European Council at the end of the Netherlands Presidency (December 1991), for ratification in 1992–3.[16]

In all this there was no specific mention of strengthening the Commun-ity's foreign-policy making capabilities. 'Political union' was still at this

[12] Cf. the Franco-German initiative shortly before the Milan European Council in 1985: Nuttall, *European Political Co-operation*, 246.

[13] Attali, *Verbatim III*, 326 ('Il faudrait qu'après l'économique on aille vers un projet politique européen'). See also *Deutsche Einheit*, no. 70, 472. Kohl had told Italian Prime Minister Andreotti the week before (18 Oct. 1989) that the Single Market was not enough, and that much greater progress towards political union had to be made: *Deutsche Einheit*, no. 62, 453.

[14] Attali, *Verbatim III*, 331, 354–5, 389.

[15] Mitterrand, *De l'Allemagne, de la France*, 83–4; Teltschik, *329 Tage*, 54; *Deutsche Einheit*, no. 100A, 566–7.

[16] Teltschik, *329 Tage*, 68–9; Mitterrand, *De l'Allemagne, de la France*, 85; *Deutsche Einheit*, nos. 108, 108A, 596–600, and no. 111, 614–15; compare Attali, *Verbatim III*, 357–8. For a different view on the relative enthusiasm for political union of Mitterrand and Kohl, see Doutriaux, *Le Traité sur l'Union européenne*, 19.

stage mainly about strengthening the powers of the Parliament, a reform more likely to appeal to German than to French élites.[17] In this it followed the agenda set by the European Parliament in its resolution of 23 November. Kohl was of course as much concerned with domestic opinion as with handling relations with France, and knew that action to repair the 'democratic deficit' would be a political necessity for him.[18]

Immediately after the Strasbourg European Council Mitterrand gave instructions to his staff to work for a serious commitment to the political strengthening of the Community as early as the forthcoming Irish Presidency (the first half of 1990). This task was given to the Foreign Minister, Roland Dumas, and to Jean-Louis Bianco, Jacques Attali, Élisabeth Guigou, and Hubert Védrine, all on the President's staff at the Élysée.[19] On the German side, the counterparts were Horst Teltschik, director of the foreign and security policy section at the Federal Chancery, and his colleague Joachim Bitterlich, to whom he left most of the EC business.[20] The fact that the responsible officials worked directly for the President and the Chancellor, and not in the respective Foreign Ministries, was not without significance, as will be seen.

The need for a gesture to cement the Franco-German relationship became more acute towards the end of 1989, as relations between Mitterrand and Kohl, already poor following the Bundestag speech and Mitterrand's visit to East Germany, deteriorated further because of the Chancellor's continued refusal to give public recognition to the Oder–Neisse line as the frontier of a united Germany.[21] In a meeting on 4 January 1990 at Mitterrand's country retreat at Latché, designed to repair the relationship between him and Kohl, the French President insisted on the need

---

[17] *Deutsche Einheit*, no. 70, 472–3, 474, 476; no. 108, 598; no. 111, 614; no. 213, 929. For the dogma, long held in German élite circles, that monetary union would follow a process of economic and political union (the 'coronation' theory), see Dyson, 'Chancellor Kohl as Strategic Leader', 39. For an interesting observation on the echoes of the 1848 Paulskirche Parliament with the German élite, referred to by Kohl, see Pedersen, *Germany, France, and the Integration of Europe*, 153–4.

[18] Delors, *L'Unité d'un homme*, 239. Kohl was particularly concerned to secure the support of the Bundesbank, which was insisting on a strong political union to complement EMU, and that of the SPD, which could block ratification in the Bundestag and Bundesrat: Mazzucelli, *France and Germany at Maastricht*, 117, 118; Moravcsik, *The Choice for Europe*, 395.

[19] Védrine, *Les Mondes de François Mitterrand*, 433; Lequesne, 'Une lecture décisionelle', 140–1, and the remarks in Cohen, *Mitterrand et la sortie de la guerre froide*, 149 and 154. For a discussion of the precise date at which the initiative for a parallel conference on political union took shape, see Ch. 3, n. 52 above.

[20] Confirmed to the author by Mr Teltschik; see also Küsters, *Entscheidung . . .* , 31.

[21] Favier and Martin-Roland, *La Décennie Mitterrand*, iii. 190–1, 203.

to strengthen the existing Community, and to find solutions simultaneously for the problems of Germany and Europe as a whole.[22] He returned
to this theme at a meeting with Kohl on 15 February 1990, at which both
supported the idea (launched two days earlier by the Irish Presidency) of
holding an extraordinary meeting of the European Council.[23] From there
it was but a step to deciding on a joint Franco-German initiative on
political union. The idea had been in the air for some time. Mme Guigou
had submitted a proposal to that effect to the President on 6 February
1990 and had received an encouraging response, and Bitterlich had
also aired the possibility on a visit to Paris on 13 February. Arrangements
for preparing the initiative were put in hand following a meeting in
Paris on 15 March between Teltschik and the Secretary General of the
Élysée, Jean-Louis Bianco. The decision was hailed in Bonn as a means
of demonstrating to the world 'the continued close friendship and co-
operation' between France and Germany, after a tense period in their
relationship.[24]

It remained to discuss the contents of the initiative. The Germans
wanted to keep them as general as possible, and leave the details to be
worked out between the Foreign Ministries at a later stage. Kohl's reluctance to see Genscher too closely involved certainly contributed to this attitude. Mitterrand, on the other hand, was anxious to have clearly stated
objectives, especially regarding institutional reform. On the whole, the
German view prevailed.[25] What is not certain is where the initiative to
include a common foreign and security policy came from. The available
documents indicate rather clearly that the driving force behind the concept
of political union came from the staffs at the Élysée and the Chancellery,
especially Guigou and Bitterlich. Védrine tells us that he was in charge of
the external relations aspects of the initiative, but gives no details about
his instructions or the negotiations.[26] For his part, the Chancellor showed
no signs of being interested in more than the broad concept of European
foreign policy. Certainly as late as his Camp David meeting with Bush
on 24 February 1990, Kohl was still thinking exclusively in terms of
strengthening the powers of the European Parliament,[27] and in the

[22] *Deutsche Einheit*, no. 135, 689; Favier and Martin-Roland, *La Décennie Mitterrand*, iii.
225–7.
[23] *Deutsche Einheit*, no. 187, 849–50.
[24] Attali, *Verbatim III*, 412 and 419–20; Védrine, *Les Mondes de François Mitterrand*, 438;
Teltschik, *329 Tage*, 175–6.
[25] *Deutsche Einheit*, nos. 241 and 241A, 1005–7, and no. 243, 1010–1.
[26] Védrine, *Les Mondes de François Mitterrand*, 438.
[27] *Deutsche Einheit*, no. 192, 861.

working elements for the initiative later submitted to him for approval, the future CFSP lurks coyly under the heading 'unity and consistency of the Union' ('Einheit und Kohärenz der Union'), backed up by references to the planned revision of the EPC provisions of the Single Act and to the Belgian Memorandum.[28] In a later letter to Delors, the Chancellor attributes the paternity of the idea to the President of the Commission.[29] The most likely explanation is that the idea of a common foreign and security policy was included at the instigation of the Élysée and Chancellery officials, confronted with the European Parliament's resolution and the Belgian Memorandum. If indeed, as seems to be the case, the decision was taken suddenly and little thought had been given to what was implied by a transformation of EPC, the subsequent delays and uncertainties are more easily explained.

Kohl announced the forthcoming initiative on a visit to the Commission on 23 March,[30] thus pipping Mitterrand at the post, to the disgust of the latter, who had intended to make a splash with it on French television two days later.[31]

The letter which Mitterrand and Kohl sent on 19 April to the Irish President of the European Council, Charles Haughey, was concise to the point of abruptness:

In the light of far-reaching changes in Europe and in view of the completion of the single market and the realization of economic and monetary union, we consider it necessary to accelerate the political construction of the Europe of the Twelve. We believe that it is time 'to transform relations as a whole among the member States into a European Union . . . and invest this union with the necessary means of action', as envisaged by the Single Act.

With this in mind, we should like to see the European Council deciding as follows on 28 April:

(1) The European Council should ask the competent bodies to intensify the preparations for the intergovernmental conference on economic and monetary union, which will be opened at the end of 1990 at the invitation of the Italian Presidency, as decided by the European Council at Strasbourg.

(2) The European Council should initiate preparations for an intergovernmental conference on political union. In particular, the objective is to: strengthen

---

[28] *Deutsche Einheit*, no. 241A, 1006–7.   [29] 13 Mar. 1990: Ibid. no. 215, 936.

[30] Teltschik, *329 Tage*, 181.

[31] Attali, *Verbatim III*, 449–50. One may speculate that Mitterrand also wished to use the initiative to distract attention from his previous leaning towards maintaining the GDR for as long as possible as an independent state, the impossibility of which had finally been demonstrated by the East German elections on 18 Mar.

the democratic legitimation of the union, render its institutions more efficient, ensure unity and coherence of the union's economic, monetary and political action, define and implement a common foreign and security policy.[32]

The Foreign Ministers should be instructed to prepare an initial report for the meeting of the European Council in June and to submit a final report to the meeting of the European Council in December. We wish the intergovernmental conference on political union to be held in parallel to the conference on economic and monetary union.

(3) Our aim is that these fundamental reforms—economic and monetary union as well as political union—should enter into force on 1 January 1993 after ratification by the national parliaments.

The Foreign Ministers of the French Republic and the Federal Republic of Germany, Roland Dumas and Hans-Dietrich Genscher, will present these ideas for discussion at the forthcoming informal meeting of the Council of Ministers (General Affairs) on 21 April.[33]

The concision was deliberate, to avoid an 'ill-prepared, confused, and counter-productive' discussion at the European Council.[34] But it also concealed the fact that ideas about what political union might mean in practice were relatively undeveloped. This was to lead to difficulties later. For the time being, in so far as it dealt with external relations, the initiative was limited to calling for coherence ('consistency'), and fixing the definition and implementation of a common and foreign security policy as an objective. The contrast with the Belgian Memorandum could not have been more striking. Whereas the Belgians argued in favour of a pragmatic strengthening of the Community's foreign-policy making capability, without amending the Treaty at this stage, and made a number of concrete suggestions for achieving this, Mitterrand and Kohl declared themselves in favour of a common foreign and security policy and proposed an intergovernmental conference to bring this about, implying Treaty amendment but without giving any indication of what should actually be done.

Most of the Heads of State and Government were prepared to give it a try, without at this stage committing themselves to a common foreign and security policy. The exceptions were the Prime Ministers of the United Kingdom, Denmark, and Portugal.[35] Mrs Thatcher pointed out

---

[32] The CFSP did not figure among the original elements approved by Kohl: *Deutsche Einheit*, no. 241A, 1006–7.

[33] Corbett, *The Treaty of Maastricht*, 126; Gerbet, de la Serre, and Nafilyan, *L'Union politique de l'Europe*, 289–90.

[34] Attali, *Verbatim III*, 455.   [35] Teltschik, *329 Tage*, 211.

perspicaciously but no doubt unwisely that neither of the authors of the initiative knew what political union was; she did, and she was having none of it. Her tactics in the discussion were to state very plainly what for her political union could not mean. As far as foreign policy was concerned, this included any weakening in the role of NATO and any restriction on the right of Member States to conduct their own foreign policies.[36] In return, Chancellor Kohl pointed out that she could not have it both ways: both to be mistrustful of Germany and to oppose European integration.[37]

The European Council 'confirmed its commitments to political union', and decided to put in hand a detailed examination 'on the need for possible Treaty changes with the aim of strengthening the democratic legitimacy of the union, enabling the Community and its institutions to respond efficiently and effectively to the demands of the new situation, and assuring unity and coherence in the Community's international action.' (The objective of a CFSP was not taken over from the Mitterrand–Kohl text.) The examination was to be undertaken by Foreign Ministers, who would report to the European Council in June, with a view to a decision on a second IGC in parallel to that on EMU, for ratification in the same time-frame.[38]

In the event, the Foreign Ministers chose to limit themselves to setting out a list of questions about political union.[39] A first informal meeting of Foreign Ministers at Parknasilla on 18–19 May held out scant prospects for far-reaching reform. Delors was moved by the discussions to say that 'it was more efficient to start from the weaknesses and gaps of the current institutional system and to see how gradual progress can be made'. Everyone agreed on strengthening political co-operation, but, as the French Foreign Minister Roland Dumas said: 'Everyone is aware of the fact that it is too soon to speak of external policy and security in terms of Community integration: no country is ready to delegate its sovereignty in these matters'. On the other hand, the idea of giving the Commission a non-exclusive right of initiative was already being aired.[40]

The Irish Presidency attempted to draft a note setting out the minimum of consensus, but this proved to be a bare minimum indeed. After Parknasilla discussions at the level of officials passed to the 'personal repre-

---

[36] Thatcher, *The Downing Street Years*, 761–2; Cloos *et al.*, *Le Traité de Maastricht*, 54.

[37] *Deutsche Einheit*, no. 266, 1082.   [38] *Bull. EC*, Apr. 1990, 1.12.

[39] Corbett, *The Treaty of Maastricht*, 137–9.

[40] *EUROPE*, no. 5259, 21–22 May 1990, 3–4.

sentatives',[41] who preferred an approach which, by asking questions rather than finding answers, kept more ideas open for discussion.[42] The report they produced for Foreign Ministers to forward to the European Council was particularly prudent on foreign policy. Under the section headed 'Unity and coherence of the Community's international action', the Ministers divided the questions to which the proposal for a CFSP gave rise into three categories:

Scope

(i) the integration of economic, political and security aspects of foreign policy;

(ii) the definition of the security dimension;

(iii) the strengthening of the Community's diplomatic and political action *vis-à-vis* third countries, in international organizations and in other multilateral forums;

(iv) the evolution of the transfer of the competences to the union and in particular the definition of priority areas where transfer would take place at an initial stage.

Decision-making

(i) use of the Community method (in full or in adapted form) and/or a *sui generis* method, bearing in mind the possibilities offered by the evolution over time of the degrees of transfer of competence to the union, referred to above;

(ii) the Commission's role, including the faculty of launching initiatives and proposals;

(iii) establishment of a single decision-making structure; central role of the General Affairs Council and the European Council in this context; preparatory bodies; the organization and strengthening of the Secretariat;

(iv) modalities aimed at ensuring the necessary flexibility and efficiency to meet the requirements of formulation of foreign policy in various areas; consideration of decision procedures including the consensus rule, voting practices involving unanimity with abstentions, and qualified majority voting in specific areas.

Implementation

There is a recognised need for clear rules and modalities for the implementation of the common foreign policy; the following are to be examined in this context:

---

[41] At this stage, these were, with the exception of Portugal, the Permanent Representatives, i.e. the members of Coreper: Cloos *et al.*, *Le Traité de Maastricht*, 55 n. 14. Later France, Denmark, and Spain were represented by senior officials from capitals: Doutriaux, *Le Traité sur l'Union européenne*, 32. According to de Schoutheete ('The Creation of the CFSP', 44), the preparation of the early stages was entrusted to the Political Committee and Coreper.   [42] Cloos *et al.*, *Le Traité de Maastricht*, 56–7.

(i) role of the Presidency (and of the 'Troika'), and of the Secretariat;
(ii) role of the Commission;
(iii) role of national diplomatic services in a strengthened collaboration.

Some of the ideas which popped up in the Ministers' report were later to be taken into the CFSP, but on the whole the report provided little guidance about how to take the discussion further. Interestingly, the gradual transfer of competences to the union figured as a question to be explored, but this never really happened. The role of national diplomatic services also sank without trace.

The report was duly presented to the European Council meeting at Dublin on 25 and 26 June, and resulted in agreement that a second intergovernmental conference would be convened, this one on political union, opening on 14 December 1990. The Heads of State and Government did not, however, provide any guidance for the Conference, which would adopt its own agenda.[43]

Preparations under the Italian Presidency

The Italian Presidency of the second half of 1990 was devoted to preparing the ground for the formal launching of the two intergovernmental conferences at the European Council meeting in December. It did this, as regards political union, by collating and organizing discussions on the contributions from Member States which now began to flow in. The process was evolutive. The Italians chose to allow the substance of the negotiation to take shape, rather than to enunciate an *ex cathedra* Presidency objective. Instead, successive Presidency drafts summing up the state of the discussions imperceptibly consolidated a common basis of what was generally acceptable. This was not only consistent with the Italian diplomatic tradition; as regards foreign policy it reflected the absence of any fixed idea in advance of the form which change might take. This was the more noticeable because of the failure of France and Germany to follow up their previous initiative.[44] One might have expected Mitterrand and Kohl to flesh out their letter of 19 April with some concrete ideas, but there was silence from that quarter until shortly before the December European

---

[43] *Bull. EC,* June 1990, 1.11.
[44] Kohl perciepiently remarked, at his meeting with Mitterrand in Munich on 17–18 Sept. 1990, that he 'had the feeling that without a new Franco-German initiative reasonable progress would not be made', but this was not followed up until the end of the year: *Deutsche Einheit,* no. 424, 1545.

Council. The other Member States were therefore led to 'conclude that the main purpose of the [April] letter had been to proclaim a common purpose but that there was, in fact, no political concept agreed upon between Paris and Bonn as to what a common foreign and security policy should be'.[45] This gave added importance to the exercise engaged in by the Italian Presidency. By December, with the exception of the defence and security aspects, the contours of what was to become the common foreign and security policy were already visible without there having been a clear, agreed formulation of the desired aim of the operation.

In so far as there was an agenda for change in foreign-policy making, it had been set by the European Parliament in the Resolution it adopted on 11 July 1990, on the basis of the second Martin Report.[46] The Parliament considered that matters 'currently dealt with under EPC [should] be dealt with in the Community framework with appropriate procedures'. It believed

that the current division between external economic relations handled by the Community institutions with the Commission acting as the Community's external representative, and political cooperation handled by EPC with the EPC President acting as external representative, is increasingly difficult to maintain in practice,' and considered 'that any genuine attempt 'to assure unity and coherence in the Community's international action' must abolish this increasingly artificial distinction.

It therefore called

for the Council (rather than a separate framework of foreign ministers) to be given the prime responsibility of defining policy; for the Commission to have a right of initiative in proposing policies to Council and to have a role in representing the Community externally, including appropriate use of its external missions in third countries; and for the functions of the EPC secretariat to be absorbed by the Commission and the Council; and for the Community's foreign policy to be subject to scrutiny by the Community's elected Parliament.

On security, it called

for the scope of the Community's foreign policy to include issues of security, peace and disarmament, with a close coordination of national security policies, and to respect the principle of solidarity and the inviolability of the external borders of Member States.

---

[45] de Schoutheete, 'The Creation of the CFSP', 46–7.
[46] Corbett, *The Treaty of Maastricht*, 114.

Taking up the idea put forward by Delors in January 1990, the Parliament considered 'that in all these areas, the Community should aim to have common policies on all matters in which the Member States share essential interests.'

Finally, the Parliament considered that the Community should represent the Member States in international organizations in areas of established Community competence.

The European Parliament's Resolution contained the core agenda of those who wished EPC to be changed in the direction of integration with the EC. All that was lacking was a specific reference to decision-making by majority vote, and the military aspects of security. The latter were indeed not taken up in the debate until after Saddam Hussein's invasion of Kuwait in August 1990. It was a moderate programme, and might have produced the desired effect had the then benign atmosphere of EPC and the perception of shared views on the most important foreign policy issues persisted longer in the post-Cold War era. As things turned out, more stringent institutional arrangements would have been necessary in order to produce a genuine common foreign and security policy. The Resolution nevertheless constituted a catalogue of institutional changes around which the debate turned. Some of the ideas were generally accepted, some were disputed, and some provided scope for compromise.

The suggestions put forward by Member States were, however, largely determined by their different approaches in principle towards the concept of building the Community as a political entity, rather than an overriding concern 'to assure unity and coherence in the Community's international action'. These approaches ranged from the vociferously hostile, with the United Kingdom at one extreme, to the federally enthusiastic, with the Benelux countries at the other. The effect of this on proposals for foreign-policy making procedures can be illustrated from the submissions by Denmark and the Netherlands, who might be described as mainstream representatives of the two schools of thought. The Danish government memorandum, approved by the Market Committee of the Folketing on 4 October 1990,[47] stated a preference for a gradual development in EPC, with the consensus rule continuing to apply. Co-operation on security policy could be gradually extended, but co-operation in defence policies was rejected. Denmark favoured using the General Affairs Council as a united forum for dealing with EC and EPC business, and presciently recognized that a consequence of this would be that prior preparation of dossiers

[47] Corbett, *The Treaty of Maastricht*, 162.

would also have to be co-ordinated. The Danish government accepted the absorption of the EPC Secretariat by the Council Secretariat, and the confirmation of the Commission's 'current position as an equal partner in EPC'. Both of these were advances on previous Danish positions.

The policy document on EPU presented by the Dutch government to Parliament on 26 October 1990 addressed the question of the unity and coherence of the EC's international action in a different way.[48] There were two guiding principles: the inclusion of foreign policy and security in EPU should not lead to an increase in the intergovernmental character of European integration, and any decisions would have to be in line with NATO co-operation. Within this framework, the Dutch saw advantage in allocating EPC decision-making to the General Affairs Council, merging the Council and EPC Secretariats, and having closer alignment between Coreper and the Political Committee. As regards decision making, the Dutch argued in favour of a flexible majority vote system over time, a non-exclusive right of initiative for the Commission,[49] and a form of parliamentary control through the European Parliament. Defence co-operation in the narrow sense would remain with the WEU and NATO, but there was scope for Community co-operation on aspects of defence industry policy, arms exports, arms control, participation in UN peace-keeping forces, and joint 'out of area' operations. Greater coherence between WEU and EPU was needed, but the Dutch saw some disadvantages in formal incorporation of the WEU in EPU.[50]

As might be expected, the Commission took up position among the integrationist Member States, but with the exception of the question of a defence guarantee it remained within the integrationist mainstream. It was a long way from the full-blooded federalist approach adopted by the European Parliament in its March 1990 Resolution (which the Parliament had itself drawn back from in July). The Commission's views were expressed in the formal opinion it submitted, in accordance with the Treaty, on 21 October 1990.[51] The analysis was based on Delors' idea of acting together

[48]   Corbett, *The Treaty of Maastricht*, 184–6.

[49]   Notwithstanding this paper, the Dutch—or at least State Secretary Dankert, speaking before the 1991 Netherlands Presidency—recognized that majority voting and the exclusive right of proposal by the Commission needed to be indissolubly linked. Without that, democratic control would be impossible—as would the prime Dutch objective of ensuring that 'the interests of all member states . . . be taken into account in as balanced a manner': Dankert, 'Challenges and Priorities', 9, 10.

[50]   For an extended commentary on the Netherlands' approach, see Penders and Kwast, 'The Netherlands and Political Union', 260–70.

[51]   Corbett, *The Treaty of Maastricht*, 166–7.

to pursue vital common interests—in other words, renouncing for the time being the ambition of pursuing a universalist foreign policy, in which all matters fell within the Community's ambit.[52] Although the Treaty should, in the Commission's opinion, outline the procedures and methods for a 'common policy' leading towards European Union, it had to be recognized that Member States '[had] special relations with certain parts of the world and geopolitical positions which are firmly anchored in their history. More importantly, the Twelve do not yet share the same assessment of their responsibilities or of their general and specific commitments in various parts of the world'. On the same lines, the Commission recommended a specific approach to security matters. 'The Treaty should include a reference to this subject and might incorporate the undertaking contained in Article 5 of the 1948 Brussels Treaty on the WEU which specifies that, in the event of an armed attack against one of the contracting parties, the others are obliged to provide aid and assistance.[53] More than that, the new Treaty should, in general terms, point the way towards a common security policy, including defence.' The objective was clear, but progress towards it was to be pragmatic and gradual.[54]

In order to prepare decisions for the 'common foreign policy', the Commission proposed bringing together in the Council Secretariat the current EPC Secretariat, which would be strengthened, and representatives of the Commission. Coreper should be put in a position to take cognizance of foreign policy matters before the Council took a decision. On decision-making, the Commission advised against compiling a list of areas considered to be of vital common interest. Instead, it should be left to the European Council to decide on the areas to be transferred from the scope of political co-operation to that of a common or Community policy. The Council would then take decisions by a qualified majority,[55] except on matters directly related to security. The most important decisions could be implemented through a number of formulas, all of them involving Commission participation. Finally, the European Parliament should be consulted on foreign and security policy on a regular basis, but as a matter of practice rather than law.

---

[52] Favier and Martin-Roland, *La Décennie Mitterrand*, iv. 221.

[53] The guarantee of mutual assistance was supported only by Greece, in itself enough to make the other Member States nervous, given the state of Graeco-Turkish relations: Cloos et al., *Le Traité de Maastricht*, 473.

[54] de Schoutheete, 'The Creation of the CFSP', 47.

[55] The Commission made it clear that this was the augmented qualified majority requiring the votes of 8 Member States, stipulated by the Treaty in cases where there was no provision for a proposal from the Commission.

It has already been mentioned that references to the security dimension of a foreign policy were no more than passing until after Saddam Hussein's invasion of Kuwait. The first detailed initiative in this area was taken by Italy on 18 September 1990. The Italian Foreign Minister, Gianni De Michelis, was quick to seize the opportunity afforded by events in the Gulf to open up discussions on the security dimension of a common foreign policy—'As far as Europe is concerned, there is no doubt that the Gulf crisis has given [a] decisive impulse to the organization of the Intergovernmental Conference in Rome in December . . . the strong aggregating forces present at this stage have brought to the fore the perception that the time is ripe to discuss the substance of the future of the European dimension of security and defence'.[56] The Italians proposed extending the competences of the Union to all aspects of security without limitations; in other words 'to transfer to the Union the competences currently being exercised by WEU'.[57] This transfer would imply the following commitments:

— approve the principle of a security guarantee among Member States;
— extend our consultation and our coordination to defence and security matters and examine all practical measures to this end;
— involve the Defence Ministers and their representatives in the deliberations of the Union on matters related to security and defence;
— concert our policies on crises outside Europe insofar as they may affect our security interests, including the possibility of joint initiatives aimed at ensuring the respect of relevant decisions of the UN Security Council;
— consult and coordinate our policies in the field of disarmament and arms control, with a particular reference to negotiations in the framework of the CSCE process;
— develop industrial and technological cooperation in the military field;
— consult on arms sales policies to third countries.

This 'extensive and radical reform' would be accompanied by opt-out provisions for those who 'would wish not to share this particular aspect of the institutional reform or single actions deriving from it'.

On the basis of these and other contributions the Member States began in a series of discussions to put together an agenda for political

[56] Guazzone, 'Italy in the Gulf Crisis', 73.

[57] Laursen and Vanhoonacker (eds.), *The Intergovernmental Conference on Political Union*, 292. The EPC Secretariat also prepared about this time a paper on the implications of a security policy, which made the point that general political convergence might be achieved without formal mutual involvement between EU and WEU: van Eekelen, *Debating European Security*, 67–8.

union. The first opportunity to do this in the field of foreign affairs was the informal meeting of Foreign Ministers held at Asolo, in the hills above Venice, on 6–7 October 1990. The beginnings of consensus emerged on giving a right of initiative to the Commission. On decision making, the larger Member States stressed the importance of reserving at least the most important decisions to the European Council acting unanimously; there was an opening for majority decisions on day-to-day management issues. Italy's idea of incorporating the WEU into the EC was received frostily. Instead, more flexible ways of practical co-operation were canvassed.[58]

The Asolo meeting is remembered for having produced the eponymous 'Asolo list'. On the Delorian hypothesis, supported by Dumas and Genscher, that the core of a common foreign policy could be based on 'common values and interests', the Ministers tried their hand at drafting a list of areas in which such values and interests were deemed to apply. The result was banal, and hardly constituted a reliable pointer to effective action. As has been seen, the Commission in its October Opinion advised against attempting a catalogue of vital interests. Nevertheless, the Member States regularly reverted to the question throughout the IGC and subsequently.

These discussions led the way to a special meeting of the European Council in Rome on 27–8 October, which, with regard to foreign-policy making, made two important advances on the previous position. The European Council 'recorded consensus on the objective of a common foreign and security policy to strengthen the identity of the Community and the coherence of its action on the international scene'—the Dublin meeting of the European Council had not gone so far—and 'noted that there was a consensus to go beyond the present limits in regard to security'. On both these points, the United Kingdom delegation preferred 'not to pre-empt the debate in the Intergovernmental Conference'.[59] This was, as it turned out, the last opportunity the British Prime Minister had to bring her special view of the Community's future to bear, since she left office a few days later. The supporters of integration thus lost an effective ally, since opposition by Mrs Thatcher was a strong incentive to her colleagues to take the contrary view.[60]

The sum of all these discussions was resumed in the report of 16 November 1990 prepared for the European Council by the Italian Pres-

[58] '*EUROPE*', 8–9 Oct. 1990, 3-3bis.
[59] *Bull. EC*, Oct. 1990, 1.4; Thatcher, *The Downing Street Years*, 764–7.
[60] Cloos *et al.*, *Le Traité de Maastricht*, 63.

idency.[61] The Presidency accepted the difficulties of the Asolo exercise by admitting that 'an *a priori* definition of a list of sectors or areas considered to be of common interest would . . . raise difficulties of interpretation. Accordingly, the Community's priorities in foreign policy . . . should be determined and carried out by institutional procedures through a pragmatic evaluation (European Council and General Affairs Council)'. The report did, however, venture to set out a list of objectives based on the work at Asolo: 'consolidation of democracy, the peaceful settlement of disputes, arms reductions, the solution of crises which threaten international stability, monetary stability or economic growth, the expansion of international trade, the development of the least-favoured countries, the effectiveness of the action of international organizations, and in particular of the United Nations and the CSCE, on the basis of common positions.'

While development policy was to be consistent with the general objectives of foreign policy, it was to be the subject of a separate Treaty chapter. 'Similar consistency should be achieved with the Community's foreign policy in the economic sphere.'

The question of security was dealt with more cautiously, given the doubts expressed by Member States. The incorporation in the Treaty of a defence guarantee, together with the inclusion in security policy of arms control, disarmament, and confidence-building measures, of participation in UN actions, and of co-operation and export controls, were mentioned as possible ways of giving effect to the European Council's commitment to 'go beyond the present limits', without being clear recommendations for action. Similarly, the increasing responsibility of the union for security affairs could be achieved through gradual co-ordination between the EC and the WEU, leading to a merger in the long term, possibly on the expiry of the Brussels Treaty in 1998.

On decision making, the Presidency proposed introducing a single Council, harmonizing the preparation of the Council's work, and giving the Commission a non-exclusive right of initiative. The EPC Secretariat would be incorporated into the Council Secretariat. As to procedures, 'the present rule of consensus for decisions regarding the priorities and the basic lines of the common foreign and security policy, in particular those laid down by the European Council', should be maintained. There should, however, be a possibility of introducing the rule of qualified majority voting for decisions involving the practical application of lines of policy decided by consensus.

[61] Corbett, *The Treaty of Maastricht*, 191–3.

A week before the second meeting of the European Council in Rome on 14–15 December 1990, Kohl and Mitterrand once again circulated a letter setting out their views on the scope of the IGC on political union. The initiative seems to have come from the German side.[62] In general, emphasis was placed on the role of the European Council, which was to decide 'the essential guidelines in the main fields of action of the Union, in particular in the area of common foreign and security policy'.[63] On the CFSP itself,

its vocation would . . . be to encompass all areas. Its objective would be to present the essential interests and common values of the Union and its Member States, to strengthen their security, to promote cooperation with the other States and to contribute to peace and development in the world.

We suggest that the European Council should define the priority area of common action: for example relations with the USSR and the countries from Central and Eastern Europe, the implementation of the conclusions of the summit of the 34[64] and the follow-up of the CSCE process, the disarmament negotiations, relations with Mediterranean coastal countries . . . Foreign policy will thus be able to move towards a true common foreign policy . . .

. . . Political Union should include a true common security policy which would in turn lead to a common defence . . . We propose that the Conference should review how the WEU and Political Union might establish a clear organic relationship and how, therefore, the WEU, with increased operational capacities, might in time become part of Political Union and elaborate, on the latter's behalf, a common security policy.

The links between the WEU and the Community Member States which are not members of this organization could be gradually strengthened. Cooperation between the WEU and the European States belonging to the Atlantic Alliance but [not] to the EEC would also be enhanced.

The decisions of the intergovernmental conference should respect the commitments made to the allies of the Atlantic Alliance, as well as the specificity of the defence policy of each Member State.

We are convinced that the Atlantic Alliance as a whole will be strengthened by the increased role and responsibility of the Europeans and by the establishment within NATO of a European pillar.

Decision-making structures should notably rest on the fact that the General Affairs Council debates Community aspects and implements the common defence and security policy defined by the European Council.

[62] Attali, *Verbatim III*, 651.

[63] Laursen and Vanhoonacker (eds.), *The Intergovernmental Conference on Political Union*, 313–14; Gerbet, de la Serre, and Nafilyan, *L'Union politique de l'Europe*, 307–8; van Eekelen, *Debating European Security*, 69–70.

[64] The CSCE Summit which had taken place in Paris on 19 Nov. 1990.

The decisions would in principle be adopted unanimously, with the understanding that abstaining should not hinder the adoption of decisions. The treaty will provide for the possibility of adopting certain decision[s] at a majority as soon as the new treaty enters into force or within a period of time to be specified. More particularly, when the European Council would have to define the principles and orientations of the common foreign and security policy, or when the Council would have to adopt concrete measures required by a given specific situation, it might be decided that the implementing arrangements for these measures may be adopted through majority decisions.

The second Kohl–Mitterrand letter was a disappointment, and did not provide an adequate stimulus to take the discussion on CFSP further. Drawing for substance on the Italian Presidency's report, it took a middle-of-the-road line inconsistent with the ambitious tone of their first letter the previous April. It resembled closely the final outcome of the IGC—not because the Franco-German line determined that outcome, but because it was modelled on what was already emerging as the median position.[65] The drafting of the letter strongly suggests a compromise between the two parties, with the French securing language on the European Council and the Germans on NATO. There was a dearth of innovative thinking on what concrete reforms might be envisaged for EPC, possibly because none of the drafters had practical experience of that process. The end result was that still no one knew, beyond the *bien-pensant* verbiage, what the common foreign and security policy was for.

The first Dublin European Council had endorsed the Franco-German initiative on political union, without committing itself to a common foreign and security policy as such. The first Rome European Council had agreed on the objective of a CFSP, and on the need to go beyond existing practice on security questions. The second Rome European Council gave remarkably precise guidance on both these issues to the Intergovernmental Conference, which held its first session immediately after the closure of the European Council on 15 December 1990. The European Council

welcomes the broad agreement on basic principles concerning the vocation of the Union to deal with aspects of foreign and security policy, in accordance with a sustained evolutive process and in a unitary manner, on the basis of general objectives laid down in the Treaty.

The common foreign and security policy should aim at maintaining peace and international stability, developing friendly relations with all countries, promoting

---

[65] For a table comparing several of the positions mentioned in this section, see Remacle, *Les Négociations sur la politique étrangère*, 8–9.

democracy, the rule of law and respect for human rights, and encouraging the economic development of all nations, and should also bear in mind the special relations of individual Member States.

To this end, the Conference will in particular address the Union's objectives, the scope of its policies and the means of fostering and ensuring their effective implementation within an institutional framework.

Such an institutional framework would be based on the following elements:

(i)   one decision-making centre, namely the Council;

(ii) harmonization and, where appropriate, unification of the preparatory work; a unified Secretariat;

(iii) a reinforced role for the Commission, through a non-exclusive right of initiative;

(iv) adequate procedures for consulting and informing the European Parliament;

(v)   detailed procedures ensuring that the Union can speak effectively with one voice on the international stage, in particular in international organizations and *vis-à-vis* third countries.

The following elements should be considered as a basis for the decision-making process:

(i)   the rule of consensus in defining general guidelines; in this context, non-participation or abstention in the voting as a means of not preventing unanimity;

(ii) the possibility of recourse to qualified-majority voting for the implementation of agreed policies.

As regards common security, the gradual extension of the Union's role in this area should be considered, in particular with reference, initially, to issues debated in international organizations: arms control, disarmament and related issues; CSCE matters; certain questions debated in the United Nations, including peace-keeping operations; economic and technical co-operation in the armaments field; co-ordination of armaments export policy; and non-proliferation.

Furthermore, the European Council emphasizes that, with a view to the future, the prospect of a role for the Union in defence matters should be considered, without prejudice to Member States' existing obligations in this area, bearing in mind the importance of maintaining and strengthening the ties within the Atlantic alliance and without prejudice to the traditional positions of other Member States. The idea of a commitment by Member States to provide mutual assistance, as well as proposals put forward by some Member States on the future of Western European Union, should also be addressed.[66]

The European Council's directives to the IGC contained everything that was agreed a year later as the second pillar of the Maastricht Treaty. Indeed,

[66]   *Bull. EC,* Dec. 1990, 1.6.

in some respects it went further than the Treaty. For example, the 'elements for consideration' with regard to the decision-making procedure were framed with greater clarity than the Treaty itself, and the tone of the section on security policy was more positive. To all intents and purposes, the decisions about the CFSP had been taken by the time of the second Rome European Council. The long and difficult discussions which ensued in the course of the following year are attributable on the one hand to the Gulf War, which as it unfolded caused many Member States to think hard about hitherto unquestioned tenets of their defence policy, and on the other to the resurgence of the old ideological battle between intergovernmentalists and integrationists, which was to lead to the pillar system. These debates had remarkably little effect on the final form and content of the Treaty, but took up a good deal of political time and attention.

It is sometimes suggested that the IGC on political union was at a disadvantage compared with that on EMU because it had a scant year for its discussions with little in the way of serious preparatory work, while the latter had the comprehensive work of the Delors Committee to build on.[67] Although true, this should not be taken to imply that the job would have been better done if more time had been available. That would only have been the case had rigorous analysis of the situation and the demands it placed on the Community brought about a shared perception of the requirements.[68] Failing that, the Belgian approach of incremental reform based on the experience of dealing with Central and Eastern Europe would have been the better way. But that way was barred by the success of the Kohl–Mitterrand initiative for a political union treaty, launched for essentially domestic reasons. Had that initiative been followed up, as regards the CFSP, by a cogent demonstration of an external rationale, a more productive process might have been possible. This did not happen. As a result, Member States determined their approach to the conference negotiations, in the all-important preparatory phase under the Italian Presidency, by their own needs and foibles rather than by reference to a good defined in common. The chances of success were further diminished by the decision to entrust the negotiations to the personal representatives of Foreign Ministers, for the most part the Permanent Representatives, and certainly not the Political Directors[69]—a prudent choice when it came to keeping a firm hand on the internal constitutional development of the Community,

---

[67] See for example de Schoutheete, 'The Creation of the CFSP', 61.
[68] Mazzucelli, *France and Germany at Maastricht*, 98.
[69] Cloos *et al.*, *Le Traité de Maastricht*, 73.

but less fortunate for the task of discovering innovative techniques of European foreign-policy making.

The Gulf War

Saddam Hussein's invasion of Kuwait on 2 August 1990 was not supposed to happen. The end of the Cold War had given rise to the hope that war itself might now be a thing of the past. The Iraqi President's action not only shattered that illusion, it was a return, not to the conditions of the Cold War (a stronger and more self-confident Soviet Union might well have nipped Saddam's dangerous adventure in the bud), but to an even earlier age, which saw nothing wrong in the acquisition of territory and resources by force.

The Gulf conflict had a significant effect on the shape of the European Community's common foreign and security policy, with whose gestation it coincided. Within the IGC on political union, it gave the CFSP more importance than it might otherwise have had; it obliged the Member States to confront seriously their global responsibilities in the post-Cold War world; it concentrated the debate on the security and defence aspects of the CFSP; and it ensured that, once again, the relationship with the United States was at the heart of the argument about the nature of European foreign policy.

EPC reacted to the crisis with the polished professionalism which had been perfected over the years. Within the limits of the system, the EC Member States made an admirable display of cohesion and unity of purpose. The imposition of economic sanctions and the provision of assistance to the front-line states, in spite of some technical problems, for the most part worked well. Even the WEU naval co-ordination in the Gulf, although it fell short of joint operations, was more than satisfactory. It was only after several months that the crisis began to test the limits of EPC. The affair of the hostages, and then the succession of initiatives to resolve the crisis by diplomatic means, demonstrated that when domestic pressures became too strong they invariably prevailed over the cohesion demanded by EPC. Finally, Operation Desert Storm showed that when hostilities break out, EPC has to close for the duration. The initiative to provide safe havens for the Kurds of Northern Iraq was an attempt by the Community to reclaim a role in the aftermath of the war.

Literally within hours of the invasion of Kuwait, EPC issued a statement condemning it and calling for an immediate withdrawal of Iraqi forces from Kuwait territory. This was followed up by a special meeting of the Political Committee in Rome on Saturday 4 August, which took the decision to impose economic sanctions. A statement was issued announcing an embargo on oil imports from Iraq and Kuwait; appropriate measures aimed at freezing Iraqi assets in the territory of Member States; an embargo on sales of arms and other military equipment to Iraq; the suspension of any co-operation in the military sphere with Iraq; the suspension of technical and scientific co-operation with Iraq; and the suspension of the application to Iraq of the System of Generalized Preferences.[70]

These decisions were to be executed immediately. Already by Monday 6 August, the Commission had made a series of proposals for Council Regulations for those matters which fell indubitably within EC competence. These were superseded, however, by new proposals to align the Community's action on Resolution 661 of the Security Council, adopted the same day, which made the imposition of sanctions obligatory on all states. The Commission sent consolidated and revised proposals to the Council on 7 and 8 August. They were adopted on 8 August.[71]

The decision to wait for the Security Council Resolution before promulgating the Community acts was not just in order to ensure complete conformity with the United Nations' requirements. There was some nervousness about exposure to demands for compensation from commercial quarters, against which the Security Council Resolution gave some protection; furthermore, at least one Member State required a guarantee that the embargo would apply to all countries equally.[72] The form of the Community acts was well established by precedent: sanctions against the Soviet Union, Argentina, and especially South Africa. The national delegations in the Council, however, took care to emphasize the primacy of EPC in the decision-making process. The Commission had included a reference to a 'declaration of the Community and its Member States condemning the invasion of Kuwait by Iraq' as a basis for the measures; the Council added a phrase stating explicitly that this declaration was 'adopted on 4 August 1990 in the framework of political co-operation'. The Council also added specific justification for having recourse to Article 113 of the EC Treaty as a sovereign decision of EPC, contrary to the view traditionally held by the

---

[70] *Bull. EC,* July–Aug. 1990, 1.5.9, 1.5.11.

[71] Council Regulation (EEC) no. 2340/90 and ECSC Decision 90/414/ECSC: OJ L 213 of 9 Aug. 1990; *Bull. EC,* July–Aug. 1990, 1.4.20–22.

[72] Attali, *Verbatim III,* 549. Germany's sanctions were taken in implementation of the UN embargo, according to Genscher, *Erinnerungen,* 919.

Commission:[73] 'Whereas the Community and its Member States have agreed to have recourse to a Community instrument in order to ensure uniform implementation, throughout the Community, of the measures concerning trade with Iraq and Kuwait decided on by the United Nations Security Council'. There was to be further disagreement about the legal base of sanctions when later in the year it was decided to extend them explicitly to services. The Commission proposed the maintenance of Article 113, the Council proposed recourse to Article 235 (action to attain one of the objectives of the Community when the Treaty has not provided the necessary powers). The European Parliament on this occasion came down on the side of the Council, for the purely political reason that Article 235 provided for the obligatory consultation of Parliament, while Article 113 did not.[74]

The imposition of sanctions (through a legal act of the Community) was a traditional weapon at the disposal of EPC in the face of international crisis. The other classic response was to reach for the chequebook. The immediate need was to help cope with the refugees. From 11 August the Iraqi government allowed nationals from Arab and Third World countries to leave, and a stream of impoverished expatriates began to flow out of Iraq and Kuwait, mostly to Jordan and Egypt but also to Turkey. Some returned to their homes in these countries, but many used them as staging-posts to their final destinations. Jordan in particular was faced with horrific problems of managing the transit. On 23 August, King Hussein said that 185,000 refugees had arrived in Jordan and only 67,000 had been moved on. By the middle of September the estimates of those stranded in Jordan varied from 70,000 to 105,000.[75]

Almost immediately the Commission began to grant emergency aid. Following the Commission's decision of 21 August and the conclusions reached by the Community Foreign Ministers at their meeting the same day, 1 million ECU was made available under Article 950 of the Community budget. The aid was to be implemented by the Commission's usual partners (NGOs, Red Cross/Red Crescent, UN) or the Jordanian and Egyptian governments.[76] This was followed up by further grants. By mid-November, when the situation was stabilizing, the Community and the

---

[73] The Commission acknowledged the right of EPC to decide the principle of sanctions, but not to choose the legal form they should take if the matter fell within EC competence: Nuttall, 'The Commission: The Struggle For Legitimacy', 138–9. The issue was settled in Art. 228a of the Maastricht Treaty.

[74] Nuttall, *European Political Co-operation*, 265.

[75] Freedman and Karsh, *The Gulf Conflict*, 132–4.

[76] Commission Press Release IP(90)710 of 22 Aug. 1990; *Bull. EC*, July–Aug. 1990, 1.4.67.

Member States together had provided 98 million ECU, of which 58.5 million ECU had come from the EC budget. This was some 30 per cent of the international effort, the second in size after Saudi Arabia, and greater than all the other industrialized countries and NGOs combined.[77]

Even more serious than the plight of the refugees was the parlous economic situation of the front-line states. The temporary rise in the price of oil and the imposition of sanctions had an effect on the economies of both the industrialized and developing worlds. Particularly hard hit were Iraq's immediate neighbours, who also lost the income remitted by their workers in Kuwait and Iraq as well as income from tourism. Jordan's losses for the current year were estimated at 1 billion ECU, and Egypt's at 2 billion ECU. Turkey estimated its potential loss, which included loss of revenues from the pipeline, at $4.5 billion over a longer period. The European Community had been directly approached for aid by these and other countries, and was disposed to respond favourably to at least the three most seriously affected, the more so since short-term economic assistance was clearly within the EC's capabilities. However, the Community could not carry all these losses alone, and envisaged taking part in an international effort. The United States was particularly anxious that the financial burden should be widely distributed.[78] Indeed, a Financial Co-ordination Group was subsequently set up at American initiative, involving the OECD states, including the EC, and the larger Gulf states, which by the beginning of November had agreed on an aid package of $13 billion, most of which was to go to Turkey, Egypt, and Jordan.[79]

A decision in principle to grant aid was taken at a special meeting of Foreign Ministers in the EPC framework at Rome on 7 September 1990. The discussion took place on the basis of 'working hypotheses' presented by the Commission, which had assembled the necessary economic data and advanced suggestions as to how the Community's aid might be structured. The Commission was, however, cautious about seeming to present a formal proposal, since it feared being accused of overstepping the mark in a case in which the borders between EPC and EC were particularly fuzzy. In particular the choice of beneficiaries, in which the Ministers followed the Commission, was as much political as economic (Turkey's insistence on being rewarded for its accession to the Western camp, Jordan's support of Iraq). It will be recalled that the notion of a non-exclusive right

[77] Commission Press Release IP(90)924 of 15 Nov. 1990.
[78] *Deutsche Einheit*, no. 423, 1542–3.
[79] Freedman and Karsh, *The Gulf Conflict*, 186–7; *EUROPE*, 5320 (3/4 Sept. 1990), 5–6; 5321 (5 Sept. 1990), 5–6; 5322 (6 Sept. 1990), 5–6.

of initiative for the Commission in common foreign policy questions was circulating about this time in discussions preparatory to the convening of the IGC.[80]

To take a decision in principle was one thing; to implement it proved to be another. It had been expected that the first operational decisions on aid would be taken at the next meeting of the General Affairs Council, scheduled for 17 September. The Commission proposed a total contribution of 1.5 billion ECU, shared equally between the Community (the contribution to be financed as far as possible by savings on existing budget lines) and the Member States. In the event, the decision was put off. Although many Member States could accept the Commission's proposals as they stood, others wished first to get a better idea of what other contributions would be forthcoming internationally, and the United Kingdom insisted on allowances being made for those Member States who were individually committed to military expenditure in the region.[81] It was not until 1 October that the Foreign Ministers, who happened to be in New York for a CSCE meeting, decided on how the aid of 1.5 billion ECU should be split up—not half and half, as the Commission had proposed, but 500 million ECU (grants and loans) from the EC budget, and the remaining 1 billion ECU from the Member States.[82] This reflected concerns about the strains a greater contribution would place on the EC budget (a revision of the financial perspectives would be required), but also gave satisfaction to the United Kingdom's desire to pay a smaller contribution in view of its military commitments. Arguments continued about how the national contributions should be shared out, and the formal decision on the Community contribution was not taken until December, given the need for concertation with the European Parliament. The disbursement of the Community aid gave rise to further delays as Member States argued about apportionment. In the end the decision was left to the Commission, which allotted 175 million ECU to Egypt in grant aid, 150 million ECU to Jordan in grant aid, and 175 million ECU to Turkey in interest-free loans. The bulk of Community aid was paid by February 1991; by the end of January, only one-third of the 1 billion ECU from the Member States had been disbursed.[83]

The positive diplomatic effect of the Community's initial decision to

---

[80] *Bull. EC*, Sept. 1990, 1.4.4; *EUROPE*, 5322 (6 Sept. 1990), 5.

[81] *Bull. EC*, Sept. 1990, 1.3.20 and 1.4.9; *EUROPE*, 5330 (17/18 Sept. 1990), 7–8.

[82] *EUROPE*, 5341 (3 Oct. 1990), 7.

[83] Freedman and Karsh, *The Gulf Conflict*, 187–8; Commission Press Release IP(91)76 of 30 Jan. 1991.

provide significant economic assistance to those countries suffering most directly from the Iraqi invasion of Kuwait—all of which were, in their different ways, to play significant parts in the development of the crisis— was thus dissipated by internal wrangling and delays. The absence of EC budget provision for crises of this sort, and the reluctance of Member States, for reasons of their own, to make use of what did exist, were to be a recurrent theme in the evolution of European common foreign-policy making, and the question was not adequately addressed until the Amsterdam Treaty.

An interesting tailpiece to the saga of the Community's aid to the front-line states is the decision in February 1991 to grant financial aid to Israel and the Occupied Territories. Following guidelines adopted by the Foreign Ministers on 4 February, the Commission forwarded to the Council proposals for a total of 250 million ECU in loans and grants from the EC budget to Israel and the Palestinian population in the Occupied Territories. This came about entirely as the result of a heavy intervention from Hans-Dietrich Genscher, the German Foreign Minister, who wanted significant compensation for Israel. Germany was guiltily aware that German companies had been involved in Iraq's chemical weapons programme and in the extension of the Scud missile's range, and had offered Israel substantial sums in aid. Securing an additional contribution from the Community was a way of increasing this assistance at less cost to the federal budget. The move was contested by Douglas Hurd and Delors on budgetary grounds, but accepted by the other Ministers on condition, as proposed by France, that the Palestinians should get an equal amount. The significance of the incident lies in its demonstration of the primacy of political reality over institutional propriety. The Commission could have refused to make the necessary proposals for the aid, and perhaps, since it knew the funds were not available, should have done so, but was no more able than the other Ministers to withstand the demands of a determined representative of a great power.[84]

The Community was quick off the mark in imposing sanctions, but had no powers to enforce them. The question of enforcement rapidly became the centre of diplomatic debate, and it was one in which the Community had no standing to intervene. To be effective, the embargo had to be turned in effect into a blockade, although the term was avoided, and this meant essentially the operational deployment of naval forces in the Red Sea and

[84] *Bull. EC*, Jan.–Feb. 1991, 1.3.23; Commission Information Memo P-13 of 1 Mar. 1991; David Usborne, 'Palestinians and Israel To Get Equal Aid', *Independent*, 6 Feb. 1991; Freedman and Karsh, *The Gulf Conflict*, 339.

the Persian Gulf. Individual Member States (Belgium, France, Italy, the Netherlands, Spain, and the United Kingdom) were prepared to take part in these operations, but could not, according to the rules, discuss their intentions in EPC. Nor could they tackle with the requisite authority the question of whether authority over and above what had already been given by the Security Council was required for enforcement operations, an issue over which the members of the Council were divided.[85] The fact that the WEU provided a forum for the co-ordination, however limited, of the Member States' naval efforts in the region heightened the interest of that organization as a potential component of the Union's potential security and defence identity.

As early as 7 August, the United States, recalling the successful work done by the WEU in the Gulf during the Iran–Iraq war, had signalled to the WEU Secretariat its interest in co-ordinating US naval deployments in the area.[86] The French Presidency of WEU[87] decided to convene a meeting of WEU Foreign and Defence Ministers in Paris on 21 August. In addition to the WEU members, invitations to attend as observers were issued to the three non-WEU EC Member States—Denmark, Greece, and Ireland—and, because of the special circumstances, to Turkey. Only Ireland declined. At this meeting, held back-to-back with an EPC Ministerial Meeting in Paris to discuss the question of hostages, it was decided to set up an *ad hoc* group of representatives of Foreign and Defence Ministries, drawing on the experience gained during the Iran–Iraq war, and to designate points of contact in Defence Ministries to facilitate technical aspects of this co-operation. The French Presidency was prepared to envisage rotating tactical control of all WEU ships, but this was opposed by the United Kingdom.[88] Instructions were given that 'co-ordination within WEU should also facilitate co-operation with other countries deploying forces in the region, including those of the United States'. The WEU Council meeting was followed up on 27 August by a meeting of Chiefs of Defence Staff, a first for the WEU, at which the principles of a joint specific guideline on the enforcement of the embargo were drawn up, and adopted by the end of the month. The guideline laid down harmonized procedures for the conduct of checks on vessels in the Gulf. On 4 and 10

---

[85] Freedman and Karsh, *The Gulf Conflict*, 143–53.

[86] Jacomet, 'The Role of WEU in the Gulf Crisis', 162. The chapter by Jacomet gives a full account of WEU's activities during the Gulf crisis, on which these paragraphs largely draw.

[87] France chaired the WEU for the 12 months beginning 1 July 1990, i.e. throughout the Gulf crisis.   [88] van Eekelen, *Debating European Security*, 52–3.

September representatives of the naval forces present in the Gulf met in Bahrein, at the suggestion of the Americans, and under joint American, Arab, and European (WEU) chairmanship to settle questions of operational co-ordination. The meeting was preceded by a co-ordination meeting of WEU participants at the French Embassy in Bahrein.[89]

What was not done, however, was to go a step further and agree on a joint operation involving specific command and control procedures. This would not have been acceptable to France. President Mitterrand made it clear that co-ordination of national activities was desirable, but to do more was out of the question. It was bad enough that the Americans were clearly in the lead; the ideal would have been a UN-controlled operation, but better that France shared the chairmanship with the Americans than that the latter should preside alone. It was a fortunate coincidence that it was France's turn to take the Presidency of the WEU, which may explain the unusual French enthusiasm for that organization.[90]

The relative efficiency with which WEU was able to organize the co-ordination of naval and air surveillance in the Red Sea and the Gulf made an impression on EC Member States preparing to negotiate in the IGC. It led Italy to propose in its initiative of 18 September 1990 the transfer of WEU's responsibilities to the EU. Yet in a way the horse had already bolted. WEU in principle acknowledged the primacy of EPC in deciding on policy.[91] But now activity on the ground was generating a need for spontaneous policy-making. Furthermore, the close association with the Americans, and the consequent tendency to have recourse to NATO-type procedures, were establishing habits of independence which in the period after Maastricht were to make their mark on the security debate.

If co-ordination of enforcement measures was beyond the powers of the Community, at least it could be done by the WEU, all of whose members were members of the EC. The WEU action could therefore be cited as an example of 'flexibility'—the procedure whereby some but not all EC members engage in joint action—before the term had come into general use. It was, however, well within the powers of the Community—it was indeed a typical activity for EPC—to establish a common line for all Member States on the attitude to be taken with regard to the European hostages which Saddam Hussein had taken in Iraq and Kuwait. But it was

[89] Jacomet, 'The Role of WEU in the Gulf Crisis', 164–5; Attali, *Verbatim III*, 570.

[90] Attali, *Verbatim III*, 569, 570; Jacomet, 'The Role of WEU in the Gulf Crisis', 164; Heisbourg, 'France and the Gulf Crisis', 35 n. 39.

[91] Jacomet, 'The Role of WEU in the Gulf Crisis', 162, 167.

on this issue that the foreign policy of the Twelve in the Gulf crisis began to fall apart.

There were nearly 8,000 EC nationals in Kuwait and Iraq at the beginning of August, over half of them from the United Kingdom.[92] At first it was not clear whether they, and other Western nationals, were to be prevented from leaving. An interview the Troika had with the Iraqi Vice-Minister for Foreign Affairs was not promising.[93] Hardline pronouncements by the Iraqi régime soon left no room for doubt, and at the initiative of the Italian Presidency, acting on behalf of the Community, the Security Council adopted on 18 August 1990 Resolution 664 calling for the immediate departure of third-state nationals.[94] Already in their statement of 10 August the Twelve had expressed their concern for the situation of foreigners, held the Iraqi authorities accountable for the safety of EC citizens, and entrusted the Presidency with the appropriate coordination. Now they held a special EPC Ministerial Meeting in Paris on 21 August,[95] which was devoted in particular to the situation of foreign nationals. In the statement issued after the meeting, the Community and its Member States, after renewing their condemnation in strong terms, 'warn[ed] the Iraqi Government that any attempt to harm or jeopardize the safety of any EC citizen will be considered as a most grave offence directed against the Community and all its Member States and will provoke a united response from the entire Community'. They also 'warn[ed] Iraqi citizens that they will be held personally responsible in accordance with international law for their involvement in illegal actions concerning the security and life of foreign citizens.'[96]

Among Saddam Hussein's various motives for retaining the hostages was a desire to split the alliance which had formed against him. By releasing them in dribs and drabs, in response to pleas accompanied preferably by a recognition of the merits of Iraq's case but certainly by a boost to Saddam's international prestige through high-profile visits to Baghdad, Saddam hoped to explore cracks in the unity which had taken him and the world by surprise. Thus began the 'long procession of foreign dignitaries making a pilgrimage to Baghdad'.[97] The most high-ranking, if not the most prestigious, was President Waldheim of Austria, but he was not

---

[92] Freedman and Karsh, *The Gulf Conflict*, 140–1.
[93] Attali, *Verbatim III*, 556.   [94] Freedman and Karsh, *The Gulf Conflict*, 137.
[95] This was the meeting which immediately followed the extraordinary meeting of the WEU Council.
[96] *Bull. EC*, July–Aug. 1990, 1.5.14, 1.5.16.
[97] Freedman and Karsh, *The Gulf Conflict*, 137–9, 156.

alone. Emissaries from EC countries also took up their pilgrims' staves. Indeed, following the Community's statement of 21 August the Iraqis let it be understood that they might be ready to release the nationals of some, but not all, EC Member States. Those of countries which had taken a strong line in support of the United States, including the United Kingdom and Germany, were excluded.[98]

Technically there was nothing in the statement of 21 August to prevent Member States from undertaking or conniving at missions to secure the release of their own nationals, but such a course of action was certainly in contradiction with the message of a united Community front which the statement gave out, as well as the general obligation of Community solidarity. When the former French Foreign Minister Claude Cheysson went to Tunis to see Yasser Arafat, and did not immediately exclude the idea of a separate negotiation on the French hostages which Arafat put to him, Mitterrand reacted violently: 'Ce serait honteux, honteux de se séparer des autres!'[99] As time wore on, visitors to Baghdad from the EC countries began to accumulate. A representative of the Franco-Iraqi Friendship Group, a former member of the East German Parliament, the former Cat Stevens, and a Spanish Parliamentary delegation all returned with their modest hauls.[100] The *coup de théâtre*, however, was the release of all 327 French hostages announced by the Iraqi government on 22 October. France's partners were unable to believe that there had been no secret deal, and the resentment was intense.[101]

It so happened that the former British Prime Minister Edward Heath was in Baghdad at the time the liberation of the French hostages was announced. Compared with the French, his haul of 33 sick and elderly British citizens was meagre. The British government had not been keen on his mission, but had not told him not to go.[102] Combined with the French release, the Heath mission showed the Community that its line on hostages

---

[98] Freedman and Karsh, *The Gulf Conflict*, 139.

[99] Attali, *Verbatim III*, 569, 571, 572, 586. Freedman and Karsh, *The Gulf Conflict*, 157–8, imply a more flexible attitude on the part of French diplomacy. One can exclude neither a difference of approach between the Élysée and the Quai d'Orsay, nor more wide-ranging contacts by the French President than have been recorded.

[100] Freedman and Karsh, *The Gulf Conflict*, 251.

[101] There had certainly been continuing contacts between Arafat, accompanied on occasion by the Iraqi Foreign Minister Tariq Aziz, and first Cheysson and then Edgar Pisani, believed to be an emissary of Mitterrand. Both denied that they had held out any inducement to the Iraqis. This was at first confirmed by Baghdad, and later denied, when indeed France made no payment: Freedman and Karsh, *The Gulf Conflict*, 170–2; Attali, *Verbatim III*, 625; Favier and Martin-Roland, *La Décennie Mitterrand*, iii. 459.

[102] Freedman and Karsh, *The Gulf Conflict*, 173.

was getting out of hand. An EPC statement was accordingly issued on 28 October 1990 by the European Council meeting in Rome which in effect set out guidelines on the hostage question: 'The Member States of the European Community reaffirm their total solidarity in achieving the freedom of all foreign citizens trapped in Iraq and Kuwait and denounce the unscrupulous use which Iraq is making of them with the sole and vain purpose of trying to divide the international community . . . They affirm their determination not to send representatives of their governments in any capacity to negotiate with Iraq the release of foreign hostages and to discourage others from doing so.'[103]

The roots of this initiative lay in the declared intention of former German Chancellor Willy Brandt to follow the example of his friend Edward Heath and travel to Baghdad 'on a humanitarian and political mission'. Out of solidarity with allies, Foreign Minister Genscher had already declined, on 26 October, an Iraqi offer to come to Baghdad to collect the German hostages. Anxious to deny Brandt and his political friends in the SPD the kudos a mission to Baghdad would bring, with elections coming up in a couple of months, Chancellor Kohl pressed his fellow Heads of Government in Rome to take a stand which would in effect cut the ground from under Brandt's feet. Having achieved his aim in Rome, Kohl found himself confronted with serious domestic difficulties. Brandt told the hostages' families that the German government was preventing him from carrying out his mission. Faced with the ensuing public outcry, Kohl felt he had no choice but to back down. In order to square this about-face with the Rome guidelines, the Chancellor tried to give the mission a European gloss. Using the Christian Democrat network, he tried to persuade the former Italian Foreign Minister, Emilio Colombo, to go along, and Genscher did the same but on the Liberal network, with former Commissioner Willy De Clercq. Both declined. The Italian Presidency, approached by the Germans, explored the possibility of securing cover from the UN Secretary General, but when this failed they refused to go any further with the idea, even though there was also pressure in Italy for action to release the hostages. At this point the German government threw in the towel, gave Brandt their blessing, and hired an Airbus from Lufthansa to bring the hostages back. The other members of the Community were outraged, and a special EPC Ministerial Meeting was called in Rome to discuss the question (at the request of the Dutch Foreign Minister Hans van den Broek, whose relations with Genscher were poor).

---

[103] *Bull. EC,* Oct. 1990, 1.15.

Genscher brazened it out, on the grounds that Brandt 'did not intend to negotiate but instead express expectations'.[104]

The incident had important implications for EPC and the developing debate about a common foreign and security policy. It impaired the effectiveness of the Community's stand on the hostages, and thereby brought EPC into disrepute. But it also encouraged cynical views about the seriousness of France and Germany in promoting a CFSP. There were suspicions that French diplomacy had at the least connived at the release of French nationals, but at any rate, if that was indeed the case, the French had had the sense to cover their tracks. The Germans had shown that they had no scruples about breaking the Community line when needs must; indeed, Kohl toyed with the idea of sending his own emissary to Baghdad to match the domestic impact of the Brandt visit.[105] Perhaps the most important conclusion to be drawn from the affair, once again, is that EPC only worked so long as it remained the domain of the foreign policy élite. Once it was exposed to domestic pressure, discipline broke down.

In the early days of the invasion, as soon as it became obvious that his action did not command general support in the Arab world, Saddam launched a diplomatic initiative linking the Kuwait issue with the problem of Palestine. He suggested a comprehensive solution for 'all issues of occupation, or the issues that have been depicted as occupation in the entire region'. The issues would be dealt with serially, that of Kuwait being tackled last.[106] He could not lose. If he succeeded, he would be the Arab hero; if he failed, he would still retain control of Kuwait; in either case, he would divide his opponents.

The issue of linkage was a tricky one for the European Community. They had long taken a position on the Middle East more favourable than the Americans to the Palestinian cause, although in recent years there had not been agreement on whether the time was right to press for an international conference to look at the question. France was in favour, the United Kingdom and in particular the Netherlands were against. The question of whether to take the idea further, and run the risk in the present context of appearing to propitiate Saddam, which no one wanted, divided

---

[104] Freedman and Karsh, *The Gulf Conflict*, 172–5; Guazzone, 'Italy in the Gulf Crisis', 79; Joseph Fitchett and Barry James, 'Chagrined, Bonn Aids Brandt Trip', *International Herald Tribune*, 6 Nov. 1990; Ian Murray, 'Bonn Urges EC to Temper Anti-Iraq Line to Avert War', *The Times*, 6 Nov. 1990.
[105] Bush and Scowcroft, *A World Transformed*, 406, 408.
[106] Freedman and Karsh, *The Gulf Conflict*, 100–1.

the Twelve over the coming months and coloured the debate over whether they should attempt a diplomatic effort to avert armed conflict.

In early September 1990 the Iraqis let fall copious hints that a French initiative enabling Saddam to get off the hook might be favourably received in Baghdad. The French did not fall into this trap, but Mitterrand was nevertheless tempted to launch a diplomatic initiative of his own. He did so in his speech to the General Assembly of the United Nations on 24 September 1990. In particular he said that, if Iraq announced its intention to withdraw from Kuwait and release the hostages, 'everything becomes possible'.[107] In a second stage, Kuwaiti sovereignty (not necessarily Al-Sabah rule) would be restored, and finally 'the moment [would come] when, in place of the confrontation afflicting the Near East, there would be a dynamic of good neighbourliness in security and peace for all'.[108] This position diverged significantly from that hitherto adopted in Political Co-operation, and had not been communicated in advance to France's European partners. In that they were not discriminated against: the Quai d'Orsay was equally in the dark, the speech having been worked and reworked in the Concorde which took the President to New York. Mitterrand's objective seems on the one hand to have been to demonstrate that, although of necessity taking a forward position by sending French forces to the Gulf, he was not as a result subservient to American policy, which he thought to be drifting away from the liberation of Kuwait towards the crushing of the Iraqi régime, and on the other hand to maintain an international profile by holding on to the initiative—and in a way which would bring dividends in the Maghreb, where public opinion was strongly pro-Iraqi. He also had to guard against disaffection within his own ranks, where the Defence Minister, Jean-Pierre Chevènement, consistently adopted a softer line, and against pro-Iraqi business interests.[109] The important point for the Community was not the difference on substance, which could have been bridged easily enough in the Political Committee, but the blatant flouting of EPC discipline. It was another demonstration that EPC failed to operate outside the insider circle.

The Community was ready enough to engage in diplomacy for peace, while insisting on compliance with the Security Council Resolutions, but

[107] Freedman and Karsh, *The Gulf Conflict*, 166–7. Taken aback by the wave of criticism which followed his initiative, Mitterrand was later to qualify his position: Lacorne, 'Le Rang de la France', 342–4.

[108] Lacouture, *Mitterrand*, ii. 339–40; Favier and Martin-Roland, *La Décennie Mitterrand*, iii. 452–4.

[109] Védrine, *Les Mondes de François Mitterrand*, 534; Attali, *Verbatim III*, 598; Heisbourg, 'France and the Gulf Crisis', 19; 'Hubel, Europa, Japan und der Krieg um Kuwait', 489.

had difficulty in finding a willing interlocutor, whether the Arabs collectively or Iraq individually. Forcing the hand of their partners, the Italian Presidency in a ham-handed and ill-prepared move invited the Arab League to a Euro–Arab Dialogue meeting to be held in Venice on 7–8 October 1990. The Arab League courteously accepted the invitation in principle, but found that the date was 'not propitious'. The Arabs particularly objected to the Community's attempt to exclude Iraq from the meeting, whereas Iraq, together with Kuwait, was still taking part in meetings of the League.[110]

Nor did the Community have greater success in offering dialogue to Iraq. As the date set for resolving the issue by force grew closer, the Europeans joined the many others endeavouring to persuade the Iraqis to withdraw peacefully from Kuwait. On 5 December 1990 the Twelve invited Iraqi Foreign Minister Tariq Aziz to meet them in Rome, following his visit to Washington, which was then being discussed. Worried that Saddam would use the European invitation as a pretext for procrastination, Bush wrote to Andreotti as President of the European Council warning against any weakening of the coalition. When Saddam finally called off talks with the Americans, the Community had no choice but to cancel their own invitation. They were not prepared to engage in a dialogue without the Americans. Although the Italian Foreign Minister, De Michelis, was prepared to try, he was vehemently opposed by van den Broek (causing Mitterrand to enquire acidly how many divisions the Dutch had). In the New Year the Twelve tried again. On 4 January 1991 they once more issued an invitation to Tariq Aziz, who declined to meet the Troika, whether in Luxembourg or in Algiers, but was prepared to meet Dumas. He also accepted the American invitation while declining the European, which for the Twelve was the ultimate humiliation.[111]

Finally, on 14 January, the day before the Allies' ultimatum was due to expire, the Community threw in the towel. While faintly continuing to hold out the prospect of a Troika meeting with Tariq Aziz, the Ministers, meeting in Geneva, said: 'In the face of the continued refusal of the Iraqi authorities to implement the resolutions of the Security Council and in the absence of any signal in this sense, the European Community and its Member States regret to have to conclude that the conditions for a new European initiative do not exist as of this moment'.[112]

[110]   *EUROPE*, 5332 (20 Sept. 1990), 7, and 5335 (24/5 Sept. 1990), 6.
[111]   *Bull. EC*, Jan.–Feb. 1991, 1.4.4, 1.4.5, 1.4.8; Freedman and Karsh, *The Gulf Conflict*, 243–5; Attali, *Verbatim III*, 659, 661; Védrine, *Les mondes de François Mitterrand*, 536.
[112]   *Bull. EC*, Jan.–Feb. 1991, 1.4.11.

Dumas arrived late at this meeting—he had waited to hear the results of the UN Secretary General's mission to Baghdad, and to accompany Mr Perez de Cuellar from Paris to Geneva—but by all the rules of EPC France was bound by the decision taken by the Twelve. France now, however, launched a new initiative in the form of a draft Security Council Resolution. This consisted of a renewed appeal for withdrawal in return for a guarantee of non-aggression, to be followed by efforts to resolve 'other regional problems', by convening an international conference. The initiative had been under preparation for some days, and Mitterrand had wanted to launch it earlier, but had not found the right opportunity.[113] It was unfortunate that the eventual timing, coming as it did immediately after the 'Community and its Member States' had renounced any further initiative, gave the appearance of being in flagrant contradiction with France's obligations to its European partners.[114] It was even more unfortunate that, as ill luck would have it, the draft was finally circulated as the British Prime Minister, John Major, was leaving the Élysée after lunch with Mitterrand during which not a word had been breathed about French intentions.[115] The incident confirmed the suspicions of the partners, observing the flow of semi-, demi-, and quasi-official French emissaries to Baghdad, that French diplomacy had for some time being ploughing a lone furrow.[116] The Netherlands in particular took a jaundiced view of these efforts,[117] but the inconsistency between Mitterrand's call for a common foreign and security policy and French diplomatic practice was clear to all.

When Operation Desert Storm began, the French forces, by dint of flair and improvisation, gave a good account of themselves, thus securing the position of France as a country that mattered. This had been the prime

---

[113] Mitterrand was influenced, among other considerations, by the fact that, according to the most recent polls, 57% opposed French military involvement: La Balme, 'L'Influence de l'opinion publique daus la gestion des crises', 415. See also Favier and Martin-Roland, *La Décennie Mitterrand*, iii. 488 n. 1. According to one account, the inspiration for the last-ditch initiative came from Dumas: Lacouture, *Mitterrand*, ii. 350–1.

[114] The French could have justified their action by referring to their obligations as a permanent member of the Security Council. But it is doubtful whether they would have bothered. The option of a renewed Community *démarche* had indeed been considered in Paris, but rejected on the grounds that the Twelve had so far been 'absent' from the conflict: Favier and Martin-Roland, *La Décennie Mitterrand*, iii. 485. The argument did not lack force for being circular.

[115] Attali claims that Hurd (and Genscher) had been informed, but the ordering of his account of events is ambiguous: Attali, *Verbatim III*, 690.

[116] Freedman and Karsh, *The Gulf Conflict*, 270–4; Attali, *Verbatim III*, 660–3, 676–8, 681, 683, 687–95; Védrine, *Les Mondes de François Mitterrand*, 534–7; Favier and Martin-Roland, *La Décennie Mitterrand*, iii. 479–81, 483–7.

[117] Neuman, 'The Gulf War', 105.

motivation for Mitterrand's early military commitment.[118] After the dis-appointments of German unification, the United Kingdom was only too happy, through a substantial military effort, to resume its position as America's best friend in Europe, while Germany, still wrestling with the problems of bringing the country together again, and anxious not to go against the Soviet Union until the last legal knot in unification had been tied,[119] was not yet prepared to seek the constitutional reinterpretation which would allow it to take part in military operations outside NATO, and had to salvage its honour by financial contributions. Italy was the only other European country engaged in combat in the Gulf.

The 'Big Four' were therefore, in their individual ways, involved in the affair in a way which cast the rest of the Community into the shade, in spite of the latter's undeniable contribution. It was they alone who were informed of a later Soviet initiative to avert the land war, with strict injunctions to maintain confidentiality, which proved embarrassing in the subsequent EPC meeting.[120] It was this separation of those Member States which still had the means for a credible national foreign policy from those which did not, as well as the unavailability of military force, which cast doubt on the Community's ability to conduct a foreign policy, and led Delors to say to the European Parliament on 21 January 1991 that 'To be brutally frank, public opinion sensed that Europe was rather ineffectual'. He followed this up in his Alastair Buchan Lecture at the International Institute for Strategic Studies on 7 March 1991 by saying that 'The Gulf War has shown beyond doubt the limits to the influence and action of the European Community . . . This is one more reason for moving towards a form of political union with a common policy for external relations and security'.[121]

Although the Community had no role to play in the aerial bombardment and the land war, it did in fact continue to work in a useful if not headline-catching way. As early as 17 January 1991, the day after the aerial attacks began, a special EPC Ministerial Meeting was held in Paris following a WEU Ministerial Meeting. The Ministers were already bending their mind to what the Community's policy might be after the crisis was over.

[118] Heisbourg, 'France and the Gulf Crisis', 18–19; Védrine, *Les Mondes de François Mitterrand*, 523; Favier and Martin-Roland, *La Décennie Mitterrand*, iii. 479, 502–3.
[119] The Soviet Parliament did not ratify the treaties, on which the withdrawal of Soviet troops from the former GDR depended, until 4 Mar. 1991: 'Hubel, Europa, Japan und der Kreig um Kuwait', 490; Genscher, *Erinnerungen*, 907.
[120] Freedman and Karsh, *The Gulf Conflict*, 381 and 481 n. 31.
[121] Freedman and Karsh, *The Gulf Conflict*, 358; speech by Jacques Delors to the International Institute for Strategic Studies, 7 Mar. 1991 (translation mine).

This was not just forward planning; the Ministers were anxious to display a positive attitude towards the Arab world even while the fighting was still going on. The Community and its Member States 'will develop a global approach towards the region through a renewed Mediterranean policy, a relaunched Euro-Arab dialogue and a reinforced cooperation with the Gulf Co-operation Council and the Arab Maghreb Union and all countries concerned in the region . . . [They] renew their full commitment for the convening of an international peace conference on the Middle East, at the appropriate moment'.[122]

Following this up, the Luxembourg Presidency circulated on 19 February 1991 a note on an overall approach for a post-crisis scenario, the economic section of which had been contributed by the Commission. The main lines were adopted by the Ministers on 4 March 1991, and confirmed at the special meeting of the European Council on 8 April 1991.[123] As a result, missions were dispatched throughout the Middle East—the Troika had talks at Damascus on 6 March with Syria, Egypt, and the Gulf countries, and at Tripoli the next day with the Arab Maghreb Union, while Foreign Minister Poos and Commissioner Matutes went to Amman and Jerusalem.[124] The Community was returning to what it could do well— long-term diplomacy, mainly economic.

The special meeting of the European Council had been called for by France while the fighting was still going on. Now that it had stopped, there was some uncertainty about what it might be expected to achieve. The day was saved by an eye-catching initiative of John Major, to set up safe havens for Kurds in the northern part of Iraq. Following the defeat of the Iraqi forces by the coalition, Saddam had moved fast to stem disaffection in both the north and south of the country, thus allowing the Republican Guard to regain its morale. The treatment of the Kurds in the north was particularly harsh, and the press and television screens were full of harrowing pictures. The United States was reluctant to intervene. For the Americans, to liberate Kuwait was one thing, to interfere in the internal affairs of a sovereign state was another. They had deliberately chosen not to pursue the Iraqi forces to the gates of Baghdad, given the doubts of the international community and uncertainty about the future stability of Iraq should Saddam's régime fall. Were they now to get involved in protecting an oppressed minority within Iraq's borders?

Public pressure to do something was mounting, however, and the British

---

[122] *Bull. EC*, Jan.–Feb. 1991, 1.4.17. [123] Clesse, 'Europe and the Gulf War', 91–3.
[124] Remacle, *Les Négociations sur la politique étraugère*, 23.

Prime Minister's idea proved to be a timely move. Unveiled to a surprised European Council, it commanded general support. The creation of safe havens would allow the Kurdish refugees to come down from the mountains and return to their homes. The responsibility for protecting the safe havens would be awarded to the United Nations; how this was to be assured was not clear. The Heads of State and Government allocated 150 million ECU in support of the refugees, and Prime Minister Santer and President Delors, who were scheduled to visit New York and Washington the next day, were charged with convincing the UN Secretary General and President Bush of the merits of the plan.[125] The meeting of the European Council was immediately followed by a meeting of the WEU Council hastily convened by France[126] in order to give operational expression to the decisions taken a few moments previously by the European Council. Although described as a 'stunt', the meeting was invested with deep symbolic significance as an example of how the relationship between WEU and the EC, proposed by France and Germany in the IGC, might work in practice.[127]

From the British point of view, Operation Safe Haven was a success. Here was a striking response on a matter of grave public concern; here was a demonstration of the importance the United Kingdom attached to the European foreign policy process;[128] and here was, if need be, a surefire way of preventing the French from turning the European Council meeting into a platform for forestalling the Americans by launching an initiative for an international conference. From the European point of view, the operation was equally successful. It allowed a veil to be drawn over the divisions of the Twelve over the preceding months, and it showed that European foreign policy was capable of acting as well as talking. It even brought some relief to the beleaguered Kurds.

---

[125] Freedman and Karsh, *The Gulf Conflict*, 421–5; *EPC Documentation Bulletin*, 1991, Vol. 7, 91/098, 91/099; James Bone, 'UK Plan to Save Kurds Came After US warning', *The Times*, 12 Apr. 1991; David Usborne, 'EC's War Wounds Start to Heal', *Independent*, 10 Apr. 1991; Sarah Helm, Leonard Doyle, and Edward Lucas, 'US Cool over Proposal for Kurds' Haven', *Independent*, 10 Apr. 1991; Peter Hort, 'Die Zwölf in ihrem Element: Symbolik statt klarer Antworten', *FAZ*, 10 Apr. 1991.

[126] As WEU Presidency, France was in a good position to emphasize the connection between EC foreign policy and the WEU: van Eekelen, *Debating European Security*, 81–2.

[127] De Gucht and Keukeleire, 'The European Security Architecture', 57–9; Remacle, *Les Négociations sur la politique étraugère*, 23–4.

[128] The French and Germans were given advanced warning, the Americans were 'told, but not consulted'. One cannot help agreeing with David Owen's comment, 'As far as the Americans were concerned, this was a deliberate but well-judged bounce': *The Times*, 12 Apr. 1991.

The Gulf conflict exerted a determining influence on the course of the debate on a common foreign and security policy. Before Saddam Hussein's invasion of Kuwait, it had been possible to take the view that the European Community's foreign policy vocation lay on peaceful lines. The trend of history lay in disarmament and the dismantling of military alliances. The Warsaw Pact was in a state of collapse, and NATO was engaged in transforming itself from a purely defensive organization to an active proponent of peace and stability. The Community's contribution to the new European architecture was through non-military means—G24, the Association Agreements, and the successful absorption of East Germany. In academic terms, the Community was evolving as a 'civilian power'. This was not to say that there were not many supporters of a defence and security role for the Community—the 'Platform on European Security Interests' of the WEU, otherwise known as the 'Hague Platform', adopted on 27 October 1987, had stated that 'the construction of an integrated Europe will remain incomplete as long as it does not include security and defence'[129]—but events were not flowing in their direction, and the security dimension did not figure prominently in the common foreign and security policy debate.[130]

The conflict in the Gulf changed all that. The Europeans were quick to draw the conclusion that a recognized international policy role depended on the ability to project power, and that collectively they did not have that ability. The Italian paper of 18 September 1990, which proposed the transfer of the powers of WEU to the Community, was an early recognition of this. More significant was the paper submitted by France and Germany in February 1991. France had discovered from its experiences in the Gulf not only that its forces were ill adapted to fighting small wars for the preservation of international order, but that it was disagreeably dependent on American intelligence and transport capacities. Germany was sensitive to the widespread criticism it received for its failure to participate militarily, in spite of its substantial financial contribution. For both, recourse to the WEU in liaison with the European Community was the answer. For France, it was a way of preserving a defence personality independent of the United States; for Germany, it was a means of assum-

[129] van Eekelen, *Debating European Security*, 11, 359.

[130] It is indeed the case that the Foreign Ministers discussed security and defence at their informal meeting in Luxembourg in Apr. 1990, and that the United Kingdom—or at any rate Foreign Secretary Hurd—submitted ideas the following month about a defence role for the WEU within NATO: van Eekelen, *Debating European Security*, 42–3. But the debate was lukewarm at the time.

ing a defence personality which overcame decades of post-war inhibition, minimized domestic criticism, and disarmed fears abroad of German revanchism.[131]

All this meant that the common foreign and security policy took on much more importance in the IGC on political union, and the security and defence dimension within the CFSP.[132] It also meant that the United States took an enhanced, and not always friendly, interest in the Europeans' efforts to achieve political union. Whereas the attitude of the US Administration had initially been one of benign encouragement, it became more reserved when the Europeans showed an active interest in building up WEU separately from NATO. The Americans sent a tough memorandum to the members of WEU in advance of the special WEU Ministerial Council on 22 February making clear their opposition to the Europeans' going it alone.[133] In what had become one of the crucial points under discussion by the time the Intergovernmental Conference got under way, the Member States' positions were governed less by their views on the objective merits of the case than by their attitude to Europe's relations with the United States.

---

[131] Heisbourg, 'France and the Gulf Crisis', 30–2, 34–6; Kaiser and Becher, 'Germany and the Iraq Conflict', 65–9; Hubel, 'Europa, Japan und der Krieg um Kuwait', 501. Germany was only able to play a role at all, in a purely humanitarian capacity, through its participation in WEU: Hubel, 'Europa Japan und der Krieg um Kuwait', 492; Kaiser and Becher, 'Germany and the Iraq Conflict', 53–4.   [132] Grant, *Delors*, 207.
[133] Gnesotto and Roper (eds.), *Western Europe and the Gulf*, 4; Guazzone, 'Italy in the Gulf Crisis', 80–1.

6

The Intergovernmental Conference

The Italian Presidency report of 16 November 1990 and the conclusions of the Rome European Council of 14–15 December 1990 already contained the substance of the common foreign and security policy as adopted in the Maastricht Treaty. The long debate throughout the Intergovernmental Conference, which lasted for the whole of 1991, was devoted on the one hand to refining these points, and on the other to two major issues of principle: to what extent should the Community's foreign policy be assimilated to EC mechanisms and procedures, and how far should the Community go in acquiring its own security and defence capability? The first issue, a continuation of the argument over 'consistency', was fought out in what came to be known as the 'pillars' debate, and the second, stimulated by experiences in the Gulf War, over the Community's relationship with the WEU. A third issue, the degree of democratic control to be exercised over the activities of the Community, constituted the main part of the remainder of the agenda on political union, and spilled over from time to time to foreign policy questions.

The IGC had been called as a result of a move by Germany and France, and these two countries were anxious not to lose the initiative as the conference proceeded. They therefore tabled a number of joint papers, quite often at crucial moments in the debate. It was not always easy, however, for Paris and Bonn to agree on the line to take, since their approach to political union differed in fundamental respects. These may be set out schematically in the following way:

France
- lukewarm on democratic control;[1]
- in favour of an intergovernmental CFSP;
- strong on an independent European defence capability (WEU).

Germany
- strong on democratic control;
- in favour of an integrationist CFSP;

[1] Favier and Martin-Roland, *La Décennie Mitterrand*, iv. 159, 182.

- ambiguous on an independent defence capability (NATO).

These different attitudes led ineluctably to the following result, which can be clearly seen in the Maastricht Treaty:

- quite strong on democratic control;
- an intergovernmental CFSP;
- the defence question postponed.

It might even be said that there was a tacit bargain between Germany and France, whereby the French gave the Germans something on democratic control, the Germans gave the French something on the CFSP, and there was a stand-off on defence, which was too sensitive and important for a compromise to be possible.

The other Member States did not count for as much as might have been expected, since their positions on foreign-policy making cancelled each other out and varied depending on whether classic foreign policy or defence questions were being addressed. On what might be called the subject area of old-style EPC, the line-up was as follows:

(a) United Kingdom, Denmark, Greece, and Portugal: improve EPC on existing lines, no alignment with EC mechanism and procedures;
(b) Germany, Benelux, Italy, and the Commission: a strong common policy aligned with EC mechanisms and procedures;
(c) France: a strong common policy focused on the European Council.

On the new defence area of policy, the line-up was slightly different:

(a) United Kingdom, Netherlands, and Portugal: an Atlanticist defence, relying on NATO;
(b) France and all other countries except for (c) below, with some heart-searching in the case of Germany: an independent defence capability, based on the WEU;
(c) Denmark, Greece, and Ireland: distinctive national positions.

These basic positions were adhered to, with few changes of substance, throughout the IGC negotiations. As far as the foreign policy aspects of political union were concerned, these may for convenience be divided into four stages:

1. the 'first reading', from the beginning of the conference to the publication of the Luxembourg Presidency's non-paper of April 1991 (a pre-draft of the Treaty);

2. the period up to the Luxembourg European Council of June 1991, which failed to reach agreement on the structure of the Treaty, especially as regards the CFSP;
3. the period up to the presentation of the Netherlands Presidency's alternative draft in the early autumn;
4. the final negotiations, culminating in the Maastricht European Council in December 1991.

The 'first reading'

The opening discussions in the IGC were not taking place in a political and diplomatic vacuum. They coincided with the Community's frenzied last-minute attempts to avert hostilities with Iraq by diplomacy, France's even more last-minute attempts to do the same, and Desert Storm itself—the brief burst of fighting which as one of its more noteworthy side-effects gave a new twist to the debate about a European defence capability. Indeed, the rapidity with which the new Luxembourg Presidency tabled a first paper on the CFSP, on 16 January 1991, was attributed to the urgency imparted by the situation in the Gulf.[2] CFSP, and in particular the security dimension, acquired a greater relative importance in the overall agenda for political union than had originally been the case.[3] Indeed, Delors was later to say that the Member States became obsessed with defence during the IGC, to the extent that the opportunities afforded by the previously promising prospect for foreign policy were lost.[4]

The main part of the detailed negotiations was entrusted to the Personal Representatives of the Foreign Ministers. These were mostly the people who had served the same function during the preparatory period. Apart from the Representatives from Denmark, France, and Italy, they were all Permanent Representatives to the European Community. No Political Director was involved, and, with the exception of the Belgian Philippe de Schoutheete and later of the Irishman Padraig MacKernan, none had previously been a Political Director. Although no doubt the different Foreign Ministries sought the views of their Political Director on CFSP questions, the Political Committee as such was not directly associated with the IGC. This was a different procedure from that adopted

[2] Cloos *et al.*, *Le Traité de Maastricht*, 77.
[3] Laursen and Vanhoonacker, *The Intergovernmental Conference on Political Union*, 12.
[4] Grant, *Delors*, 207.

for the Single European Act, and helps to explain the occasional clumsiness on technical questions.[5]

After one meeting on the CFSP at the level of Personal Representatives, the Foreign Ministers had their first discussion of substance on 4 February 1991. This gave Ministers the opportunity to say on what points the negotiations should in their view concentrate. France, Spain, and Germany stressed the need for a gradual approach to the setting up of a CFSP; all referred to the need to distinguish between different types or levels of action; France and Germany wanted to have common defence included as an objective; the United Kingdom stressed the role of the WEU; and Belgium insisted on including voting by qualified majority among the decision-making procedures. The French and German Foreign Ministers argued at this meeting in favour of discussions on security being extended to cover defence questions. A common security and defence policy should be developed by the WEU, which would receive general guidelines from the European Council. Areas of security to be subject to a common policy were suggested, based on the ideas put forward by the Italian Presidency the previous autumn. The WEU would finally be integrated into the European Union in 1998, taking advantage of the provision which allowed for denunciation of the WEU Treaty at that date.[6]

A revised Franco-German paper setting out these proposals in detail was tabled in February.[7] A common security policy implied that 'political union should implement a common security policy in the aim of setting up a common European defence system in due course without which the construction of European Union would remain incomplete'. However, 'the Atlantic Alliance, and notably a permanent US military presence in Europe, remains indispensable for European security and stability'. WEU was to become 'the co-operation channel between Political Union and NATO'. The Atlantic Alliance 'should be strengthened by a more impor-

---

[5] Cloos *et al.*, *Le Traité de Maastricht*, 73–4. Unlike in the EMU IGC, there was no group below the level of the Personal Representatives working on the technical details of political union. The 'Friends of the Presidency', active especially during the Luxembourg Presidency, did not have any particular technical expertise: Mazzucelli, *France and Germany at Maastricht*, 19 n. 36; 136.

[6] Laursen and Vanhoonacker, *The Intergovernmental Conference on Political Union*, 79; 12–13.

[7] Corbett, *The Treaty of Maastricht*, 240–2; Gerbet, de la Serre, and Nafilyan, *L'Union politique de l'Europe*, 311 (version of 4 Feb. 1991); Laursen and Vanhoonacker, *The Intergovernmental Conference on Political Union*, 333–5 (revd. version of 19 Feb. 1991). The revised version was considerably toned down following criticism by the United Kingdom and the Netherlands, echoing that of the United States. In particular, the ultimate integration of WEU into the EC was abandoned: Guazzone, 'Italy in the Gulf Crisis', 81.

tant role and greater responsibilities for Europeans . . . a European identity for security and defence should be reflected in the development of
a European pillar within the Alliance'. The European Council should
'have the jurisdiction to decide what areas of security policy should be
the subject of a common policy'. Disarmament and control of armaments
in Europe; security questions, including peace-keeping measures in
the context of the United Nations; nuclear non-proliferation; and
economic aspects of security, namely co-operation concerning armaments
as well as the control of arms exports (with recognition of the possible
involvement of EC external policy), were given as examples. While the
responsibilities and activities of WEU would be maintained, it would
be brought closer to Political Union through 'cooperation in the sense of
coordination of work and complementarity in the distribution of tasks'.
In particular, 'European Council decisions on the principles and guidelines
of common foreign and security policy should serve as a guideline for
cooperation in the framework of the Treaty of Brussels'. In order to
promote co-operation, WEU administrative divisions could be transferred
to Brussels.

The Franco-German paper, like the Italian initiative of the previous
autumn (confirmed by a new paper on 5 February[8]), arose out of the
events in the Gulf. The pressure was the greater since the United States and
its partners had now launched their attack on Saddam Hussein's forces.
Desert Storm clearly showed that the United States was now the world
leader, and that its leadership rested primarily on its military capability.
For France, this implied that the Europeans should make an effort to
pool their military capabilities to form some sort of counterweight to
American power. This line was consistent with the recent French policy
of bolstering the WEU, at least since the WEU common platform at The
Hague in 1987.[9] At least France was militarily engaged in the Gulf;
Germany believed itself to be constitutionally prevented from doing any
more than providing moral and financial support, to a partner to which
it had recently owed so much. A European defence policy might help it to
resolve this dilemma. Furthermore, support for the WEU helped to keep
the French in a good mood. Behind the initiative lay the feeling that Political Union would not be worthy of the name without a defence dimension.[10] The words already quoted—'a common defence system . . . without

[8] Laursen and Vanhoonacker, *The Intergovernmental Conference on Political Union*, 13, 322–4.

[9] Doutriaux, *Le Traité sur l'Union européenne*, 56.

[10] Anderson and Goodman, 'Mars or Minerva?', 43, 49.

which the construction of European Union would remain incomplete'—
are significant in this respect.

The concept of using the WEU as a means of approaching a common
defence was supported in a long and philosophical address delivered to the
International Institute for Strategic Studies on 7 March 1991 by Jacques
Delors.[11] Delors took as his starting-point the Gulf War, which had shown
up the limits of the Community's influence and power to act. At the same
time, Europe was both surrounded by dangers of all kinds, and expected
by its partners to exercise its responsibilities. In the last analysis, the only
way to ensure security was to defend oneself, weapon in hand. The Gulf
War had shown, when it came to fighting, that the Community had neither
the institutional tools nor the military capability it needed to act as a
Community. The only option compatible with the European Union's
global ambition was to embed a common security policy firmly within it.
Tactics could vary, and transitional formulas could be considered, but the
ultimate goal should be clear. A common defence policy only made sense
if it combined a unity of analysis and action in foreign policy, and a
commitment to mutual assistance if a Member State was threatened.
The wording of Article 5 of the WEU Treaty[12] should be taken up into the
EU Treaty.

To discuss European defence only made sense when combined with
the reform of NATO. Delors here referred to some of the ideas in Baker's
Berlin speech of December 1989. Delors complained that the Europeans
had not responded adequately to Baker's offer—the Transatlantic
Declaration of November 1990 was not enough, and did not deal with
the problem of how a multifarious Europe was to deal with an America
united in policies and action. Nevertheless, a start had to be made with
what was to hand—the WEU. Of the two concepts of the WEU under
discussion in the IGC—as a forum for co-operation among European
countries and a bridge to NATO, or as the crucible of a European defence,
rooted in the Community, and the second pillar of the Atlantic Alliance—
Delors preferred the latter. WEU, the existing organization together
with any future progress in the setting up of multinational and intervention forces, should be gradually incorporated into the Community. Questions of common defence should be discussed by the European
Council and by joint Councils of the Foreign Ministers and
the Ministers of Defence. Delors specified that, unlike for the CFSP,
defence policy questions should be decided unanimously, while

---

[11] Delors, *Le Nouveau concert européen*, 290–309.
[12] Art. 5 of the WEU Treaty provides for a mutual defence guarantee.

any Member State could be excused the obligations resulting from a decision.

The fact that the President of the European Commission spoke in public on matters of security was considered shocking by many, and alerted professional diplomats to the Commission's new-found self-confidence in foreign affairs. It was not that the views expressed were particularly heretical: as well as France and Germany, they were broadly shared by Spain, Italy, Greece, Belgium, and Luxembourg.[13] It was rather that for the Commission to venture on this terrain was foreign to the EPC ethos, and upset the diplomatic conventions of twenty years. By taking such a high profile, Delors was exposing the Commission to a snub.

This was all the more likely to come as two Member States, the United Kingdom and the Netherlands, very definitely did not hold these views. They were in favour of the concept of WEU as a bridge to NATO. The British Foreign Secretary, Douglas Hurd, explained how this might be achieved in his Churchill Memorial Lecture in Luxembourg on 19 February 1991. Ambassadors to NATO could be appointed concurrently to WEU, which could be enlarged to include all European members of NATO, including Norway and Turkey. At the same time, co-operative links should be developed between WEU and the Community.[14] The British defence White Paper, published in July 1991, made the United Kingdom's stand clear:

In the British view the WEU can serve as a bridge between the transatlantic security and defence structures of NATO and the developing political and security policies of the Twelve ... Building totally distinct Western European Defence identities, involving the eventual absorption of the WEU by the Twelve, would be disruptive of NATO ... A defence organization based on the Twelve would need to set up its own separate defence structures. To follow this route would be to invite confusion and a less reliable defence than we have enjoyed over the last 40 years.

For the British defence establishment, the incorporation of WEU into the Community on Franco-German lines was the more ineligible as it was supported by the Commission. The mistrust of the European institutions which permeated Mrs Thatcher's Bruges speech had survived her departure from office.[15]

---

[13] Grant, *Delors*, 186.
[14] Laursen and Vanhoonacker, *The Intergovernmental Conference on Political Union*, 13.
[15] Richardson, 'British State Strategies after the Cold War', 162–3.

The Netherlands stood by their traditional policy of firm support for NATO, and therefore backed the position taken on defence by the United Kingdom. According to the Netherlands' Foreign Minister Hans van den Broek, 'We have to offer stronger political co-operation, not a threat of rivalry, if we want to keep the US guarantees that Europe needs'.[16] The Dutch were so concerned about the support which the Franco-German proposal was attracting that, as well as seeking US intervention,[17] they asked for a special session of Foreign Ministers to be convened, which took place at Senningen (a castle in Luxembourg) on 26 March 1991. Genscher and Dumas called for progress on defence; Hurd and van den Broek expressed their doubts. There was no meeting of minds.

Behind the concerns of the United Kingdom and the Netherlands, always stalwart supporters of the Atlantic Alliance, lay considerable unease in the United States about the turn the discussion on security was taking. This unease was variously described as 'a blend of cautious observation and interested concern'[18] and 'a minor rampage'.[19] What particularly disturbed the Americans was that the CFSP might become a European caucus for NATO discussions, thus reducing the influence the United States could bring to bear on the final decision. The US made it clear that it viewed NATO as the paramount institution for Atlantic security.[20] This concern was expressed in a State Department telegram sent to the eleven European members of NATO on 20 February 1991—the missive which became famous as the Bartholomew/Dobbins telegram.[21] Using strong language, the telegram declared that 'efforts to construct a European pillar by redefining and limiting NATO's role, by weakening its structure, or by creating a monolithic bloc of certain members would be misguided', and 'we are concerned over the proposals that the WEU should be subordinated

---

[16] Wester, 'The Netherlands and European Political Union', 172; Favier and Martin-Roland, *La Décennie Mitterrand*, iv. 164–5.

[17] Pijpers, 'The Netherlands', 253.

[18] Murray, 'View from the United States', 214. Chris Murray, a perceptive and well-informed observer of Community affairs, was posted to the US Mission to the EC at the time.

[19] Ross, *Jacques Delors and European Integration*, 68. George Ross was attached to the Delors Cabinet for the first half of 1991.

[20] Murray, 'View from the United States', 216–19; Anderson and Goodman, 'Mars or Minerva?', 412 n. 36. The US State Department had expressed its concern the previous year that the EPC Ministerial Meeting of 20 Jan. 1989 had come out in support of an early CSCE Summit while the matter was still under discussion in NATO: *Deutsche Einheit*, no. 153, 743.

[21] Nye and Keohane, 'The United States and International Institutions', 120; Edwards, 'European Political Co-operation', 236; van Eekelen, *Debating European Security*, 78–81. The text of the telegram is reproduced at van Eekelen, *Debating European Security*, 340–4.

to the European Council, thereby developing a European security component—solely within the EC—that could lead to NATO's marginaliza-
tion'. Jim Dobbins, then in charge of European Affairs in the State
Department, followed this up with a tour of EC capitals to argue against
anything which might weaken NATO.[22]

The IGC discussions on foreign policy at this stage and later were
dominated by security matters. The other main issue still unresolved, the
extent to which foreign-policy making could be assimilated to the Community system, and the treaty form by which this should be expressed,
attracted less attention in this early phase of the Conference. The Italian
proposal on common foreign and security policy of 5 February, mentioned
above, presented a draft of provisions on the CFSP without specifying how
these might be incorporated into a treaty.[23] Building on the work done by
the previous Italian Presidency, the draft incorporated the few procedural
changes which met with general agreement—a non-exclusive right of initiative for the Commission, a foreign policy secretariat set up as part of the
General Secretariat of the Council (but staffed by seconded diplomats),
mutual provision of diplomatic and consular assistance in foreign countries[24]—and for the rest set out an interesting structural approach which
could have been explored further with advantage. Drawing on ideas first
publicly advanced by Delors, the Italians suggested that the European
Council should 'define the priorities and areas of application of the
common foreign and security policy on the basis of general interests
common to the Community/Union and its Member States'. On this basis,
the General Affairs Council should 'formulate and conduct the CFSP as the
single source of decisions'. Decisions on the principles and general
guidelines, and any decisions on security, were to be taken by consensus,
abstention by one or more Member States not preventing the consensus;
decisions on implementation were to be adopted by a qualified majority.

So far, so conventional. The Commission Opinion of 21 October 1990
had taken a similar line. Where the Italian draft interestingly differed is in
point 7 of the text: 'The provisions of Title III of the Single Act . . . shall
continue to apply to areas of foreign policy which are not part of the

---

[22] Buchan, *Europe*, 37. David Buchan was at that time the Brussels correspondent of the
Financial Times, and closely involved with the events here described. See also Favier and
Martin-Roland, *La Décennie Mitterrand*, iv. 165.

[23] Laursen and Vanhoonacker, *The Intergovernmental Conference on Political Union*,
322–4.

[24] This is ascribed to experience of mutual consular assistance in Kuwait after the Iraqi
invasion (Buchan, *Europe*, 34), but in fact the discussion had been going on for years in
EPC.

common policy'. This shows that the common foreign and security policy was conceived of as being qualitatively different from the old EPC, the 'value added' being conferred by the role given to the European Council and the real possibility of qualified majority voting. The CFSP would therefore not be global in ambition, but would confine itself to those areas where the Member States have agreed at the highest level that they have general interests in common. The continued existence alongside it of EPC, operating according to the old rules (with the procedural amendments mentioned above), would be a perpetual reminder of the difference between the two. The Maastricht Treaty, however, abrogated Title III of the Single Act, thereby sacrificing the clarity of the distinction between old EPC and new CFSP. The Italian draft also provided for the Council to ensure consistency with EC external relations, which would be an integral part of the common foreign policy, and for the proceedings of the Council's preparatory bodies (Coreper and the Political Committee and their subsidiary bodies) to be closely co-ordinated and, where necessary, integrated.

The first attempt to elaborate an overall structure for foreign-policy making in the Community was made by the Commission, which tabled a 'contribution' at the beginning of March 1991 in the form of a draft legal text on the development of a common external policy.[25] The text did not deserve the reputation it acquired of being a federalist coup mounted by a power-crazed Commission. Indeed, it was distinguished by its gradualism, reaching back to the Spinelli approach in the European Parliament's draft treaty of 1984. What it did was to bring under a single section of the Treaty all the Community's external policies (common foreign and security policy, external economic policy, and development co-operation), while preserving the procedures proper to each. As far as the CFSP was concerned, the European Council was to fix the limits of the Union's powers. The principle of subsidiarity would be applied, so that Member States would act in those areas where there was no need for the Union to take responsibility. There would thus be a common policy, not a single policy, which would be implemented through the existing institutional framework. On matters identified as being of 'vital common interest' by the European Council, the Council would decide on common action by

---

[25] Corbett, *The Treaty of Maastricht*, 218–29. The text was available on 28 Feb.; it appeared in Agence Europe on 7 Mar., the day Delors delivered his speech on security at the IISS: Ross, *Jacques Delors and European Integration*, 93; *Europe Documents* no. 1697–1698, 7 Mar. 1991. For an overall assessment of the Commission's contribution to the IGC on political union, see Endo, *The Presidency of the European Commission under Jacques Delors*, 170–90.

augmented qualified majority (at least eight Member States voting in favour). Other matters would be dealt with under intergovernmental co-operation, it being provided that abstention would not prevent consensus. The right of initiative, whether for the definition of matters of vital common interest or actions to be decided in consequence, would lie with the Presidency, the Commission, or a simple majority of Member States. (This limitation of the right of initiative of the Member States, invented by the Commission, would have increased substantially the influence of that institution.) Responsibility for preparing the Council's deliberations would rest with Coreper, not the Political Committee. The European Court of Justice would not have jurisdiction; and CFSP would be represented jointly by the Presidency and the Commission. Common security policy would guarantee assistance in the event of an armed attack; a list of matters of vital common interest would be adopted, as defined by the December 1990 Rome European Council; and there would be regular meetings of Foreign and Defence Ministers. For security policy, decisions would be unanimous, and dispensation might be granted in special cases. Articles 223 and 224 of the EEC Treaty[26] would be repealed, since their contents would be subsumed under the new policy.

The section on external economic policy took up existing Treaty provisions, but amended Article 113 (on the common commercial policy) to put an end to controversy over the scope of the article, in particular as regards investment, services, export credits, and intellectual property. The jurisprudence of the Court, whereby for every power conferred on the Union internally there is a corollary external and exclusive power (the 'ERTA effect'), would be enshrined in the Treaty. For all these areas, the Commission would be recognized as alone responsible for representing the Union. The Commission would be able to act on its own authority in accordance with the delegation of powers ('hierarchy of norms') proposals it had made in another context in the IGC. Development co-operation policy would be specifically included in the Treaty—it had previously been conducted under the catch-all Article 235. Both action specific to the Union, and joint action by the Union and its Member States, were envisaged in this field, but the Union would have the sole power to conclude international agreements whether it acted alone or jointly with the Member States.

Seen objectively, the Commission's text was bold, but not over-bold, and certainly did not amount to making the whole of the CFSP subject to EC

---

[26] The 'reserve of sovereignty' articles, providing for derogations from the Treaty for reasons of national security.

procedures, as some were later to claim. The very fact that the European Council would have control by unanimity over the choice of 'vital common interests' was in itself a guarantee of this.[27] However, the dictatorial tone of much of the document, the emphasis on the Commission's role throughout, and some unrealistic and naïve provisions[28] combined to provoke the Member States' contumely.[29] They may have been right to suspect concealed ambition. At an office meeting shortly after the paper was completed, François Lamoureux, President Delors' Deputy Chef de Cabinet, gave an inside view of how the paper had been prepared and what it was designed to achieve:

We've been working on it for nearly a year in our small group . . . and I wrote the whole thing myself . . . It was only when we knew what we wanted to go [*sic*] that we brought in the Andriessen, Matutes and Marin cabinets, who edited a few things . . . the Marin people were no use at all . . . We tried to set up a genuine Communitarization of foreign policy. The European Council will identify applicable areas by unanimity and then the Council will work via qualified majority to create policy. And we were careful not to set out an *a priori* list of areas where the CFSP would work. We avoided the list Rome II set out last year in order to prevent member states fighting about it at the IGC. First get the treaty, then we'll specify the areas . . . The most important thing is to link foreign policy and security. We judged that we needed a mutual assistance pact, and we knew that it wouldn't be much use to have one until we had a common military operation, so to get both we imported the mutual assistance clause of the WEU Treaty. The Community will simply absorb WEU, and this, in turn, will give the Community a common position in NATO.[30]

Whatever the Commission's intentions, the draft was badly received by the delegations to the IGC. Carlos Westendorp, the Spanish Secretary of State for EC Affairs, said that the Commission's chief concern seemed to have been to give themselves more power, instead of searching for common ground; it was acting like a thirteenth Member State.[31] Consulting the other Personal Representatives on 25 March, the Luxembourg Presidency concluded that only Italy and the Commission were not content to leave foreign and security policy to be dealt with outside the EC Treaty.[32]

[27] de Schoutheete, 'The Creation of the CFSP', 53–4.

[28] e.g. Art. Y4: 'the Member States shall consult each other and the Commission on all national foreign policy measures they intend to take'.

[29] The author, present at a diplomatic reception in Brussels the day the document was launched, was struck by the unanimous venom with which it was greeted.

[30] Ross, *Jacques Delors and European Integration*, 95.

[31] Grant, *Delors*, 189; Doutriaux, *Le Traité sur l'Union européenne*, 53–4.

[32] Buchan, *Europe*, 38.

The upshot was that the Commission's paper was not taken seriously into account in the IGC discussions. The blow was the more serious for the Commission in that, intent on maintaining its freedom to manœuvre, it had declined the invitation to join with the Presidency and the Council Secretariat in producing the papers which from now on were to be the basis of discussion in the IGC on Political Union. This was the reverse of the procedure followed in drafting the Single Act, when the Commission's participation in drafting Presidency texts had enabled it to exercise significant influence on the final result. On that occasion, however, the Commission had not been associated by the Presidency with the preparation of the foreign policy section; it is all the more surprising that the Commission now elected to forgo the real opportunity of affecting from behind the scenes the future shape of foreign-policy making.[33]

At this stage the Luxembourg Presidency tabled 'draft Treaty articles with a view to achieving political union'.[34] This was the Luxembourg 'non-paper', dated 12 April 1991 and first discussed on 17 April. The Presidency was concerned that, although the EMU and Political Union IGCs were supposed to run in parallel, the EPU IGC was well behindhand since unlike EMU, it had no formal Treaty drafts to base its discussions on. Furthermore, the preliminary discussions which had taken place so far could continue indefinitely unless delegations had something on which to concentrate their minds.[35] Although purportedly only a compendium of the most commonly held views, the 'non-paper' rapidly became the only basis for discussion. Such is the power of the pen.

The method followed by the Presidency in drafting the non-paper was to include those positions supported by a majority of delegations, and when it was necessary to decide among them, to follow the requirements of a coherent and rational presentation.[36] Thus the European Council was to define the principles and general guidelines of the CFSP, on the basis of which policy would be conducted by the Council, in particular through joint actions. It would have the power to decide that the detailed arrangements for carrying out a joint action should be adopted by a majority to be defined. The Union would be represented externally by the Presidency, assisted by the Commission. Coreper would be responsible for preparing Council meetings and carrying out instructions given it by the Council,

---

[33] Cloos *et al.*, *Le Traité de Maastricht*, 75; Grant, *Delors*, 189–90; David Buchan, 'Jacques Delors: Blowing his Top, but Surely Bluffing', *Financial Times*, 23 Nov. 1991; Endo, *The Presidency of the European Commission under Jacques Delors*, 180–1.

[34] Corbett, *The Treaty of Maastricht*, 267–88.

[35] Cloos *et al.*, *Le Traité de Maastricht*, 81.   [36] Ibid. 81–2.

while the Political Committee would formulate opinions. The Council and the Presidency would be assisted by the General Secretariat of the Council in the preparation and implementation of the Union's common foreign and security policy. On security, the 'draft Treaty provisions' were laconic, reflecting the deeply divided views on the subject. It was merely stated that 'decisions by the Union on security matters which have defence implications may be wholly or partly implemented in the framework of the Western European Union, insofar as they also fall within that organization's sphere of competence', without existing obligations deriving from membership of NATO or WEU being affected. There was a provision—in square brackets—for a review of the situation in 1996.

The Presidency's claim to have engaged in a technical exercise setting out the views of the majority of delegations was somewhat disingenuous. The limitation of the possibility of voting by qualified majority, the dominant role of the Presidency in external representation, and the role in preparation and implementation of the CFSP assigned to the General Secretariat of the Council, all betokened an intergovernmentalist view which was strongly held by some Member States, but not necessarily the majority. Above all, however, the fact that the Luxembourg Presidency had chosen to structure the Union in three separate compartments—soon to become known as 'pillars'—devoted respectively to the European Community as such, the CFSP, and home affairs and judicial co-operation, was taken as a decisive indication that the draft was intended to be intergovernmentalist. To be sure, this was doing no more than perpetuating the structure of the Single European Act, but several delegations had been led to believe by the events in Central and Eastern Europe and the political initiatives taken as a result, especially by France and Germany, that higher ambitions were in order. It is difficult to resist François Lamoureux's embittered assessment that Luxembourg was 'in the pocket of the French and the Council Secretariat'.[37] For his part, Pierre de Boissieu, the French Personal Representative, later said that 'the negotiation on political union is the only one the Commission neither understood nor controlled.'[38] No doubt both views were correct.

[37] Grant, *Delors*, 188–90; de la Serre, 'La Politique européenne de François Mitterrand', 116. For a justification of the Presidency's tactics, and a fuller account of the reaction to them, see Cloos *et al.*, *Le Traité de Maastricht*, 107–13.

[38] Védrine, *Les Mondes de François Mitterrand*, 470. With the concentrated venom made possible only by a deep personal knowledge of the Institution, where he had for four years been Vice-President Ortoli's Chef de Cabinet, Pierre de Boissieu was later (25 Nov. 1991) to write of the Commission: 'Sur l'Union politique, elle est systématiquement à contretemps, à contre-procédure et à contre-priorité' (Favier and Martin-Roland, *La Décennie Mitterrand*, iv. 220–1).

Belgium, the Netherlands, and Italy disliked the structure of the draft, as did the European Parliament. Most virulent in criticism was the Commission, which complained about the Presidency's 'minimalist' approach; the structure, which blocked the way to any development of the Community on federalist lines; and above all the proposals regarding decision-making procedures (this did not concern the CFSP), which considerably diminished the Commission's right of initiative.[39] These defects were advantages in the eyes of the United Kingdom and Denmark. The British in particular opposed any form of majority voting in CFSP. The proposals concerning security, modest as they were, went too far for the British and the Dutch, and not far enough for the French, the Spanish, and others.[40]

The Luxembourg European Council

The Luxembourg Presidency pressed ahead with consultations with a view to presenting a final draft Treaty for approval by the European Council in June. The next meeting at Ministerial level, which dealt with security, was the informal Gymnich-type meeting at Mondorf-les-Bains on 27–8 April. The discussion made some progress because in the meantime American thinking about the conditions under which the United States might be reconciled to a European defence identity had advanced. On 17 April Secretary Baker had met EC Foreign Ministers and argued: that European foreign and security policies should not weaken NATO; that NATO's integrated military structure should be maintained; that any new European defence structures should be open to all the European members of NATO; that these structures ought to facilitate the protection of vital interests outside Europe; and that if changes to existing military structures were envisaged, they should be discussed within NATO as well. This was an improvement on the previous US position of opposition to even limited autonomy for WEU.[41]

The crucial discussion on the structure of the Treaty came at a special

[39] The Belgian parliamentary delegation to the COSAC (Conférence des organes spécialisés des Assemblées de la Communauté) on 6–7 May 1991 supported an exclusive right of initiative for the Commission: Lequesne, *Paris–Bruxelles*, 256.

[40] Cloos *et al.*, *Le Traité de Maastricht*, 82–3; Laursen and Vanhoonacker, *The Intergovernmental Conference on European Union*, 15; de Schoutheete, 'The Creation of the CFSP', 54–5.

[41] Ross, *Jacques Delors and European Integration*, 147; Cloos *et al.*, *Le Traité de Maastricht*, 83–4. The Luxembourg Presidency remained in close contact with the Americans throughout: Lorenz, 'Luxembourg', 239.

meeting of Foreign Ministers held at Dresden on 3 June 1991. Hans-Dietrich Genscher had invited his colleagues to meet in the former DDR to allow the inhabitants to see what sort of Community they had just joined. One wonders what they made of it. This was the meeting at which Marc Eyskens, the Belgian Foreign Minister, consecrated the phrase 'the three pillars' to describe the structure followed in the Presidency draft. Mr Eyskens likened the non-paper proposals to a Greek temple with different columns, while he preferred a tree with several branches. A few days later, he was to write in *Le Figaro*, 'We must at all costs maintain the unity of the European Community and avoid the establishment of a Political Union with its own mechanisms, some of which would be intergovernmental, alongside the existing Communities'.

The debate turned on the difference of approach between the Presidency non-paper and the amendments tabled by the Commission on 21 May 1991.[42] The Commission noted that 'it is somewhat paradoxical that the current trend in the Intergovernmental Conference favours a kind of revision of the Treaty of Rome that would depart from this general unification process and keep the Community no longer as the focal point but simply as one entity among others in a political union with well-defined objectives and a variety of institutional schemes'. The CFSP would certainly involve adjustments to traditional practice, but 'this adjustment to the Community approach cannot be allowed to go so far as to break up the existing model'. The Commission stood by the view that 'the central objective of transforming the Community into a European Union should be to ensure the unity, the consistency and, as a result, the efficiency of its international activities. It is, of course, clear that a common foreign and security policy is a *sui generis* policy that can be implemented only gradually; but it is not possible to affirm the identity of the Union and the consistency of its international personality simply by adding a foreign and security policy to existing policies . . . there can be no question of grafting the Union concept onto the existing Treaty; the Union must absorb the Community and all that it has achieved'.

Delors engaged in heavy political lobbying before the Dresden meeting in favour of the Commission's approach. He was rewarded by support from the Netherlands, Belgium, Greece, Spain, Italy, Portugal,[43] and Germany. France, supported by the United Kingdom and Denmark, took

---

[42] Corbett, *The Treaty of Maastricht*, 289–92.

[43] The sources differ as to the camp into which Portugal fell. There may have been some ambiguity about its position. Delors' count was 9 to 3 in his favour: Endo, *The Presidency of the European Commission under Jacques Delors*, 188.

the opposite view. Foreign Minister Dumas warned of a treaty with multiple 'exceptions, special regimes and dispensatory clauses from EC mechanisms—thus a judicial imbroglio'. As a compromise, the Presidency suggested maintaining the pillars, but strengthening the provisions for a single institutional framework, and underlining the evolutive nature of the Union by inserting appropriate revision clauses.[44]

These conclusions were reflected in the revised draft which the Presidency tabled on 18 June 1991.[45] The new Article A set the tone: 'By this Treaty, the High Contracting Parties establish among themselves a Union. The Union shall be founded on the European Communities supplemented by the policies and co-operations established by this Treaty. It shall have as its task to organize, according to the principles of consistency and solidarity, the relations among the Member States and among their peoples. This Treaty marks a new stage in a process leading gradually to a Union with a federal goal.' Article C further stated: 'The Union shall be served by a single institutional framework which shall ensure the consistency and continuity of the actions carried out in order to reach its objectives while respecting and developing the *acquis communautaire*. The Union shall in particular ensure the consistency of its external actions as a whole in the implementation of its external relations, defence, economic and development policies.' The detailed provisions on the CFSP were for the most part unchanged, but the section on security now contained the specification that 'The common foreign and security policy includes all questions related to the security of the Union'. In Article B, the framing of a defence policy is stated as a long-term objective. A review with a view to the eventual framing of a defence policy was proposed for 1996 at the latest.[46]

In spite of these efforts it was clear by the time of the Foreign Ministers' meeting on 23 June 1991 that there was not going to be agreement at the European Council on 28–9 June. The Presidency calculated that too many Member States were playing for time: the British wanted more time to work on the draft on the table before the moment for political decisions came, given the divisions on Europe within the Conservative Party; the

[44] Cloos *et al.*, *Le Traité de Maastricht*, 84–5, 112–13; Laursen and Vanhoonacker, *The Intergovernmental Conference on Political Union*, 16; Grant, *Delors*, 190; Ross, *Jacques Delors and European Integration*, 145–7; Delors, *L'Unité d'un homme*, 271–2; de Schoutheete, 'The Creation of the CFSP', 55; Doutriaux, Le *Traité sur l'Union européenne*, 59; Buchan, *Europe*, 39; Favier and Martin-Roland, *La Décennie Mitterrand*, iv. 181.

[45] Corbett, *The Treaty of Maastricht*, 293–320; Grant, *Delors*, 191.

[46] de Schoutheete, '*The Creation of the CFSP*', 56–7; Cloos *et al.*, *Le Traité de Maastricht*, 85–6.

Germans were sufficiently sympathetic to the British difficulties not to want to put them under too much pressure, and in any case the German internal position was not yet decided; the Spaniards thought the necessary balance was lacking; and the Belgians and Dutch, together with the Commission, still hoped to claw back something more on the structure.[47]

As it turned out, the attention of the Luxembourg European Council was fully devoted to the Yugoslav crisis, which had just broken out. The Heads of State and Government soon resigned themselves to postponing a decision until the European Council at Maastricht in December, only President Mitterrand saying that he could accept the Presidency text as it stood. The European Council's conclusions did not significantly advance the debate on the CFSP, although it was agreed that 'the Community Member States which are party to the Treaty on the Atlantic Alliance, in accordance with the guidelines established at the recent meeting of NATO Foreign Ministers in Copenhagen, regard the ultimate reinforcement of a European defence identity as an important contribution to the strengthening of the Atlantic Alliance. In the immediate future, they will endeavour to work out common guidelines with a view to the forthcoming NATO Summit in Rome'.

The most significant passage in the conclusions was, however, an innocent-seeming little passage which read: 'The European Council considers that the Presidency's draft forms the basis for the continuation of negotiations, both as regards most of the principal points contained in it and the state of play at the two Conferences, on the understanding that final agreement by the Member States will only be given to the Treaty as a whole.' This sentence represents the outcome of an epic but ultimately vain struggle by the Dutch and Belgian Prime Ministers to secure that the Presidency's draft would be, not *the* basis for the continuation of negotiations, but *a* basis, the implication being that competing drafts might still be tabled. It is difficult to avoid the conclusion that the future Netherlands Presidency, already at this stage, intended doing precisely that.[48]

The Netherlands Presidency draft

In spite of their tactical defeat at the Luxembourg European Council, the Netherlands, which took over the Presidency on 1 July 1991, set about

---

[47] Cloos *et al.*, *Le Traité de Maastricht*, 86; Grant, *Delors*, 191; Doutriaux, *Le Traité sur l'Union européenne*, 61.

[48] *Bull. EC*, June 1991, 1.3; Cloos *et al.*, *Le Traité de Maastricht*, 87; Buchan, *Europe*, 39.

immediately to producing a new draft Treaty more in line with their own way of thinking. They had been encouraged by the line-up in the discussions at Dresden[49] to believe that there was a possibility of securing an outcome on more integrationist lines than had seemed realistic to the Luxembourg Presidency. The redrafting operation was under the direct control of Pieter Dankert, the Minister responsible for Europe in the Netherlands Foreign Ministry, who had immense experience of European politics, not least as President of the European Parliament. This did not mean, however, as some have claimed, that Hans van den Broek, the Foreign Minister, was so preoccupied with the Yugoslavia crisis that he failed to keep an eye on what his junior Minister was up to; on the contrary, he was completely informed throughout. Nor did the Presidency act entirely on its own; the Commission is reported to have given strong support and even to have lent a hand with the drafting, although Delors denied this.[50]

A revised draft was finally circulated towards the beginning of September, after the Presidency had already put off two negotiating sessions. In spite of the cries of horror and outrage with which it was received, the text was far from being the expression of federal orthodoxy it was made out to be, and, from the strict integrationist point of view, was modest in its ambition.[51] The objective was stated to be, not to set up a Union, but to establish a European Community as 'a new stage in a process leading gradually to a European Union with a federal goal'. The pillars disappeared, the section on CFSP being placed within the chapter devoted to the external relations of the Community, as had been proposed in the Commission's March draft. Within the CFSP section, the Dutch returned to the idea of the Italian proposal of the previous February, of gradually introducing a qualitatively different common foreign and security policy through the means of 'joint action', in all areas where the Member States have essential interests in common, the conditions for the implementation of which may be fixed by the Council either unanimously or by a qualified majority— the choice was left open. For all other areas, Article 30 of the SEA would

[49] Eight against three, with the hapless Luxembourg Presidency struggling to find a position which would achieve a result. There was at this stage a clear majority in favour of an integrated structure: *EUROPE*, 5504 (3–4 June 1991), 3.

[50] de Schoutheete, 'The Creation of the CFSP', 57; Grant, *Delors*, 194–5; Ross, *Jacques Delors and European Integration*, 171–2; Endo, *The Presidency of the European Commission under Jacques Delors*, 185. For a different view, which stresses van den Broek's preoccupation with other matters and his intransigence when the Netherlands paper was finally debated, see Pijpers, 'The Netherlands', 253–5.

[51] Corbett, *The Treaty of Maastricht*, 329–40.

continue to apply. The Court of Justice would have jurisdiction, but only to review the legality of the application of the procedures for deciding on the joint action.

By comparison with the Luxembourg draft, these provisions were closer to the model put forward by the Commission and supported by the 'integrationist' Member States. On security, however, the Dutch reverted to their Atlanticist preferences. The common security policy was to 'complement the security policy resulting from the obligations flowing for certain Member States from the Treaties establishing the North Atlantic Treaty Organization and the Western European Union', and the Council was to ensure that cohesion was promoted between the Community security policy and the policy followed within those organizations. The idea of using the WEU as a means of implementing Community security policies was dropped.

The Dutch draft demonstrated the dilemma faced by those who wished to graft the CFSP onto a Community framework. This had been pointed out already by Roland Dumas at the Dresden meeting in the remark quoted above, and is best explained by Philippe de Schoutheete:

On the general issues of principle concerning European integration, there is much to be said in favour of the Dutch draft treaty text. It is certainly consistent with views long held and always vigorously defended by that country in its approach to European affairs. In the specific field of foreign and security policy, however, the practical consequences of such an approach are on the negative side. Since such a policy does not fit easily into the Community procedural framework, which was not conceived with that sort of policy in mind, and since the Dutch approach had as its main objective excluding a separate procedural framework within the Union, little more could be done than to maintain the informal consensual rules that have governed political co-operation in the course of the years. In the Dutch approach, there was no question of a real breakthrough in common foreign and security policy.[52]

The validity of this argument depends upon acceptance of the premise that 'such a policy does not fit easily into the Community framework'. Such had always been and certainly remained the political reality, and integrationists were forced to accept this. Where they went wrong was in believing that it was possible to achieve some sort of halfway house, combining some Community features with other features inherited from traditional diplomatic consultation, and yet achieve a satisfactorily efficient result. But this premise is not a truth for all time, and the attempt to introduce a new

[52] de Schoutheete, 'The Creation of the CFSP', 58.

way of doing things in strictly limited areas to be selected by the European Council might have dented its validity. It should be noted that the CFSP provisions finally agreed in the Maastricht Treaty are subject to their own dilemma, since they fail to tackle effectively the problem of consistency, in the sense of using the Community's legal and economic potentiality as a vehicle for foreign policy.

The Netherlands Presidency draft was finally available at the beginning of September, and was energetically commended to partners in a round of diplomatic visits over the next few weeks. As a result of this campaign, the Dutch thought that they had secured four delegations in favour of taking the new draft as a basis for discussion, with four against and the remainder hesitant. The overall assessment was that there was a clear majority in favour of the draft, including Germany.[53] But when it came to the first discussion by the Personal Representatives, on 26 September, the Presidency tactics, as well as its text, were heavily criticized. At the Ministerial-level meeting four days later, on 30 September, only Belgium (and the Commission) was prepared to continue to work on the basis of the Presidency draft. All the others called for a return to the Luxembourg paper. Genscher spoke last, saying that since everyone else was against the Netherlands paper, then he was too.[54] On 'Black Monday' for Dutch diplomacy, Mr van den Broek withdrew the draft.

One can only speculate about what went wrong. Certainly Dutch diplomacy was not so incompetent as to have completely misread the signals. The Dutch representative in Brussels sent a warning to his authorities, passing on the negative views with which he had been favoured by his colleagues during an excursion to the Netherlands Antilles, but he was known to have personal doubts about the course of action being followed in The Hague, and his advice may therefore not have carried the weight it should. The hard reality was that the delegations had got used to the Luxembourg text, and were worried about the delays which would be caused by having to start working with a new one. Member States may have been reluctant to express themselves as clearly to Mr Dankert in their own capitals as they were constrained to do when the time for decisions came at the Ministerial meeting. While the Dutch were campaigning in favour of their text, others were certainly campaigning against it; indeed, the last-minute change of heart by Germany, which particularly grieved the Dutch, has

---

[53] George Brock, 'Federal Camp Wins First Round', *The Times*, 26 Sept. 1991; Mazzucelli, *France and Germany at Maastricht*, 159, 167; personal conversation with Mr Dankert.

[54] Klaus-Peter Schmid, 'Der Haager Selbstmord', *Die Zeit*, 11 Oct. 1991; Mazzucelli, *France and Germany at Maastricht*, 149–50.

been ascribed to French pressure in the form of personal lobbying of Genscher by Dumas in New York the previous weekend (Genscher was much closer personally to Dumas than to van den Broek). But the underlying reason may perhaps be found in the prescient observation of the Foreign Minister of Luxembourg, Mr Poos, who as early as the European Council at Dublin in June 1990 had said that unlike the Tour de France, where you can start with twelve riders and arrive with seven, the IGC can start with seven but has to arrive with twelve. It may be that the other Member States were simply not ready to sacrifice the rest of the Treaty to integrationist principle, when even a small number of their partners were irrevocably opposed.[55]

The final negotiations

The immediate effect of the failure of the Dutch draft was to confer on the Luxembourg draft a legitimacy it had not earned at the Luxembourg European Council. Nearly three months had gone by since then, without any progress having been made. Only two months were left before the Maastricht European Council in December. It was unthinkable either to separate the EMU and EPU IGCs, or to postpone the whole thing once again. Foreign Ministers would have to get a move on if the deadline was to be met. This involved concentrating only on the major points of difference, and taking the details of the CFSP on trust more or less as they stood in the Luxembourg draft. It has to be said, however, that there was a general acceptance that the important discussions on the defence of Europe were taking place in NATO. Significant progress on a European security and defence identity had been made at the NATO Foreign Ministers' meeting at Copenhagen on 6–7 June 1991, and there was hope of agreeing a satisfactory formula with the United States at the NATO Summit scheduled to take place on 7–8 November 1991 at Rome.[56]

There was of course no question now of finding an alternative to the 'pillar' structure, so that difficulty was removed. Two main questions therefore remained to be resolved: security and defence, and qualified majority voting for the implementation of CFSP measures. The Netherlands

---

[55] Cloos *et al.*, *Le Traité de Maastricht*, 88–90, 83; de Schoutheete, 'The Creation of the CFSP', 58; Doutriaux, *Le Traité sur l'Union européenne*, 63; Buchan, *Europe*, 39–40; Wester, 'The Netherlands and European Political Union', 174; van Wijnbergen, 'Germany and European Political Union', 59; Mazzucelli, *France and Germany at Maastricht*, 158–9.

[56] Doutriaux, *Le Traité sur l'Union européenne*, 64.

Presidency tabled a revised version of the Luxembourg paper on 3 October, but no longer enjoyed sufficient credibility to provide more than technical guidance for the discussions. More important contributions, especially on defence, came in the shape of an Anglo-Italian declaration of 5 October 1991 and a Spanish-French-German communiqué of 11 October. A decisive intervention was the joint initiative by Kohl and Mitterrand, also dated 11 October.

The Anglo-Italian declaration[57] was on the face of it a bizarre coupling of the federalist De Michelis with the definitely non-federalist Hurd. But on closer examination the alliance made political sense. It had been in gestation since the previous April, when Hurd and De Michelis, both nervous about Franco-German occupation of the diplomatic high ground, had met in a *trattoria* near Rome airport to consider the possibility of a joint initiative on defence.[58] With the United States now more relaxed about European ambitions for a security and defence identity, as shown by the progress in discussions in NATO,[59] the United Kingdom became in turn more ready for compromise with its partners in the Community, and was anxious to avoid whenever possible the high-profile isolation of the Thatcher years. Italy was a relatively Atlanticist Member State, with which a common position might be stitched together. The Italians, for their part, saw the early leading position they had taken on security and defence the previous year fading in the shadow of the Franco-German partnership, and were looking for ways of strengthening their position in the negotiation.[60] The paper recognized that 'Political Union implies the gradual elaboration and implementation of a common foreign and security policy and a stronger European defence identity with the longer term perspective of a common defence policy compatible with the common defence policy we already have with our allies in NATO'. The special relationship between Western Europe and North America remained a key element of the European identity. 'The development of a European security identity in the field of defence should be construed in such a way

[57] Corbett, *The Treaty of Maastricht*, 341–2; Laursen and Vanhoonacker, *The Intergovernmental Conference on Political Union*, 413–14; Gerbet, de la Serre, and Nafilyan, *L'Union politique de l'Europe*, 312–13.

[58] Buchan, *Europe*, 37.

[59] The US had not taken long to row back from the extreme positions taken in the Bartholomew telegram. As early as 16 Apr. 1991 Secretary Baker had communicated to the Europeans his Five Points on ESDI, which expressed support for a CFSP with NATO both the principal venue for consultations on security issues and the ultimate provider of defence: van Eekelen, *Debating European Security*, 83.

[60] Martial, 'Italy and European Political Union', 149.

as to reinforce the Atlantic Alliance . . . WEU should be entrusted with the task of developing the European dimension in the field of defence, it will develop its role in two complementary directions: as the defence component of the Union and as the means to strengthen the European pillar of the Alliance'. Not surprisingly, few details were given about how this double act might be achieved: WEU would 'take into account in its activities' the decisions of the European Council; for the rest, there would be increased co-ordination, facilitated by the transfer of the WEU Ministerial organs to Brussels. But the EU was to remain independent; the new reaction force which was proposed was to be under the exclusive control of its members.

The Anglo-Italian declaration was published on the eve of the informal meeting of Foreign Ministers at Haarzuilens (5–6 October 1991), and was welcomed as progress even though it was thought to be too Atlanticist. It stimulated France and Germany, however, to recall that their own concept of European defence was different. Following a meeting of the French and German Foreign Ministers in Paris on 11 October 1991, which the Spanish Foreign Minister also attended,[61] a joint communiqué was issued which stated that 'the WEU, which is an integral part of the process leading to European Union, could be given the responsibility of setting up the defence and security policy'. In a reference to the other issue still under hot debate, the three Ministers pleaded 'for qualified majority voting over the modalities in setting up the common foreign and security policy'.[62]

On the same day Chancellor Kohl and President Mitterrand sent to Prime Minister Lubbers as President of the European Council a joint proposal on the CFSP designed to get the process moving. This initiative, the seeds of which had been sown the previous June by developments in NATO,[63] had been under active consideration since the two had met in Bonn on 18 September. 'Our partners will be annoyed,' said the President, 'but we must have everything settled before Maastricht.' Kohl and Mitterrand took care, whatever the European partners might think, to make sure that the United States would not be annoyed by being presented with a *fait accompli*: before the drafting was finalized, two emissaries (Védrine and Hartman) were dispatched to Washington to put the

---

[61] This was all that remained of a Franco-German attempt to sideline the Netherlands Presidency by bringing together in Paris 'those Member States who wish to make a success of the Maastricht Summit': Christian Chartier, *Le Monde*, 9 Oct. 1991.

[62] Corbett, *The Treaty of Maastricht*, 343.

[63] Favier and Martin-Roland, *La Décennie Mitterrand*, iv. 167–8.

Americans in the picture.[64] Brent Scowcroft, the National Security Adviser, was grateful for the advance warning but made it plain that WEU could be no more than a hinge between the Community and NATO, not an instrument of the EC. The message was followed up by a personal letter from Bush to Mitterrand.[65]

The Franco-German initiative[66] included a draft article on security and defence, a list of priority areas for the CFSP, and a draft statement to be made by WEU. The draft article provided that 'the decisions and measures taken by the Union in this area [security and defence] may be developed and implemented entirely or in part by the EU, which is an integral part of the process of European Union'.[67] These provisions 'shall present no obstacle to closer bilateral co-operation . . . within the WEU and the Atlantic Alliance'. They were to be reviewed by 1996. The draft WEU statement made several concrete proposals for the development of a 'clear organic relationship' between the WEU and the Union,[68] involving the transfer of the WEU's General Secretariat to Brussels, but, at the suggestion of Mitterrand, also included measures to strengthen co-operation between WEU and NATO. At the same time, the upgrading of the Franco-German brigade into an army corps was announced, to 'serve as the core of a European corps, including the forces of other WEU Member States'.

The Netherlands Presidency tabled a final draft on 8 November 1991.[69] This was to be the basis of the remainder of the discussion in the IGC, although there were parallel discussions in NATO—culminating in the Rome Summit of 7–8 November at which the United States recognized the European vocation to a security and defence identity, albeit as a component of a transatlantic security role[70]—and in WEU, chaired by Germany,

[64] Mitterrand had been less than enthusiastic about Kohl's initial proposal that the two of them should take the Concorde to Washington to make a joint pitch to Bush: Favier and Martin-Roland, *La Décennie Mitterrand*, iv. 203.

[65] Védrine, *Les Mondes de François Mitterrand*, 466; Favier and Martin-Roland, *La Décennie Mitterrand*, iv. 206.

[66] Corbett, *The Treaty of Maastricht*, 344–6; Gerbet, de la Serre, and Nafilyan, *L'Union politique de l'Europe*, 313–16.

[67] The last phrase is the significant addition to language otherwise found in the Luxembourg text.

[68] Harmonization of Presidencies; synchronization of sessions and working methods; closer co-operation between Secretariats; creation of a military planning group in WEU.

[69] Corbett, *The Treaty of Maastricht*, 348–74.

[70] 'We believe that the best way, the most effective way of [the Europeans' playing a greater role in their defence] is for there to be a European security identity which is complementary with the Alliance': Secretary Baker, 7 Nov. 1991 (*Atlantic News*, no. 2368 (9 Nov. 1991), 3). For the NAC declaration, see Gerbet, de la Serre, and Nafilyan, *L'Union poli-*

to finalize the text of its own declaration. As far as the CFSP was concerned, the Presidency text followed fairly closely the Luxembourg draft. The final negotiation really began at the 'conclave' at Nordwijk on 12–13 November 1991, at which the Foreign Ministers attempted in windy isolation to prepare the ground for the European Council scheduled for 9–10 December. The CFSP was of course only one of the points which remained undecided, and by no means the most important of them (there were still serious problems over the passage to the third stage of EMU, 'cohesion'— the financial compensation sought by Spain and others—and the Social Chapter). After the Ministers' next meeting, at the Palais d'Egmont in Brussels on 2–3 December 1991, only two items under this heading remained for the Heads of State and Government to deal with: the question of majority voting, to which the United Kingdom remained strictly opposed, and the language to be used in the section on defence—some (the UK, the Netherlands, Denmark, and Portugal) talked of a 'common defence policy', while others (France, Germany, Belgium, Spain, Luxembourg, and Greece) talked of a 'common defence'.[71] Italy hovered between the two, and Ireland took refuge in its neutrality. The question had become a semantic one, especially since the NATO meeting in Rome, but that did not prevent delegations from engaging in passionate debate on the relative merits of the two formulas.

The European Council settled both questions by a form of words which enabled agreement to be reached, but did nothing to resolve the underlying differences of opinion.[72] Qualified majority voting was admitted for the implementation of joint actions, but only if a decision to do so had been reached by unanimity;[73] and in a triumph of Janus-like ingenuity, put forward by the Belgian delegation,[74] it was enacted that 'The common

---

tique de l'Europe, 316–18. Para. 34 of the Rome 'Strategic Concept' states: 'The potential of dialogue and co-operation within all of Europe must be fully developed in order to help to diffuse crises and to prevent conflicts since the Allies' security is inseparably linked to that of all the other states in Europe. To this end, the Allies will support the role of the CSCE process and its institutions. Other bodies including the European Community, Western European Union and United Nations may also have an important role to play': Dorman and Treacher, *European Security*, 166–7. The Italian Foreign Minister De Michelis said that the results of the Rome Summit were 'a good premise for subsequent discussions at Community level in view of the European Council in Maastricht': *Atlantic News*, no. 2368 (9 Nov. 1991), 4.   [71]Doutriaux, *Le Traité sur l'Union européenne*, 93.

[72] For a detailed and well-informed account of the negotiations at Maastricht, see Mazzucelli, *France and Germany at Maastricht*, 174–95.

[73] Spanish responsibility for this 'complex and paralysing' formula (to use Delors' words) was ruefully admitted by Prime Minister Gonzáles: Barbé, 'Spain', 117.

[74] Doutriaux, *Le Traité sur l'Union européenne*, 210; Luif, *On the Road to Brussels*, 42.

foreign and security policy shall include all questions related to the security of the Union, including the eventual framing of a common defence policy, which might in time lead to a common defence'. This was achieved by establishing a sequential relationship between the most that the recalcitrant Member States (the United Kingdom and the Netherlands) could be induced to accept, namely a 'common defence policy', and the least with which the more enthusiastic Member States (France and Germany) could be satisfied, namely a 'common defence'. To borrow a phrase from Wim van Eekelen, the common foreign and security policy had been hustled into existence;[75] there remained the bagatelle of ratifying the Treaty and putting the CFSP into effect.[76]

[75] van Eekelen, *Debating European Security*, 118.
[76] Doutriaux, *Le Traité sur l'Union européenne*, 66–71; de Schoutheete, 'The Creation of the CFSP', 58–61; Cloos *et al.*, *Le Traité de Maastricht*, 90–3; Corbett, *The Treaty of Maastricht*, 47–8.

7

The Treaty on European Union

The Maastricht Treaty was agreed by the European Council in December 1991, but it was to be two months more before the text could be finalized and signed. Inevitably, given the fraught conditions in which the final bargains were struck late on 10 December, there was subsequent disagreement on what the precise terms of the deal had been, and officials argued long and hard over drafting points which concealed real difficulties of substance. These only marginally affected the CFSP, however; just as in the IGC itself foreign policy had not really constituted more than a tactical obstacle to final agreement, so the drafting group did not have to spend too much time on that section in the weeks after Maastricht.

This was perhaps a pity. The section of the Treaty dealing with foreign policy was particularly opaque, and a training in archaeology rather than political science or law would no doubt be of more assistance in its comprehension. The text represented what was left of successive strata of discussion after anything which did not achieve consensus had been cut away. It suffered, unlike the EMU parts of the Treaty, from never having had a clear objective generally agreed, and a single draftsman to interpret that objective. It was not easy to follow the structure of the CFSP provisions of the Maastricht Treaty. One of the tasks of the subsequent Amsterdam IGC was to reorder the articles to make some sort of logical sense.

A result of this was not so much to make the provisions on the CFSP—essentially but not exclusively Title V of the Treaty ('Provisions on a common foreign and security policy')—difficult to understand as almost impossible to track down through the meanderings of the text. The purpose of this chapter is not to give a comprehensive commentary on the text, but to present the main features of the CFSP, culled from the different parts of the Treaty in which they can be found, and to attempt to explain their origins. The features selected are those which mark the principal innovations compared with EPC.

Security and defence

The bitter arguments on security and defence, which continued right up to the end of the IGC negotiations, have tended to conceal the fact that considerable progress had been made in this area since the Single European Act. Then, it was not possible for the Member States to do more than confirm the previously agreed readiness to discuss the political and economic aspects of security, mainly but not exclusively because of the position of neutrality adopted by Ireland. Now, after the end of the Cold War and following the experiences in the Gulf, there was general agreement that the Union's range should extend to all aspects of security, including the military ones. Where there was disagreement was over the way in which the Union's activities in this area should be articulated, and whether there should be a commitment to mutual defence, going so far as a defence guarantee. The reason for this disagreement was differing views about the Union's relationship with the Atlantic Alliance. The problem was quite simply shelved until a future date.

One of the objectives the Union set itself was 'to assert its identity on the international scene, in particular through the implementation of a common foreign and security policy including the eventual framing of a common defence policy, which might in time lead to a common defence' (Article B) [Art. 2][1]. This takes up the wording used in the CFSP section of the Treaty ('The common foreign and security policy shall include all questions related to the security of the Union, including the eventual framing of a common defence policy, which might in time lead to a common defence': Article J.4.1 [Art. 17]), and was deliberately included in the general provisions of the Treaty (the 'chapeau') to emphasize that the CFSP was an integral part of the Union, and not a self-standing pillar. The distinction between 'a common defence policy' and 'a common defence' was not purely semantic, although it came close to this in the closing stages of the IGC; it involves the relationship with NATO, and the question of whether, in time, the Union should assume a defence commitment and thereby become an alliance.[2] Both were aspirations for the future, rather than commitments for the present, but the two are sequential, and the degree of enthusiasm for each differed markedly. A 'common defence

---

[1] The numbers in square brackets refer, where appropriate, to the corresponding articles (sometimes amended) in the numbering of the Consolidated Treaties established following the adoption of the Treaty of Amsterdam.

[2] de Schoutheete, 'The Creation of the CFSP', 59; Cloos *et al.*, *Le Traité de Maastricht*, 471–2.

policy' is something that will definitely be framed—eventually; a 'common defence' *might* in time be the result—but there is no guarantee that that will happen. Perhaps the most interesting implication of the Treaty in this respect was that the Union appeared to deny itself the option of being a civilian power. The aspiration to a defence role, however hedged about, became part of the *acquis*, and as such something that candidate members of the Union are obliged to take on board, regardless of whether or not they are neutrals.

The responsibility for this part of the CFSP was delegated to the WEU: 'The Union requests the Western European Union (WEU), which is an integral part of the development of the Union, to elaborate and implement decisions and actions of the Union which have defence implications. The Council shall, in agreement with the institutions of the WEU, adopt the necessary practical arrangements.' This appears to follow the French view, which caused so much concern to the United States, that WEU should be the defence arm of the Union. There were no provisions, however, specifically enabling the European Council to give directives to WEU, or even to fix general guidelines, so the US fear of a European caucus was allayed. Even the interpretation of the word 'requests' was contested. France maintained that the EU thereby acquired the possibility of making a specific request to the WEU whenever the need arose. The United Kingdom believed that the request had been made, once and for all, in the Maastricht Treaty.[3] Furthermore, 'The policy of the Union in accordance with this Article shall not prejudice the specific character of the security and defence policy of certain Member States and shall respect the obligations of certain Member States under the North Atlantic Treaty and be compatible with the common security and defence policy established within that framework'. Similarly, closer bilateral co-operation was authorized between two or more Member States in the framework of WEU and the Atlantic Alliance (Articles J.4.2, 4, and 5) [Arts. 17.3, 1, and 4].

The way in which WEU organized itself so as to be able to play the role assigned to it was a matter for the members of that organization, not the EU as a whole. Two declarations were made by WEU, and noted by the Intergovernmental Conference (Declaration No. 30).[4] The first declaration concerned the role of the WEU and its relations with the EU and the

---

[3] Dumond and Setton, *La politique étrangère et de sécurité commune*, 113–14.

[4] The declarations attached to the Treaty, unlike the Protocols, do not form an integral part of the Treaty and their status in international law is less secure. They were originally unnumbered; the numbering was added to make reference easier when the Treaty was officially published.

Atlantic Alliance, and explained in more detail the philosophy underlying the defence provisions of the Maastricht Treaty. The first two paragraphs stated:

1. WEU Member States agree on the need to develop a genuine European security and defence identity and a greater European responsibility on defence matters. This identity will be pursued through a gradual process involving successive phases. WEU will form an integral part of the process of the development of the European Union and will enhance its contribution to solidarity within the Atlantic Alliance. WEU Member States agree to strengthen the role of WEU, in the longer term perspective of a common defence policy within the European Union which might in time lead to a common defence, compatible with that of the Atlantic Alliance.

2. WEU will be developed as the defence component of the European Union and as a means to strengthen the European pillar of the Atlantic Alliance. To this end, it will formulate common European defence policy and carry forward its concrete implementation through the further development of its own operational role.

After having noted the provisions of Article J.4 of the TEU [Art. 17], the declaration stated that 'the WEU is prepared, at the request of the European Union, to elaborate and implement decisions and actions of the Union which have defence implications'. To this end, a number of practical measures, largely inspired by the Kohl–Mitterrand letter of 11 October 1991,[5] were announced to develop a close working relationship with the EU:

— as appropriate, synchronization of the dates and venues of meetings and harmonization of working methods;
— establishment of close co-operation between the Council and Secretariat-General of WEU on the one hand, and the Council of the Union and General Secretariat of the Council on the other;
— consideration of the harmonization of the sequence and duration of the respective Presidencies;
— arranging for appropriate modalities so as to ensure that the Commission of the European Communities is regularly informed and, as appropriate, consulted on WEU activities in accordance with the role of the Commission in the common foreign and security policy as defined in the Treaty on European Union;
— encouragement of closer co-operation between the Parliamentary Assembly of WEU and the European Parliament.

[5] The provisions regarding the Commission had not appeared in the Kohl–Mitterrand text: Corbett, *The Treaty of Maastricht*, 345–6.

Whereas WEU's objective in relation to the EU was to become its defence component, its objective in relation to the Atlantic Alliance was 'to develop WEU as a means to strengthen the European pillar' of the Alliance. Closer working links were therefore to be developed, and the role of WEU Member States in the Alliance to be strengthened, 'on the basis of the necessary transparency and complementarity between the emerging European security and defence identity and the Alliance. WEU will act in conformity with the positions adopted in the Atlantic Alliance'. 'WEU Member States will intensify their co-ordination on Alliance issues which represent an important common interest with the aim of introducing joint positions agreed in WEU into the process of consultation in the Alliance which will remain the essential forum for consultation among its members and the venue for agreement on policies bearing on the security and defence commitments of Allies under the North Atlantic Treaty.' In other words, WEU—not the EU—was allowed to be a caucus but within strictly defined limits.

Several administrative arrangements were announced for co-operation between the EU and NATO, rather similar to those between WEU and the EU, as well as some improvements in WEU's operational capability, including the setting up of a planning cell. It was decided that the seat of the WEU Council and Secretariat should be transferred to Brussels.

Conforming to General Scowcroft's preference, WEU was more a hinge than an instrument of the EU. In fact it served a double role, that of defence component of the EU and European pillar of the Alliance. The question of enlarging the membership of WEU therefore arose. Hitherto it had been composed, almost by accident, of all the members of the Community except those which for one reason or another had no wish to take part in enhanced security activities. Such a limited membership now seemed rather odd, given that all Member States had signed up to the Maastricht Treaty. In a second declaration, therefore, WEU held out the possibility of enlarged membership according to different formulas:

States which are members of the European Union are invited to accede to WEU . . . or to become observers if they so wish. Simultaneously, other European member States of NATO are invited to become associate members of WEU in a way which will give them the possibility of participating fully in the activities of WEU.

This was a significant change in policy, and one that was hotly debated within the WEU in the run-up to the Maastricht Treaty.[6] Previously,

---

[6] van Eekelen, *Debating European Security*, 114–17.

membership had been offered to Member States of the Community who so wished (the 'Cahen doctrine').[7] Thus, although WEU membership was not coterminous with membership of the Community, it remained within the Community perimeter. Now, a status which was practically as good as membership (and better than that of observer, which was offered to EC members like neutral Ireland) was available to members of NATO which were not members of the Union. WEU membership had gone outside the perimeter of the Union. Only on paper was this compatible with the WEU's role as an instrument of the EU, and it was a good indication that the Atlanticists, led by the United Kingdom, had had the best of it in the IGC.

The integrationists were however determined to fight again another day. The provisions of Article J.4 [Art. 17] were to be reviewed on the basis of a report to be presented to the European Council in 1996, bearing in mind that from 1998 it would, by the terms of the Brussels Treaty, become possible for WEU Member States to announce their withdrawal from that organization (Article J.4.6) [Art. 17.5]. The WEU undertook in its declaration to mount a similar review, taking account of 'the progress and experience acquired and [extending] to relations between WEU and the Atlantic Alliance' (Declaration No. 30, I).

Consistency

The decision not to incorporate the CFSP into the Community framework was made more palatable to the integrationists by the inclusion of a reference to it in the general introductory provisions to the Treaty as a whole.[8] This furnished the columns of the Greek temple with an appropriate pediment, and provided the legal basis for the 'single institutional framework' which had been accepted for all three pillars of the Union structure. The problem of 'consistency' naturally remained: if there were still to be two modes of foreign-policy making, the question of how to ensure cohesion

---

[7] Remacle, *L'UEO*, 35; Franck, 'Belgium', 155. It is not certain that the 'Cahen doctrine' did not also apply to members of NATO (van Eekelen, *Debating European Security*, 14). Since the doctrine was never formally adopted, the question is unlikely to be settled. Different parties may have had different interpretations, and indeed the same parties may have had different interpretations depending on their interlocutors. On the occasions on which the author heard Ambassador Cahen speak on the subject, the possibility of enlargement referred exclusively to members of the EC.

[8] Art. B [Art. 2] quoted above, and Art. D [Art. 4], which confirms the European Council as a body defining the general political guidelines of the Union as a whole.

between them had to be addressed. This was done in two ways: by the very fact of the new institutional arrangements which were introduced, and by specific requirements laid down to ensure consistency.

The general obligation was expressed in Article C [Art. 3]:

The Union shall be served by a single institutional framework which shall ensure the consistency and continuity of the activities carried out in order to attain its objectives while respecting and building upon the *acquis communautaire*.

The Union shall in particular ensure the consistency of its external activities as a whole in the context of its external relations, security, economic and develop-ment policies. The Council and the Commission shall be responsible for ensur-ing such consistency. They shall ensure the implementation of these policies, each in accordance with its respective powers.

This provision was on the face of it inconsistent with Article J.8.2 [Art. 13.3], which provided that 'The Council shall ... ensure the unity, con-sistency and effectiveness of action by the Union', where the role of the Commission is not mentioned. It may be argued that this is because the context is concerned exclusively with the functions of the Council, but the Commission's role is not mentioned in the article devoted to that either (Article J.9) [Art. 27].

Furthermore, Article C differed from the corresponding article in the Single European Act[9] in that the responsibility for ensuring consistency was assigned, not to the Presidency and the Commission, but to the Council and the Commission. The negotiators of the SEA deliberately chose the Presidency in preference to the Council because they wanted to create an operational responsibility, and believed that the Council was too diffuse a body adequately to shoulder such a responsibility. The effect of the change in the TEU, presumably not deliberate, was to transform an obligation of ensuring compliance into one of merely observing it.

The introduction of a single institutional framework had the effect of abolishing the old Ministerial Meetings of EPC and substituting in prac-tice the General Affairs Council (Foreign Ministers) as the sole decision-making body (at Ministerial level) for all matters concerning foreign affairs.[10] This was not stated in so many words, but can be deduced from the economy of Title V, and in particular Article J.11.1 [Art. 28.1]. This article reads: 'The provisions referred to in Articles 137, 138, 139 to 142,

---

[9]   Nuttall, *European Political Co-operation*, 254–5.
[10]   With the exception of development questions, which remained with the Development Council, and the new provisions for the external relations of EMU, for which Ecofin was responsible.

146, 147, 150 to 153, 157 to 163 and 217 of the Treaty establishing the European Community shall apply to the provisions relating to the areas referred to in this Title'. Articles 146, 147, and 150 to 153 [Arts. 203, 204, and 206 to 209 EC] govern the functioning of the Council.

Contrary to suggestions made in some of the previous drafts, the single institutional framework did not penetrate lower than the Ministerial level. The decision on the respective roles of the Political Committee and Coreper was put off until a later date, as was, implicitly, the question of whether and how the EPC and Council Working Groups should be merged. Declaration No. 28 read: 'The Conference agrees that the division of work between the Political Committee and the Committee of Permanent Representatives will be examined at a later stage, as will the practical arrangements for merging the Political Co-operation Secretariat with the General Secretariat of the Council and for co-operation between the latter and the Commission'. The problem was whether the Political Committee or Coreper should have the last word on a CFSP dossier before it was submitted to the Council. The text of the Treaty gave support to both theses. On the one hand, Article J.8.5 [Art. 25] provided that 'Without prejudice to Article 151 of the Treaty establishing the European Community, a Political Committee consisting of Political Directors shall monitor the international situation in the areas covered by common foreign and security policy and contribute to the definition of policies by delivering opinions to the Council at the request of the Council or on its own initiative'. On the other hand, the specific reference to Article 151 [Art. 207 EC], which provides, in the version amended by the TEU, that 'A committee consisting of the Permanent Representatives of the Member States shall be responsible for preparing the work of the Council and for carrying out the tasks assigned to it by the Council', suggested that the role of Coreper extended also to CFSP matters. The Political Committee's access to Foreign Ministers was no longer exclusive.

On the other hand, the merger of the EPC Secretariat with the General Secretariat of the Council was decided by the TEU. This results, not only from Declaration No. 28 quoted above, but also from Article 151, which went on to state in its second sub-paragraph: 'The Council shall be assisted by a General Secretariat, under the direction of a Secretary-General'. Article 151 applied to the CFSP by virtue of Article J.11 [Art. 28] quoted above.

The attempt made in the first Netherlands Presidency draft to secure at least partial oversight of the activities of CFSP by the European Court of Justice failed. This results from Article L [Art. 46], in which Article J (governing the CFSP) is excluded from the provisions to which the powers of the Court shall apply. It can be argued, however, that were a dispute to arise as to whether an action by the Union under Article J, including the use of the Community budget, affected the EC Treaty contrary to the provisions of Article M [Art. 47], then the Court could be called upon to decide (Article L (c)) [Art. 46 (e)].

Common positions and joint actions

The Treaty introduced two new instruments of action for the CFSP: common positions and joint actions. These were meant to be qualitatively superior to what had existed in EPC, but the failure to agree on a limited, operational list of important interests in common, and on qualified majority voting, left them empty shells.

The TEU established two modes of pursuing the objectives of the CFSP: (1) by establishing systematic co-operation between Member States in the conduct of policy (Article J.2) [Art. 16], leading when appropriate to common positions, and (2) by gradually implementing (Article J.3) [Art. 14] joint action in the areas in which the Member States have important interests in common (Article J.1.3) [Art. 13.2].

Articles J.2.1 and J.2.2, first subparagraph, provide that 'Member States shall inform and consult one another within the Council on any matter of foreign and security policy of general interest in order to ensure that their combined influence is exerted as effectively as possible by means of concerted and convergent action', and that 'Whenever it deems it necessary, the Council shall define a common position'. No further details were given about common positions, which led to difficulties in implementation.

As for all matters concerning the CFSP, except for procedural questions[11] and some aspects of joint actions, decisions under this heading are taken unanimously (Article J.8.2, second subparagraph). Member States are enjoined, but not constrained, to abstain in order to facilitate consensus. Declaration No. 27 on voting in the field of the common foreign and security policy stated: 'The Conference agrees that, with regard to Council de-

---

[11] It was not clear how procedural questions were to be decided in the CFSP. By analogy with the Community, it should be by simple majority, but Art. 148.1 of the EC Treaty [Art. 205.1 EC], which contains this provision, was not among those EC articles which applied to Title V of the TEU (Art. J.11) [Art. 28.1]. The question was settled, in favour of a simple majority of members, by the Amsterdam Treaty [Art. 23.3].

cisions requiring unanimity, Member States will, to the extent possible, avoid preventing a unanimous decision where a qualified majority exists in favour of that decision'. Some Member States wanted this proviso to be in the Treaty, but the United Kingdom and its supporters would only agree on condition that it was relegated to a Declaration, and therefore non-binding.[12]

The conditions for the adoption of joint actions were set out in Article J.3, and will be discussed later.

The institution of the mode of operation described as 'joint action' derived from the idea that the common foreign and security policy had to differ qualitatively from what had been done in Political Co-operation.[13] From the beginning of the debate the presumption had been that a number of topics representing important interests which the Member States had in common would be selected and that in those areas there would be provision for a more effective policy, with its own decision-making procedures, at Union level. Proposals on these lines were found, for instance, in the Italian paper of February, the Commission draft of March, and the first Netherlands draft of September 1991, demonstrating the integrationist origin of the idea. A reflection of this can be found in the proposal, contained in the Luxembourg Presidency non-paper of April, to introduce 'joint action in all areas where the Member States have essential interests in common'.[14]

The interest of the concept of a 'joint action' depends on three conditions: the parallel existence of other types of activity, less qualitatively advanced; agreement on the areas of essential common interest; and a qualitatively different decision-making procedure. The IGC created a category of 'joint actions', but respected none of these conditions.

The parallel existence of other types of activity would have been ensured if 'joint actions' had been superimposed on the existing activities of EPC, for it is only by comparison that qualitative difference can be perceived. This would have required the continuation in force of the provisions of Title III of the SEA (governing EPC), which is precisely what the Italian and Netherlands drafts proposed. The IGC chose instead to repeal that Title (Article P.2) [Art. 50.2]. In its place there came the general faculty for

---

[12] Buchan, *Europe*, 46.

[13] The terminology 'joint action' had been used in previous EPC texts (see, for example, Art. 30.1 of the SEA), but with a different connotation from that which prevailed in the Maastricht debate.

[14] Corbett, *The Treaty of Maastricht*, 283. For a discussion of the characteristics of common positions and joint actions, see Cloos *et al.*, *Le Traité de Maastricht*, 476–9.

information and consultation and the new category of activity of 'common positions' described above. This did not merely replace the old EPC activity, it added a new form of activity, common positions, itself designed to be qualitatively superior. The problem, astounding for a legal text, was that no definitions were provided for any of these terms. When it came to implementing the Treaty, this led to interminable discussions about what precisely common positions and joint actions were, and what activities could be assigned to each category. The idea of the joint action as something qualitatively different was lost.

As late as the Kohl–Mitterrand letter of October 1991 the inclusion in the Treaty of a list of essential interests in common, first discussed at Asolo the previous autumn, was still under active consideration. For example, the Franco-German draft suggested political and economic relations and co-operation with the Soviet Union; political and economic relations and co-operation with the countries of Central and Eastern Europe; the CSCE process, including the implementation of the results of the Paris CSCE Summit of November 1990; relations with the United States of America and Canada on the basis of joint declarations of November 1990; political and economic relations with the Mediterranean region and with the Middle East; policy and co-operation within the United Nations and other international organizations; participation in humanitarian measures; and, on the security side, disarmament policy and arms control in Europe, including: confidence-building measures; participation in peace-keeping measures, especially within the framework of the United Nations; nuclear non-proliferation; and the economic aspects of security, i.e. co-operation regarding arms exports and the control of arms exports.[15] In the end, it proved to be too difficult to reach agreement on a list, and it was left to the European Council to issue general guidelines for joint action as and when (Article J.3.1). The European Council had a first bite at the cherry at its meeting at Lisbon in June 1992, when it approved a report by Foreign Ministers on the subject. It followed this up at its special meeting at Brussels on 29 October 1993, immediately before the entry into force of the TEU, when it issued a list of priority areas for joint action, defined as: the promotion of stability and peace in Europe; the Middle East; South Africa; the former Yugoslavia; and Russia.[16]

An attempt was made to provide joint actions with a qualitatively different decision-making procedure, but this essentially failed. The operative paragraphs of Article J.3 read:

[15] Corbett, *The Treaty of Maastricht*, 345.
[16] *Bull. EC*, June 1992, 1.31; *Bull. EC*, Oct. 1993, 1.4.

1. The Council shall decide, on the basis of general guidelines from the European Council, that a matter should be the subject of joint action.

Whenever the Council decides on the principle of joint action, it shall lay down the specific scope, the Union's general and specific objectives in carrying out such action, if necessary its duration, and the means, procedures and conditions for its implementation.[17]

2. The Council shall, when adopting the joint action and at any stage during its development, define those matters on which decisions are to be taken by a qualified majority.

Where the Council is required to act by a qualified majority pursuant to the preceding subparagraph, the votes of its members shall be weighted in accordance with Article 148(2) of the Treaty establishing the European Community, and for their adoption, acts of the Council shall require at least 62 votes in favour, cast by at least 10 members.[18]

This tortuous construction, whereby the Council first determined by unanimity those aspects regarding the implementation of a joint action which may subsequently be decided by qualified majority, was forced upon the IGC by the rocklike determination of in particular the United Kingdom to exclude any danger of being put in a minority in the CFSP. It gave only verbal satisfaction to those who wanted a more dynamic policy, and the procedure has never been used.[19] It does not provide a qualitative advance on the practices of EPC. It has been mercilessly deflated in Delors' compelling parody of the decision-making process as applied to an EU meeting with the East European countries:

First we would have to decide, unanimously, whether the meeting was to be in Warsaw, Budapest or Prague. Then we would have to agree whether we were going by plane. Lunch? We would need an opt-out for vegetarians. No doubt, we could use majority voting to decide where the smoking and non-smoking sections should be.[20]

The absence of effective qualified majority voting was, however, not the only feature which impaired the effectiveness of joint actions. Although lacking a legal definition, a joint action may be presumed to be specific and to concern something which is to be done. In this it differs from the

---

[17] In practice these requirements have not been regularly observed.

[18] The numbers given here are those resulting from the amendment to the TEU to take account of enlargement to include Austria, Sweden, and Finland. The requirement for at least 10 members to vote in favour is the normal EC provision in the absence of a proposal from the Commission: Art. 148.2 of the EC Treaty [Art. 205.2 EC].

[19] The joint action on anti-personnel landmines provided for implementation by qualified majority voting, but it was never necessary to have recourse to this: Ginsberg, 'The EU's CFSP', 21; OJ L115 1–3, Art. 6.3.   [20] Buchan, *Europe*, 46.

concerted viewpoints familiar from EPC. Unlike viewpoints, which can arise from discussion and be collectively drafted, actions need to be proposed by a body designated for that purpose. In the case of the CFSP, the right of initiative is shared by the Member States and the Commission. Article J.8.3 [Art. 22.1] provided that 'Any Member State or the Commission may refer to the Council any question relating to the common foreign and security policy and may submit proposals to the Council'. A shared right of initiative is very different from the exclusive right of initiative enjoyed by the Commission in the Community system. It is not just a question, as the vulgar interpretation has it, of where the power lies, nor is it even of the Commission's representing the Community interest, which is beyond the power of even the most well-intentioned Member States. It is that an exclusive right of initiative encourages the construction of an active rather than a reactive agenda, and above all pinpoints the responsibility for proposing action. When responsibility is shared by all, the danger is that it will be exercised by none. The proposal contained in the Commission's draft of February 1991, that the right of initiative should lie with the Presidency, the Commission, or a simple majority of Member States, reflected this analysis, although it was politically a non-starter. In practice, the responsibility has lain with the Presidency, with the difficulties of lack of continuity and uneven levels of resources caused by the system of rotation. Throughout the CFSP debate the Member States in general failed to apprehend the link in the Community system between majority voting and the exclusive right of initiative.[21]

Subsidiarity and commitment

The CFSP is a common policy, not a single policy. The Union's competence is not exclusive; Member States retain their own foreign policies. The question therefore arises to what extent and under what circumstances these national foreign policies and the CFSP may differ. Although the Treaty included exhortations to discipline and observance of the common line, no effective provision was made for policing these. Inevitably, therefore, discipline was sporadic.

Like all the sections of the Maastricht Treaty, the CFSP is subject to the principle of subsidiarity. Article B, second subparagraph [Art. 2], provided

[21] For the function, in the context of the CFSP, of the exclusive right of initiative in preserving the Community legal order, democratic control, and the interests of smaller states, see Dankert, 'Challenges and Priorities', 9–10.

that 'The objectives of the Union shall be achieved as provided in this Treaty and in accordance with the conditions and the timetable set out therein while respecting the principle of subsidiarity as defined in Article 3b[22] of the Treaty establishing the European Community'. The Treaty made, however, additional provision for cohesion with regard to the CFSP, combined with limited exceptions in specific circumstances.

A general exhortation to cohesion was contained in Article J.1.4 [Art. 11.2]: 'The Member States shall support the Union's external and security policy actively and unreservedly in a spirit of loyalty and mutual solidarity. They shall refrain from any action which is contrary to the interests of the Union or likely to impair its effectiveness as a cohesive force in international relations. The Council shall ensure that these principles are complied with'.

There was a specific obligation in the case of common positions (Article J.2.2, second subparagraph) [Art. 15]: 'Member States shall ensure that their national policies conform to the common positions'. The obligation in the case of joint actions was formulated differently again (Article J.3.4) [Art. 14.3]: 'Joint actions shall commit the Member States in the positions they adopt and in the conduct of their activity'.

An interesting comparison can be made with the corresponding text in the Single European Act, Article 30.2(c) of which provided that 'In adopting its positions and in its national measures each High Contracting Party shall take full account of the positions of the other partners and shall give due consideration to the desirability of adopting and implementing common European positions . . . the determination of common positions shall constitute a point of reference for the policies of the High Contracting Parties'.

The Maastricht texts were on the face of it more constraining than the SEA, although one may speculate that the latter was closer to the reality. That is indeed the problem; if there are no provisions for enforcement, then the more realistic wording is likely to be the more credible. Compliance with the principles referred to in Article J.1.4 was to be ensured by the Council, that is by its members collectively; but what band of poachers makes an effective gamekeeper, given that each one individually may some day have need to resort to poaching?

---

[22] The relevant provisions of Art. 3b [Art. 5 EC] read: 'In areas which do not fall within its exclusive competence, the Community shall take action, in accordance with the principle of subsidiarity, only if and in so far as the objectives of the proposed action cannot be sufficiently achieved by the Member States and can therefore, by reason of the scale or effects of the proposed action, be better achieved by the Community'.

Two derogations were provided for. One, discussed in the section on security and defence, reserved the position with regard to obligations under NATO; the other provided a procedure in case of difficulty over a joint action: 'Should there be any major difficulties in implementing a joint action, a Member State shall refer them to the Council which shall discuss them and seek appropriate solutions. Such solutions shall not run counter to the objectives of the joint action or impair its effectiveness'.

The provisions on subsidiarity and commitment contained in a nutshell the essential flaw in the structure of the CFSP. By wishing to maintain simultaneously an effective EU foreign and security policy and unrestricted national foreign policies, the Member States secured for themselves the worst of both worlds. Had there been agreement to reserve a limited number of issues exclusively to the EU level; had there been agreement to deal at the EU level only with topics, or only in a way, which did not overlap with national policies; had there been agreement to construct an EU CFSP on its own merits, with no obligation to mirror it at the national level—then in none of these cases would serious difficulties have arisen. What Member States did, however, was to lock their national policies on paper into a common European policy, with minimal chances of escape. Since real life declined to abide by the paper commitments, the CFSP fell into disrepute.

Representation and implementation

In a further example of the problems presented by consistency, the arrangements for representation and implementation of the CFSP left important questions of responsibility undecided.

Article J.5.1 [Art. 18.1] provided that 'The Presidency shall represent the Union in matters coming within the common foreign and security policy'. In this task the Presidency 'shall be assisted if need be by the previous and next Member States to hold the Presidency. The Commission shall be fully associated' (Article J.5.2) [Art. 18.4]. The Treaty was clear, but not sufficiently so. What happens when an activity combines CFSP elements, and EC elements in respect of which the Community would normally be represented by the Commission? It can be argued that the political element provided by the CFSP confers primacy on the Presidency. Against that, however, may be adduced the provision of Article M [Art. 47], whereby 'nothing in this Treaty shall affect the Treaties establishing the European Communities or the subsequent Treaties and Acts modifying or supplementing them'. In other words, in case of discrepancies, Paris and Rome prevail over Maastricht. In practice, *ad hoc* solutions are sought, sometimes with considerable acrimony.

The same observations apply to implementation. Article J.5.2 [Art. 18.2] provided that 'The Presidency shall be responsible for the implementation of common measures[23]; in that capacity it shall in principle express the position of the Union in international organizations and international conferences'. Here again, the Presidency is responsible, but pragmatic solutions have to be found.

The situation is complicated in that it appears from provisions elsewhere in the text that the Presidency was not alone in its responsibility for implementing at any rate joint actions. Member States must be presumed to do so too: see Article J.3.5 [Art. 14.5] ('Whenever there is any plan to adopt a national position or take national action *pursuant to a joint action . . .*') and Article J.3.7 [Art. 14.7] ('Should there be any major difficulties in *implementing a joint action*, a Member State shall refer them to the Council'). In practice, decisions on implementation have been taken, after collective discussion, having regard to the characteristics of the case.

The most important question regarding implementation of the CFSP was that of finance. Article J.11.2 provided that

Administrative expenditure which the provisions relating to the areas referred to in this Title entail for the institutions shall be charged to the budget of the European Communities.

The Council may also:

— either decide unanimously that operational expenditure to which the implementation of those provisions gives rise is to be charged to the budget of the European Communities; in that event, the budgetary procedure laid down in the Treaty establishing the European Community shall be applicable;

— or determine that such expenditure shall be charged to the Member States, where appropriate in accordance with a scale to be decided.

These provisions put an end to the convoluted system of finance under which EPC operated,[24] and were innocently believed to be a neutral and objective way of describing the different modes of finance available. They turned out to be some of the more contentious ones in the Maastricht Treaty.

[23] These 'common measures' are a mystery. They do not appear elsewhere in Title V. Can 'common measures' refer to all CFSP activities? Or is it a mistranslation of 'joint actions'? In the French-language version there is no difference between the two ('actions communes').

[24] Nuttall, *European Political Co-operation*, 258.

Foreign policy provisions outside Title V

In addition to the CFSP provisions in Title I (common provisions) and Title V, the Maastricht Treaty legislated for other important areas of foreign policy. New sectors, like culture, the environment, and development co-operation, were for the first time given a solid legal base, and each had provision for the conduct of international relations.[25] In addition to some changes in EC external relations, Pillar III (Justice and Home Affairs) and EMU were provided with particularly elaborate procedures for the conduct of international relations. CFSP was directly concerned, however, only with the imposition of sanctions.

A specific procedure for the imposition of economic sanctions was introduced, replacing, but modelled on, the EPC practice. Article 228a of the EC Treaty [Art. 301 EC] stipulated that 'Where it is provided, in a common position or in a joint action adopted according to the provisions of the Treaty on European Union relating to the common foreign and security policy, for an action by the Community to interrupt or to reduce, in part or completely, economic relations with one or more third countries, the Council shall take the necessary urgent measures. The Council shall act by a qualified majority on a proposal from the Commission.'

The new article precisely reflected the practice which had grown up over the years through the experience acquired with, successively, the Soviet Union (imposition of martial law in Poland), Argentina (the Falkland Islands), South Africa (apartheid), and Iraq and Kuwait. Following consensus in EPC, sanctions were imposed by Council Regulation, which could in theory, as a trade policy measure, be adopted by a qualified majority. The requirement for a unanimous decision to adopt the common position or joint action (it is unlikely that the joint-action majority-voting provisions could apply in this case) made the Article 228a provision for qualified majority voting singularly devoid of content. The fact that the Commission retained its right of initiative was nevertheless important.

Corresponding provisions were made in the part of the Treaty dealing with EMU. Article 73g.1 [Art. 60.1 EC] stipulated: 'If, in the cases envisaged in Article 228a, action by the Community is deemed necessary, the Council may, in accordance with the procedure provided for in Article 228a, take the necessary urgent measures on the investment of capital and on payments as regards the third countries concerned'. The Council

---

[25] See, for example, Arts. 128.3, 130r.4, and 130y of the EC Treaty [Arts. 151.3, 174.4, and 181 EC]: Doutriaux, *Le Traité sur l Union européenne*, 130–2.

concerned is not the General Affairs Council, but Ecofin. This results from Declaration No. 3, which stipulates that for provisions on capital and payments, which include the sanctions provisions of Article 73g, the Council meets in the composition of Economic and Finance Ministers. One might argue that the common positions and joint actions referred to in Article 228a are the property of the Foreign Ministers, but this has to be deduced from practice rather than from any text attached to the Treaty.

8

Ratification

The Treaty on European Union had been signed; now it had to be ratified. This was expected to be a formality, with national parliamentary procedures concluded in time for the Treaty to come into force at the same time as the introduction of the Single Market on 1 January 1993. At first, all went well. There was a general absence of public debate and enquiry outside specialized circles, which had become traditional in European constitutional legislation. The situation changed after the Danish electorate rejected the Treaty in a referendum held on 2 June 1992, followed two months later by a wafer-thin majority in a referendum which President Mitterrand called in France. Overnight, the very principles of European integration were brought into question.

These developments coincided with the worsening of the situation in Yugoslavia. International attention had been concentrated on that country since June 1991. The European Community had been the first to enter the diplomatic fray, with six months still to run before the IGC was due to draw to a close. It might be supposed that the events in Yugoslavia, and the Community's efforts to bring order to a troubled and dangerous situation, would have a deep impact on the course of the debate on the Community's incipient common foreign and security policy. In fact, the reverse was the case. By June 1991, the shape of the CFSP had been pretty well determined by the draft treaty which the Presidency had laid before the European Council in Luxembourg. The remaining points at issue—the position of the CFSP in the Community legal order, the question of majority voting, and the Community's security and defence personality—were not affected by what happened in Yugoslavia. Indeed, the reverse occurred: it was the Community's policy towards Yugoslavia which was affected, some would say adversely, by the positions of principle adopted by some Member States, especially the United Kingdom and France, in the discussions in the IGC. The influence of Yugoslavia was seen at a later stage, when public disillusionment about the Community's failure to achieve a peaceful solution to the conflict contributed to the climate of moroseness which made the ultimate ratification of the Maastricht Treaty so difficult.

Yugoslavia

The headline-catching response of the European Council on 28 June 1991 to the declarations of independence by Slovenia and Croatia a few days earlier has given rise to the impression that the Community was taken by surprise by these events. The failure to forecast them, it is said, can be attributed to EPC's lack of intelligence-gathering capabilities. This was not the case. There had been plenty of predictions of the violent break-up of Yugoslavia, which cannot have escaped the attention of the Member States.[1] The Community had been expecting the worst since at least the previous autumn, and had been engaged in diplomatic activity in an effort to prevent the collapse of the Federation. On 4 February 1991, the Community had made representations to the federal and republic author-ities 'stressing their commitment to the evolution of Yugoslav society towards a democratic settlement acceptable to the whole of Yugoslavia, in line with the Paris Charter'. The hope was that the dialogue between the parties in Yugoslavia 'would lead to constitutional arrangements which would ensure the establishment of a new Yugoslavia based on the prin-ciples of freedom and democracy'.[2] This line reflected the consensus of the Member States. Even Germany at this stage was still urging the Republics which wished to secede to look for arrangements which would keep the Federation together.[3]

An EPC statement of 26 March 1991, on which the Troika drew in its meeting with the Yugoslav authorities on 4 April, encouraged 'the efforts under way to resolve the constitutional crisis in the country by way of dia-logue', and gave a broad hint that the process of reform based on political dialogue would 'enable the full development of the co-operation which already exists between the Community and the Federal authorities. In the view of the Twelve, a united and democratic Yugoslavia stands the best chance to integrate itself in the new Europe'.[4] The point was reinforced a few days later by Jacques Poos, the President of the Council: Yugoslavia 'could have expectations with respect of its association with the Commun-ity if its territorial unity and integrity are safeguarded. Any other attitude could jeopardize internal frontiers in Europe.'[5] This was a sizeable carrot, albeit unaccompanied by any stick; Yugoslavia was currently under con-

---

[1] Maull, 'Germany in the Yugoslav Crisis', 100, 127 n. 2; Gow, *Triumph of the Lack of Will*, 204. [2] *EPC Documentation Bulletin*, 1991(7), 91/083.

[3] Genscher, *Erinnerungen*, 931; Gow, *Triumph of the Lack of Will*, 167.

[4] *Bull. EC*, Mar. 1991, 1.4.6; *EPC Documentation Bulletin*, 7 (1991), 91/114, 91/122.

[5] Edwards, 'European Responses to the Yugoslav Crisis', 168.

sideration for an Association Agreement of the kind then being negotiated with some of the Central and East European countries, and the Third Financial Protocol was due to be agreed.[6] The Community's inbuilt distaste for the dismantling of any federation, especially at a time when it would set a bad example to the decaying Soviet Union, was reinforced by the fact that it was the Federal Yugoslav Prime Minister, Ante Marković, who had launched a programme of economic liberalization and democratic reform.[7] Indeed, Marković had counted on American and EC support for his reform programme to counter the fissiparous tendencies of his country, and was disappointed that support, although not requested until December 1990, had come too late and with too many conditions attached.[8] Ironically, the Slovenians felt that their aspirations to join European organizations could not be fulfilled as long as they were held captive in Yugoslavia, and the confederal models put forward by Slovenia and Croatia were in part patterned on the EC.[9]

The Third Financial Protocol was finally initialled on 3 April 1991, despite the continued uncertainty about the political and economic situation. It provided for a total of 730 million ECU in European Investment Bank loans over a period of five years, with a possible additional 77 million ECU from the EC Budget for an interest-rate subsidy for loans for transport infrastructure.[10] On 29–30 May 1991 the President of the European Council, Jacques Santer, and the President of the Commission, Jacques Delors, made a joint official visit to Yugoslavia to impress on both the federal and the republic authorities that the EC's continued support depended on a settlement of the country's problems in the manner indicated in the EC's statements.[11] It can be argued that the visit came too late for warnings, even at the highest political level, to have much effect. Delors had in fact been pressed by his staff to make the visit the previous autumn, but had hesitated, not wanting the Commission to take too high a political profile in the circumstances of the time. The Commission had submitted its formal opinion on the forthcoming IGC in October 1990,

---

[6] Lukic and Lynch, *Europe from the Balkans to the Urals*, 262.

[7] Chenu, 'Les Hommes en blanc', 85.

[8] Lukic and Lynch, *Europe from the Balkans to the Urals*, 183; Crnobrnja, *The Yugoslav Drama*, 149–50.

[9] Lukic and Lynch, *Europe from the Balkans to the Urals*, 18, 169–70.

[10] *Bull. EC*, Apr. 1991, 1.3.27.

[11] van Eekelen, *Debating European Security*, 141; Woodward, *Balkan Tragedy*, 160; Ross, *Jacques Delors and European Integration*, 168 and 292 n. 5; Grant, *Delors*, 191. For written confirmation of the message passed during the visit, see Santer's subsequent letter to the Yugoslav Prime Minister: *EUROPE*, 5510 (12 June 1991), 5.

and its 'contribution' on the development of an external relations policy of the Union, which was to cause such trouble, was tabled in March 1991. It can be imagined that this inhibited the Commission from getting too far in front of the Member States on such a delicate issue.

The Community therefore had a policy towards Yugoslavia, which relied on the overwhelming need for European support felt by both the federal authorities and the would-be breakaway republics of Slovenia and Croatia. Furthermore, it was the only policy which could reasonably have been followed in the circumstances, and it was in line with the positions of the United States and the CSCE.[12] It is all very well with hindsight to say that the Community should have foreseen the bloodbath to come and acted accordingly, but to build into policy the possibility of a bloodbath would have run the risk of encouraging the developments it was designed to forestall. Furthermore, it was important to maintain consistency with the policy applied to other countries of Central and Eastern Europe at the time, of support for pluralist democracy and moves towards a market economy. President Tudjman of Croatia complained in April 1991 'that the West talks only of the need for democracy and a free market in Yugoslavia, and ignores the national question'.[13] To act otherwise would have been irresponsible: stability in the CEECs was more important to the Community than stability in Yugoslavia.

At their 'conclave' on 24 June in Luxembourg, the Foreign Ministers agreed that the Twelve would not acknowledge any unilateral declarations of independence by Croatia and Slovenia, as 'a unilateral act could not bring any solution'. Furthermore they would refuse any contact with secessionists. As a counterpart, the Community offered to help with drawing up a democratic constitution, and with economic restructuring.[14] The next day, the Assembly of the Republic of Slovenia and the Sabor of the Republic of Croatia adopted declarations establishing sovereign and independent republics, and the federal forces responded by securing ostentatiously the external borders of Yugoslavia.[15] The European Council, which met on 28–9 June 1991, was forced into the position of responding to the new

[12] Ramelot and Remacle, *L'OSCE et les conflits en Europe*, 72.

[13] Edwards, 'European Responses to the Yugoslav Crisis', 165. In return, the Yugoslavs seemed to the Western Europeans to be ignoring economics. When asked at the end of his visit to Yugoslavia in May what his strongest impression had been, Delors told the Yugoslav Ambassador to the EC that it was the lack of interest in the economic aspects of the situation and the overriding importance given to the symbols of nationalism: Crnobrnja, *The Yugoslav Drama*, 272 n. 1.

[14] Edwards, 'European Responses to the Yugoslav Crisis', 169; *EUROPE*, 5519 (24–5 June 1991), 4–5.　　　　[15] Trifunovska, *Yugoslavia through Documents*, 286–304.

situation with no time for measured assessment and preparation by the habitual EPC machinery. It chose to adopt an activist line to enforce the policy of support for the federal institutions of Yugoslavia which was already in force. The Troika of Foreign Ministers was dispatched to Belgrade *séance tenante* and returned in triumph before the close of the session, thus enabling the Presidency to declare that the European Council had 'heard a report from the ministerial Troika on its return from Belgrade and Zagreb, and expressed satisfaction at the results of this mission'. It was nevertheless prudent enough to add that it remained 'concerned about the situation in [Yugoslavia] and requests the relevant organs of European co-operation to remain seized of this situation and follow developments closely'.[16] This prudence was not misplaced, as the Troika was obliged to resume its mission the next day.

In sending the Troika to negotiate a cease-fire, the European Council established a pattern of active intervention in the affairs of Yugoslavia, setting the norm for the international community which has persisted to this day. Why did it choose to go down this road? The most common explanation is that the Heads of State or Government wanted to compensate for the failure of the Community in the Gulf crisis, prove by demonstration that an active common foreign and security policy was a real possibility, and thus mask the failure, precisely at the Luxembourg meeting, to agree on the final shape of the Treaty on European Union. The fact that the Luxembourg European Council coincided with the outbreak of fighting was the proximate cause of precipitate action by the Heads of State and Government, which led to far-reaching, unforeseen, and disastrous consequences.[17]

Certainly, this theory is given credence by the declaration of the President of the European Council, Jacques Santer, that the action taken added up to 'a common foreign and security policy even before . . . [it] had found its way into the future treaty on the Union'.[18] The reality is likely to have been more subtle and more confused. The Member States did indeed act with precipitation, under pressure to be seen to be doing something in any forum which came to hand, the CSCE as much as the European Council. Further reflection might have revealed more aspects of the decision to inaugurate a highly active policy, but the decision is unlikely to have been any different, even had it been postponed. Rightly or wrongly,

---

[16] *Bull. EC*, June 1991, 1.25.
[17] This argument is expressed in its most extreme form in Gow, *Triumph of the Lack of Will*, 46–50. For a less ferocious version, see Crnobrnja, *The Yugoslav Drama*, 190.
[18] Edwards, 'European Responses to the Yugoslav Crisis', 184.

the Community had for six months been warning against any move to break up the Yugoslav federal system, with promises of further assistance conditional on the warning's being heeded. Now that those moves had been made, with an immediate military response by the federal authorities, the Community could not abandon its position without incurring severe damage to its credibility, regardless of whether or not progress towards a CFSP was being made.

It has not yet been revealed precisely how the European Council reached its decision. Italy is reported to have been behind the move to send the Troika to Belgrade. The Italian Prime Minister, Giulio Andreotti, said that 'a simple appeal was not enough. The world is full of appeals which are ignored and what is happening on our doorstep requires more than a "bureaucratic diplomatic" approach'.[19] Indeed, the Italian initiative may have been prepared well in advance. The Italian delegation had brought to Luxembourg a suspiciously large aircraft into which the Troika, attendant officials, and a contingent of journalists were hastily bundled and whisked away to Belgrade while the European Council was still in progress.[20] The Foreign Minister, Gianni De Michelis, said that the rapid dispatch of the Troika constituted an EC diplomatic rapid reaction force.[21] Certainly Italy may be supposed to have had an interest in demonstrating the potential for an active CFSP, given its overall approach in the IGC. In this particular case, however, more immediate national interests were at stake. Italy shared a border with Slovenia, where it had important economic interests, and on the eve of the European Council meeting had with Austria activated the CSCE mechanism to require Yugoslavia to explain its military activity on the frontier.[22] As Andreotti had said, the trouble was on the doorstep. And there were only three days remaining during which De Michelis would be a member of the Troika.[23] Whatever the motivation, the Italian initiative at the European Council showed once again that EPC suffered from the lack of an objective mechanism to define the European interest and make the necessary proposals.

There was another element behind the European Council's decision: the attitude of the United States. There can be little doubt that part of the Community's activism can be ascribed to a desire to prove that it was as

[19] Ibid. 170. The order of the agenda had been altered so that a decision on Yugoslavia could be taken right at the start of the meeting: *EUROPE*, 5523 (29 June 1991), 3–4.

[20] Buchan, *Europe*, 72.   [21] Gow, *Triumph of the Lack of Will*, 48–9.

[22] Ramelot and Remacle, *L'OSCE et les conflits en Europe*, 77.

[23] At the time of the European Council, the Troika was composed of Luxembourg, Italy, and the Netherlands. From 1 July 1991 it was composed of the Netherlands, Luxembourg, and Portugal.

capable as the Americans of playing a part in international affairs. The cry of Jacques Poos, the Foreign Minister of Luxembourg and President of the Council, on the return of the Troika from Belgrade—'C'est l'heure de l' Europe'—has gone down in history. It has been glossed as a proof of misplaced triumphalism. In fact, the full quotation puts the European action in a different light. What Poos said was: 'It is the hour of Europe, not the hour of the Americans.'[24] He elaborated on this for reporters: 'If one problem can be solved by the Europeans, it's the Yugoslav problem. This is a European country and it's not up to the Americans and not up to anybody else.'[25] In fact, the Americans were more than happy to leave Yugoslavia to the Europeans, and had told them so. For the Bush Presidency, Yugoslavia was a minor regional difficulty compared with the other grave problems the United States was facing, chief among them being the imminent collapse of the Soviet Union. The United States' interests were not involved in Yugoslavia to the same extent. In spite of the public rhetoric, if the Community was out to steal the Americans' thunder, it was with the connivance of Washington. This was to have serious repercussions later, as Clinton, in opposition to Bush, included a more activist policy on Yugoslavia in his election campaign, and was thus committed to it when he became President, with disastrous consequences for the Europeans' own diplomatic efforts. For the time being, however, the Community had the field to itself.[26]

At first sight, the Troika mission appeared to be successful. Admittedly the Ministers had to go back twice to Yugoslavia before a deal among the parties to the dispute was finally achieved, but following the meeting at Brioni on 7 July 1991 there seemed to be the basis for a peaceful settlement of the crisis.[27] The mission marked a significant stage in the institutional development of EPC. It was the first time that the Community had delegated authority to a non-collective body to engage in negotiations with a third party on its behalf. Admittedly, EPC had negotiated the Helsinki Final Act, but it had done so collectively, with all the Member States present. The EPC Troika had been essentially a representative, not a negotiating, body. For example, in the Euro–Arab dialogue it expressed the positions which had previously been worked out in EPC, but could not

---

[24] Edwards, 'European Responses to the Yugoslav Crisis', 170.

[25] Gow, *Triumph of the Lack of Will*, 50 n. 11.

[26] Ibid. 29, 48 n. 7, 203–4, 206; Gnesotto, *Leçons de la Yougoslavie*, 26–7; Glitman, 'US Policy in Bosnia', 70–1.

[27] For a disillusioned but well-informed account of the Troika's diplomatic efforts, which makes much of the naïveté of the Europeans, see Silber and Little, *The Death of Yugoslavia*, 174–84. The account displays the dangers of not having deep briefing-books.

modify them as part of a negotiation. At Belgrade and Brioni the Member States allowed the Troika room for manoeuvre to enable it to come up with the desired result. The situation was therefore conceptually similar to that in the Community when the Commission engages in trade negotiations on behalf of the EC.

In the Community system, the Commission negotiates on the basis of a mandate, which it has taken the initiative of proposing itself, and which may be adapted in the course of the negotiations on reference to the Council. For its negotiations in Yugoslavia the Troika had a mandate, which was revised in the course of the negotiations.[28] The analogy with the Community is, however, not perfect. The mandate given to the Troika by the European Council was not initiated by the negotiator but arose through collective discussion, the draft having been prepared under the authority of the Presidency. It took the form of a declaration which was ready to be issued on the first day of the European Council's meeting, but which was in the event withheld because of the Troika's mission. On the Troika's return from Belgrade, Mr Poos confirmed that the principles of the declaration were: a cease-fire and a return of the troops to their barracks; a three-month moratorium to be devoted to dialogue and the practical effects of the declaration of independence; and the lifting of Serbia's reservation against the election of a Croat as president of the Federation.[29] The negotiating objectives were not, however, the Community's own; they had been taken over *en bloc* from the Federal Prime Minister, Ante Marković (although Marković opposed the Troika's proposals at Brioni, as he saw the Federation's interests disappearing from view in the course of the negotiations).[30] One may doubt the wisdom of this course of action; certainly to declare a moratorium of three months as good as condemned the EC to recognize Slovenia and Croatia at the expiry of that period, during which there would be open season on the internal frontiers of Yugoslavia. But EPC did not have its own policy-making capacity, and so was obliged to get policy where it could.[31]

---

[28] The Foreign Ministers held a special EPC meeting on 5 July 1991 at which the decision to suspend the second and third financial protocols with Yugoslavia, which had eluded the European Council, was finally taken. At the suggestion of the United States, an arms embargo was also introduced: *Bull. EC,* July–Aug. 1991, 1.4.3; Nuttall, 'The EC and Yugoslavia', 19.

[29] *EUROPE,* 5524 (30 June 1991), 3. The text of the unpublished declaration is at *EUROPE,* 5523 (29 June 1991), 8.

[30] Woodward, *Balkan Tragedy,* 168; Gow, *Triumph of the Lack of Will,* 50–1; Silber and Little, *The Death of Yugoslavia,* 181.

[31] The idea of a moratorium was the more attractive to the Community as it furnished

The Troika's efforts were hampered by suspicions on the part of the breakaway Yugoslav republics that the Community's negotiating position was not rock-solid. The German government in particular, under severe domestic pressure in favour of Slovenia and Croatia, gave the impression in its declarations and contacts that independence for the republics could not be excluded as an outcome. This made the republican leaders more disinclined to make concessions to the Troika than if they had been convinced there was no alternative. On the eve of the Slovene and Croatian declarations of independence Genscher telephoned[32] the Federal Yugoslav Foreign Minister, Budimir Lončar, to make two points: that the Yugoslavian people had the right to decide their own future, and that the use of force was totally excluded. This could well be interpreted as a green light for independence, especially when compared with the official EC position. Genscher intervened again in the middle of the Troika's series of visits to Yugoslavia. He visited Belgrade, and had planned to visit Ljubljana but was deterred by a cleverly orchestrated display of the military risk, on 1 July 1991, the day the Troika returned from its second visit.[33] Genscher bitterly resented the affront, which was to colour his subsequent attitude to the crisis.[34] At the Ministerial Meeting on 5 July he was quoted as saying that 'If it had been left to me alone, specific mention would have been made of the need to recognize the independence of Slovenia and Croatia in the event of future military action'.[35] And on 18 July President Tudjman of Croatia left Bonn after a meeting with Kohl and Genscher, encouraged to step up confrontation with the Yugoslav People's Army (JNA) and effectively put an end to the ongoing efforts to find a compromise solution among the republics.[36] This is not to say that the Germans did not have every right to take the line they did, but the fact that the Community could not speak with a single voice impaired the effectiveness of EPC.

a useful compromise between those who wished to preserve Yugoslavia's federal structures and those (Germany) who wished to recognize Slovenia and Croatia as quickly as possible: Favier and Martin-Roland, *La Décennie Mitterrand*, iv. 187–8.

[32] From Rome, where he was in a meeting with the Italian Foreign Minister Gianni De Michelis, who backed up Genscher's line: Genscher, *Erinnerungen*, 936–7.

[33] Ibid. 938–40; Silber and Little, *The Death of Yugoslavia*, 179–80. His mission was justified by the fact that Germany chaired the new CSCE Committee of Senior Officials (crisis mechanism)—a function which Genscher elevated for the occasion to that of President of the Council of Ministers of the CSCE: Remacle, *Les Négociations sur la politique étrangère*, 35, 45 n. 6.

[34] Libal, *Limits of Persuasion*, 16–17, 40.

[35] Edwards, 'European Responses to the Yugoslav Crisis', 171.

[36] Crnobrnja, *The Yugoslav Drama*, 194.

In addition to a cease-fire, the suspension of the declarations of independence for three months, and agreement on the election of the Croatian representative as President of the collective federal presidency, the Brioni declaration provided for negotiations on the future of Yugoslavia by the parties concerned to begin not later than 1 August 1991, and for a monitoring mission to 'become operational as soon as possible in order to help stabilize the cease-fire and to monitor the implementation of the remaining elements of the agreement reached between Yugoslav parties with the contribution of the European Community'[37]—essentially the return to barracks of the JNA. The European Community Monitoring Mission (ECMM) was the EC's most distinctive contribution to a settlement of the Yugoslav problem, and marked an important step towards an active foreign policy.

Technically speaking, the ECMM was not a European Community mission at all. It had been set up by the recently created Committee of Senior Officials of the CSCE, which, at its Prague meeting on 3–4 July 1991, 'welcomed the readiness expressed by the EC-Member States, building on their initiatives, to organize a mission to help stabilize a cease-fire and to monitor the implementation of the above-mentioned elements of the agreement'. The Committee also 'welcomed . . . the interest of other CSCE participating States to take part in the mission on the basis of the arrangements between the European Community and Yugoslav authorities', and 'requested the mission to inform the Committee on the progress of its work at the earliest opportunity'.[38] In fact, although officers from Canada, Sweden, Poland, and Czechoslovakia later joined the Mission, it remained, at the request of the Yugoslav hosts, primarily a Community affair.[39]

The first thing to do was to settle the legal basis on which the ECMM was present in Yugoslavia. Agreement on this was achieved in a Memorandum of Understanding (MOU), concluded on 13 July 1991, between the Community and its Member States and the Commission, on the one hand, and the federal and republic authorities, on the other, after the text had been approved at the Ministerial Meeting on 10 July.[40] It is interesting to note that EPC appears to have experienced no *états d'âme* about committing the Community in this way. This is in marked contrast

[37] Trifunovska, *Yugoslavia through Documents*, 311–15.   [38] Ibid. 308–10.
[39] Ramelot and Remacle, *L'OSCE et les conflits en Europe*, 88.
[40] *EUROPE*, 5532 (11 July 1991), 3; Trifunovska, *Yugoslavia through Documents*, 317–22. The MOU was signed for the Twelve by the Dutch Ambassador-at-Large Christiaan Kroener: *EUROPE*, 5535 (15–16 July 1991), 3.

with the soul-searching which went on a few years later, after the introduction of the CFSP, when it came to concluding a similar agreement
regarding the EU administration of Mostar. The main features of the
MOU, from the administrative point of view, were that the monitors were
to enjoy freedom of movement in the Mission area, display the flag of the
European Community, and enjoy diplomatic privileges and immunities.
The Mission would operate under the responsibility of a national from the
country holding the EC Council Presidency, who would report, through
the Presidency, to all the Participating Parties. The monitors were not to
carry arms, and would wear civilian dress. The question of costs was left
'to be decided on'.

The Community had entered into an obligation without the means
readily available to carry it out. The Monitoring Mission had to be impro-
vised from scratch. There was no question of turning to NATO, and though
the possibility of using the WEU was raised (by the WEU), it was never
seriously considered. Even if the Yugoslav hosts had not insisted on the
monitors' being unarmed, there would have been no consensus in the EC
for arming them. The IGC debate on a defence capability for the Community was at its height, and the Netherlands was firmly opposed to any
strengthening of WEU's role at the expense of NATO. The Netherlands
Foreign Minister, Hans van den Broek, could use his position as EC
Presidency to ensure that no awkward precedents were set.[41] The Mission
therefore had to be constituted by an *ad hoc* appeal for volunteers in the
Member States. Although there was a leavening of civilians, the larger
number were soldiers in mufti. By December 1991, by which time the
mission had, with difficulty, been extended to Croatia, there were 190
observers and 150 support staff.

Making a virtue of necessity, the Mission exploited its civilian character to good effect. The monitors were dressed in white uniforms, drawn
from stocks which the Dutch Navy had conveniently to hand, and wore
the blue brassard of the European Community.[42] It was the first time the
EC had deployed forces identifiable as its own, bearing no weapons and
arrayed in garments symbolic of peace. This was subsequently turned to
derision, as the Croatians dubbed the white-clad monitors 'the men from
the ice-cream factory', who only appeared when the sun shone—they were
present to observe peace but absent from where the fighting was going on.

---

[41] van Eekelen, *Debating European Security*, 143.
[42] A stock of EC flags, caps, brassards, and stickers had been provided by the Commission's Directorate General for Information, and taken out by one of the Commission's first
observers: EC Commission, *Courrier du personnel*, no. 533 (Dec. 1991), 2–6.

This was inevitable, given that the Mission's initial mandate was to keep the peace, not make it, but that inconvenient fact was forgotten under pressure from the highly efficient Croatian propaganda machine, directed to ensuring that the Mission's remit was extended to Croatia, where the situation was more difficult than in Slovenia and where an effective cease-fire did not exist.[43]

Although the Mission was constituted and deployed so hastily, it had a surprisingly elaborate structure which reflected the Member States' dislike of delegation. It was headed by an ambassador from the Presidency, who changed with the Presidency every six months. The Head of the ECMM was assisted by a 'Policy Committee' made up of representatives of the contributors, which in turn controlled a 'working unit' ('cellule de travail') and several 'technical units' in charge of practical questions. The monitors operated in pairs, always of mixed nationality, and were regularly rotated. Headquarters were in Zagreb. Materiel was provided nationally, which led to an interesting and varied transport pool, and, at the insistence of the United Kingdom, the Mission was financed by national contributions.[44] It should not have worked, but it did, and does—the Mission is still deployed in and around former Yugoslavia—and was a good example of how EPC could improvise effectively and create new forms of Community activity, even without the benefit of a formal framework.[45]

The Mission did more than establish the identity of the Community on the ground. It performed a number of functions, some of which had not been foreseen at the start.[46] One of the most important was to provide the Community and the Member States with a constant stream of information about what was happening. This was influential in changing the Community's view of Serbia and demolishing any remaining support for the federal authorities, and culminated in a damning report attacking the activities of the JNA which was sent to Brussels in November 1991.[47] The Mission also found itself involved in a myriad acts of mediation which served to reduce local tension,[48] as well as full-scale negotiations like those which brought about the withdrawal of the JNA from the Prevlaka Penin-

[43] Wynaendts, *L'Engrenage*, 50; Chenu, 'Les Hommes en blanc', 93–4; Nuttall, 'The EC and Yugoslavia', 21–2.

[44] 'Envoi d'une mission européenne de "surveillance"', *Le Figaro*, 11 July 1991, 2.

[45] Chenu, 'Les Hommes en blanc', 87–8; Nuttall, 'The EC and Yugoslavia', 22.

[46] Edwards, 'The Potential and Limits of the CFSP', 184; Libal, *Limits of Persuasion*, 49.

[47] Gow, *Triumph of the Lack of Will*, 56; Lukic and Lynch, *Europe from the Balkans to the Urals*, 192–3; Chenu, 'Les Hommes en blanc', 90, 101.

[48] Gow, *Triumph of the Lack of Will*, 56, 124; Chenu, 'Les Hommes en blanc', 88.

sula in September 1992.[49] At the initiative of a Belgian monitor, a 'humanitarian unit' was set up, and proceeded to issue guidelines for the application of the Geneva Convention and investigate human rights violations.
This had not been foreseen in the Mission's mandate.[50]

Troika diplomacy had succeeded in Slovenia largely because the Serbs
wanted it to. The situation was more difficult in Croatia, where there
were important Serb minorities which were not prepared to settle for
autonomous status. Faced with increasing violence on the ground, including the excesses of Vukovar which, through the media, for the first time
brought the situation in Yugoslavia to the horrified attention of the public
at large, the Community held fast to its determination to seek a solution
by negotiation. At a special EPC meeting on 27 August 1991 the Foreign
Ministers called for a cease-fire by 1 September, to be monitored by the
ECMM. This would allow the Community 'to convene a peace conference
and establish an arbitration procedure'. The peace conference would bring
together the federal and republican authorities in Yugoslavia and, on the
European side, 'the President of the Council, representatives of the
Member States and the Commission'. Within the framework of the Conference an Arbitration Commission was to be set up, composed of two
members appointed unanimously by the Federal Presidency and three
appointed by the Community and its Member States, and required to give
its decision within two months.[51]

This decision was the result of two competing proposals, launched
respectively by Germany and France, which were merged after bilateral consultations between Genscher and Dumas into a not entirely
satisfactory compromise. The idea of a peace conference came from
Germany. It had already been mooted by the Twelve at their meeting on
6 August, but now the Germans pressed hard, nervous at the public
outcry over the reports of bloodbaths in Croatia and confident that
Community support for the federal authorities was on the wane. The Conference would provide the framework for the parties to reach a constitutional settlement, doubtless based on independence for the breakaway
republics.

The Arbitration Commission had a different origin and purpose. The
brainchild of Robert Badinter, former French Minister of Justice, it had
been taken on board by Mitterrand and Dumas and defended as a French
initiative. The tasks of the Commission were not clear, and were not

---

[49] Gow, *Triumph of the Lack of Will*, 106; Chenu, 'Les hommes en blanc', 98.
[50] Chenu, 'Les Hommes en blanc', 107–8, 236.
[51] *Bull. EC*, July–Aug. 1991, 1.4.25.

specified in the EPC decision setting it up. The original idea, of Slovenian inspiration, had been for it to pronounce on the legal rights of successor states and thus help negotiate the distribution of assets and debts of the former federation, but it soon found itself charged by the Conference and by the Community with other tasks, including the knotty question of borders and the criteria for recognition.[52] The situation was complicated by difficulties over composition. Agreement was soon reached on the Community representatives, in the shape of the Presidents of the Constitutional Courts of France, Germany, and Italy, but the Yugoslav side could not agree on its own representatives, who in the end were replaced by eminent constitutional lawyers from Belgium and Spain. The difference was crucial: a body in which the Yugoslavs were represented and working with the Europeans might have been able to work out some sort of arrangement to which, through their representatives, they were committed. An external arbitration body whose authority was not accepted would have a totally different, and not necessarily constructive, function.[53]

The Arbitration Commission and the Conference represented different diplomatic approaches to the Yugoslav question. The Commission's role was to arbitrate; what was to happen if its findings were ignored was left unclear. The Conference, on the other hand, provided a forum and encouragement for negotiations among the parties concerned, and in theory its task was over when the negotiations were successfully concluded. Although both suffered from an inability to impose their views, essentially their functions were contradictory. The fact that they formed part of a package, stitched together by Dumas and Genscher to maintain the illusion that EPC policy was being driven by the Franco-German tandem, barely served to conceal this. As a result, there were bitter discussions about the relationship between Commission and Conference. Germany and France insisted on the greatest possible independence for the Commission, while the Netherlands as Presidency saw the Commission as an instrument at the disposal of the chair.[54] The compromise decision, which sought to square the circle by leaving the Commission's mandate to the Presidency while providing that it should report to the Conference, and at the same time have control over its own procedures and organization, was less than satisfactory and showed the sort of difficulties which could arise in EPC when more than one Member State launched competing proposals. The

---

[52] Debie, 'De Brioni à Dayton', 51–3; Védrine, *Les Mondes de François Mitterrand*, 610; Genscher, *Erinnerungen*, 946–8; Woodward, *Balkan Tragedy*, 250, 465 n. 87.

[53] Remacle, *Les Négociations sur la politique étrangère*, 39; Nuttall, 'The EC and Yugoslavia', 16.　　　　　　　　　　　　　　[54] Genscher, *Erinnerungen*, 948.

problem arose through the absence in EPC of an exclusive right of initiative.

The Conference was formally set up on 3 September 1991 and held its inaugural session in The Hague on 7 September.[55] The former British Foreign Secretary, Lord Carrington, was appointed its Chairman. He himself modestly attributed the choice to the fact that he had become well known to the Foreign Ministers during his period as Secretary General of NATO. The Conference met in the Peace Palace at The Hague; its infra-structure was provided by the hasty but effective improvisation which characterized EPC. There were two Vice-Chairmen, one Dutch and one Spanish, and a small standing Secretariat headed by a young and active Luxembourg diplomat and made up of officials seconded from Member States and the Commission. Later in the month, as it became clearer that a successful outcome would preserve only the most tenuous appearance of the survival of Yugoslavia as a state, three working groups in which all par-ticipants were represented were set up to organize the dissolution. One, dealing with human rights and the rights of minorities, was chaired by a German diplomat, Gert Ahrens; the second, responsible for institutional aspects, was conducted by Brian Crowe, British Ambassador to the inter-national organizations, including the CSCE, in Vienna; and the third, on economic co-operation, was attributed to Jean Durieux, Counsellor *hors classe* (in effect a Director General) at the European Commission. Henry Darwin, Deputy Legal Adviser at the Foreign and Commonwealth Office, was appointed legal adviser to the Conference, and Ambassador Henry Wynaendts, while continuing to carry out his duties as representative in Yugoslavia of the Netherlands Presidency, was asked to co-ordinate the three working groups.[56]

The machinery and the good intentions were in place, but the Confer-ence could not succeed in the absence of willingness on the part of the belligerents to reach a negotiated settlement. A durable cease-fire was a condition of this, and the Community put a great deal of diplomatic effort into securing a succession of truces which were regularly broken. This was not surprising, as continued fighting was seen by each of the warring parties to be to its potential advantage. The Conference's only hope of success was to be perceived as a neutral ringholder, to which the parties could turn when exhausted. As the autumn wore on, however, this be-came increasingly difficult for the Member States, subjected to intense

---

[55] *Bull. EC*, Sept. 1991, 1.4.2; *EPC Documentation Bulletin*, 7 (1991), 91/256-8, 91/260.
[56] Wynaendts, *L'Engrenage*, 118–19; Nuttall, 'The EC and Yugoslavia', 15–16.

domestic political pressure from public opinion revolted by the carnage and swayed by the media to attribute blame exclusively to Serbia. The Community had recourse to sanctions to induce the republics to come together in the Conference, but the pressure was selective.

Since the Community had never tried to run a conference like this before, the *modus operandi* had to be invented from scratch. Lord Carrington had his own ideas about how to carry out the job, which consisted in concentrating on bilateral contacts with the various factions, the results of which were reported to infrequent and short plenary sessions, lasting no more than two hours, and with little debate. Although this way of proceeding was in keeping with the arbitration mode, it contributed little to a result by negotiation and startled the Yugoslav participants. Mihailo Crnobrnja, who was the Yugoslav Ambassador to the EC at the time, makes the point that 'all of them, except the President of BiH, had been seasoned Communist Party officials in the past, quite accustomed to long, tiresome, and gruelling sessions that would, with great effort and considerable time, produce platforms and statements indicating political agreement. The elegant conference format that Carrington pursued was wasted on the Yugoslav participants and certainly did not help in finding a solution.'[57]

The same comment might have been made of those officials with equally gruelling experience of EC meetings. Although Carrington kept the Council fully informed of progress, and certainly did not overstep his mandate, his reluctance to engage in long plenary sessions in the presence of the Member States reduced the opportunities available to him to secure their commitment to the line he was following. The effects of this were shown most strikingly in the recognition *débâcle*. Even when the Member States were in agreement, the Council remained the forum for EC policy making, while Lord Carrington was responsible for negotiations. The relationship between the two was not always clear.

Nor was the Community as a whole sufficiently effective in obtaining international support for its activities. The United States was happy for the Community to get its feet wet, and the Soviet Union was in the final stages of collapse—the attempted *coup d'état* in Moscow took place at the height of the EC's diplomatic efforts in mid-August, and the state was to be dissolved by the end of the year. The Presidency nevertheless took care to keep the Community's partners informed. Van den Broek visited Washington on 3 July and a joint statement was issued, and great pride was taken in

[57] Crnobrnja, *The Yugoslav Drama*, 195.

the joint statement issued on 18 October 1991 by the Community and its Member States, the United States, and the USSR—the first of its kind— but the EC's partners were not made to feel that they shared responsibility for efforts to tackle the problem.[58] The philosophy of Mr Poos' 'heure de l'Europe' still held sway. The Community paid for its failure to insist on its partners' being more closely involved when the United States declined to support the Vance–Owen plan just over a year later.

Equally unfortunate was the implicit rivalry with the United Nations. Although Secretary General Perez de Cuellar was no more anxious than the Americans to get involved in Yugoslavia, and only reluctantly accepted the European proposal in September 1991 to put the subject on the Security Council agenda,[59] his organization seems to have resented the appearance on the scene of this new peace-keeping body which showed no enthusiasm for learning from those with more experience in the field.[60] The Secretary General's Special Representative, Cyrus Vance, was appointed on 8 October 1991,[61] the very day the three months' moratorium negotiated at Brioni expired. It was as though the EC's time was up. Certainly the fact that henceforth two parallel negotiations were proceeding with the Yugoslav parties could only complicate the situation. Even though personal relations between Carrington and Vance were good, and the two had professed a commitment to joint action,[62] accidents were bound to happen, as in December 1991 when the Secretary General demanded the withdrawal from the cease-fire negotiations of two EC diplomats from the ECMM,[63] or in July 1992 when Lord Carrington secured from the Serbs, reputedly without prior consultation with the UN, a cease-fire agreement which required them to place their heavy arms under UN supervision.[64] More seriously, the deployment of UN forces in Croatia in the winter of 1991 and the spring of 1992, by freezing the position of the Serbian enclaves, countered the Community's attempts to reestablish Croatian administration with guarantees for the Serb minority population.[65] This is not to say which policy was the correct one, only that

---

[58]   *EPC Documentation Bulletin*, 7 (1991), 91/202, 333, and 91/312, 512.

[59]   The EC wished to secure an internationally binding arms embargo. An earlier attempt by France at the beginning of August to inform the Security Council officially of the Community's activities had been opposed by the United States and the United Kingdom: Védrine, *Les Mondes de François Mitterrand*, 609–10; Genscher, *Erinnerungen*, 945.

[60]   Woodward, *Balkan Tragedy*, 462 n. 65; Wynaendts, *L'Engrenage*, 138.

[61]   Following a call from the Community: *EPC Documentation Bulletin*, 7 (1991), 91/295.

[62]   Crnobrnja, *The Yugoslav Drama*, 206.   [63]   Chenu, 'Les Hommes en blanc', 102.

[64]   Lukic and Lynch, *Europe from the Balkans to the Urals*, 282.

[65]   Guicherd, *L'Heure de l'Europe*, 36.

the two were incompatible. And the more the United Nations were impli-
cated, the more fissile became the Community, given the ambivalent
allegiance of France and Britain as permanent members of the Security
Council as well as members of the EC.[66]

It was the United Nations, not the Community, which was in the spring
of 1992 to deploy an armed force in former Yugoslavia to supervise
the cease-fires in Croatia brokered by Cyrus Vance. The failure of the Community to do so has been criticized in retrospect, and regardless of whether
military intervention would have been any more successful than civilian
action—the experience of UNPROFOR is not encouraging in this
respect—it certainly contributed to the Community's loss of credibility
over Yugoslavia. Several attempts were made to secure a decision in favour
of armed intervention, but agreement could not be reached because of the
opposition of some Member States, led by the United Kingdom. The
British had a number of reasons for this; high on the list was their unwill-
ingness, at a crucial stage in the Maastricht negotiations, to show by a
practical demonstration that military action by the Community was
feasible. The Yugoslav crisis did not have a significant impact on the
IGC negotiations on a common foreign and security policy, but the negotiations certainly had an impact on the Community's policy towards
Yugoslavia.

The idea of military action undertaken on behalf of the EC to intervene
between Serbs and Croats in support of the Monitoring Mission was first
advanced by France in late July 1991. At the extraordinary EPC Ministerial Meeting on 29 July 1991 Dumas set out three options, including a
peace-keeping force, even though President Mitterrand a few days earlier
had excluded the use of force to keep the federation in being. This proposal attracted little support from the other Member States. Dumas
returned to the charge at the Ministerial Meeting on 6 August, proposing
that recourse should be had to the WEU for the purpose. The United
Kingdom, Denmark, Germany, and Portugal were against; Germany did
not exclude intervention by either the EC or the CSCE.[67] The Community
could only note that 'the Member States of the WEU have decided to
instruct their representatives to take stock of the present situation in
Yugoslavia and to examine whether there is any contribution which the
WEU could make to the maintenance of an agreed cease-fire'.[68]

---

[66] Gnesotto, *Leçons de la Yougoslavie*, 19; Nuttall. 'The EC and Yugoslavia', 23.

[67] Favier and Martin-Roland, *La Décennie Mitterrand.* iv. 189–90; Guicherd, *L'Heure de l'Europe*, 18–19; Genscher, *Erinnerungen*, 945.

[68] *Bull. EC*, July–Aug. 1991, 1.4.15; *EPC Documentation Bulletin*, 7 (1991), 91/243.

The French suggestion was taken up again by the Netherlands EC Presidency at the beginning of September, in part, it has been suggested, to test the French resolve and to explore the position of Germany in favour of doing more for the Slovenes and the Croats. Goaded by the refusal of two German monitors to go where they had been directed on the grounds that it was too dangerous, van den Broek had secured from Genscher an emergency meeting of the WEU Council immediately following an EPC Ministerial Meeting.[69] The two meetings took place on 19 September 1991. The Netherlands Presidency proposed the dispatch of a lightly armed force under the banner of the WEU. This time, the United Kingdom did agree to studies being made by the WEU, it being understood that forces would only be sent for peace-keeping duties, and only in the event of a cease-fire, and that a final decision on this had not yet been taken. The Community expressed its satisfaction 'that the WEU explores ways in which the activities of the monitors could be supported so as to make their work a more effective contribution to the peace-keeping effort. It is their understanding that no military intervention is contemplated and that, before a reinforced monitor mission were established, a cease-fire would have to be agreed with a prospect of holding and that all Yugoslav parties would have expressed their agreement. The Community and its Member States would wish to have the opportunity to examine and endorse the conclusions of the study'.[70]

The discussion in the WEU not unnaturally reflected that which had just taken place in EPC. Germany was hesitant; the Netherlands was prepared to supply a battalion almost immediately, and Belgium promised its support. The United Kingdom's position remained negative. An *ad hoc* group was set up to study the question, and reported on 30 September. The group's report contained four options, mirroring those which Dumas had already presented in July, and ranging from logistic underpinning of the monitors through armed escort and protection (3,000–5,000 men) and a peace-keeping force in support of the monitors (over 10,000) to an expanded peace-keeping force (over 20,000). None of the options was accepted. National positions remained unchanged, with most Member States accepting at least one of the more modest options, but the United Kingdom remaining opposed. Responsibility for the whole affair was shuffled off onto Lord Carrington, who was desired to give the Presidency a call if he saw a chance of a cease-fire holding. Even this would do no more than trigger a further EPC meeting.

[69] Germany at the time held the Presidency of the WEU.
[70] *Bull. EC*, Sept. 1991, 1.4.7; Libal, *Limits of Persuasion*, 54–5.

There can be no doubt that in pressing for an armed force in Yugoslavia the French were attempting to prejudge through concrete action the outcome of the debate which was at this time still raging in the IGC about whether the Community should have a security and defence personality. The author of the French plan of action in preparation for the emergency meetings on 19 September, Hubert Védrine, has explained that the idea was to have an 'intervention force' set up by the Security Council and then confirmed by EPC, to be implemented by those WEU members who so wished.[71] A decision by the Security Council was necessary to provide international legitimacy and to ensure that no one country found itself on its own; the European Council's endorsement would be consistent with the greater foreign policy role which France was trying to secure for it in the Maastricht negotiations; and the WEU, although it existed only on paper, nevertheless provided a setting for those countries which wished to do something.[72]

Equally there can be no doubt that British resistance to the French proposals for armed intervention derived at least in part from their opposition to the concept of a security and defence dimension for the Community. Certainly, Douglas Hurd expressed a number of other reasons—the need to avoid open-ended commitments which were sure to escalate; the difficulty of extracting oneself once committed; the futility of 'doing something' just for the sake of it—with the shadow of Northern Ireland hanging over all.[73] These objections were no doubt sincere, but they were reinforced by the need not to give away a trick in the Maastricht end-game. Opinions differ as to whether an armed intervention by the WEU, acting on behalf of the Community, could at this stage have had any effect on the course of the conflict, but it was British institutional fears which prevented the experiment from taking place.[74]

It was understandable that there was no agreement on whether to make

---

[71] France did indeed launch this proposal in New York, but could find no support. The initiative ended up in Security Council Resolution no. 713 (25 Sept. 1991), expressing encouragement for European efforts but limiting specific action to the imposition of an arms embargo: Favier and Martin-Roland, *La Décennie Mitterrand*, iv. 235–6; Trifunovska, *Yugoslavia through Documents*, 349–50.

[72] Védrine, *Les Mondes de François Mitterrand*, 611.

[73] Gow, *Triumph of the Lack of Will*, 179; Edwards, 'European Responses to the Yugoslav Crisis', 180, 186.

[74] The account given in these paragraphs has been pieced together from the following, sometimes contradictory, sources: van Eekelen, *Debating European Security*, 145–9; Gow, *Triumph of the Lack of Will*, 160, 162, 176; Guicherd, *L'Heure de l'Europe*, 18–19; Remacle, *Les Négociations sur la politique étrangère*, 38, 40–1; Favier and Martin-Roland, *La Décennie Mitterrand*, iv. 189–90, 196–7, 235.

use of the WEU as the armed branch of the Community when the principle involved was still under discussion in the IGC. It might have been supposed, however, that once that principle was admitted in the Maastricht Treaty, albeit hedged round with provisos and conditions, the Community would have taken advantage of the new possibilities and addressed itself to WEU when military intervention was necessary. It was not to be. The WEU was indeed to engage in military activities in connection with Yugoslavia, but on its own initiative, not at the request of the Community. In so doing it found itself, not an arm of the Community, but an arm of NATO.

This came about through the requirement to enforce the arms embargo on former Yugoslavia, and the wider embargo on Serbia and Montenegro, especially in the Adriatic. The Community decided to apply trade sanctions to the two republics on 27 May 1992, adopting them formally on 1 June in the light of Security Council Resolution No. 757, which had been adopted in the meanwhile.[75] The WEU thereupon decided to engage its forces in the monitoring of this Resolution in the Adriatic. On 10 July 1992 it announced the dispatch of naval and air forces to monitor commercial traffic to the ports of Montenegro. NATO announced a similar decision the same day. This could have led to unseemly and possibly even dangerous competition, but some *ad hoc* co-operation procedures were cobbled together, taking advantage of the fact that Italian officers were strategically placed in both operations. The WEU's Sharp Fence and NATO's Maritime Monitor patrolled the Straits of Otranto and the Montenegrin coast turn and turn about.[76]

This somewhat haphazard co-ordination might be adequate for simple monitoring; it would not do when the mission was extended. This became necessary in order to implement the strongly reinforced sanctions imposed by the Security Council in Resolution No. 319 of 17 April 1993.[77] Such at any rate was the view expressed by Admiral Boorda (US Navy), the Commander of the Allied Forces in Southern Europe (CINCSOUTH), who took advantage of a lunch at Mons to convince Willem van Eekelen, the WEU Secretary General, that things were now getting serious, and that a seamless command structure was necessary if lives were not to be lost.

[75] *Bull. EC*, June 1992, 1.4.12; Trifunofska, *Yugoslavia through Documents*, 593–9.

[76] Cremasco, 'La Comunità europea', 117–19; van Eekelen, *Debating European Security*, 155.

[77] Trifunofska, *Yugoslavia through Documents*, 909-15. Authorization to 'stop and search' had already been given by Security Council Resolution no. 787 of 16 Nov. 1992: Trifunofska, *Yugoslavia through Documents*, 757–61.

Van Eekelen represented to Alain Juppé, the French Foreign Minister, and Douglas Hurd, his British counterpart, strolling in the gardens of the Villa Madama before the WEU ministerial meeting at Rome on 19 May 1993, that the only alternative to setting up a complicated command arrangement for two separate operations was to accept unity of command under NATO, with political supervision of both forces entrusted to the NATO and WEU Permanent Councils jointly. The second option was immediately attractive to Juppé, because it gave WEU political visibility, and to Hurd, because it made use of the NATO command structure. The concept was approved on 8 June at a joint session of the NATO and WEU Councils, and Operation Sharp Guard came into existence on 15 June.[78] No request had been made by the Community to WEU, which at American insistence became both politically and operationally the junior partner in a joint exercise. This was no doubt the most practical way of meeting an urgent operational need, but it was not what Mitterrand had in mind in launching the CFSP.

The embargo was also enforced on traffic on the Danube. Initially, the operation was seen as a purely customs one. The Community sent sanctions assistance missions to Romania, Bulgaria, and Hungary, to encourage and support the local customs administrations. These missions, later extended to Albania, Croatia, Macedonia, and Ukraine, were organized in co-operation with the CSCE, the Commission financing the communications and co-ordination centre (SAMCOMM) in Brussels.[79] The measures proved inadequate to prevent breaches of the embargo, however. At the beginning of 1993, therefore, the WEU Secretary General raised the possibility of a WEU action on the Danube. This was followed up by a report by the CSCE sanctions co-ordinator and the Italian Presidency of the WEU, proposing the permanent deployment on the Danube of eight patrol boats and 250 customs officers. The British at first preferred to leave the operation in the hands of the Community, and the Russians not surprisingly showed their sensitivity about military action in the Black Sea and the Danube basin. The Danube countries also required some convincing. The offer of a WEU operation was finally made at a meeting of the WEU Council on 5 April 1993, and Hungary, Bulgaria, and Romania all signed up by 20 May—just at the time WEU was losing its autonomy

---

[78] van Eekelen, *Debating European Security*, 155–6; Leurdijk, *The United Nations and NATO in Former Yugoslavia*, 24–31; Cremasco, 'La Comunità europea', 122; Gow, *Triumph of the Lack of Will*, 129–31.

[79] Commission Press Release IP(92)798 (7 Oct. 1992); Ramelot and Remacle, *L'OSCE et les conflits en Europe*, 90–1.

in the operation in the Adriatic. Any appearance of a military operation was carefully avoided, since that would have excluded German participation, and the host countries still remained sensitive about the use of force. The WEU force was therefore composed of police and customs officers, not military personnel, and it was only later that they were even allowed to carry small arms. Where the WEU acted alone, it was obliged to adopt a non-military posture. And, once again, the force had been set up *proprio motu* and not at the invitation of the Community. Neither WEU nor the EC Member States showed any enthusiasm for the early implementation of the Maastricht Treaty provisions.[80]

The Community's decision not to embark on armed intervention in the early stages of the Yugoslav crisis, even in support of its monitors, has been sharply criticized with hindsight but did not at the time bring European foreign policy into disrepute. Its failure to hold to a consistent line on the recognition of the breakaway republics, ending in the shambolic recognition of Slovenia and Croatia and the later destructive recognition of Bosnia-Herzegovina, did. It was this, as much as the failure of successive peace plans, which gave rise to the common perception that the European Community had failed over Yugoslavia.

It will be recalled that in the first half of 1991 the Community's policy had been to support the preservation of a federal system for Yugoslavia. This policy had been fully supported by the German government. Indeed, on 20 March Foreign Minister Genscher had warned the President and Foreign Minister of Slovenia that they should not be in a hurry to take any unilateral steps but rather to look for ways of giving the Yugoslav Federation a new constitutional form.[81] Public sympathy for Slovenia and Croatia was, however, beginning to mount. Sensing the mood, and spotting an opportunity to make up some of the ground lost to the government over the unification of Germany the previous year, the opposition SPD party decided as early as May to campaign for the recognition of Slovenia and Croatia as soon as they had formally declared independence.[82] Feeling in Germany was strong on the issue, which was the subject of an intensive media campaign led by *Die Welt* and the *Frankfurter Allgemeine Zeitung*. Sympathy for the Croatians was particularly pronounced, stimulated by

---

[80] Ramelot and Remacle, *L'OSCE et les conflits en Europe*, 91–2; van Eekelen, *Debating European Security*, 157–9; Edwards, 'The Potential and Limits of the CFSP', 182; Nuttall, 'The EC and Yugoslavia', 24; Maull, 'Germany in the Yugoslav Crisis', 108–9.

[81] Genscher, *Erinnerungen*, 931.

[82] Woodward, *Balkan Tragedy*, 177, 185; Genscher, *Erinnerungen*, 932; Libal, *Limits of Persuasion*, 6–7.

the presence in Germany of a large and closely knit Croatian *émigré* community.[83]

The German government stuck to the Community position, subscribing to the line taken by both the Foreign Ministers at the 'conclave' on 24 June and the European Council itself on 28–9 June.[84] The Chancellor and his Foreign Minister nevertheless ran into heavy criticism on their return to Bonn after the European Council, this time not only from the SPD but also from the Chancellor's own CDU. Volker Rühe, the Secretary General of the CDU, said on 1 July: 'We won unification through the right to self-determination. If we Germans now think that everything may remain as it is in Europe, that we may pursue a policy of the status quo without recognising the right to self-determination of Croatia and Slovenia, we lose our moral and political credibility . . . We should start a movement in the EC to lead to such recognition. It can't be done alone.'[85] Caught between the CDU and the SPD, Genscher thought it prudent to make a smart about-turn. On 3 July he wrote to his fellow Foreign Ministers calling for the immediate recognition of Slovenia and Croatia,[86] leading to the Troika's adoption of the concept of a three months' moratorium.

From then on, Germany was engaged in a struggle with its EC partners over the question of recognition, which was amply documented in the public press. At first it was supported only by Denmark, to be joined later in the autumn by Belgium and Italy. The other Member States and Lord Carrington argued in vain that to recognize Slovenia and Croatia at this stage would be to discard one of the few cards which the Community held and would destroy any chance of a successful outcome of the Conference. Unable to stand against the tide of public opinion, the German government increased the diplomatic pressure on its partners until by the end of the year they were obliged, against their better judgement, to accept recognition.

[83] For a comprehensive and subtle analysis of German public opinion and policy, see Maull, 'Germany in the Yugoslav Crisis'. Maull is inclined to downplay the influence of domestic politics. A contrary view is taken by Gow, *Triumph of the Lack of Will*, 166–9.

[84] Védrine maintains that Genscher urged recognition on 23 [*sic*] June and Kohl at the European Council: Védrine, *Les Mondes de François Mitterrand*, 606. If they did, neither pressed his position to the extent of blocking the consensus. It seems unlikely that Genscher at least did so, since independence was not declared until 25 June, and he makes no mention of it in his memoirs. On the other hand, he did telephone Lončar at that time to remind him of the right to self-determination (see above).

[85] Maull, 'Germany in the Yugoslav Crisis', 117; Libal, *Limits of Persuasion*, 19; Reuters, Bonn, 1 July 1991.

[86] Favier and Martin-Roland, *La Décennie Mitterrand*, iv. 187.

The Community was not against recognition as such. Indeed, it was implicit in the terms of the Brioni Agreement, and was spelled out in the agreements reached between Croatia and Serbia at The Hague on 4 October 1991: 'it was agreed that a political solution should be sought in the perspective of recognition of the independence of those republics wishing it, at the end of a negotiating process conducted in good faith and involving all parties'.[87] But the Ministers went on to recall that 'the right to self-determination of all the peoples of Yugoslavia cannot be exercised in isolation from the interests and rights of ethnic minorities within the individual republics'. This was the point which separated Germany from its partners: was recognition to wait until the problem of minorities could be settled, or was it to take place before then, as an act of justice?

The German view prevailed. The pace was accelerated by Kohl's commitment, made under intense domestic pressure in a speech in the Bundestag on 27 November and confirmed to President Tudjman on a visit to Bonn early the following month, to recognize Slovenia and Croatia by Christmas.[88] It was tacitly agreed, not least by Kohl, that the question of recognition had to be kept off the agenda of the Maastricht European Council,[89] but it was finally tackled at an extraordinary EPC Ministerial Meeting in Brussels on the night of 15–16 December. After lengthy and difficult discussions the Foreign Ministers agreed to recognize those republics which applied for Recognition by 23 December, and which accepted the commitments laid down in the 'Guidelines on the Recognition of New States in Eastern Europe and in the Soviet Union', which the Ministers had adopted at the same meeting. The decision to recognize would be implemented on 15 January 1992, on the basis of advice to be given in the meanwhile by the Badinter Commission.[90]

Genscher had made it quite clear during the meeting that this formula in no way prevented Germany from announcing its recognition of

---

[87] Statement at the informal meeting of Foreign Ministers at Haarzuilens, 6 Oct. 1991: *Bull. EC*, Oct. 1991, 1.4.7.

[88] Maull, 'Germany in the Yugoslav Crisis', 104; Genscher, *Erinnerungen*, 958. The German position was not inconsistent with the line taken by the Presidency. Van den Broek had said on 10 Oct., and repeated a few days later in an interview with the Austrian press, that the political process should be completed within one month, or at the most two, whereupon the time would come for the Twelve to decide about recognition. The deadline, whether intentionally or not, was set to expire just after the European Council: Genscher, *Erinnerungen*, 954; Libal, *Limits of Persuasion*, 65. In the subsequent recriminations, Germany placed excessive reliance on the Presidency's commitment, which had not been endorsed by the Twelve.   [89] Genscher, *Erinnerungen*, 955.

[90] *Bull. EC*, Dec. 1991, 1.4.5 and 1.4.6; *EUROPE*, 5631 (16–17 Dec. 1991), 3–4, and 5632 (18 Dec. 1991), 3–4.

Slovenia and Croatia before Christmas. This was done on 23 December. In an attempt to draw a rather frayed figleaf over the shattered remains of the Community's position, the actual establishment of diplomatic relations was delayed until the Community deadline of 15 January. The other Member States duly followed suit three days later,[91] after the Badinter Commission had on 11 January taken the view, surprisingly in the case of Croatia stipulating only a strengthening of the constitutional provisions protecting minorities, that the two republics fulfilled the criteria. The *débâcle* on recognition, following on the heels of the agreement at Maastricht to establish strengthened foreign policy disciplines, attracted disobliging comment from diplomatic observers and did a great deal to discredit the fledgling CFSP. Not only had Germany blatantly ignored the outcome of the Ministerial Meeting as regards timing,[92] which had been reached only at German insistence in the face of serious doubts on the part of many of the Member States, but it had also, to make a deal possible, given Greece *carte blanche* to block the recognition of Macedonia at will.[93] Furthermore, the spectre of renewed German power, which the CFSP had precisely been designed to ward off, had once more reared its head. How could this have come about?

Part of the answer lies in Germany's overriding need to secure Community cover for its own decision. Another Member State might simply have recognized the two republics, and *tant pis* for the Community. This was not something that Germany felt capable of, and it was strongly discouraged by France. As Genscher himself said, in such an historically sensitive relationship as that between Germany and Yugoslavia two aspects were of particular importance: not to encourage centrifugal tendencies, and not to go it alone. 'Unity in the EC was absolutely essential, if the old rivalries of the First and Second World Wars were not to be revived and imperil the new Europe. A common position had to be found, primarily in the EC, but also in the CSCE.'[94]

So Germany had to have a European decision. But why did the other Member States cave in, against their better judgement and in spite of the

---

[91] *Bull. EC*, Jan.–Feb. 1992, 1.5.10.

[92] For a brave attempt to justify the German action, see Genscher, *Erinnerungen*, 960–6, echoed by Libal, *Limits of Persuasion*, 83–6, 152–4.

[93] Maull, 'Germany in the Yugoslav Crisis', 104.

[94] Genscher, *Erinnerungen*, 932. Woodward attributes this to Genscher's need, under pressure from the FDP, to reassert foreign policy leadership after Kohl's successes over unification: Woodward, *Balkan Tragedy*, 185–6. However that may be, a common decision was still Germany's preference at the time of the 16 Dec. Ministerial Meeting: Libal, *Limits of Persuasion*, 152.

admonitions of Lord Carrington and the United States?[95] The popular interpretation is that there had been a trade-off at Maastricht: German readiness to concede the demands of its partners on the Treaty, especially the United Kingdom, against their acceptance of recognition.[96] This seems to be too crude a description of what happened. If deal there was, it was between France and Germany. And the deal was no more than to prevent the issue of recognition from coming to a head until the Maastricht European Council was out of the way. The object was to preserve the unity of the couple in order to avoid endangering the greater goal of the Maastricht Treaty.

By Védrine's own account, the difference of approach between France and Germany, or to be more accurate between Kohl and Mitterrand, to the question of Yugoslavia was a greater threat to the relationship and to the preparations for Maastricht than was the unification of Germany.[97] Mitterrand believed that there could be no stability in Yugoslavia without agreed borders and firm guarantees for the rights of minorities. Kohl was more concerned about his domestic political situation, where he was, as he told Mitterrand, under heavy pressure from his own party as well as the FDP, the Church, the press, and the 500,000 Croats living in Germany. The differences between the two men were caricatured in the press as Germany supporting Croatia and France supporting Serbia, just like 1914. Mitterrand remarked acerbically to John Major that he supposed the Germans would send their army to Croatia, and the French and British theirs to Serbia. Choosing not to regard this as a joke, Major said that he had no intention of sending the British army anywhere it was not already.

Kohl and Mitterrand confronted their differences frankly at a meeting in Bonn on 18 September 1991. Mitterrand accused Kohl of pursuing a German national policy in the Balkans, which could break up the Community. To avoid that, he was prepared to compromise. For his part, Kohl promised not to go it alone. He said that, for him, the priority was

[95] Gow, *Triumph of the Lack of Will*, 209; Woodward, *Balkan Tragedy*, 183–4; Maull, 'Germany in the Yugoslav Crisis', 104.

[96] See for example Gow, *Triumph of the Lack of Will*, 170; Woodward, *Balkan Tragedy*, 184. Douglas Hurd has, in the author's hearing, denied that any such deal was made. This is confirmed by German participants at the 16 Dec. meeting: Libal, *Limits of Persuasion*, 182 n. 10.

[97] The admittedly speculative account of events given in these paragraphs has been assembled from the following sources: Védrine, *Les Mondes de François Mitterrand*, 612–13, 615–22; Favier and Martin-Roland, *La Décennie Mitterrand*, iv. 198–9, 226, 235, 240, 243–4.

Maastricht, and if the two of them didn't do it, it would take a long, long time. The compromise which the French saw emerging was that the question of recognition should be put off until after Maastricht, while France gave up its attempts to secure an armed intervention force with a clear UN mandate.[98] The subject was briefly raised again at the Franco-German Summit in Bonn on 14 November, at which Mitterrand continued to call for the Community to take a joint decision based on agreed frontiers and respect for minority rights. Kohl's response was to repeat his difficulties with public opinion.

The Maastricht European Council was now fast approaching, and Genscher had warned Dumas that Germany would recognize Croatia immediately afterwards, between 16 and 24 December. What could be done to ensure that the discussions at Maastricht were not disturbed by the recognition question, and to prepare the debate on recognition which would inevitably follow? Mitterrand broached the subject at dinner with Kohl in Paris on 3 December. To avert the danger of divisions in the Community which German recognition would cause, he said he was prepared to look for ways of avoiding a Franco-German split. Kohl was above all anxious that the subject should not be raised at Maastricht. Mitterrand reassured him on that point.

Pierre Morel, the Diplomatic Adviser at the Élysée, had refurbished an idea whereby France and Germany should prepare a joint initiative, intended originally to be launched after Maastricht, based on the granting of recognition in exchange for prior guarantees of minority rights and agreed borders. These guarantees would be inferred from a general statement regarding the criteria for the recognition of new states in Europe. The proposal was approved by Mitterrand and forwarded to the Presidency on 5 December. It was discussed by the Foreign Ministers themselves at their European Council dinner on 10 December, and approved in principle. The Heads of State and Government did not tackle the issue, although it was of course at the back of everyone's minds and was raised in bilateral contacts. The French believed they had secured a minimum position which would preserve the appearance of unity, and intensive negotiations on the list of principles ensued in Bonn under the aegis of the respective Political Directors.[99]

It was a forlorn attempt to preserve the appearance of unity. Once the

[98] A different interpretation of the outcome of the meeting, with no mention of a deal, is given by Michael Libal, who was at the time the official responsible for Yugoslavia in the German Foreign Ministry: Libal, *Limits of Persuasion*, 53–4.

[99] Libal, *Limits of Persuasion*, 83.

European Council was out of the way, the Germans felt that they had kept their part of the bargain—to hold off until after Maastricht—and made it plain that German recognition would brook no further delay. On 15 December—the day before the Foreign Ministers were due to meet to decide the issue—Kohl announced at a charity concert for Croatian refugees that Germany would recognize Croatia and Slovenia before Christmas. Genscher said the same in a radio interview. In the circumstances, it was not surprising that the Foreign Ministers' discussion the next day was difficult. France did manage to secure agreement that the Badinter Commission should determine whether the republics seeking recognition met the criteria, but this was neglected as a procedural detail by Genscher on the grounds that an equally respectable German expert had already settled the issue in favour of Croatia, so the Badinter verdict could only be a formality.

There was no deal trading agreement on recognition against a favourable German attitude to the Maastricht negotiations. The deal, between Kohl and Mitterrand, was that recognition should be set to one side until agreement had been reached on the Treaty. Germany was thereafter able to force through a decision on the lines it preferred because its partners feared the criticism that would surely come if the Community was publicly split so soon after having decided on a common foreign and security policy. Dumas put it in a nutshell: 'une fracture au sein des Douze et singulièrement entre la France et l'Allemagne sur la question des Balkans me paraît beaucoup plus dangereuse que les risques . . . d'un embrasement accéléré de l'ex-Yougoslavie. L'éclatement de la Yougoslavie est un drame, celui de la Communauté serait une catastrophe'.[100]

The decision to submit the republics' applications for recognition to the Badinter Commission for assessment, taken to solve the imminent German problem rather than as a considered act of policy, had other unforeseen and highly undesirable effects. In the view of the Commission, Macedonia fulfilled the criteria, but recognition was prevented by the Greek veto. As regards Bosnia-Herzegovina, the Commission declared the situation was uncertain, and might be clarified by holding a referendum on independence. This was duly held on 29 February and 1 March, and resulted in a 99.7 per cent vote in favour of independence. However, the

---

[100] '. . . for the Twelve, and especially for France and Germany, to split over the Balkans seems to me to be much more dangerous than the risk of hastening the conflagration in former Yugoslavia. For Yugoslavia to split up is tragic; for the Community to do so would be catastrophic': note from Dumas to Mitterrand, 14 Dec. 1991 (Favier and Martin-Roland, *La Décennie Mitterrand*, iv. 244).

overwhelming majority of the Serbs, who constituted almost one-third of the total population of Bosnia, did not take part in the referendum.[101] The result, combined with strong pressure from the United States, already devoted to the Bosnian cause, pushed the Community into recognizing a country ripe for civil war. A legal device had been converted into a political blunder.

It is going too far to claim that the referendum precipitated the outbreak of conflict in Bosnia. But it was yet another blow to the Community's claim to be operating an intelligible foreign policy with regard to Yugoslavia. In the first months of the crisis, the Community's policy might have been wrong-headed, and had certainly been unsuccessful, but it had not been discreditable and was not believed to be incompetent. Even the failure to deploy armed force was not at the time a stick to beat the Community with. The recognition of the republics, however, whether Slovenia and Croatia, Macedonia, or Bosnia-Herzegovina, was very publicly bungled, and brought the notion of an EC foreign policy into disrepute.

It also undermined what remaining chances the EC Conference chaired by Lord Carrington had of securing peace in former Yugoslavia. The cease-fire in Croatia had been negotiated by the UN envoy, Cyrus Vance, and there was a move in the UN Secretariat in May to start up diplomatic negotiations again at a UN-sponsored Peace Conference in Geneva. These were stopped by the Secretary General, but there was a general feeling nevertheless that the wider international community, including Russia, had to be more closely involved. The Serbs were the first to move in this direction, followed by the French. Mitterrand launched the idea at the Western Economic Summit at Munich on 7 July 1992, and it was taken up in the Summit's declaration on former Yugoslavia.[102] The incoming President of the European Council (since 1 July 1992), John Major, took the initiative to call a conference in London on 26–7 August 1992, co-chaired by himself and UN Secretary General Boutros Boutros-Ghali. The conference established a set of principles and the organizational framework for a UN-EC Conference which would replace the EC Conference and sit permanently in Geneva. The Co-Chairmen were to be, for the UN, Cyrus Vance, and for the EC, David Owen. The 'hour of Europe' had lasted barely fourteen months.[103]

[101] Gow, *Triumph of the Lack of Will*, 78–9, 83–4.
[102] Libal, *Limits of Persuasion*, 95–6.
[103] Woodward, *Balkan Tragedy*, 286–7; Gow, *Triumph of the Lack of Will*, 223–9; Wynaendts, *L'Engrenage*, 178–83.

The conflict in Yugoslavia did not affect the discussions in the IGC on the aims and substance of a common foreign and security policy, but those discussions certainly affected the Community's policy towards Yugoslavia and the course of events there. Early armed intervention was excluded, most significantly because the United Kingdom was determined to avoid creating a precedent for CFSP, and the thorny issue of recognition was postponed because Kohl and Mitterrand were determined not to allow it to affect the delicate negotiations at the Maastricht European Council. Once the Treaty was signed, however, the embarrassing failures of European diplomacy provided material for use in the ratification debate, although opposite conclusions could be drawn. On the one hand they could be adduced as proof that EPC was in need of strengthening; on the other, that to conceive of an effective CFSP was a hopeless task. The EC record in Yugoslavia was far from being the main reason for the unexpected difficulties in ratification, but it did contribute to the general climate of dissatisfaction which beset the Community in the wake of the Maastricht Treaty.

Ratification

Surely no Head of Government, as he left the Maastricht meeting of the European Council in December 1991, could forecast the trials and tribulations attendant upon the ratification process. There had never been any particular difficulty before. Admittedly, EMU was a bold step forward, but after more than two years of difficult negotiations the governments of the Community had reached a satisfactory conclusion; since they all commanded working majorities in their national parliaments, why should there be a problem? Ratification of the Single European Act had been a routine event. There had been an unexpected constitutional hiccup in Ireland, precisely over what was held to be a transfer of sovereignty in the field of foreign affairs, but this had been rapidly and easily dealt with thorough a favourable referendum. In Denmark, the government lacked the necessary parliamentary majority for constitutional change, but was able to secure approval through a referendum with a majority which, if not lavish, was at least not embarrassing. These feats could no doubt be repeated if required. The only country which expected trouble after Maastricht was the United Kingdom, and Prime Minister Major thought he had done enough to pre-empt it by securing an opt-out on the Social

Chapter and an opt-in on the single currency. 'Game, set, and match'[104] proved to be over-optimistic as a description of the United Kingdom's part in the Maastricht process, but it was accurate enough as a forecast of the outcome of ratification, even though the general election of April 1992, by reducing his majority to 21, left him in a tricky situation in Parliament.

The bombshell came, not from the United Kingdom, but from Denmark. Given the deep suspicion of the European Community which prevailed in that country, this might have been expected. In fact, it was not. If the Danish government had secured ratification of the Single Act by referendum, presumably the feat could be repeated for the Maastricht Treaty. The Danish Constitution provides that powers may be transferred to supranational organizations by a five-sixths majority of the Folketing, or by referendum if the five-sixths majority in the Folketing is not achieved, but the normal majority is. There was neither a five-sixths nor a normal majority for the Single Act, but the members of the Folketing had undertaken to respect the outcome of a consultative referendum. When this gave a vote of 56.2 per cent in favour, the necessary five-sixths majority was thereby achieved.

The situation was different with regard to the Maastricht Treaty. With the exception of the extreme right and left wings, all the political parties had come round to supporting it. However, the government was just short of a five-sixths majority in the Folketing. At the close of the parliamentary procedure (12 May 1992), the bill authorizing ratification of the Maastricht Treaty was passed by 130 votes in favour, 25 against, 23 absent, and one abstention. A referendum was therefore necessary to determine the issue (and no doubt would have been a political necessity in any case). The Danish people made their decision known on 2 June 1992: 1,606,442 voted in favour (49.3 per cent), and 1,653,289 voted against (50.7 per cent). By a majority of fewer than 50,000 votes, out of a total electorate of 3.9 million, the Danes had tipped over the construction which twelve governments had spent four years laboriously assembling.

The reasons for the rejection were varied and have been much discussed.[105] The basic cause could well have been that, having worked hard to bring round the political parties, the government had neglected the ordinary people. It was the first salutary lesson that the élitist approach to the EC was no longer going to work as well as it had in the past—a

---

[104] A sound-bite attributed to the Prime Minister, but in fact the work of his spokesman: Young, *This Blessed Plot*, 432.

[105] For the background, see Heurlin, 'Denmark and the Ratification of the Maastricht Treaty', 172–8.

phenomenon common to many Member States which was soon to give birth to a new EC rhetoric. Some features of the debate, however, were more strongly marked in Denmark than in the rest of the Community, and reflected the traditional Danish approach to the EC. This applied to foreign policy, and in particular to defence. During the Folketing debate, all parties mentioned this aspect of the Maastricht Treaty. The Conservative and Liberal Parties were in favour of strengthened security and defence co-operation, albeit on the intergovernmental basis guaranteed by the three-pillar structure. The Socialists, the Progress Party, and the Radical Liberals, as well as the Social Democrats, all had doubts about the inclusion of a defence dimension. The Radical Liberal spokesman, although satisfied with the existing EPC, thought that it had not done very well in Yugoslavia. These considerations undoubtedly weighed, among others, in the 'No' vote.

Shocked as they were by the Danish result, the other Member States were by no means inclined to renegotiate the Treaty. The door was left open for Denmark to come back in, and cosmetic touches could always be found, but the clear message was that the Danes themselves had to find the solution to the difficulties they had got into. Meeting in Oslo on 4 June 1992, the Foreign Ministers

noted that 11 Member States have expressed the desire for European Union involving all the Member States. They rule out any renegotiation of the text signed at Maastricht.

The ratification procedure will continue in the Member States on the basis of the existing text and in accordance with the schedule agreed on, before the end of the year.

They all agree that the door should be left open for Denmark to participate in the Union.[106]

The Danish government produced in October 1992 a paper analysing the situation following the referendum. This contained a number of options, ranging from leaving the Community to accepting the Maastricht Treaty but with some special provisions for Denmark. An interesting thing now happened. It was the main opposition parties which took the initiative of working out a position on the basis of which, after agreement by the other Member States, the Danish people could be asked to reconsider its verdict. This was the so-called 'national compromise', which was forwarded to the other Member States on 30 October 1992 with the support

---

[106] *Bull. EC*, June 1992, 1.1.3; Laursen and Vanhoonacker (eds.), *The Ratification of the Maastricht Treaty*, 70.

of all the political parties but one. Among other issues designed to make the EU more accessible to ordinary people, the 'national compromise' sought four opt-outs for Denmark, of which the first concerned security and defence. The other three were the single currency, EU citizenship, and any transfer of sovereignty in the area of justice and home affairs. The paragraph concerning security and defence read: 'Denmark does not participate in the so-called defence policy dimension, which involves membership of the Western European Union and a common defence policy or a common defence.'[107]

Intense diplomatic activity followed, which resulted in a face-saving formula adopted by the European Council at Edinburgh in December 1992. In a nutshell, nothing in the Maastricht Treaty was altered, but various existing and self-evident features were given prominence, thus allowing the Danish government to claim that Denmark would not be forced into anything it really did not want, and on that basis to put the question to the Danish people in a second referendum a year later. In particular as regards defence, the Edinburgh European Council noted that Denmark had, at the invitation of the WEU, become an observer to that organization; it further noted that 'nothing in the Treaty on European Union commits Denmark to become a member of the WEU', which had always been obvious not only in the case of Denmark but also for all other Member States. The Heads of State or Government nevertheless spelled out that 'Accordingly, Denmark does not participate in the elaboration and implementation of decisions and actions of the Union which have defence implications, but will not prevent the development of closer co-operation between Member States in this area'.[108] The only practical implication was recognized in a Declaration on defence, in which the European Council noted 'that Denmark will renounce its right to exercise the Presidency of the Union in each case involving the elaboration and the implementation of decisions and actions of the Union which have defence implications. The normal rules for replacing the President, in the case of the President being indisposed, shall apply. These rules will also apply with regard to the representation of the Union in international organizations, international conferences and with third countries'.[109]

Such a case has never arisen. The arrangement was important, nevertheless, for two reasons. First, it joined the list of precedents authorizing a Member State to opt out of obligations—and opportunities—which had

---

[107] 'Denmark in Europe', submitted to the Member States on 30 Oct. 1991: Laursen and Vanhoonacker (eds.), *The Ratification of the Maastricht Treaty*, 505–9.
[108] *Bull. EC* 12-1992, 1.37, p. 25.   [109] *Bull. EC*, Dec. 1992, 1.41, p. 26.

been agreed to by the great majority of Member States. The United Kingdom had its dispensation from the Social Chapter and the single currency, Denmark from the single currency and now the defence aspects of foreign policy. Those countries which wished to go further and faster began to wonder whether they could always be held back to the pace of the slowest. Second, the institutional arrangements consequent on the opt-out were set out in a binding, public text. No longer could *sub rosa*, nudge-and-wink solutions be found to obviate passing embarrassment experienced by one or the other Member State. Everything had, for legal and political reasons, to be set out openly in black and white. This was desirable for the Social Chapter, for otherwise laws could not be passed. It was harmful to the CFSP, which, since the principle of consensus was maintained, inevitably suffered from the public dissociation of a Member State from a given policy area. It could only hamper the free flow of foreign-policy making, as the Irish position had done in the old days of EPC. Both these inconveniences were to surface again, in an acute form, in the Intergovernmental Conference leading to the Amsterdam Treaty.

The stage was now set for the Danish people to express their views in a second referendum. Most political parties at least had now realized that to reject the Maastricht Treaty a second time would be tantamount to withdrawal from the Union, and made the best of the deal secured at Edinburgh. It is difficult not to sympathize with the Progress Party, which maintained its opposition on the grounds that the Danes would be voting a second time about the same thing: 'not a single comma had been changed in the Maastricht Treaty'. But there was a comfortable five-sixths majority in the Folketing for the bills which would permit Danish ratification. A referendum had been provided for, however, and on 18 May 1993, 56.7 per cent of the Danish electorate voted in favour of the Maastricht Treaty, as interpreted by the Edinburgh agreement, while 43.3 per cent voted against.

It would be going too far to claim that the Maastricht provisions for a common foreign and security policy played a crucial part in the Danes' initial rejection, and that the subsequent dispensation from its defence side swung the balance in favour. The Danish public's disenchantment with an EU defence capability was part and parcel of a general concern that political power was slipping out of control. This covered the single currency, policing, and European citizenship as well as a future European army. Approximately one-third of the voters were in favour of the inclusion in EC competence of each of the areas of common foreign policy, common defence policy, the single currency, and the social dimension, but there is no guarantee that it was the same third in each case.[110] What swayed the balance was the fear that the economic costs of rejection would be too high, and the Edinburgh formula was sufficient to allow a new campaign in favour of Maastricht to be conducted.

President Mitterrand did not need to call a referendum to secure ratification of the Maastricht Treaty by France, but he did. His reasoning was a curious amalgam of committed propaganda for the European idea and wanting to pull a fast one on the opposition. The adventure was to backfire, in conditions which brought the Treaty, and all its component parts, into further disrepute.[111]

The President of the Republic, as was his right and arguably his duty, first consulted the Constitutional Council as to whether the Treaty was consistent with the Constitution. If the Constitutional Council found that certain provisions were not consistent, then the Constitution would have to be amended. The Constitutional Council gave its ruling on 9 April 1992. It found that the provisions relating to Community citizens' right to vote and stand in municipal elections, the introduction of a monetary policy and a single exchange-rate policy, and the free entry and movement of persons were contrary to the Constitution. Interestingly, the Council did not extend its observations to the provisions on foreign policy and defence, which caused so much trouble in Denmark. It may be that the Council took the view that previous treaties, for example the Single European Act, on which it had not been consulted, could not now be put into question: *pacta sunt servanda*.

President Mitterrand therefore had to decide how the Constitution was to be amended. Two ways were open to him. He could either submit identical proposals to both the National Assembly and the Senate, the result then being submitted to a referendum. If the President chose to forgo the referendum, the text had to be adopted by a three-fifths majority of both houses meeting as the Congrès du Parlement. Alternatively, and more doubtfully, he could submit the question to a referendum directly. Mitterrand chose the first alternative, thereby running the risk of providing a platform for anti-European views, and also of incurring unwanted

---

[110] Laursen, 'Denmark and the Ratification of the Maastricht Treaty', 80.

[111] The following paragraphs draw on Keraudren and Dubois, 'France and the Ratification of the Maastricht Treaty', and Védrine, Les Mondes de François Mitterrand, 552–61. See also Grunberg, 'Le Trouble des opinions publiques', 112–13, 119, and Favier and Martin-Roland, *La Décennie Mitterrand*, iv. 310–32. For a thoughtful and penetrating account of the ratification debate in France, see Mazzucelli, *France and Germany at Maastricht*, 207–25.

constitutional changes. This is precisely what happened. Not surprisingly, the parliamentarians took the opportunity of writing further powers for themselves into the Constitution, together with a number of other amendments which, while not necessarily affecting the text of the Treaty, betrayed concern about the slippage of powers from the national to the European level.

The revision of the Constitution was voted on 25 June 1992. In spite of a rearguard action which lasted over the summer, there were no further constitutional obstacles to the ratification of the Maastricht Treaty. Mitterrand had decided, however, to submit directly to a referendum the law authorizing ratification of the Treaty. His decision was announced the day after the negative result of the Danish referendum on 2 June 1992. It could therefore be presented as an attempt to secure a popular vote of confidence in the government's policy over Europe, which had been shaken by the failure in Denmark. But there was a deeper constitutional motive for Mitterrand's action: the direct appeal to the people was designed to counter the Senate's growing tendency, as shown by the debate on the revision of the Constitution, to intervene in matters which the Fifth Republic order had intended should be reserved to the President. At a still deeper level of political advantage, Mitterrand believed that there was an opportunity here to divide his political opponents and distract attention from the parlous situation in which the Socialist government found itself after the disastrous local election results and the departure of Edith Cresson as Prime Minister in April.

The opposition of the Communist Party to the Treaty was traditional and clear-cut. The Socialist Party, as the party of government, could be expected to support the Treaty. In fact, many Socialists, scenting the popular mood and fearful of the outcome of the elections due in March 1993, were anxious to avoid a high profile, and the left wing, led by Jean-Pierre Chevènement, was opposed for reasons of national sovereignty. Mitterrand believed, however, that these differences would not be significant. He counted on a decisive split in the ranks of the conservative opposition. The liberal centre parties (UDF), led by Valéry Giscard d'Estaing, were strongly and traditionally in favour of Europe and the European Community. The Gaullists (RPR), however, led by Jacques Chirac, had always found Europe a sensitive subject, and although Chirac finally came out in favour of the Maastricht Treaty senior members of the party took a prominent role in the anti-Maastricht campaign. The split even carried through to the RPR's allotted broadcasting time, with half going to the anti-Maastricht camp and half to supporters of the party's official line.

It looked, therefore, as though Mitterrand's tactics were going to pay off. But although the opposition was indeed split, the forces supporting the government were not united, and the opinion polls began to show alarmingly high 'No' voting intentions. The supporters and opponents of the Maastricht Treaty found themselves with some strange cross-party bedfellows, and the arguments which were deployed during the referendum debate were not the usual political currency. When Mitterrand announced the referendum, he justified further progress in European integration, embodied in the Maastricht Treaty, by the need to ensure peace in Europe, especially since the fall of the Berlin Wall in 1989. Those in favour of the Treaty argued that the European Union needed to be strong in order to counterbalance rising nationalism, as exemplified by the conflict in Yugoslavia. Opponents of the Treaty adduced against this the Community's failure to deal adequately with the Yugoslavia problem. The two sides were in fact saying the same thing—that the EC in its present shape had failed to produce, over Yugoslavia, the results which could properly be expected of it—but reached diametrically opposite conclusions about the ratification of the Maastricht Treaty. Yugoslavia provided the stick with which both sides could beat each other indiscriminately. Other issues were of course discussed, economic and monetary union being naturally prominent, together with fears of the centralization of the Community in Brussels, as well as the unpopularity of Mitterrand and his government, but Yugoslavia played an important part.[112]

The Maastricht Treaty, especially its foreign policy provisions, owed its existence in great measure to French fears of domination by a united and strengthened Germany, and it might have been expected that this would have been produced as an argument in favour of the Treaty in the course of the ratification debate. In fact, although the argument was deployed on both sides of the debate, Mitterrand himself declined to make use of it. In a newspaper interview a week before the referendum, he complained that he personally had been hurt by the way in which supporters of the Treaty almost as much as opponents had used the argument of mistrust of the Germans. 'To begin with, it is a sign of lack of confidence in oneself. And then it gives the impression that Germany has its special devils (the expression has been used), whereas every nation must master its own. To understand Germany and the Germans requires greater respect.'[113] This fairly breathtaking sublimation of the role he had himself played in the making

---

[112] Guicherd, *L'heure de l'Europe*, 57; Gnesotto, *Leçons de la Yougoslavie*, 25.
[113] Védrine, *Les Mondes de François Mitterrand*, 560.

of the Treaty may be ascribed to the need to preserve publicly the rosy aura surrounding the Franco–German relationship; it may also reflect a realization that fear of Germany was not likely to weigh heavily in the decision of the French people.

The CFSP provisions of the Treaty do not appear in themselves to have presented any special difficulty to the French electorate. This may have been because they were not perceived as presenting any particular threat to French sovereignty or the interests of France. Indeed, a senior French official close to the campaign later claimed that one of the reasons France had fought so hard for the three-pillar structure was in order to take popular attitudes into account.[114] While one may suspect that this is a justification after the event for a position which was in any case firmly held by the French negotiating élite, the three-pillar structure no doubt denied opponents of the Treaty an additional stick with which to beat the government.

When the referendum took place on 20 September 1992, France voted by a whisker in favour of ratifying the Maastricht Treaty (51.04 per cent in favour and 48.95 per cent against). The result, profoundly disturbing to the French political establishment since the electorate split on lines completely different from the traditional party-political structure, has been analysed and explained *ad infinitum*. Its effect on the development of the European Union was serious. This applied less to economic and monetary union, for which the Treaty set deadlines which one day were sure to arrive, as to the new areas introduced into the Union by the Treaty—the common foreign and security policy and co-operation on justice and home affairs. Unlike EMU, the CFSP had no institutional deadlines. It remained in essence not so different from its predecessor, EPC, and like it depended for its effectiveness on a common approach of the Member States and a solid public reputation. Now the instigator of the CFSP, François Mitterrand, had come within a hair's breadth of destroying his brainchild at birth. Not only was the standing of the CFSP affected by the grudging assent given to the Union, but the Member States, recalling the public doubts expressed in the ratification process, proved to be cautious and unwilling to take risks in the subsequent management of the CFSP.

The other Member States had less difficulty in ratifying the Treaty, even though the question was the subject of fierce debate throughout the Community. The British government had to lead a tough and epic struggle in the face of resistance from the so-called Euro-sceptics, who carried

---

[114] Mazzucelli, *France and Germany at Maastricht*, 224.

more weight in Parliament after the April 1992 elections had left the Major government with a severely reduced majority, but victory was never in doubt given the support of the Liberal Democrats. The CFSP was not an issue in the debate. By and large, it can be said that the Maastricht Treaty was ratified because no other government pursued the hazardous course of a referendum. The exception was Ireland, which had learnt from its experience of ratifying the Single European Act that an attempt to amend the country's position on foreign affairs by state prerogative rather than popular consultation ran the risk of being overturned by the courts.[115] The Irish government did not intend to make the same mistake twice, and a referendum was announced, which was held on 18 June 1992. Although the Treaty's CFSP provisions were attacked in some political quarters, most parties accepted the government's view that they did not, at this stage, compromise Irish neutrality, on which in any case views were evolving.[116] The leader of the Labour Party, Dick Spring, said that 'the Maastricht Treaty *per se* will not endanger Irish neutrality in the period leading up to a further Intergovernmental Conference'.[117] The result of the referendum was a 69 per cent vote in favour. Those in favour had been swayed by economic considerations. Those against were influenced by a variety of considerations, of which defence was but one.

The greatest surprise, and potentially the greatest obstacle, on the road towards ratification occurred in Germany, the country on the face of it least likely to present difficulties as the originator, with France, of the Maastricht Treaty.[118] Although the political establishment, with few exceptions, supported the Treaty, public opinion, rattled by the unexpectedly high cost of unification, was reluctant to abandon the anchor of the Deutschemark. Sixty-two economists of high repute issued, rather late in the day,[119] eleven theses why EMU would do more harm than good. As Kohl had feared, the argument was brought forward that EMU, whether or not desirable in itself, was dangerous in the absence of measures to strengthen democratic control in the Community. In contradistinction to their views on EMU, the German people, when asked, expressed themselves strongly and increasingly in favour of a common foreign and security policy. In spring 1992 61 per cent were in favour of a common foreign

---

[115] Nuttall, *European Political Co-operation*, 256–7.

[116] Keatinge, 'Ireland and Common Security', 218–19.

[117] van Wijnbergen, 'Ireland and the Ratification of the Maastricht Treaty', 185–6.

[118] These paragraphs are drawn from Beuter, 'Germany and the Ratification of the Maastricht Treaty', See also Mazzucelli, *France and Germany at Maastricht*, 243–72.

[119] June 1992, four years after the debate had been launched at the European Council in Hanover.

policy, and 71 per cent (West Germany) and 81 per cent (East Germany) in favour of a common security and defence policy.

In spite of the hesitations about EMU, the Treaty was ratified in December 1992 by an overwhelming majority in the Bundestag and unanimously by the Bundesrat. The ratification certificate could not, however, be signed by the Federal President because the legality of the Treaty had been challenged before the Constitutional Court. More than a score of constitutional cases were brought, by plaintiffs ranging from the Greens to the Republicans to Manfred Brunner, former Chef de Cabinet of Martin Bangemann, Vice-President of the European Commission. All these cases were based on arguments that the Maastricht Treaty violated fundamental and unamendable principles of the German Constitution. Ratification was delayed until the Court had delivered its opinion, which it did not do until 12 October 1993, making Germany the last Member State to deposit its instruments of ratification.

Although the Constitutional Court rejected the challenges to the Treaty, it did so in an 85-page opinion which significantly altered the way in which the fundamental structures of the Community had hitherto been regarded by the integrationist school.[120] In brief, the Court insisted on the primacy of national citizens acting through their national systems for securing the legitimacy of the Union,[121] side by side with a European Parliament which would be (but was not yet . . .) increasingly in a position to perform similar functions; at the same time, and as a consequence, progress in integration through interpretation of the texts or incrementally was frowned on. Although specific conclusions with regard to the CFSP were not drawn, the emphasis on the nation state as the basic building block of the structure of the Union goes in the direction of foreign-policy making as organized under EPC, rather than a genuine common foreign and security policy of the Union as such.

The process of ratification of the Maastricht Treaty was a sad and anxious time for the supporters of European integration, and a salutary one for its negotiators. The situation was indeed paradoxical. Support for the unification of Western Europe was stationary or in decline, and

---

[120] Laursen and Vanhoonacker (eds.), *The Ratification of the Maastricht Treaty*, 515–16.

[121] 'If a union of democratic states performs sovereign tasks through the exercise of sovereign authority it is first and foremost the citizens of the Member States who must legitimize such action through a democratic process via their national parliaments' (Headnote 3 (a)); 'The Treaty on European Union establishes a union of countries in order to create an ever closer union among the peoples of Europe (organized as states) (Art. A TEU), rather than a state based upon a European people' (Headnote 8).

attitudes towards the Treaty were little more than lukewarm. Only in the Netherlands, Ireland, and Italy did public opinion polls show an absolute majority in favour.[122] And yet heavy and increasing majorities expressed themselves in favour of the European Community being responsible for foreign policy towards countries outside the EC and for a common policy in matters of security and defence. Support for EC policy responsibility in both areas was generally in the 60–80% range, with security coming higher than foreign policy. The exceptions were Ireland and Denmark, both non-members of the WEU, where security scored below foreign policy and both were at lower levels (50–55% by October 1992). Even in the United Kingdom, in general so mistrustful of the Community and all its works, support for EC foreign policy responsibility approached 50%, and for security was well on the way to 60%.

The only explanation of the phenomenon of comparatively low levels of support for European unification and Maastricht, and high levels of support for EC foreign and security policy responsibility, is, first, that the foreign policy and security question did not enter the ratification debate to any appreciable extent (with the exception of Denmark and Ireland) and, second, that, when it did, public opinion was not convinced that the Maastricht Treaty provided an adequate response to what the public claimed to want. Yugoslavia was an argument which cut both ways. As was stated above with reference to France, those who in any case opposed the Treaty claimed that the Community's failure in Yugoslavia proved its incapacity to conduct a sensible foreign and security policy, while those in favour of the Treaty said that this was precisely what Maastricht was supposed to remedy. The truth no doubt lay in an amalgam of the two: a successful foreign policy needed the self-confidence and sureness of purpose furnished by a confident and prosperous Community recognized as legitimate by its citizens, and the Community needed for the sake of legitimacy the capacity to intervene effectively in grave situations external to it. As the CDU politician Schäuble said, 'How can I tell people at home we should abandon the D-mark for a currency union, when Europe is not in a position to stop a war?'[123]

---

[122] This paragraph is taken from Knoben, 'Public Opinion in the European Union'.
[123] Beuter, 'Germany and the Ratification of the Maastricht Treaty', 105.

9

Implementation

Principles and guidelines

Not all of the constituent parts of the CFSP were settled at Maastricht. Some important elements were held over until the following year, and some were not in place until after the Treaty was ratified, on the eve of its coming into force.

It will be recalled that one of the ideas behind instituting 'joint actions' in the CFSP had been to provide an enhanced decision-making procedure in those areas of policy where Member States had agreed in advance that they had important interests in common.[1] Although hopes of significant improvements in decision-making had been dashed, the Treaty still required that priority areas should be defined. There had been agreement at Maastricht on a residual list of security areas, derived from the 'Asolo list', but it was felt that more was needed.[2] In response to an invitation by the European Council, the Foreign Ministers therefore drafted over the next few months a report establishing a general framework in which the CFSP could operate, and identifying some areas suited for joint action. This report was submitted to and approved by the European Council at Lisbon on 26–7 June 1992.[3]

In addition to recalling the general objectives laid down by the Treaty for the CFSP, the report suggested some specific objectives:

  (i) strengthening democratic principles and institutions, and respect for human and minority rights;
 (ii) promoting regional political stability and contributing to the creation of political and/or economic frameworks that encourage regional co-operation or moves towards regional or sub-regional integration;
(iii) contributing to the prevention and settlement of conflicts;

---

[1] Art. J.1.3.
[2] Dumond and Setton, *La Politique étrangère et de sécurité commune*, 86; Luif, *On the Road to Brussels*, 68.
[3] *Bull. EC*, June 1992, I.16 and annex 1 (18–22).

(iv) contributing to a more effective international co-ordination in dealing with emergency situations;

(v) strengthening existing co-operation in issues of international interest such as the fight against arms proliferation, terrorism and the traffic in illicit drugs;

(vi) promoting and supporting good government.

This catalogue of sentiments appropriate to a post-Cold War power, while admirable in itself, did not provide much guidance for the selection of joint actions. Three additional factors were therefore identified:

(i) the geographical proximity of a given region or country;

(ii) an important interest in the political and economic stability of a region or country;

(iii) the existence of threats to the security interests of the Union.

Using these criteria, the report identified a limited number of geographical areas in which joint action could be undertaken in the short term: Central and Eastern Europe, in particular the Commonwealth of Independent States and the Balkans; the Mediterranean, in particular the Maghreb; and the Middle East. This at least was clear: CFSP would deploy its new instrument of joint action with respect to its geographical neighbours. Unfortunately, the clarity thus achieved was immediately muddied by a series of provisos: the selection of areas was merely illustrative; the European Council could always change it to take developments into account; and in any case one should not forget relations with the developing world, both Lomé and non-Lomé countries, nor indeed the United States, Canada, and Japan. The CFSP's reach was to be truly global, covering all parts of the world with the exception, no doubt unintentional, of Australia, New Zealand, and the Antarctic. The genesis of the report helps to explain this. The Portuguese Presidency's intention had been to secure a balance between East (Eastern Europe, reputed to be of greater concern to the northern members of the EC) and South (the Mediterranean and developing worlds, of greater interest to the southern members). This led to an extensive enumeration of areas of interest. In the third draft, tabled for the meeting of Foreign Ministers at Guimarães, pretty well all regions of the world were cited as possibilities for joint action. This, and the draft's inadequate treatment of security issues, attracted criticism, and the number of priorities was reduced for the final document adopted by the European Council at Lisbon. The price to be paid, however, was the inclusion of the above-mentioned provisos, diluting the list of 'joint action' areas to the point where the concept lost significance.[4]

More detailed indications were given about potential objectives for joint action for each of the selected areas. For example, the following text was adopted with reference to Russia and the former Soviet Republics (similar texts were provided for other countries in Central and Eastern Europe, including the Balkans; former Yugoslavia; the Maghreb; and the Middle East):

Hitherto, the action of the Community and its Member States in the political field has been dominated by the need to assure the area's stability, with particular attention to the preservation of European security. With a view to strengthening the Union's capacity for influence *vis-à-vis* this group of countries, joint action might be envisaged in the following areas:

  (i) support for the setting up of a framework of harmonious relations between the European Union and the new States, taking into account the different interests and historical experiences of the States concerned;
 (ii) reinforcing existing patterns of co-operation and trade between the new States themselves;
(iii) encouraging full compliance with all the treaties on disarmament and arms control to which they are parties, including those on non-proliferation;

This text has all the resonance of a mission statement dutifully penned by an old-fashioned manager dragooned into the best business-school practices. Given the circumstances, it was no doubt unrealistic to hope for better, although the absence of any reference to Russia in a text supposedly devoted to it, and the failure to implement the commitment to open joint facilities and missions in the CIS, were disappointing.

The final section of the report, devoted to domains within the security dimension, for the most part limited itself to repeating the language of the Maastricht Treaty. It did reveal that the European Council had indicated the domains within the security dimension which might be the object of joint actions:

---

[4] de Vasconcelos, 'Portugal: A Case for an Open Europe', 129–30; de Vasconcelos, 'Portugal: Pressing for an Open Europe?', 279–80; Barbé, 'Spain', 125. The degree of attention which the report attracted at Ministerial level has, however, been doubted: Dumond and Setton, *La politique étrangère et de sécurité commune*, 26.

(i) the CSCE process;
(ii) the policy of disarmament and arms control in Europe, including confidence-building measures;
(iii) nuclear non-proliferation issues;
(iv) the economic aspects of security, in particular control of the transfer of military technology to third countries and control of arms exports.

The Foreign Ministers had been invited by the European Council to 'begin preparatory work with a view to defining the necessary basic elements for a policy of the Union by the date of entry into force of the Treaty'. To assist in the work, it was decided at the initiative of France to create an *ad hoc* working group on security under the Political Committee.[5]

The drafters of the report were handicapped by the need to achieve consensus and by the absence of clear ideas about what would constitute a joint action. Already the language of the report revealed the difficulties which would attend the implementation of the CFSP over ensuring the application of consistency in practice. Could joint actions formally incorporate Community instruments? And if they did, was it CFSP or EC procedure which was to apply? If, for example, a joint action with regard to a CIS republic were to incorporate a Trade Agreement with the EC, would the Commission be legally bound to make the corresponding proposal?

A more serious difficulty, however, lay in the impossibility of working out in the abstract, and by a consensus procedure, what the Member States' 'important interests in common' were. This could only be done by a distillation of often-competing national interests, and to be effective required the presence of a body serving a function similar to that of the Commission in the EC. But perhaps, in view of the absence of a system for genuine majority voting on joint actions, it was not so crucial to work out what 'important interests in common' were, after all.

It had been expected that the Treaty on European Union, and with it the CFSP, would enter into force on 1 January 1993, at the same time as the completion of the Single Market. In selecting areas suited to joint action in a report prepared well before the European Council in June 1992, the Foreign Ministers could not foresee that delays in the ratification of the Treaty would put back its entry into force by ten months. As noted in the previous chapter, Germany was the last Member State to deposit its instruments of ratification, and the Treaty came into force on 1 November 1993.

---

[5] Dumond and Setton, *La politique étrangère et de sécurité commune*, 115.

To mark the event, the European Council met on the eve of the new era, on 29 October 1993. It adopted a number of guidelines for the 'rapid implementation of the measures which we regard as priorities under the new Treaty', including some on the CFSP. In doing so it reviewed its decision at Lisbon in June 1992, and this time was concise and practical in specifying joint actions to be undertaken, although still making sure that the range was sufficiently wide to cater for Member States' special interests:[6]

The CFSP will be developed gradually and pragmatically according to the importance of the interests common to all Member States; the European Council asks the Council, as a matter of priority, to define the conditions and procedures for joint action to be undertaken in the following areas:

Promotion of stability and peace in Europe

Stability, reinforcement of the democratic process and development of regional co-operation in Central and Eastern Europe. A stability pact to resolve the problem of minorities and to strengthen the inviolability of frontiers will be a staple component of these measures.

Middle East

Accompanying the Middle-East peace process by use of the political, economic and financial means provided by the Union in support of a comprehensive peace plan.

South Africa

Support for the transition towards multiracial democracy in South Africa through a co-ordinated programme of assistance in preparing for the elections and monitoring them, and through the creation of an appropriate co-operation framework to consolidate the economic and social foundations of this transition.

Former Yugoslavia

Search for a negotiated and durable solution to the conflict; contribution to the implementation of a peace plan and support for humanitarian action.

Russia

Support for the democratic process initiated in Russia; in accordance with the wishes of the Russian authorities, dispatch of a team of observers for the parliamentary election on 12 December. This action will be co-ordinated with

---

[6] Dumond and Setton, *La politique étrangère et de sécurité commune*, 128.

the European Parliament and the international organizations that will also be involved.[7]

The European Council had fulfilled its obligation under Article J.3.1 to issue general guidelines. It was now up to the Council to adopt the corresponding joint actions.

As regards security, the initiative to prepare for the entry into force of the Maastricht Treaty lay, not with the European Council, but with WEU. It will be recalled that WEU was to serve both as the defence component of the EU and the European pillar of NATO; it was to be a hinge, not an instrument. In its dual capacity it had two immediate problems to resolve: the question of membership and the nature of its tasks.[8]

Membership had become a problem because of WEU's dual role straddling the EU and NATO. If WEU had only been the defence component of the EU, the problem could have been easily solved by adapting the original Cahen doctrine: members of the EU who so wished were entitled to full membership of WEU, and those who did not could be observers. Under this formula, Greece, which had in effect made membership a condition of its accepting the Maastricht security provisions,[9] would join as a full member and Denmark and Ireland as observers. The only political problem would be the application of Article V of the WEU Treaty. Would the defence guarantee hold in the case of armed conflict between Turkey and Greece?

Matters were not so simple, however. Since WEU also had to serve as the European pillar of NATO, a way had to be found of associating those European members of NATO which were not members of the EU (Iceland, Norway, and Turkey). This made the Article V question even more complicated, as well as seriously impairing WEU's image as the security face of the EU. However, this was the decision which had been reached in the IGC, and the new status of associate member was therefore invented. The German Presidency of WEU lost no time in writing to those concerned, in the EU and in NATO, to draw their attention to the new possibilities which were open to them, as set out in the second WEU Declaration annexed to the Maastricht Treaty.

What's in a name? The distinction between full and associate members was hard to discern, and gave rise to much discussion. Those who

---

[7] *Bull. EC*, Oct. 1993, I.4.

[8] For the debate within the WEU, see van Eekelen, *Debating European Security*, 119–39, on which these paragraphs draw. There is a useful summary of developments in Luif, *On the Road to Brussels*, 74–82.

[9] van Eekelen, *Debating European Security*, 114.

leaned towards the WEU's EU role, like France, tended to maximize the points of difference; those who preferred to emphasize the NATO aspect, like the United Kingdom, tended to play it down. The WEU Declaration itself had made it clear that associated membership would be conceived 'in a way which will give [the associated members] the possibility of participating fully in the activities of WEU'. What did this mean in practice? By the end of May a compromise had been reached, and was formalized by the WEU Ministerial Council meeting at the Petersberg on 19 June 1992. The most important arrangements were as follows:

- WEU Council meetings would normally be held in enlarged format, including the associate members and observers,[10] but restricted meetings could be held at the request of the majority of full members, or half of them if that included the Presidency. (One single member sufficed to call a meeting of the enlarged Council, but a higher threshold was fixed for the restricted Council to prevent Greece from systematically excluding Turkey from the discussions.)
- Associate members would have access to the Planning Cell, but would not provide regular members to it.
- They could take part in forming the consensus, but could not block it.
- They would take part on the same basis as full members in WEU military operations to which they committed forces.
- They would make a financial contribution to the operation of the WEU.

Above all it was made clear that NATO and WEU defence guarantees could not be invoked in the case of disputes between members of either organization.

The new arrangements were not formally applied for some time. Although most of them could have been handled by administrative means, the accession of Greece required ratification by all the full members and, because of hesitations on the part of the Netherlands, this was not achieved until 1995. In the meanwhile, Greece became an 'active observer', and the arrangements for associates and observers were applied provisionally.

The other main question which the WEU had to decide after Maastricht was what it was supposed to do. This too was settled in the Petersberg

---

[10] Unlike the associate members, the observers can only speak on invitation, but intimations on their part that they would like to take the floor are unlikely to be ignored.

Declaration. In addition to fulfilling defence obligations in accordance with Article V,

military units of WEU member states, acting under the authority of WEU, could be employed for:

— humanitarian and rescue tasks;
— peacekeeping tasks;
— tasks of combat forces in crisis management, including peacemaking.[11]

These tasks would be carried out by units drawn from the forces of WEU member states, designated to that effect, whether or not they also had NATO missions.

In order to carry out these tasks, WEU needed a planning capability, and steps were taken to set up a Planning Cell, as foreseen in the Maastricht Declaration. The United Kingdom wanted it to be in physical proximity to SHAPE, but the WEU Secretary General, Willem van Eekelen, successfully insisted that it should be located with the Secretariat, for which new premises were being sought in Brussels. With forty officers the new Cell was almost as large as the rest of the Secretariat put together, and was headed by two generals. Its mission was defined in the Petersberg Declaration as:

— preparing contingency plans for the employment of forces under WEU auspices;
— preparing recommendations for the necessary command, control and communications arrangements, including standing operating procedures for headquarters which might be selected;
— keeping an updated list of units which might be allocated to EU for specific operations.

The decision at Maastricht to treat the WEU as the defence arm of the Union had implications for the practical relations between the two organizations. Co-operation with the EU Council Secretariat was provided for in the WEU Maastricht Declaration, but the Commission was only to be 'regularly informed and, as appropriate, consulted'. A report on practical measures to develop the relations with the EU and NATO was adopted by the WEU Ministers at the Petersberg meeting, and the EU part evolved into an Annex attached to the Document on the Implementation of the TEU adopted by the EC Council on 26 October 1993 and confirmed by

---

[11] In the sense of peace enforcement, including coercive measures: van Eekelen, *Debating European Security*, 127. For the Petersberg Declaration itself, see Gerbet, de la Serre, and Nafilyan, *L'Union politique de l'Europe*, 342–7.

the European Council on 29 October. It was further confirmed by the WEU Council on 22 November. The Annex gave an expanded version of the type of activity which the WEU might undertake, not excluding recourse to means other than military personnel. Examples given included situations in which:

- the security interests of the Union are directly concerned;
- the Union is politically and economically involved in a specific crisis or conflict and acknowledges that additional WEU support is necessary (military observers, cease-fire, peace-keeping, sanctions monitoring, and peace enforcement);
- the Union is asked by the UN/CSCE to make a contribution and it concludes that WEU, in a cohesive division of labour, could make a specific contribution; or
- humanitarian efforts need logistic support.

If the request to the WEU was part of a broader action which the EU would continue to conduct, special attention would be required: 'In this case mutual information and consultation procedures will ensure the coherence of the action as a whole, whilst ensuring that WEU take in an autonomous way the operational decisions, including military planning, rules of engagement, command structures, deployment and withdrawal.' Mutual information would be assured by the respective Presidencies. In addition, the Secretaries General of the WEU and the Council would keep each other fully informed and exchange written material in the relevant areas. Cross-participation by staff in meetings, however, would be decided on a case-by-case basis after consultation of the two Presidencies, and the staff concerned would not take part in their own right, but would form part of the Presidency delegation. Attempts would be made to co-ordinate dates and venues of meetings. The arrangements for Commission participation were not finalized until October 1994.

The arrangements were reasonable on paper, but proved inadequate in practice. One problem was the absence of security clearance for Commission and Council Secretariat staff. Although appropriate Commission staff were given national security clearance for EPC material classified 'confidential' and above, no such system applied in the Council, and in any case did not come up to NATO standards. Since WEU valued the NATO documents it received, it tended to be strict with classified material and parsimonious in its selection for onward transmission. Furthermore, while association via the back door, as it were, might suffice for the Council Secretariat, it was not good enough in the eyes of the Commission, which resented being obliged to attend WEU meetings as part of the Presidency delegation on the same footing as the Head of the CFSP Secretariat. A more dignified status was blocked by those Member States—Britain and France—which opposed strengthening the Commission's role in the security field. It has to be said that the EU was no more welcoming to the WEU Secretary General, who only once attended a meeting of the EU Council, and the fact that EPC/CFSP set up its own Working Group on security tended to drain the corresponding, and pre-existing, WEU Working Group of its interest.[12]

The implementation of the Maastricht Treaty did not, therefore, contribute to bringing the EU and WEU closer together. The disagreements among Member States about a security role for the Union had only been papered over by the Treaty; in reality they continued to prevent concrete progress in that direction. WEU's relations with NATO, on the other hand, proceeded apace. This was partly because operational requirements brought them together, partly because the pro-NATO camp in the WEU were winning the battle of minds, partly because the United States was cunningly making NATO more attractive to the Europeans. As early as May 1992 there was a joint meeting of the WEU and North Atlantic Councils, and the practice was institutionalized in the NATO Summit Declaration of 10 January 1994. The network of contacts was dense, although not necessarily rich.[13]

Administrative structures

Coreper and the Political Committee

Although the foreign-policy making methods introduced by the Maastricht Treaty remained firmly intergovernmental, they none the less represented a significant change in comparison with the now defunct EPC.[14] A telling indication of the change can be found in the reform of

[12] The source for the Annex, extensively quoted here, is van Eekelen, *Debating European Security*, 212–15. See also ibid. 185–6, 199–200; *EPC Documentation Bulletin*, 9 (1993), 93/407; Jopp, 'The Defense Dimension of the European Union', 157; Dumond and Setton, *La politique étrangère et de sécurité commune*, 121–2.

[13] van Eekelen, *Debating European Security*, 199–200; Dumond and Setton, *La politique étrangère et de sécurité commune*, 119.

[14] For an overview of the implementation of the CFSP from the integrationist point of view, see Regelsberger, 'Reforming CFSP', and Regelsberger and Wessels, 'The CFSP Institutions and Procedures', 34–43 Compare Bretherton and Vogler, *the European Union as a Global Actor*, 179–83.

the administrative structures of both Council and Commission. The new structures introduced by both Institutions in themselves had an influence on the way policy was made.

Respectful of the Commission's autonomy, the IGC did not discuss changes in the structure of that institution. It did, however, address the question of the relationship between Coreper and the Political Committee, without coming to a conclusion. The matter was left to subsequent negotiation.[15] In the event, it took until May 1992 to reach a first agreement, confirmed by the European Council on 29 October 1993, just before the entry into force of the Maastricht Treaty,[16] and considerably longer in practice to settle down into a fixed *modus operandi.* It was not until January 1996 that a working compromise was set down in black and white.

The difficulty arose because of rivalry between the two bodies over which should have the final say before a matter was submitted to the Council for decision. The question was not just a battle over turf, although that counted; it also involved a debate on the style and culture of foreign-policy making in the EU. The Political Committee represented the old ways of EPC—a highly flexible and pragmatic decision-making process, still lightly burdened with precedent and neglectful of legal form, in which considerations of 'high policy' came foremost. Coreper, while not precisely avant-garde, stood for a way of doing business which was grounded in law and procedure, in which most issues were long- to medium-term, and in which greater attention had to be paid to opinion outside the charmed circle of diplomacy. Coreper was in a strong legal position to assert its claim to have the last word on any matter submitted to the Council, based on Article 151 of the EC Treaty and Article 19 of the Council's Rules of Procedure.[17] The tension between the two bodies was reflected in a passage which Coreper added at the last minute to the report adopted by the Council on 27 October 1993, whereby 'the opinions of the Political Committee setting out, inter alia, its conclusions or recommendations intended for the Council will appear on the agenda for the Permanent Representatives Committee to ensure that they are forwarded to the Council in good time (pursuant to Article J.8.5). The Permanent Representatives Committee will attach to them comments and recommendations which it deems necessary and (under Article 151 of the EC Treaty) will endeavour, as need be, to reach an agreement at its level to be submitted to the Council for

[15] Declaration No. 28.
[16] Text at Westlake, *The Council of the European Union*, 178.
[17] 'All items on the agenda for a Council meeting shall be examined in advance by Coreper unless the Council decides otherwise.'

approval.'[18] In spite of the reference to Article J.8.5 of the Maastricht Treaty, which gave the Political Committee the right to submit opinions to the Council on its own initiative, this appeared to subordinate the Committee to Coreper. The waters were still further muddied by the fact that, as experience over the past few years had shown, EPC activity increasingly relied on EC instruments for their effectiveness. The Political Committee was therefore obliged in any case to construct a relationship with those able to deploy the instruments, including Coreper. Finally, account had to be taken of the feeling commonly held by the Permanent Representatives that, as career diplomats, their views on foreign policy issues were likely to be as authoritative as those of their Political Director colleagues.[19]

In the end the deal was that Coreper made a final check on matters submitted to the Council, particularly regarding their institutional, financial, and Community aspects, but by a sort of gentleman's agreement did not make any alterations to the Political Committee's political judgement. The Political Directors were magnanimously allowed to attend sessions of the Council for CFSP items, sitting alongside the Permanent Representative. The Political Committee had therefore lost the exclusivity it had enjoyed in the palmy days of the EPC Ministerial Meetings. It nevertheless clawed back some influence by organizing its meetings on the eve, and if necessary on the morning, of the Council sessions, in order to take account of the latest international events, which meant that for practical reasons Coreper could not always fully exercise its *droit de dernier regard*. And of course the Political Committee retained its power of day-to-day management of the CFSP through decisions which did not need to be submitted to Ministerial level.[20]

The Permanent Representatives discovered that they needed assistance in keeping track of what the Political Committee was up to, let alone in preparing for Ministerial discussion those aspects of CFSP questions which were their proper concern. They therefore set up at the initiative of Germany a working party of CFSP Counsellors, or 'Groupe de Conseillers', which was given formal status by a decision of 26 July 1994. There was already a precedent for this in the 'Groupe de Conseillers' which had been the channel for the Commission to communicate with the Member

---

[18] Dumond and Setton, *La politique étrangère et de sécurité commune*, 46–7.

[19] Nicoll, 'Representing the States', 195.

[20] For informed studies of the relationship between the Political Committee and Coreper, see Dumond and Setton, *La politique étrangère et de sécurité commune*, 48–50; Kiso, 'An Uncosy Relationship', and Galloway, 'Common Foreign and Security Policy', 220–1.

States on the political aspects of its management of the PHARE programme. These officials are posted to the Permanent Representations and though they can address themselves both to Coreper and to the Political Committee, are in fact an emanation of Coreper and act under the instructions of the Ambassadors in Brussels. They attend the meetings of both the Political Committee and Coreper, and time their own meetings between those of the two bodies 'in order to review points on which the Political Committee is submitting opinions to the Council, thereby ensuring that all Permanent Representations are sensitized to the conclusions of the Political Committee and the ground it has already covered in preparing the Council'.[21] The Group is itself responsible for advising on horizontal (legal, institutional, and financial) problems concerning CFSP, and for co-ordinating the agendas of Coreper and the Political Committee.

The Group of Counsellors is an important element in ensuring 'consistency' in the sense of the Maastricht Treaty. By its very existence, however, it has detracted from the role of both the European Correspondents and the Commission. The European Correspondents used to be the motor of institutional progress. They would formulate procedures as these developed through experience, and would usually be called on to do the groundwork of preparing documents like the successive Reports (Copenhagen, London, the decision accompanying the SEA) which marked the development of EPC. This is no longer part of their duties. Whereas in the past the Correspondents' role was balanced between their responsibility for co-ordination within the Foreign Ministry and their function as part of a collective European enterprise, the balance now tips to the side of domestic responsibility, in importance if not in time.[22] Similarly, the Commission used to be able to draw considerable advantage from its position as bridge between EPC and the Community. Its representatives were the only officials to take part in meetings of both the Political Committee and Coreper, and their advice to the Political Committee on the EC aspects of EPC activities was usually well received. The existence of the Group of Counsellors means that this exclusivity has been lost. The Commission naturally retains the authority which comes from its mastery of many of the EC instruments, but it is no longer the sole and privileged exegete of Community lore.

[21] Galloway, 'Common Foreign and Security Policy', 221; Dumond and Setton, *La politique étrangère et de sécurité commune*, 46
[22] Dumond and Setton, *La politique étrangère et de sécurité commune*, 51.

Working Groups

Unlike in the case of the Political Committee and Coreper, the Maastricht Treaty and its accompanying documents did not provide for any administrative action with regard to the Groups of EPC and the Working Parties of the Council. Yet it became obvious on reflection that close cooperation between the two, or even an outright merger, would be necessary if the principle of consistency was to be paid more than lip service. The former EPC Groups were an indispensable forum for the exchange of views and information on the international issues of the day, and for preparing recommendations for submission to the Political Committee. They tended to be undervalued by the larger Member States, but were highly appreciated by the smaller ones whose networks of diplomatic missions were less extensive. The Council Working Parties had a different function: working on the basis of a proposal from the Commission, they were in a position to request any additional information and explanation that might be necessary, clear up any technical problems, and ensure that only issues of substance went forward. The work of the two might seem to be complementary, and their merger an easy matter. That this was not so was the result once again, not only of turf battles, but of a difference in culture. In this case, the turf battles were the more significant.

The merger was decided by the European Council on 29 October 1993. The Presidency Conclusions baldly stated: 'As from the entry into force of the Treaty, all working parties will be Council working parties.' Those former EPC Groups which had direct counterparts in the Council structure were to be merged with them; those which did not continued a separate existence, but were expected to organize joint meetings whenever 'mixed' subjects were to be discussed, and in any case to follow Council working practices. Thus, for example, meetings were to be called by a note from the Council Secretariat, as well as by the traditional Coreu.

The detailed implications of the merger decision were set out by Coreper in conclusions adopted on 2 February 1994. By and large the Groups with a geographical remit were merged. Thus, for example, the EPC Latin America Working Group and the EC Working Parties on Latin America were merged to form the Standing Working Parties on Latin America; the EPC Asia Group merged with the EC Working Party on Asia to form the Standing Working Party on Asia; and so on. Former EPC Groups without counterparts simply underwent a change of name and became the Standing Working Parties on Protocol, Human Rights,

Consular Affairs, etc. A new Standing Working Party on Security was set up, confirming the existing *ad hoc* EPC body.[23]

The system did not work, and Working Groups that had supposedly merged in effect operated separately for years afterwards. The main problem was the question of attendance. The old EPC Groups had been attended by officials from the Foreign Ministries who travelled to Brussels for the purpose from their national capitals,[24] whereas the Council Working Parties were for the most part attended by officials from the Permanent Representations. Who was going to attend the meetings of the merged Working Parties? Were delegations to comprise both someone from Brussels and someone from the capital? If so, who was to be the spokesman? And above all, in the case of the Presidency, who was to chair the meeting?

To deal with these difficulties, the practice grew up of separating CFSP from EC items on the agenda, and having a different person in the chair depending on the nature of the topic. Indeed, many Working Parties went further, and organized occasional meetings to deal with CFSP questions, with attendance and chair predominantly from capitals, the majority of the other meetings being manned by the Permanent Representations. This became more than a practice which was tolerated; it was specifically endorsed by the Political Committee. It flew in the face of the move towards bringing together the political and economic sides of foreign policy questions, and was neither efficient nor edifying, but it reflected the difficulties inherent in trying to meld a foreign policy process run by home-based diplomats and one managed by staff permanently in Brussels, compounded by the division of responsibilities within the Foreign Ministries of most Member States.[25]

The Council Secretariat

It had been agreed at Maastricht that, as part of the single institutional framework, the former EPC Secretariat, which had been set up under the

[23] For overviews of the structure of CFSP Working Parties, see *CFSP Forum*, 2/1994, 2, and Regelsberger, 'The Institutional Setup and Functioning of EPC/CFSP', 78. The expression 'Standing Working Party' is the officially consecrated one used by the General Secretariat of the Council, but most practitioners continued to call them Working Groups ('Groupes de travail'), on the old EPC model.

[24] On the entry into force of the Single European Act, Working Group meetings had ceased to be held in the capital of the Presidency.

[25] On the CFSP Working Parties see in particular Galloway, 'Common Foreign and Security Policy', 216–18, and Dumond and Setton, *La politique étrangère et de sécurité commune*, 52–4 and 65.

Single European Act, should be merged with the General Secretariat of the Council. The decision was surprisingly uncontroversial, when one considers the political anguish, particularly on the part of Denmark, which had accompanied the establishment of the EPC Secretariat, leading to such gems of folklore as the symbolic half-yearly payment by the Presidency to the Council of one ecu in return for services rendered by the General Secretariat, and the sealing off of the EPC Secretariat wing of the Council building (*odi profanum vulgus et arceo*) by a special combination lock. The practical arrangements for the new dispensation were left by the IGC to further discussion (Declaration No. 28), and the general principles of the new dispensation were fixed by the Council on 11 May 1992.[26]

The EPC Secretariat had been composed of five seconded diplomats from the enlarged Troika (the current Presidency and the two Presidencies on either side of it), who rotated with mathematical precision, together with seconded support staff. At its head was a senior diplomat from a Member State, Ambassador Giovanni Jannuzzi from Italy, who was subsequently succeeded by Ambassador Pierre Champenois from Belgium.[27] Elements of this system were taken over, in that the CFSP part of the General Secretariat, unlike the remainder of the organization, was partially manned by seconded diplomats, causing some dismay to proponents of an independent Community civil service, but on balance the practices, ethos, and culture of the old Council Secretariat have tended to prevail.

Under the new regime, the external relations part of the General Secretariat (Directorate General E) was placed under a Director General. There has been only one occupant of the post so far, a former senior British diplomat, Ambassador Brian Crowe. The services under his control were divided into two branches, one dealing with external economic relations and the other with the CFSP. The latter was placed under a Deputy Director General, the first holder of this post being Ambassador Champenois (former Head of the EPC Secretariat). By keeping separate the services dealing with the political and economic aspects of EU foreign policy, the opportunity was lost of taking a significant step towards consistency. Both services were relatively small, and co-ordination should have been easy, but for one reason and another was limited in practice. The symbolic effect, reflecting as it did the wish of Foreign Ministries to maintain a role in the servicing of the CFSP, was significant.

[26] Dumond and Setton, *La politique étrangère et de sécurité commune*, 40.
[27] Nuttall, *European Political Co-operation*, 257–8; Franck, 'Belgium', 157–8.

The CFSP Secretariat itself is currently[28] divided into four Directorates, two with geographical responsibilities, one covering security and the United Nations, and one dealing with general affairs. The total staff is around 50, of whom half are administrative grade. Of these, in addition to the Deputy Director General, 11 are established EC officials from the Council Secretariat (one is from the Commission), and 12 are seconded diplomats with the EC status of 'temporary agents': the number of the latter chosen at the time allowed each Member State to second one official. On enlargement in 1995, the three new Member States provided one additional seconded diplomat each. Practically all the support staff are drawn from General Secretariat permanent staff.[29]

The new Secretariat, which began to be established at the beginning of 1994, found itself in a difficult situation. Its predecessor, the EPC Secretariat, had been smaller in size, and not all the enlarged Troika staff stayed on. Those who did provided a valuable element of continuity, but this expertise was gradually lost as their term of duty came to an end. Nor was there any clear mandate as to what the new Secretariat should do. The CFSP Secretariat clearly had to be different from its predecessor, just as the CFSP was intended to be qualitatively different from EPC, but how was this to be given concrete expression? The new staff were left to improvise. Over the years a pattern of behaviour evolved. On the basis of both the EPC experience and traditional Council practice, the Secretariat serviced the CFSP machine from Working Groups to the Political Committee and beyond. It took over from most Presidencies the responsibility for drafting agendas, and also provided position papers and other drafts for those Presidencies which felt nervous about doing this unaided.[30] The Secretariat relied heavily for material for this purpose on national input from those Member States who possessed the information and were prepared to make it available. The British were particularly forthcoming in distributing national telegrams and exercised corresponding influence over drafting, an advantage forgone by the more parsimonious Member States.[31] There

---

[28] 1999, before the post-Amsterdam changes.

[29] Galloway, 'Common Foreign and Security Policy', 223–4; Luif, *On the Road to Brussels*, 50. An early version of the structure of DG E, comprising at that stage only three Directorates, can be found at *CFSP Forum*, 3/1994, 2.

[30] Personal interviews; Dumond and Setton, *La politique étrangère et de sécurité commune*, 27, 40–1. The practice varies with the Presidency: Dumond and Setton make the point that the British jealously guard their Presidency privileges. British sources say the same about the French.

[31] Personal interviews; Dumond and Setton, *La politique étrangère et de sécurité commune*, 41–2.

were few links in this respect with the Commission, which did not encourage contact. The only activity at which the Secretariat drew the line, on the grounds of limited resources, was preparing briefings for contacts with third countries below the level of Political Director.

The absorption of the EPC Secretariat by the General Secretariat of the Council had an unexpected impact on the atmosphere of the CFSP. The account just given of the way in which the practice of the CFSP Secretariat developed indicates that, notwithstanding the presence of a considerable number of professional diplomats, CFSP in the Council has tended increasingly to be handled on traditional Council Secretariat lines. The traditional General Secretariat provides the Presidency and the national delegations with a professional if conservative business management service, and plays an undervalued but crucial role in sorting out problems and presenting issues in ways conducive to compromise. But it depends for its effectiveness in having an authorized proposal on the table. In the absence of such an institutional phenomenon in the CFSP, and given the Commission's reluctance to fill the gap, it has in effect filled the vacuum by assisting the Presidency to write its own proposals, thus assuming in practice the right of initiative without any formal change in its status.[32] This is an activity in which the permanent Council staff have felt more ill at ease than the diplomats. The difficulty arises from the existence of a gap in the system.

The Commission[33]

The second Delors Commission was due to finish its term of office at the end of 1992. This coincided with the accomplishment of the Single Market, and was due to coincide with the introduction of the CFSP, had the Maastricht Treaty been ratified according to plan. The need for a second referendum in Denmark and the recourse to the Constitutional Court in Germany meant that the CFSP was delayed by ten months, not technically becoming operational until 1 November 1993.

The outgoing Commission thus had plenty of time—indeed more time than it expected—to organize itself the better to carry out its new foreign policy responsibilities. The appointment of Jacques Delors as President of the Commission for a further two years, and the fact that his personal

[32] Dumond and Setton, *La politique étrangère et de sécurité commune*, 42.
[33] In addition to the references quoted in this subsection, see Cameron, 'Building a Common Foreign Policy', 62–4; Nuttall, 'The European Commission's Internal Arrangements'; Nuttall, 'The Commission', 145; Holland, *European Union Common Foreign Policy*, 84–5.

foreign policy advisers remained the same, provided an element of continuity in the concept the Commission had of its foreign policy role. In spite of the shaking the Commission had undergone in the ratification debate, this was still fairly ambitious. An indication of this was the appointment of Hans van den Broek, the Netherlands Foreign Minister, to the new Commission, in the confident expectation that he would be given the foreign policy portfolio. The distribution of portfolios was to be settled by the incoming Commission at an informal meeting at the Palais d'Egmont in Brussels in December 1992.

The original intention of the President and his advisers was to set up a new Directorate General for external relations, covering most of the EU's bilateral responsibilities. Only trade and development policies would remain with the existing Directorates General. The new Directorate General would answer to Mr van den Broek, who would be responsible for organizing the Commission's input into the new CFSP; he would be, as it were, the 'Foreign Minister of Europe'. The assumption was that the Commission's new right of initiative would require it to adopt a different foreign policy style which the existing structures did not adequately reflect.

Things did not work out like that. The other Commissioners were reluctant to entrust such a far-reaching and high-profile portfolio to one of their colleagues; those Commissioners who would lose geographical responsibilities they had counted on were particularly opposed. Since the distribution of portfolios was traditionally agreed by consensus, a compromise had to be found *in extremis*. A new Directorate General was set up—DG IA—responsible for external political relations and the CFSP, and put under the control of Mr van den Broek, while DG I, under the control of Sir Leon Brittan and Abel Matutes, and DG VIII, under that of Manuel Marin, were made responsible for the common commercial policy and external economic relations with the developed and developing world respectively. Geographical responsibility remained divided; the split between political and economic aspects of relations with the same countries was an unintended accident.

The structure of the new Directorate General was not agreed by the Commission until the following March. It had a Director General (Dr Günter Burghardt, the former Deputy Chef de Cabinet of Jacques Delors and Director in the Secretariat General responsible for the EPC unit) and two Deputy Directors General.[34] It was divided into five Directorates, of which two had horizontal and three geographical responsibilities. The

---

[34] Only one ever materialized.

horizontal units were mostly taken over from existing structures—the European Correspondent's unit, Protocol, the Inspectorate of Delegations, and the Planning Staff all came from the Secretariat General, while Directorate E, responsible for the management of the external Delegations, was transferred from the DG for Personnel and Administration (DG IX).[35] The geographical units had to be built up from scratch.

This proved a difficult task. The budgetary authority was not disposed to provide any extra posts for the purpose, so the new Directorate General—346 strong by July 1994,[36] of which rather more than 200 were in place on the eve of entry into force of the Treaty—had to be scraped together from a variety of sources. Where units were bodily transferred from other services, there was no particular difficulty. It was harder to persuade other Directorates General to sacrifice their staff to redeployment to the new DG. Not only did they resent the loss of prestige in becoming once again only 'economic' services, their workload had been scarcely if at all reduced by the reorganization. Some redeployment did take place, but the shortfall was for the most part made up by 'experts' on contract, mostly seconded national diplomats. It would be unfair to call the result a ragbag, but there was certainly a diversity of origin and experience which made it difficult to forge a team culture in short order. The delay in the coming into operation of the CFSP did not help. While the new Directorate General certainly benefited from having more time to get established, for the first crucial months of its existence it suffered from not having an obvious purpose in life and all the enthusiasm of a new enterprise.

Nor did the separation between the political and the economic make institutional sense. The Commission's weight in EPC had stemmed, not from its superior political wisdom, but from the fact that it largely controlled the EC instruments to which the Member States needed access if they wanted to conduct effective policies. These instruments were in the hands, not of DG IA, but of the other DGs which retained responsibility for external economic relations. It was asking too much of human nature to expect there to be full co-operation between the two, and, although co-ordinating mechanisms were set up, there was not. It was particularly dam-

[35] Cameron, 'Where the European Commission Comes In', 101–2. For a staff plan of DG IA see Edwards and Spence (eds.), *The European Commission*, 286. Control over senior appointments in the Commission's overseas delegations, which fell to DG IA after a hotly contested internal struggle, was significant in bureaucratic terms: Holland, *European Union Common Foreign Policy*, 105.

[36] Hagleitner, 'Les Rôles du Parlement européen et de la Commission', 36, 66.

aging for the prestige of DG IA to have little say in policies towards Central and Eastern Europe, which remained firmly within the remit of Sir Leon Brittan and DG I.

This exclusion encouraged the natural inclination of DG IA officials to engage in tactics of complicity with regard to the Member States in CFSP. Commission officials involved in EPC, while trying to be as constructive as possible, had always been punctilious in observing the niceties of institutional competence, even to the point of being criticized for excessive pedantry. DG IA officials had no reason to adopt a similar approach towards the CFSP, partly because of their different institutional background and submission to the new doctrine of 'consistency', but above all because they had no prerogatives to protect, and could the more easily turn for support to the surroundings with which they were most familiar and in which their daily business lay.

The Commission was also criticized by Member States, remarkably, for making too little use of its new right of initiative. It is true that the first formal use of the right did not come until 1995.[37] This was attributed by some to a desire on the part of the Commission to avoid what were in its view the less desirable in features of 'consistency', namely the acceptance of a greater degree of control by the Member States. However, other explanations seem preferable. For a start, Mr van den Broek, with the support of the President, was anxious to avoid attracting adverse comment by adopting too high a profile. But more important was the confusion about what an 'initiative' was.[38] Were straightforward EC proposals, of which there were a good many, to count as CFSP initiatives simply because they had a political angle?[39] Were informal ideas floated at the level of officials, most often at Working Party level, or even in the Political Committee, to count as CFSP initiatives, even though they were not presented in due official form? Were inputs made by Coreu, of which there were more than 40 examples between November 1993 and March 1995, to count as initiatives? The advantage of these last two methods was that they did not involve seeking formal approval by the College, but the attendant

[37] The proposal for EU participation in KEDO.
[38] Cameron, 'Where the European Commission Comes In', 102.
[39] The Commission developed the practice of 'mixed communications', in which overall policies with regard to a particular question covered both EC and CFSP subjects, but in which no specific proposals for CFSP legal acts were made. It was left to the Council to deduce what should be the form and precise content of acts consequent upon the Commission's broad policy initiative. It is supposed that the Commission feared being considered too forward: Hagleitner, 'Les Rôles du Parlement européen et de la Commission', 40–2; Luif, *On the Road to Brussels*, 56.

drawback was a lack of profile. Certainly, the College devoted remarkably little time at its meetings to CFSP affairs.[40]

A scant two years' experience of the split between the political and economic aspects of foreign policy convinced the Commission that the experiment was not a success, and the Santer Commission which took office at the beginning of 1995 reverted to the old system of combining both political and economic aspects in the same geographical desk. DG IA remained in being, still under the supervision of Mr van den Broek, who retained overall supervision of relations with the CFSP, and in addition acquired geographical responsibility for the important areas of Russia, the CIS, and Central and Eastern Europe, as well as former Yugoslavia.[41]

Difficulties in implementation

The introduction of the Common Foreign and Security Policy was, and was meant to be, an ambitious undertaking. In a world full of problems, there were bound to be difficulties in its early implementation. But a lack of clarity in drafting the Treaty, the product of the search for language to reconcile inherently divergent positions, meant that homemade difficulties were encountered in particular in three areas: the nature and content of common positions and joint actions and the extent to which CFSP activities could properly incorporate those of the Community; the financing of the CFSP; and the degree of commitment of the Member States.[42]

Common positions and joint actions

Those responsible for the implementation of the CFSP were anxious to make early use of the new instruments, intended to distinguish the CFSP from EPC, of common positions and joint actions.[43] The trouble was that

[40] Hagleitner, 'Les Rôles du Parlement européen et de la Commission', 36.

[41] Ibid. 37–9, 65.

[42] For an excellent concise account of these issues, see Spence and Spence, 'The CFSP from Masstricht to Amsterdam'.

[43] For common positions and joint actions in general, see Krenzler and Schneider, 'The Question of Consistency', 138–41; Ryba, 'La Politique étrangère et de sécurité commune', 24–32; Holland, *Common Foreign and Security Policy*, 18–21; Luif, *On the Road to Brussels*, 65–74; Dumond and Setton, *La politique étrangère et de sécurité commune*, 80–9. Dumond and Setton's book, which provides the best insight into the process, albeit from an inter-governmentalist point of view, contains a list of common positions and joint actions up to 15 Dec. 1998 (143–52). A list up to mid-1995 appears in Galloway, 'Common Foreign and Security Policy', 227–32. Similar lists appear in the *CFSP Forum* at regular intervals.

no one knew what these were.[44] The drafters of the Maastricht Treaty had forborne from defining the terms, so it was a case of *solvitur ambulando*. In the absence of legal definition, the Member States had to fall back on pragmatic experiment.

In the first six months following the entry into force of the Maastricht Treaty, the EU adopted five joint actions—in chronological order, humanitarian aid to Bosnia, observers for the elections in Russia, support for democratic transition in South Africa, the Stability Pact, and support for peace in the Middle East. Each of these drew its authority from the European Council's general guidelines of 29 October 1993. Subsequent joint actions required separate prior decisions by the European Council, although the practical difficulties this created could be overcome to an appreciable extent by a broad interpretation of the original guidelines. Each of the first five joint actions demonstrated in its own way the two problems the CFSP immediately faced in making use of its new instruments—the question of finding something to do which gave 'added value' compared with what would have been possible under EPC, and the extent to which EC instruments and institutions could be commanded under the new procedures.

The first joint action concerned the convoying of humanitarian aid in Bosnia, in support of the UNHCR. This was only a part of the Union's policy with regard to former Yugoslavia, and indeed coincided with the ill-fated Kinkel–Juppé plan (the 'EU Action Plan'). But the need to ensure that humanitarian aid reached its intended destination was obvious, and the joint action made the most of the opportunity. The action in itself was not new, however. A four-point plan to assist the UNHCR had been agreed by the European Council at Birmingham in October 1992, and an EC task force to help to distribute aid began to operate two months later.[45] Where the joint action would have been useful would have been if it had been able to produce additional resources and manpower. This was not the case, however. Indeed, the internal disagreements about financing were to mar the public impact of the joint action. Although it was decided on 8 November 1993, it was not until 20 December that the Member States were able to agree that the action, the total cost of which amounted to 48.3 million ECU, should be financed half out of the EC budget and half by the Member States. Even then, the Member States could not agree how

---

[44] The European Council on 29 Oct. 1993 approved the Council's conclusions, which *inter alia* described the nature and functioning of joint actions (internal Council document), but these said rather less in two pages than the Treaty had in a single article.

[45] Edwards, 'The Potential and Limits of the CFSP', 184.

their contributions should be calculated. The impasse continued for a further five months, by which time the need had passed and the money was diverted to other purposes.[46]

The second joint action, adopted a day later, concerned the dispatch of a team of observers for the elections in Russia. This was in line with the European Council's guidelines, which had indeed laconically confined itself to supporting Russian democracy and sending a team of observers to the elections, due to be held on 12 December. The choice of subject was imposed by the international timetable, and the action was no doubt useful in itself, but one may wonder about the merits of a procedure which requires a joint action to be preceded by European Council guidelines, when the guidelines and joint action are practically coterminous. The observers' expenses were met by the Member States which provided them; administrative costs were charged to the Council's own budget.[47]

The third joint action provided support for democratic transition in South Africa. Again, the timing was fortuitous. The Community had since 1991 been revising its policy towards South Africa to take into account prospects for the dismantling of apartheid and the transition to majority rule. More than the two previous joint actions, however, the European Council's guidelines on South Africa made an attempt at a comprehensive strategy (support for the transition to a multiracial democracy, preparation for and monitoring of elections, and creation of an appropriate co-operation framework). This may have been because a considerable amount of preparatory work had been done by the Commission, the results of which were set out in Commission Communication to the Council of 29 September 1993.[48] Nevertheless, the joint action confined itself to arrangements for the programme of assistance for the elections, together with a cursory undertaking to debate further the appropriate co-operation framework in the light of any proposals from the Commission.[49]

This apparent obsession with technicalities at the expense of the wider view was the result of a difficult procedural debate over whether joint actions could legitimately engage EC instruments and commit EC Institutions. This was the first joint action in which the question had seriously arisen. Most Member States were in favour of an integrated approach, but the United Kingdom wanted to restrict the joint action to the monitoring

---

[46] Monar, 'The Financial Dimension of the CFSP', 38–9.
[47] Allen, 'EPC/CFSP, the Soviet Union, and the Former Soviet Republics', 230–1.
[48] Holland, *European Union Common Foreign Policy*, 239–45.
[49] Ibid. 248–51.

of elections.[50] The more restrictive view prevailed. 'South Africa found itself in the precarious position of being the subject of a co-ordination and competences experiment; the practice of joint action on South Africa addressed these organizational questions in an incremental and exploratory manner, a characteristic perhaps not best suited to either policy efficiency or appropriateness.'[51] As a result the joint action confined itself to an activity that was not new and did not require the legal under-pinning of the Maastricht Treaty. The Danish Presidency of the first half of 1993 had already raised the possibility of observing the elections, and ECOMSA,[52] on whose work the election monitors built, had been in posi-tion since the previous October. Nor was a joint action indispensable for legal reasons; in July 1994 the Council decided to provide technical assist-ance for the elections in Mozambique, even though a Portuguese proposal for a joint action had been vetoed by the United Kingdom.[53] The travel costs and salaries of the observers in South Africa were met by their home governments; local expenses were covered by the pre-existing EC budget line for the Special Programme for the Victims of Apartheid. This meant that differences over financing the operation could be avoided.

The fourth joint action concerned the Stability Pact.[54] This joint action differed from its predecessors in that it was practically from the start designed to exploit the new possibilities of the CFSP. The initiative came from France. The new cohabitation Prime Minister, Édouard Balladur, used his inaugural speech before the French National Assembly on 8 April 1993 to announce an initiative to convene a conference in the framework of the European Council to forestall conflicts in Central and Eastern Europe to which unresolved minorities and border issues might give rise. The domestic political motive was clear: Balladur wished to cut some of the foreign policy ground from under the feet of President Mitterrand. But there was a deeper rationale: events in former Yugoslavia had shown that the collapse of Communist régimes could let loose horrifying bloodshed

---

[50] Holland, *European Union Common Foreign Policy*, 138. The British position is super-ficially surprising, since the United Kingdom was usually in favour of an expansionist inter-pretation of intergovernmental procedures. Fears of allowing the Commission too great a part in the operation for the time being carried the day: cf. Holland, 'The Joint Action on South Africa', 177–8, 180.

[51] Holland, *European Union Common Foreign Policy*, 76.

[52] The EC Observer Mission to South Africa.

[53] de Vasconcelos, 'Portugal: Pressing for an Open Europe', 280–1. Compare Ryba, 'La Politique étrangère et de sécurité commune', 31 n. 24.

[54] Ueta, 'The Stability Pact'; Karnitschnig, *Integration als Sicherheitspolitik*; Schneider, 'The Twelve/Fifteen's Conference Diplomacy', 253–6; Rummel, 'The CFSP's Conflict Pre-vention Policy', 113–15; Cameron, 'The Stability Pact'; Ramelot and Remacle, *L'OSCE et les conflits en Europe*, 29–33.

and violence wherever nations and boundaries did not run together. The European Community, now beginning to contemplate enlargement to at least some countries of Central and Eastern Europe, had to take care not to import the risk of violence. The French government accordingly submitted a memorandum to the European Council at Copenhagen in June 1993, in which it was stated that 'actively seeking this result [the stability and security of the continent] would be the first task of the Common Foreign and Security Policy of the Maastricht Treaty'.

The European Council endorsed the French proposal, at the same time as it opened the door, under certain conditions, to applications for membership from the CEECs. An Ad Hoc High Level Working Group was set up in July to prepare the ground, and the results of its labours were approved by the Council in October. The joint action was formally adopted in December. Its contents for the most part followed the original French proposal, except that border changes were excluded and the impression was removed that participation in the Pact was a condition for EU membership.

The Stability Pact was reputed to be cost-free, apart from the running costs of diplomacy and the expenses of the round tables and the two conferences which were held, which were borne by the host countries. In practice, however, some Community money was required to oil the wheels and make participation in the Pact more attractive to the CEECs, which with the exception of Hungary were initially rather reticent. This funding, amounting to some $300 million, came from PHARE, to the disgruntlement of the Commission, which had already committed the available appropriations in accordance with the byzantine and time-consuming procedures laid down for that purpose. Indeed, when the Council renewed the joint action on 14 June 1994 it invited the Commission to focus on achieving the 'objectives of the joint action by means of appropriate economic measures, in the framework of the implementation of Community programmes'. Financing did not provide insuperable institutional problems, however, since, as in the case of South Africa, the money was already there, and the Commission was both responsible for its management and associated with the Presidency in the diplomatic consultations with the CEECs. One of the two potential problems faced by the early joint actions was therefore eliminated. As regards the other, it would be too much to say that the Stability Pact became possible because of the new instrument of joint actions; rather the Stability Pact initiative was luckily to hand to receive the joint action label.

The fifth and final of the first series of joint actions concerned the

Middle East peace process. This was not adopted until the Greek Presidency of the first half of 1994. No one could accuse this joint action of lacking in ambition. It provided for support for the peace process by monitoring the settlements in the Occupied Territories; working to lift the Arab boycott of Israel; supporting the organization of an international economic conference on infrastructure projects; supporting a new EC–Israel agreement; participating in a future international presence in the Occupied Territories; helping to monitor elections in Gaza and the West Bank; and supporting the new Palestinian police force. The last measure required urgent financing, which at first sight could not be found within the EC budget. After some tergiversation, the Commission nevertheless agreed to provide the funds by a transfer between articles, which was within its powers to do without involving the European Parliament. This later caused the Commission considerable difficulties with the Parliament.

The first set of joint actions showed the Member States groping their way. They were not sure whether a joint action should be comprehensive or specific, a strategy or an event. Disagreement about the extent that a joint action could extend to the strictly Community sphere tended to limit both the scope of the action and the extent to which it could go beyond the familiar practice of EPC. This meant that joint actions ran the risk of trivialization with a consequent loss of credibility, a cause of concern for some Member States.[55] But if the CFSP's reach spread too far into Community territory, the reaction was equally pained. A particularly serious situation arose with the European Parliament because of the Council's habit of ignoring or bypassing EC budgetary procedures in order to finance joint actions. The difficulty was the result of the failure of the negotiators of the Maastricht Treaty to carry through the rationale on which joint actions were originally posited. This, it will be recalled, was to select a limited number of areas in which the Union had a very important interest and to conduct policy in these areas through a new instrument which would be qualitatively differentiated from its predecessors by the use of majority voting. Nothing of this was left in the Treaty. The Member States had rejected majority voting, except in conditions which precluded its practical use, and the European Council had subsequently selected a very

---

[55] For example Portugal: de Vasconcelos, 'Portugal: Pressing for an Open Europe?', 280. In due course practice settled down, and the joint actions on the nuclear non-proliferation treaty, the administration of Mostar, and the control of exports of dual-use goods (a particularly tortuous construction of CFSP and EC instruments) can be claimed to be both new and significant.

wide range of areas for joint action. Greater selectivity would have concentrated joint actions on a coherent agenda, and majority voting would have relieved fears that the intergovernmental method would prevail over that of the Community. In the absence of either, it was hard to see what joint actions were for. It was scarcely surprising, therefore, that the Council was hard put to find suitable subjects for joint actions, and yet the effort had to be made, for fear of bringing the new CFSP into disrepute through lack of use.

In the first year of operation of the CFSP, common positions were made less use of than joint actions. The first seven, up until October 1994, were all concerned with the restriction of economic relations, an uncontested use of the instrument given that it figured in Article 228a of the EC Treaty, along with the joint action, as one of the acts which could trigger EC sanctions.[56] Nevertheless, the concept of a 'common position' proved as difficult to delimit in practice as had that of a 'joint action'. The original idea had been to include in it everything that was agreed in common, including declarations. This interpretation was narrowed down, however, in the preparatory work done under the Belgian Presidency, and was given a strictly legal connotation based on Article J.2.[57] The main difficulty arose from the question whether a common position, binding on the Member States, was also binding on the Commission. If this was a merely theoretical problem in the case of the first seven common positions, it became the subject of hot debate in the two subsequent ones, concerning Rwanda and the Ukraine (October and November 1994).

In both these cases the Council had it in mind to define an overall approach combining action under both the first and the second pillars. The Commission strongly objected, not to a combined approach as such, but to the fact that this was exclusively defined under a specific provision, Article J.2, applicable only to the CFSP. Policy was held up while the institutional battle was fought out. The hostilities were conducted via the Legal Services of the two Institutions. The Legal Service of the Council took the view that it had not been the intention to exclude matters of EC competence from the CFSP provisions of the Treaty, but admitted that the Commission could not be obliged to act by a decision taken under those provisions, which would impair its autonomy under the EC Treaty. The

---

[56] The common positions relating to Libya, Haiti, and Yugoslavia were implemented by Article 228a (or its financial equivalent, Article 73g) Regulations. The common position relating to Sudan, since it concerned military equipment, was implemented by national measures: Luif, *On the Road to Brussels*, 65–6.

[57] Dumond and Setton, *La politique étrangère et de sécurité commune*, 81.

Commission Legal Service contested the view that Pillar Two provisions could apply to Pillar One subjects, and denied that the Commission could be reduced to a body for implementing CFSP policy. In its view, common positions were addressed to the Member States, not the Commission. The dilemma was not resolved until 6 March 1995, and then only partially, when the Council noted an operational guide on common positions. This provided that common positions committed the Union as a whole, and respected the consistency of the Union's external activities in accordance with Article C of the TEU. They could thus refer to the Union's external activities as a whole, but must preserve the powers specific to each Institution, including the Commission's power of initiative. On the whole, the Commission came off best; it retained a greater degree of freedom than the Member States, whose national policies had to conform, on paper, to the common position.[58]

Financing[59]

The drafters of the Maastricht Treaty did not imagine that they were in any way storing up trouble for themselves when they framed the provisions relating to the financing of the CFSP (Article J.11). Administrative expenditure was to be charged to the EC Budget, and operational expenditure was either, by unanimous decision, to be charged to the EC Budget, in which case the normal budgetary procedure was to be followed, or, failing that, it was to be charged to the Member States on a scale to be decided. This was no more than the logical extension of the practice followed hitherto. Since the Single European Act, the running costs of EPC in Brussels had been met by the Council Secretariat, and extraordinary expenses like the initial cost of setting up the Secretariat had been shared, after some wrangling over the scale, among the Member States. The same procedure was adopted to meet the costs of the ECMM in former Yugoslavia, and of the International Conference on Yugoslavia.[60] If more extensive and longer-term operational expenditure was involved—aid for Central America, positive measures in favour of the victims of apartheid, aid for the Palestinians—the Commission could be relied upon to

[58] Rummel, 'The Intergovernmental Conference 1996', 375; Schmalz, 'The Amsterdam Provisions on External Coherence', 435–6; Dumond and Setton, *La politique étrangère et de sécurité commune*, 80–3; Ryba, 'La politique étrangère et de sécurité commune', 24–5.

[59] This subsection draws principally on Dumond and Setton, *La politique étrangère et de sécurité commune*, 99–106; Monar, 'The Financial Dimension of the CFSP'; and Hagleitner, 'Les Rôles du Parlement européen et de la Commission'.

[60] Dumond and Setton, *La politique étrangère et de sécurité commune*, 101.

mobilize resources from the EC budget. The only source of friction was the degree and nature of the control of the execution of the Budget by the Member States in the EPC framework.

The new financing arrangements for the CFSP could have continued on the same lines. Administrative expenditure—the holding of meetings and suchlike—could have been financed by the Council Secretariat, drawing on the Council section of the EC Budget, which covered administrative expenditure only, while operational expenditure could have been financed by the Commission from its section of the Budget as had been done in the past. If there was no agreement on that, then the Member States would club together to provide the necessary funds for operational expenditure, replacing the informal share-out which had resulted from the system of successive Presidencies by a more formal balancing of contributions. The general expectation was no doubt that this would have been by using the GDP key, as had previously been the case.

Things did not turn out like that, because some Member States, in particular the United Kingdom and France, declined to countenance the admixture of EC procedures which the Maastricht Treaty, logically applied, would have brought about, and the majority of Member States, with the exception of the United Kingdom, were not prepared to draw the conclusion from this and finance the CFSP themselves. The French and British were particularly concerned to prevent the greater involvement of the other arm of the budgetary authority, the European Parliament, which recourse to the EC Budget would inevitably bring about. The definition of administrative expenditure was strained to breaking point, in order to allow the Council Secretariat to meet from its own administrative budget expenses which would normally have been classified as operational.[61] For example, the costs of setting up the unit in Moscow responsible for organizing the election monitors were classified as 'administrative expenditure'. If classification of expenditure as 'operational' could not be avoided, the complicity of the Commission was sought to divert operational funds from their original purposes to new CFSP requirements. Early attempts to bypass the problem by resorting to national funding met with an embarrassing lack of success. In the first joint action, support for convoying humanitarian aid to Bosnia, the compromise solution was that the cost should be split fifty–fifty between the Member States and the EC Budget. This expenditure had of course not been foreseen when the 1993 Budget had been drawn up, and could only be covered because the

---

[61] France, as the host country, was particularly anxious to secure maximum Community funding for the organizational costs of the Stability Pact.

Commission was able to make a sweep of budget lines not fully committed at the end of the year—tobacco, fishing, and PHARE were the victims. At least the money was found; the Member States had still not fully paid up their contributions a year later.

The Council did succeed in the first part of 1994 in putting its doctrine regarding the classification of expenditure at least theoretically into some sort of order. On 13–14 June 1994 it adopted four 'fiches' on, respectively, administrative expenditure, operating expenditure (financing from the Community Budget, Commission section), operating expenditure (financing from the Community Budget, Council section), and operating expenditure (financing by the Member States). These documents provided a conceptual framework for the imputation of expenditure, but did not make decisions any easier. They stressed the need to respect EC budgetary procedure, including the role of the Commission in preparing the Budget, but reserved decisions on implementation to specific cases. This document proved to be not an entirely trustworthy guide; two years later Coreper was obliged to approve a further paper, explaining in particular how to deal with the 'grey area'.

The Council's budgetary practices attracted the unfavourable attention of the European Parliament, which saw the opportunity to gain through the budgetary procedure a measure of control over the CFSP which it had been denied in the Maastricht Treaty. The operation was a delicate one: although the Parliament could pose as the guardian of budgetary orthodoxy, it would be counterproductive for it to impede unduly the carrying out of foreign policy actions of which it approved in substance. Parliament therefore took up the position that, before it agreed to make funds available for CFSP, it would need a clear indication of how they were going to be used. The Council was not willing to give Parliament the *droit de regard* over specific joint actions that this would have implied; frustrated, Parliament turned to attack the Commission, which had indeed made funds available for both the Palestinian police force and the administration of Mostar in conditions of probable legality but doubtful propriety. Even though in subsequent years greater budgetary provision for CFSP operations was approved by Parliament, a definitive settlement, in which the Parliament came out a clear winner, was only reached when an Interinstitutional Agreement was concluded in the wake of the Amsterdam Treaty.

Commitment of Member States

The difficulties experienced in the first year of implementation of the CFSP did not inspire confidence in the process. Although they passed unnoticed except by a dedicated band of foreign policy watchers, and of course by the Member States themselves, they nevertheless contributed significantly to preventing a dynamic, successful, and headline-catching European foreign policy from emerging. In this low-key environment, those Member States which had the means to conduct their own foreign policies were tempted to look elsewhere for arenas in which to deploy their diplomatic talents. This not unnaturally annoyed other Member States, which relied on the European framework for a diplomatic platform.

The CFSP was a common foreign policy, not a single policy. National foreign policies had not been abolished by the Maastricht Treaty. There was thus no legal impediment to a Member State's refraining from using the CFSP framework whenever it so chose. The only commitment in principle was to 'support the Union's external and security policy actively and unreservedly in a spirit of loyalty and mutual solidarity'; in addition the Member States 'shall refrain from any action which is contrary to the interests of the Union or likely to impair its effectiveness as a cohesive force in international relations' (Article J.1). Except on the narrowest interpretation, this does not prevent Member States from conducting their own foreign policies in other fora, and even if it did the provision would be unenforceable, since the Member States themselves, acting as the Council, are responsible for policing it ('The Council shall ensure that these principles are complied with': Article J.1). To be sure, the obligation is more binding in the case of common positions ('Member States shall ensure that their national policies conform to the common positions': Article J.2), but this provision, in addition to leaving open what happens when there is no common position, explicitly recognizes that Member States may have national policies even when there is a common position. Similar but less binding provisions apply in the case of joint actions ('Joint actions shall commit the Member States in the positions they adopt and in the conduct of their activity': Article J.2.4–6).

In the circumstances it was scarcely surprising that Member States, confronted with an apparent lack of effectiveness of the CFSP, should seek to advance their national policy aims in other fora. The most striking example, and the one that gave rise to the greatest indignation, was the Contact Group on former Yugoslavia, but other, less high-profile, cases were from time to time added to the charge-sheet—the CSCE, where the real co-ordination was done by Germany, France, the United Kingdom, and the United States; Turkey, where the Ambassadors of Germany, France, and the United Kingdom in Ankara concerted their positions outside the EU framework; the Nordic Group on US financial arrears in the UN; a group made up of Austria, Denmark, Finland, Ireland, the Netherlands, and Sweden, together with Australia, Canada, New Zealand, Norway, and Hungary, on non-proliferation; Germany, France, Italy, the United Kingdom, and Turkey, as the Cyprus Pentagonale; and the United States, Russia, and Portugal in the Angola Troika.[62] This proliferation of formations was seen, especially by integrationists, as being harmful to the image of the CFSP as a unitary policy.[63]

The Contact Group, which initially brought together the United Kingdom, France, the United States, and Russia, was set up in April 1994 in order to escape from the repeated dead-ends to which all attempts to deal with the problem of former Yugoslavia seemed condemned. Previously, one faction or the other in the Yugoslav conflict had always been able to find support from such of the powers as were not associated with the current initiative. It was hoped that if all sources of outside influence combined, this possibility would be cut off. It made sense, therefore, to invent a structure which brought together the United States and Russia. In fact, the initiative appears to have originated outside the EU, even though with the connivance of France and Britain. In February 1994 President Yeltsin had called for a summit meeting bringing together Russia, the United States, the United Kingdom, France, and Germany, and this was followed up by a proposal from the Co-Chairmen of the International Conference on Former Yugoslavia which led to their setting up the Contact Group. David Owen records that his choice of format owed something to his recollections of the Contact Group on Namibia during the 1970s. The relationship of the Namibia Contact Group with EPC is instructive; the EPC Africa Working Group was kept regularly informed of developments, and it was accepted that British, French, and German membership of the Contact Group was entirely consistent with EPC obligations. But that was two treaties earlier, and the Community was not at the time itself engaged in trying to solve the Angola problem. Two decades later the situation had changed. The creation in 1994 of the Contact Group on Yugoslavia impaired the credibility of the CFSP.[64]

---

[62] Burghardt, 'The Potential and Limits of CFSP', 322; Müller and van Dassen, 'From Cacophony to Joint Action', 66; Dumond and Setton, *La politique étrangère et de sécurité commune*, 91; de Vasconcelos, 'Portugal: Pressing for an Open Europe?', 269–70, 272.

[63] van den Broek, 'CFSP: The View of the European Commission', 28.

[64] Lukic and Lynch, *Europe from the Balkans to the Urals*, 347 n. 51; Woodward, *Balkan Tragedy*, 315–16; Debie, 'De Brioni à Dayton', 48 n. 8; Védrine, *Les Mondes de François Mitterrand*, 666 (who claims the initiative for Mitterrand and hails the setting up of the Contact Group as a triumph for French diplomacy); Owen, *Balkan Odyssey*, 275–8; Favier and Martin-Roland, *La Décennie Mitterrand*, iv. 512–13, 520–1; Neville-Jones, 'Dayton, IFOR and Alliance Relations in Bosnia', 46; Gow, *Triumph of the Lack of Will*, 156–7.

It was, however, scarcely to be expected that France and the United Kingdom, permanent members of the Security Council, would turn down such an opportunity on the grounds of EU propriety. Germany, the incoming EU Presidency, showed no greater reticence, and succeeded in remaining a member of the Group after its term of office, and membership of the Troika, were over.[65] Italy wasted no time in recriminations but set its mind to joining the Group itself, an aim in which it eventually succeeded, after an unparalleled display of diplomatic blackmail, and in spite of the opposition of the other European members, in 1997.[66] The reaction to the Group from the other Member States, in particular the Netherlands, was strong.[67] Various procedural artifices were adopted to sugar the pill. The Troika was kept informed, and sometimes involved (in spite of the unwelcome presence of Greece as Presidency); the British, French, and German members of the Contact Group were technically advisers to Lord Owen and so covered by his mandate as EU Representative; it was claimed that the EU Members of the Contact Group were merely implementing EU policy,[68] and were answerable to the institutions of the CFSP; and Carl Bildt's attendance at Dayton was in theory to ensure a collective European presence, although the French and British Political Directors warned the Americans that they should be aware that he could not speak for their governments on all issues.[69]

The setting up of the Contact Group did after all preserve a façade of EU organizational coherence and could, in different conditions, have been presented as a dynamic new form of foreign-policy making within the CFSP. Taken with the other difficulties in the implementation of the CFSP in the first twelve months of its operation, it gave the reverse impression. What had gone wrong with the CFSP?

[65] Edwards, 'The Potential and Limits of the CFSP', 189.

[66] Holbrooke, *To End a War*, 136–7; Bildt, *Peace Journey*, 101.

[67] Owen, *Balkan Odyssey*, 278; van den Broek, 'CFSP: The View of the European Commission', 24; Gallet, *La Politique étrangère commune*, 111 n. 11.

[68] The European members of the Contact Group were held to be bound by the common position on Yugoslavia: Ryba, 'La politique étrangère et de sécurité commune', 26. They were in fact given few instructions by the Council. One was that the civilian administrator should be a European: Neville-Jones, 'Dayton, IFOR and Alliance Relations in Bosnia', 50.

[69] Gow, *Triumph of the Lack of Will*, 260–1; Owen, *Balkan Odyssey*, 278; Védrine, *Les Mondes de François Mitterrand*, 669; Holbrooke, *To End a War*, 242; Bildt, *Peace Journey*, 124.

10

The nature of the CFSP

The CFSP disappointed expectations because there was no compulsion for it to exist, and therefore no consensus on the purpose it was intended to serve. In the absence of a compelling *raison d'être*, the Member States were free to allow their institutional preferences and prejudices to prevail over considerations of substance.[1]

There would not have been a CFSP had it not been for the collapse of Communism in Central and Eastern Europe. This event gave rise to a wave of public debate about the future role of Europe which emboldened those who wished to see the development of a European Union on integrationist lines to put on the table proposals for the incorporation of a reinforced foreign policy into a revised Community system. Hence the European Parliament's Resolution of March 1990, which adopted a firmly integrationist line; hence too the Belgian Memorandum of the same month, which recommended a pragmatic approach in preference to an institutional one, but tended in the same direction. Both justified their proposals by the need to make an adequate response to events to the East.

The trouble was that, in order to respond, the European Community did not need a CFSP. It had been responding perfectly adequately through its existing structures. The EC role in the G24 and its conclusion of successive generations of agreements with the CEECs, as well as the ultimate prospect of accession, were powerful incentives to think in terms of a foreign policy role for the Union, but at the same time effectively countered any move in that direction, since in themselves they provided all that was required. When subsequent events, the Gulf War and, after the conclusion of the Maastricht Treaty, the conflict in Yugoslavia, provided

---

[1] The authoritative discussion of the mismatch between expectations of CFSP and its capacity to deliver is Hill, 'The Capability–Expectations Gap', an analysis, formulated a year before the entry into force of the Maastricht Treaty, which has been a reference point for all subsequent discussion. Professor Hill intended his contribution to provide a way of measuring the CFSP's performance over time. It did not seek to establish who holds what expectations, why, and with what justification. These points are addressed in his review of developments five years on: Hill, 'Closing the Capabilities–Expectations Gap?'

confirmation of the view that foreign policy needed a military dimension to be credible, the determination of the United States to retain its dominance through NATO precluded the CFSP from advancing in that direction.

The inclusion of the CFSP in the new Union was not, or was only partially, because of ambitions along European Parliament or Belgian lines. It was rather because France and Germany took the decision to make it a part of the wider objective of political union, which they were pursuing for essentially domestic reasons. France was determined to achieve economic and monetary union; Germany was determined, and indeed needed, to extract a price for its consent. Both were in urgent need of finding an initiative to mend the rift between them caused by the movement towards German unification. To Paris and Bonn, the CFSP was more important as symbol than as substance. In the circumstances, it is hardly surprising that proposals on substance were slow to come, and when they did were of varying interest and difficult to relate to an overall scheme.

One proposal, espoused at an early stage by Delors, was to introduce a qualitatively different form of foreign-policy making, which would co-exist alongside the old style. The Member States would agree on a limited number of very important interests held in common, and in pursuit of those interests adopt a more integrated way of decision-making. The idea failed on both counts. There was no agreement to concentrate on a limited number of areas, and so the old EPC was swept away to be replaced by the CFSP across the board. And there was no agreement to take decisions in a more integrated way, so the provisions for qualified majority voting (in themselves but one feature of the Community method) were no more than an exceptionally tattered figleaf.

In the absence of genuine innovation, it is tempting to say, and has frequently been said, that the CFSP is no more than the old EPC in more grandiloquent language, and that it remains obstinately intergovernmental in nature, if not a threat then at least a rival to the EC. A closer analysis, however, suggests that, in ways unintended by its authors, the Maastricht Treaty has brought about a sea-change in the practice and ambience of foreign-policy making, which makes a reassessment of this assertion desirable. The reason is mainly bureaucratic, and is to be found in the localization of activities in Brussels. In this it continues a trend which started following the Single European Act. Three factors in particular are important: the decline in socialization, the increasing reliance on EC instruments, and the role of the Council Secretariat.

EPC worked, within its limits, because it turned those limits to advantage. Foreign Ministries made sure that it remained a self-contained operation, restricted to a small circle of initiates and powered by the forces of socialization. The secret was that, in normal circumstances, those initiates had the power to sway national policies. The Political Directors, assisted by the European Correspondents, the Heads of Department, above all the Foreign Ministers themselves, were well placed to align their countries on EPC positions if they so chose. Their task was made easier because they had control over the EPC agenda. There was nothing beyond the force of external events to oblige them to take up a subject, if it looked as though consensus would prove difficult to attain. No rules constrained them, apart from the twin precepts of intergovernmentalism and consensus; beyond that they made their own rules. Their loyalties were divided: they felt not only commitment to the national interest, but also solidarity with their partners.

This feeling of solidarity was only rarely the product of a cold calculation of reciprocal interest. It stemmed rather from the process of socialization, the feeling of belonging to a club. EPC was run by diplomats for diplomats. They organized meetings, worked out the positions, and implemented them once they had been approved. This was not enough for some, and explains in part the push in the IGC to do something more, but in its own terms it worked.

The system probably could not have endured, and was under pressure even before the Maastricht Treaty was approved. Coteries function best when they are small; EPC began to show signs of strain when adapting to enlargement. However, this did not begin to show until the Iberian enlargement of 1986. The first enlargement of 1973 had not presented any particular problems, because EPC was itself so new and had operated with the *de facto* participation of the candidate countries from the start. The problems presented by Greek enlargement were peculiar to the new member, not caused by the move from Nine to Ten. But the move from Ten to Twelve, and still more the move from Twelve to Fifteen, changed the atmosphere simply by increasing the size of the table. With each participant anxious to take the floor, discussions became a series of interventions rather than a conversation. The change in ambience was all the greater because the last enlargement took place after the new CFSP arrangements had come into force. The new members had no folk memory of the *ancien régime.*

Change was also brought about by the increasing salience of foreign policy issues, a trend which was accelerated by the events in Central and

Eastern Europe and later in Yugoslavia. Public opinion became a factor to consider, thus limiting the EPC participants' room for manoeuvre[2] and involving others, such as Prime Ministers or other Ministries, from outside the EPC circle.

But the most significant change in the ambience resulted from the decision to create in the Maastricht Treaty a single institutional framework for the CFSP and EC foreign policy. The significance lay not in the Treaty decision to merge EPC and the EC at the level of the Council—Foreign Ministers had been behaving for years as though that decision had already been taken—but in the consequences which flowed from it at the level of officials. Ironically, the Treaty refrained from setting out what these were, and the matter was left to subsequent bureaucratic negotiation and the development of everyday practice. The outcome was that the CFSP became definitively a Brussels activity, not one of the national capitals, and responsibility for servicing it passed to the Council Secretariat. The procedural device the Luxembourg Presidency had invented in order to square the circle between intergovernmentalists and integrationists was to have a greater effect on the conditions in which foreign policy was made than anyone could have imagined at the time.

The most serious effect was the decline of socialization.[3] This relied to an appreciable extent on the practice of holding EPC meetings in the capital of the Presidency. Successive Presidencies vied with each other to provide agreeable and prestigious surroundings, and if possible excursions to savour the national heritage. A great deal of importance was attached to hospitality, and the hosts' efforts in this respect were appreciated. It would be going too far to say that Presidencies were evaluated by a system of Michelin stars, but it was certainly the case that expertise in entertaining facilitated personal contacts and fostered the club atmosphere.

The decline had already begun with the Single European Act. The decision to hold all meetings of Working Groups, and some of the Political Committee, in the premises of the EPC Secretariat in Brussels meant that Presidency hospitality organized by the Protocol service of the Foreign Ministry was replaced by Presidency hospitality organized by the Council Secretariat. It was not exciting, and it was always the same. After the Maastricht Treaty came into force, working lunches were for the most part abandoned. Delegates preferred to use the time sending their reports back

[2] Allen, 'Conclusions: The European Rescue of National Foreign Policy?', 300.
[3] Regelsberger and Wessels, 'The CFSP institutions and procedures', 37. For a contrary view, see Spence and Spence, 'The CFSP From Maastricht to Amsterdam', 51–2.

to headquarters over a quick sandwich. The opportunity to engage in discussions outside the official speaking brief, to do private deals, and simply to get to know one's colleagues as people, was forgone.[4]

It is certainly excessive to claim that the CFSP failed because of the withdrawal of the gastronomic element. But in a system which had minimal institutional underpinnings, the solidarity which came from socialization supplied the want. However, socialization has to be worked for. If it atrophies, and is not replaced by institutional provisions, the system as a whole declines.

The second factor in the change of ambience was increasing reliance on EC instruments. This was not a new phenomenon; it can be observed from the beginning of the 1980s on. But it took on a new importance after the Maastricht Treaty came into force because of the arrangements for the division of labour between the Political Committee and Coreper. Under the old system, if EPC wished to make use of a Community instrument, there would be a discussion in the Political Committee to which the Commission contributed. In the case of agreement, the Commission made the necessary proposal following normal EC procedures. The Commission had the hinge role, and was in a sense a go-between linking the Political Committee and Coreper. Coreper entered the discussion at a late stage, and its input was usually technical. Under the CFSP, the Commission has to a large extent forfeited its hinge position, and Coreper has correspondingly increased in importance. The creation of the Group of Counsellors to advise on the EC, financial, and institutional aspects of CFSP proposals, reporting *de facto* to Coreper rather than to the Political Committee, is an indication of this. The more CFSP wishes to have recourse to EC instruments, the more the trend towards the EC side of the Council will be accentuated.

The shift in the Political Committee's role, to one of giving foreign policy advice to Ministers, has contributed to weakening the link with the Working Groups.[5] Following a trend which began after the Single Act, the Political Committee now only infrequently has its attention drawn to the record of a Working Group meeting. At the same time, the increase in the volume of business requires it to meet more often than ever before. This led the Political Committee to attempt to delegate some decisions to the Deputy Political Directors, but the experience proved unsatisfactory.[6] The Political Directors are at a disadvantage because their offices are in the

---

[4] Regelsberger, 'Reforming CFSP', 99.
[5] Dumond and Setton, *La politique étrangère et de sécurité commune*, 52–3.
[6] Ibid. 50.

national capitals, not Brussels. This has contributed to the increasing foreign policy importance of Coreper.

Finally, the fact that the EPC Secretariat was incorporated into the Council Secretariat has meant that the Council Secretariat ethos has prevailed, leading to a bureaucratization and legalization of CFSP proceedings. The main change remarked on by those with experience of both EPC and CFSP is the greatly increased volume of paper. This is partly because of the increase in the amount of work—unlike EPC, CFSP has difficulty in being selective about its agenda—but also because, following the well-known bureaucratic rule, staff generate paper in proportion to their numbers, not the importance of the issue. This leads to a feeling on the part of the national delegates of being out of control. The Legal Service of the Council has played an important role in ensuring that, now that the CFSP is part of the Union's legal structure, its transactions should be recorded in proper legal form. This has led to the practice, unnerving to professional diplomats, of couching foreign policy decisions in traditional EC form and of publishing them in the Official Journal (L series, reserved for legislation).[7] And the proliferation of acronyms is attributable to Council Secretariat practice.[8]

These straws in the wind, negligible in themselves, are all indications that times are changing. The administration of EU foreign-policy making is not the appanage of home-based national diplomats it once was. It is therefore not surprising that these diplomats should take a different view of a process they no longer own, and, in the case of diplomats from the larger Member States, give preference to national diplomacy. The CFSP is taking on a personality of its own, and that personality is as a member of the Community family. The failure to endow it with the recognized appurtenances of integration—the exclusive right of initiative of the Commission, qualified majority voting, subjection to the jurisdiction of the Court—should not blind us to the fact that the practices and approach of CFSP are moving in the direction of the EC. The CFSP is a halfway house—no longer the purely intergovernmental affair of the early days, but not yet a fully fledged policy arm of the Union, with its own brand of Community procedures. On two occasions, and now again at Amsterdam, the attempt to incorporate foreign-policy making into the Community family by institutional means has failed. Time, and the appointment of a Secretary General, High Representative for the CFSP, will tell whether the incremental, bureaucratic, and pragmatic approach will succeed.

[7] Ibid. 41, 49; Ryba, 'La Politique étrangère et de sécurité commune', 21.
[8] Dumond and Setton, *La politique étrangère et de sécurité commune*, 74.

BIBLIOGRAPHY

ALLEN, DAVID, 'West European Responses to Change in the Soviet Union and Eastern Europe', in Reinhardt Rummel (ed.), *Toward Political Union* (Baden-Baden, 1992), 119–38.

—— 'Conclusions: The European Rescue of National Foreign Policy?', in Christopher Hill (ed.), *The Actors in Europe's Foreign Policy* (London and New York, 1996), 288–304.

—— 'EPC/CFSP, the Soviet Union, and the Former Soviet Republics', in Elfriede Regelsberger, Philippe de Schoutheete de Tervarent, and Wolfgang Wessels (eds.), *Foreign Policy of the European Union* (Boulder, Colo. and London, 1997), 219–35.

ANDERSON, JEFFREY J., and GOODMAN, JOHN B., 'Mars or Minerva? A United Germany in a Post-Cold War Europe', in Robert O. Keohane, Joseph S. Nye, and Stanley Hoffmann (eds.), *After the Cold War* (Cambridge, Mass. and London, 1993), 23–62.

ATTALI, JACQUES, *Verbatim III, 1988–1991* (Paris, 1995).

BARBÉ, ESTHER, 'Spain: The Uses of Foreign Policy Cooperation', in Christopher Hill (ed.), *The Actors in Europe's Foreign Policy* (London and New York, 1996), 108–29.

BESCHLOSS, MICHAEL R., and TALBOTT, STROBE, *At the Highest Levels* (Boston, 1993).

BEUTER, RITA, 'Germany and the Ratification of the Maastricht Treaty', in Finn Laursen and Sophie Vanhoonacker (eds.), *The Ratification of the Maastricht Treaty* (Dordrecht, 1994), 87–112.

BILDT, CARL, *Peace Journey* (London, 1998).

BRETHERTON, CHARLOTTE, and VOGLER, JOHN, *The European Union as a Global Actor* (London and New York, 1999).

BROWN, ARCHIE, *The Gorbachev Factor* (Oxford, 1996).

BUCHAN, DAVID, *Europe: The Strange Superpower* (Aldershot, 1993).

BURGHARDT, GÜNTER, 'The Potential and Limits of CFSP: What Comes Next?', in Elfriede Regelsberger, Philippe de Schoutheete de Tervarent, and Wolfgang Wessels (eds.), *Foreign Policy of the European Union* (Boulder, Colo. and London, 1997), 321–33.

BUSH, GEORGE, and SCOWCROFT, BRENT, *A World Transformed* (New York, 1998).

CAMERON, FRASER, 'The Stability Pact', paper presented to the Defense Nuclear Agency's Fourth International Conference, Panel on Regional Security Issues, Philadelphia, 20 June 1995.

—— 'Where the European Commission Comes In: From the Single European Act to Maastricht', in Elfriede Regelsberger, Philippe de Schoutheete de Tervarent, and Wolfgang Wessels (eds.), *Foreign Policy of the European Union* (Boulder, Colo. and London, 1997), 99–108.

CAMERON, FRASER, 'Building a Common Foreign Policy', in John Peterson and Helene Sjursen (eds.), *A Common Foreign Policy for Europe?* (London and New York, 1998), 59–76.

CATTANI, A., 'Essai de coopération politique entre les Six, 1960–62, et échec des négociations pour un statut politique', *Chronique de politique étrangère*, 11(4) (July 1967).

CHENU, GEORGES-MARIE, 'Les Hommes en blanc ou l'Europe sur le sentier de la paix', in Jean Cot (ed.), *Dernière guerre balkanique?* (Paris, 1996), 85–112.

CLESSE, ARMAND, 'Europe and the Gulf War as Seen by the Luxembourg Presidency of the EC', in Nicole Gnesotto and John Roper (eds.), *Western Europe and the Gulf* (Paris, 1992), 89–96.

CLOOS, J., REINESCH, G., VIGNES, D., and WEYLAND, J., *Le Traité de Maastricht: genèse, analyse, commentaires* (Brussels, 1993).

COHEN, SAMY, 'L'Imprévision et l'imprévisible: remarques sur le processus mitterrandien d'information et de décision', in Samy Cohen (ed.), *Mitterrand et la sortie de la guerre froide* (Paris, 1998), 361–79.

—— (ed.), *Mitterrand et la sortie de la guerre froide* (Paris, 1998).

COLE, ALISTAIR, *François Mitterrand: A Study in Political Leadership*, 2nd edn. (London and New York, 1997).

CORBETT, RICHARD, *The Treaty of Maastricht* (London, 1993).

CRADOCK, PERCY, *In Pursuit of British Interests* (London, 1997).

CREMASCO, MAURIZIO, 'La Comunità europea di fronte alla crisi jugoslava', in Marco Carnovale (ed.), *La Guerra di Bosnia: una tragedia annunciata* (Rome, 1994), 109–33.

CRNOBRNJA, MIHAILO, *The Yugoslav Drama* (London, 1994).

DANKERT, PIET, 'Challenges and Priorities', in Alfred Pijpers (ed.), *The European Community at the Crossroads* (Dordrecht, 1992), 3–12.

DEBIE, FRANCK, 'De Brioni à Dayton: une très étrange diplomatie de la paix', in Jean Cot (ed.), *Dernière guerre balkanique?* (Paris, 1996), 47–83.

DE GUCHT, KAREL, and KEUKELEIRE, STEPHAN, 'The European Security Architecture: The Role of the European Community in Shaping a New European Geopolitical Landscape', *Studia Diplomatica*, 44(6) (1991), 29–90.

DE LARGENTAYE, BERTRAND, 'The European Community, the PHARE Programme, and the East–West European Partnership', in Armand Clesse and Rudolf Tökés (eds.), *Preventing a New East–West Divide: The Economic and Social Imperatives of the Future Europe* (Baden-Baden, 1992), 302–17.

DE LA SERRE, FRANÇOISE, 'A la recherche d'une Ostpolitik', in Françoise de la Serre, Christian Lequesne, and Jacques Rupnik, *L'Union européenne: ouverture à l'Est?* (Paris, 1994), 11–41.

—— 'France: The Impact of François Mitterrand', in Christopher Hill (ed.), *The Actors in Europe's Foreign Policy* (London and New York, 1996), 19–39.

——'La Politique européenne de François Mitterrand: innovante ou réactive?', in Samy Cohen (ed.), *Mitterrand et la sortie de la guerre froide* (Paris, 1998), 110–25.

DELORS, JACQUES, *Le Nouveau concert européen* (Paris, 1992).

——*L'Unité d'un homme* (Paris, 1994).

DE RUYT, J., *L'Acte unique européen* (Brussels, 1987).

DE SCHOUTHEETE, PHILIPPE, 'The Creation of the CFSP', in Elfriede Regelsberger, Philippe de Schoutheete de Tervarent, and Wolfgang Wessels (eds.), *Foreign Policy of the European Union* (Boulder, Colo. and London, 1997), 41–63.

——'Gemeinsame Außen- und Sicherheitspolitik in der Politischen Union: Machtzuwachs und politische Verantwortung', *Integration*, 14 (Jan. 1991), 3–8.

Deutsche Einheit: *Sonderedition aus den Akten des Bundeskanzleramtes 1989/90*, Dokumente zur Deutschlandpolitik (Munich, 1998).

DE VASCONCELOS, ÁLVARO, 'Portugal: A Case for an Open Europe', in Franco Algieri and Elfriede Regelsberger (eds.), *Synergy at Work: Spain and Portugal in European Foreign Policy* (Bonn, 1996), 111–36.

——'Portugal: Pressing for an Open Europe?', in Christopher Hill (ed.), *The Actors in Europe's Foreign Policy* (London and New York, 1996), 268–87.

DE WALSCHE, ALINE, 'L'Article 228 révisé par le traité d'Amsterdam', in Marianne Dony (ed.), *L'Union européenne et le monde après Amsterdam* (Brussels, 1999), 61–76.

DOCKSEY, CHRISTOPHER, and WILLIAMS, KAREN, 'The Commission and the Execution of Community Policy', in Geoffrey Edwards and David Spence (eds.), *The European Commission* (Harlow, 1994), 117–45.

DORMAN, ANDREW M., and TREACHER, ADRIAN, *European Security* (Aldershot, 1995).

DOUTRIAUX, YVES, *Le Traité sur l'Union européenne* (Paris, 1992).

DUMOND, JEAN-MICHEL, and SETTON, PHILIPPE, *La Politique étrangère et de sécurité commune (PESC)* (Paris, 1999).

DYSON, KENNETH, 'Chancellor Kohl as Strategic Leader: The Case of Economic and Monetary Union', in Clay Clemens and William E. Paterson (eds.), *The Kohl Chancellorship* (London and Portland, Ore., 1998), 37–63.

EDWARDS, GEOFFREY, 'European Political Cooperation Put to the Test', in Alfred Pijpers (ed.), *The European Community at the Crossroads* (Dordrecht, 1992), 227–46.

——'European Responses to the Yugoslav Crisis: An Interim Assessment', in Reinhardt Rummel (ed.), *Toward Political Union* (Baden-Baden, 1992), 165–89.

——'The Potential and Limits of the CFSP: The Yugoslav Example', in Elfriede Regelsberger, Philippe de Schoutheete de Tervarent, and Wolfgang Wessels (eds.), *Foreign Policy of the European Union* (Boulder, Colo. and London, 1997), 173–95.

EDWARDS, GEOFFREY, and SPENCE, DAVID (eds.), *The European Commission* (Harlow, 1994).

ENDO, KEN, *The Presidency of the European Commission under Jacques Delors* (Basingstoke, London, and New York, 1999).

FAVIER, PIERRE, and MARTIN-ROLAND, MICHEL, *La Décennie Mitterrand*, 4 vols. (Paris, 1990–9).

FRANCK, CHRISTIAN, 'Belgium: The Importance of Foreign Policy to European Political Union', in Christopher Hill (ed.), *The Actors in Europe's Foreign Policy* (London and New York, 1996), 151–65.

FREEDMAN, LAWRENCE, and KARSH, EFRAIM, *The Gulf Conflict 1990–1991* (London, 1993).

FRITSCH-BOURNAZEL, RENATA, 'Die Einigung Deutschlands aus der Sicht der Nachbarländer', in Wolfgang Heisenberg (ed.), *Die Vereinigung Deutschlands in europäischer Perspektive* (Baden-Baden, 1992), 67–82.

——*Europe and German Unification* (New York and Oxford, 1992).

FROMENT-MEURICE, HENRI, and LUDLOW, PETER, 'Towards a European Foreign Policy', paper presented to Working Group No. 2, CEPS Annual Conference Brussels, 29 November-1 December 1989.

GALLET, BERTRAND, *La Politique étrangère commune* (Paris, 1999).

GALLOWAY, DAVID, 'Common Foreign and Security Policy: Intergovernmentalism Donning the Mantle of the Community Method', in Martin Westlake (ed.), *The Council of the European Union* (London, 1995), 211–33.

GARTON ASH, TIMOTHY, *In Europe's Name* (London, 1993).

GATES, ROBERT M., *From the Shadows* (New York, 1996).

GENSCHER, HANS-DIETRICH, *Erinnerungen* (Berlin, 1995).

GERBET, PIERRE, DE LA SERRE, FRANÇOISE, and NAFILYAN, GÉRARD, *L'Union politique de l'Europe: jalons et textes* (Paris, 1998).

GINSBERG, ROY, 'The EU's CFSP: The Politics of Procedure', in Martin Holland (ed.), *Common Foreign and Security Policy: The Record and Reforms* (London and Washington, 1997), 12–33.

GLITMAN, MAYNARD, 'US Policy in Bosnia: Rethinking a Flawed Approach', *Survival*, 38(4) (Winter 1996–7), 66–83.

GNESOTTO, NICOLE, *Leçons de la Yougoslavie*, Cahiers de Chaillot 14 (Paris, 1994).

——and ROPER, JOHN (eds.), *Western Europe and the Gulf* (Paris, 1992).

GORBACHEV, MIKHAIL, *Memoirs* (London, 1996).

GOW, JAMES, *Triumph of the Lack of Will* (London, 1997).

GRANT, CHARLES, *Delors: Inside the House that Jacques Built* (London, 1994).

GRUNBERG, GÉRARD, 'Le Trouble des opinions publiques', in Françoise de la Serre and Christian Lequesne (eds.), *Quelle Union pour quelle Europe?* (Brussels, 1998), 97–124.

GUAZZONE, LAURA, 'Italy in the Gulf Crisis', in Nicole Gnesotto and John Roper (eds.), *Western Europe and the Gulf* (Paris, 1992), 71–87.

GUICHERD, CATHERINE, *L'Heure de l'Europe: premières leçons du conflit yougoslave* (Paris, 1993).

GÜNTHER, DIRK, 'Makroökonomische Implikationen der Deutschen Einheit—Anker-Rolle und Lokomitivfunktion im Test', in Barbara Lippert, Dirk Günther, Rosalind Stevens-Ströhmann, Grit Viertel, and Stephen Woolcock, *Die EG und die neuen Bundesländer: eine Erfolgsgeschichte von kurzer Dauer?* (Bonn, 1993), 115–47.

HAGGARD, STEPHAN, and MORAVCSIK, ANDREW, 'The Political Economy of Financial Assistance to Eastern Europe, 1989–1991', in Robert O. Keohane, Joseph S. Nye, and Stanley Hoffmann (eds.), *After the Cold War* (Cambridge, Mass. and London, 1993), 246–85.

HAGLEITNER, THOMAS, 'Les Rôles du Parlement européen et de la Commission dans le domaine de la Politique Étrangère et de Sécurité Commune', diploma diss., College of Europe, Bruges, 1994–5.

HAMLET, LAWRENCE L., 'The Core of Decision-making', in Reinhardt Rummel (ed.), *Toward Political Union* (Baden-Baden, 1992), 83–103.

HAYES, ERIC, 'The Internal Market and EFTA as Viewed from Brussels', in Finn Laursen (ed.), *EFTA and the EC: Implications of 1992* (Maastricht, 1990), 53–60.

HEISBOURG, FRANÇOIS, 'France and the Gulf Crisis', in Nicole Gnesotto and John Roper (eds.), *Western Europe and the Gulf* (Paris, 1992), 17–38.

HEISENBERG, WOLFGANG, 'Europäische Sicherheit als politische Aufgabe nach der Vereinigung Deutschlands', in Wolfgang Heisenberg (ed.), *Die Vereinigung Deutschlands in europäischer Perspektive* (Baden-Baden, 1992), 99–119.

HEURLIN, BERTIL, 'Denmark: A New Activism in Foreign and Security Policy', in Christopher Hill (ed.), *The Actors in Europe's Foreign Policy* (London and New York, 1996), 166–85.

HILL, CHRISTOPHER, 'The Capability–Expectations Gap, or Conceptualizing Europe's International Role', *Journal of Common Market Studies*, 31(3) (1993), 305–28.

—— 'Closing the Capabilities–Expectations Gap?', in John Peterson and Helene Sjursen (eds.), *A Common Foreign Policy for Europe?* (London and New York, 1998), 18–38.

HOFFMANN, STANLEY, 'French Dilemmas and Strategies in the New Europe', in Robert O. Keohane, Joseph S. Nye and Stanley Hoffmann (eds.), *After the Cold War* (Cambridge, Mass., and London, 1993), 127–47.

HOLBROOKE, RICHARD, *To End a War* (New York, 1998).

HOLLAND, MARTIN, *The European Community and South Africa* (London, 1988).

—— *European Union Common Foreign Policy: From EPC to CFSP Joint Action and South Africa* (London, 1995).

—— 'The Joint Action on South Africa', in Martin Holland (ed.), *Common Foreign and Security Policy* (London and Washington, DC, 1997), 174–83.

—— (ed.), *Common Foreign and Security Policy: The Record and Reforms* (London and Washington DC, 1997).

HUBEL, HELMUT, 'Europa, Japan und der Krieg um Kuwait', in Hanns W. Maull (ed.), *Japan und Europa: getrennte Welten?* (Frankfurt, 1993), 482–502.

JACOMET, ARNAUD, 'The Role of WEU in the Gulf Crisis', in Nicole Gnesotto and John Roper (eds.), *Western Europe and the Gulf* (Paris, 1992), 159–80.

JOPP, MATHIAS, 'The Defense Dimension of the European Union: The Role and Performance of the WEU', in Elfriede Regelsberger, Philippe de Schoutheete de Tervarent, and Wolfgang Wessels (eds.), *Foreign Policy of the European Union* (Boulder, Colo. and London, 1997), 153–69.

KAISER, KARL, and BECHER, KLAUS, 'Germany and the Iraq Conflict', in Nicole Gnesotto and John Roper (eds.), *Western Europe and the Gulf* (Paris, 1992), 39–69.

KARNITSCHNIG, MICHAEL, *Integration als Sicherheitspolitik: die konzeptuelle Weiterentwicklung der GASP am Beispiel des Paktes für Stabilität in Europa* (Vienna, 1999).

KEATINGE, PATRICK, 'Ireland and Common Security: Stretching the Limits of Commitment?', in Christopher Hill (ed.), *The Actors in Europe's Foreign Policy* (London and New York, 1996), 208–25.

KERAUDREN, PHILIPPE, and DUBOIS, NICOLAS, 'France and the Ratification of the Maastricht Treaty', in Finn Laursen and Sophie Vanhoonacker (eds.), *The Ratification of the Maastricht Treaty* (Dordrecht, 1994), 147–79.

KIESSLER, RICHARD, and ELBE, FRANK, *Der diplomatische Weg zur deutschen Einheit* (Baden-Baden, 1996; 1st publ. as *Ein runder Tisch mit scharfen Ecken*, Baden-Baden, 1993).

KISO, JAN OLE, 'An Uncosy Relationship: COREPER, Political Committee and CFSP', *CFSP Forum*, 2/1997, 3–5.

KNOBEN, ROGER, 'Public Opinion in the European Union', in Finn Laursen and Sophie Vanhoonacker (eds.), *The Ratification of the Maastricht Treaty* (Dordrecht, 1994), 319–48.

KOHL, HELMUT, *Ich wollte Deutschlands Einheit* (Berlin, 1996); publ. in a shortened French trans. as *Je voulais l'unité de l'Allemagne* (Paris, 1996).

KÖRMENDY, ISTVÀN, 'View from Hungary: An EC Associate's Perspective from Central Europe', in Reinhardt Rummel (ed.), *Toward Political Union* (Baden-Baden, 1992), 245–53.

KRAMER, HEINZ, 'The European Community's Response to the "New Eastern Europe"', *Journal of Common Market Studies*, 31(2) (June 1993), 213–44.

KRENZLER, HORST G., 'Die Europäische Gemeinschaft und der Wandel in Mittel- und Osteuropa', *Europa-Archiv*, 45(3) (1990), 89–96.

——'Der Europäische Wirtschaftsraum als Teil einer gesamteuropäischen Architektur', *Integration*, 15 (Feb. 1992), 61–71.

——and SCHNEIDER, HENNING C., 'The Question of Consistency', in Elfriede Regelsberger, Philippe de Schoutheete de Tervarent, and Wolfgang Wessels (eds.), *Foreign Policy of the European Union* (Boulder, Colo. and London, 1997), 133–51.

KÜSTERS, HANNS JÜRGEN, 'Entscheidung für die deutsche Einheit: Einführung in die Edition', in *Deutsche Einheit: Sonderedition aus den Akten des Bundeskanzleramtes 1989/90* (Munich, 1998), 21–236.

LA BALME, NATALIE, 'L'Influence de l'opinion publique dans la gestion des crises', in Samy Cohen (ed.), *Mitterrand et la sortie de la guerre froide* (Paris, 1998), 409–26.

LACORNE, DENIS, 'Le Rang de la France: Mitterrand et la guerre du Golfe', in Samy Cohen (ed.), *Mitterrand et la sortie de la guerre froide* (Paris, 1998), 321–46.

LACOUTURE, JEAN, *Mitterrand, une histoire de Français*, 2 vols. (Paris, 1998).

LAURSEN, FINN, 'Denmark and the Ratification of the Maastricht Treaty', in Finn Laursen and Sophie Vanhoonacker (eds.), *The Ratification of the Maastricht Treaty: Issues, Debates and Future Implications* (Dordrecht, 1994), 61–86.

—— and Vanhoonacker, Sophie (eds.), *The Intergovernmental Conference on Political Union: Institutional Reforms, New Policies and International Identity of the European Community* (Maastricht, 1992).

—— —— (eds.), *The Ratification of the Maastricht Treaty: Issues, Debates and Future Implications* (Dordrecht, 1994).

LEQUESNE, CHRISTIAN, *Paris–Bruxelles: comment se fait la politique européenne de la France* (Paris, 1993).

—— 'Commerce et aide économique: les instruments d'une politique', in Françoise de la Serre, Christian Lequesne, and Jacques Rupnik, *L'Union européenne: ouverture à l'Est?* (Paris, 1994), 43–79.

—— 'Une lecture décisionnelle de la politique européenne de François Mitterrand', in Samy Cohen (ed.), *Mitterrand et la sortie de la guerre froide* (Paris, 1998), 127–48.

LEURDIJK, DICK A., *The United Nations and NATO in Former Yugoslavia* (The Hague, 1994).

LÉVESQUE, JACQUES, *The Enigma of 1989* (Berkeley and Los Angeles, 1997; 1st publ. as *La Fin d'un empire: l'URSS et la libération de l'Europe de l'Est*, Paris, 1995).

LIBAL, MICHAEL, *Limits of Persuasion: Germany and the Yugoslav Crisis, 1991–1992* (Westport, Conn. and London, 1997).

LIPPERT, BARBARA, 'Die EG als Mitgestalter der Erfolgsgeschichte—der Deutsche Einigungsprozess 1989/90', in Barbara Lippert, Dirk Günther, Rosalind Stevens-Ströhmann, Grit Viertel, and Stephen Woolcock, *Die EG und die neuen Bundesländer: Eine Erfolgsgeschichtte von kurzer Dauer?* (Bonn, 1993), 35–101.

LOEDEL, PETER H., 'Enhancing Europe's International Monetary Power: The Drive toward a Single Currency', in Pierre-Henri Laurent and Marc Maresceau (eds.), *The State of the European Union. Vol. 4: Deepening and Widening* (Boulder, Colo. and London, 1998), 243–61.

LORENZ, PIERRE-LOUIS, 'Luxembourg: New Commitments, New Assertiveness', in Christopher Hill (ed.), *The Actors in Europe's Foreign Policy* (London and New York, 1996), 226–46.

LUDLOW, PETER, 'The European Commission', in Robert O. Keohane and Stanley Hoffmann (eds.), *The New European Community: Decisionmaking and Institutional Change* (Boulder, Colo. and Oxford, 1991), 85–132.

LUIF, PAUL, *On the Road to Brussels : The Political Dimension of Austria's, Finland's and Sweden's Accession to the European Union* (Vienna, 1995).

LUKIC, RENEO, and LYNCH, ALLEN, *Europe from the Balkans to the Urals: The Disintegration of Yugoslavia and the Soviet Union* (Oxford, 1996).

MALCOLM, Neil, 'The "Common European Home" and Soviet European Policy"', *International Affairs*, 65(4) (Autumn 1989), 659–76.

MARTIAL, ENRICO, 'Italy and European Political Union', in Finn Laursen and Sophie Vanhoonacker (eds.), *The Intergovernmental Conference on Political Union* (Maastricht, 1992), 139–53.

MASLEN, JOHN, 'The European Community and Eastern Europe in the Post-1989 Era', in Armand Clesse and Raymond Vernon (eds.), *The European Community after 1992: A New Role in World Politics?* (Baden-Baden, 1991), 225–31.

MAULL, HANNS, 'Germany in the Yugoslav Crisis', *Survival*, 37(4) (Winter 1995–6), 99–130.

MAYHEW, ALAN, 'L'Assistance financière à l'Europe centrale et orientale: le programme Phare', *Revue d'études comparatives Est–Ouest*, 27(4) (Dec. 1996), 135–57.

—— *Recreating Europe: The European Union's Policy towards Central and Eastern Europe* (Cambridge, 1998).

MAZZUCELLI, COLETTE, *France and Germany at Maastricht: Politics and Negotiations to Create the European Union* (New York and London, 1997).

MIALL, HUGH, *Shaping the New Europe* (London, 1993).

MITTERRAND, FRANÇOIS, *De l'Allemagne, de la France* (Paris, 1996).

—— *Onze discours sur l'Europe* (1982–1995) (Naples, 1996).

—— *Les Forces de l'esprit: messages pour demain* (Paris, 1998).

MONAR, JÖRG, 'The Financial Dimension of the CFSP', in Martin Holland (ed.), *Common Foreign and Security Policy* (London and Washington, DC, 1997), 34–51.

MORAVCSIK, ANDREW, *The Choice for Europe* (London, 1998).

MORGAN, ROGER, 'Das neue Deutschland in der Europäischen Gemeinschaft—politische und institutionelle Folgen', in Wolfgang Heisenberg (ed.), *Die Vereinigung Deutschlands in europäischer Perspektive* (Baden-Baden, 1992), 83–98.

MÜLLER, HAROLD, and VAN DASSEN, LARS, 'From Cacophony to Joint Action: Successes and Shortcomings of the European Nuclear Non-proliferation Policy', in Martin Holland (ed.), *Common Foreign and Security Policy* (London and Washington, DC, 1997), 52–72.

MÜLLER-GRAFF, PETER-CHRISTIAN, 'Europäische Politische Zusammenarbeit und Gemainsame Außen- und Sicherheitspolitik: Kohärenzgebot aus rechtlicher Sicht', *Integration*, 3 (1993), 147–57.

MURRAY, CHRISTOPHER, W., 'View from the United States: Common Foreign and Security Policy as a Centrepiece of US Interest in European Political Union', in Reinhardt Rummel (ed.), *Toward Political Union* (Baden-Baden, 1992), 213–19.

NELSEN, BRENT F., and STUBB, ALEXANDER C.-G. (eds.), *The European Union: Readings on the Theory and Practice of European Integration* (Boulder, Colo. and London, 1994).

NEUMAN, HENK, 'The Gulf War: A View from the Hague', in Nicole Gnesotto and John Roper (eds.), *Western Europe and the Gulf* (Paris, 1992), 97–108.

NEUWAHL, NANETTE, 'Foreign and Security Policy and the Implementation of the Requirement of "Consistency" under the Treaty on European Union', in Patrick M. Twomey and David O'Keeffe (eds.), *Legal Issues of the Maastricht Treaty* (London, 1993).

NEVILLE-JONES, PAULINE, 'Dayton, IFOR and Alliance Relations in Bosnia', *Survival*, 38(4) (Winter 1996–7), 45–65.

NICOLAÏDIS, CALYPSO, 'East European Trade in the Aftermath of 1989: Did International Institutions Matter?', in Robert O. Keohane, Joseph S. Nye, and Stanley Hoffmann (eds.), *After the Cold War* (Cambridge, Mass. and London, 1993), 196–245.

NICOLL, SIR WILLIAM, 'Representing the States', in Andrew Duff, John Pinder, and Roy Pryce (eds.), *Maastricht and Beyond* (London and New York, 1994), 190–206.

NUTTALL, SIMON J., *European Political Co-operation* (Oxford, 1992).

—— 'The Institutional Network and the Instruments of Action', in Reinhardt Rummel (ed.), *Toward Political Union* (Baden-Baden, 1992), 61–81.

—— 'The Commission and Foreign Policy-making', in Geoffrey Edwards and David Spence (eds.), *The European Commission* (Harlow, 1994), 287–302.

—— 'The EC and Yugoslavia: *Deus ex Machina* or *Machina sine Deo*?', *Journal of Common Market Studies*, 32, Annual Review (Aug. 1994), 11–25.

—— 'External Political Relations of the European Community: Institutional Aspects, Evolution and Prospects—Comments', in René Lefeber (ed.), *Contemporary International Law Issues: Opportunities at a Time of Momentous Change* (Dordrecht and London, 1994), 76–82.

—— 'The European Commission's Internal Arrangements for Foreign Affairs and External Relations', *CFSP Forum*, 2/1995, 3–4.

—— 'The Commission: The Struggle for Legitimacy', in Christopher Hill (ed.), *The Actors in Europe's Foreign Policy* (London and New York, 1996), 130–47.

NYE, JOSEPH S., and KEOHANE, ROBERT O., 'The United States and International Institutions in Europe after the Cold War', in Robert O. Keohane, Joseph S. Nye, and Stanley Hoffmann (eds.), *After the Cold War* (Cambridge, Mass. and London, 1993), 104–26.

OWEN, DAVID, *Balkan Odyssey* (London, 1995).

PATERSON, WILLIAM E., 'Helmut Kohl, "The Vision Thing" and Escaping the

Semi-sovereignty Trap', in Clay Clemens and William E. Paterson (eds.), *The Kohl Chancellorship* (London and Portland, Ore. 1998), 17–36.

PEDERSEN, THOMAS, *European Union and the EFTA Countries: Enlargement and Integration* (London, 1994).

——*Germany, France and the Integration of Europe: A Realist Interpretation* (London and New York, 1998).

PELKMANS, JACQUES, and MURPHY, ANNA, 'Catapulted into Leadership: The Community Trade and Aid Policies vis-à-vis Eastern Europe', *Journal of European Integration*, 14(2–3), 125–51.

PENDERS, JEAN, and KWAST, MARJA, 'The Netherlands and Political Union', in Alfred Pijpers (ed.), *The European Community at the Crossroads* (Dordrecht, 1992), 253–70.

PIJPERS, ALFRED, 'The Netherlands: The Weakening Pull of Atlanticism', in Christopher Hill (ed.), *The Actors in Europe's Foreign Policy* (London and New York, 1996), 247–67.

RAMELOT, VINCENT, and REMACLE, ERIC, *L'OSCE et les conflits en Europe* (Brussels, 1995).

REGELSBERGER, ELFRIEDE, 'Reforming CFSP: An Alibi Debate or More?', in Spyros A. Pappas and Sophie Vanhoonacker (eds.), *The European Union's Common Foreign and Security Policy: The Challenges of the Future* (Maastricht, 1996), 93–118.

——'The Institutional Setup and Functioning of EPC/CFSP', in Elfriede Regelsberger, Philippe de Schoutheete de Tervarent, and Wolfgang Wessels (eds.), *Foreign Policy of the European Union* (Boulder, Colo. and London, 1997), 67–84.

——and WESSELS, WOLFGANG, 'The CFSP Institutions and Procedures: A Third Way for the Second Pillar', *European Foreign Affairs Review* 1 (1996), 29–54.

REMACLE, ERIC, *La Charte de Paris pour une nouvelle Europe*, GRIP Dossier No. 150–1, (Brussels, 1990).

——*Les Négociations sur la politique étrangère et de sécurité commune de la Communauté européenne*, Dossier GRIP No. 156 (Brussels, 1991).

——*L'UEO: européenne ou atlantique?* (Brussels, 1993).

RICHARDSON, LOUISE, 'British State Strategies after the Cold War', in Robert O. Keohane, Joseph S. Nye, and Stanley Hoffmann (eds.), *After the Cold War* (Cambridge, Mass. and London, 1993), 148–69.

ROSS, GEORGE, *Jacques Delors and European Integration* (Cambridge, 1995).

RUMMEL, REINHARDT, 'Beyond Maastricht: Alternative Futures for a Political Union', in Reinhardt Rummel (ed.), *Toward Political Union* (Baden-Baden, 1992), 297–319.

——'The CFSP's Conflict Prevention Policy', in Martin Holland (ed.), *Common Foreign and Security Policy* (London and Washington, DC, 1997), 105–19.

——'The Intergovernmental Conference 1996: How to Reform CFSP?', in Elfriede Regelsberger, Philippe de Schoutheete de Tervarent, and Wolfgang Wessels (eds.), *Foreign Policy of the European Union* (Boulder, Colo. and London, 1997), 363–81.

RUPNIK, JACQUES, 'La France de Mitterrand et les pays de l'Europe du Centre-Est', in Samy Cohen (ed.), *Mitterrand et la sortie de la guerre froide* (Paris, 1998), 189–216.

RYBA, BARBARA-CHRISTINE, 'La Politique étrangère et de sécurité commune (PESC): Mode d'emploi et bilan d'une année d'application (fin 1993/1994)', *Revue du Marché commun et de l'Union européenne*, 384 (Jan. 1995), 14–35.

SCHMALZ, UWE, 'The Amsterdam Provisions on External Coherence: Bridging the Union's Foreign Policy Dualism?', *European Foreign Affairs Review*, 3(3) (Autumn 1998), 421–42.

SCHNEIDER, HEINRICH, 'The Twelve/Fifteen's Conference Diplomacy: Has the CSCE/OSCE Remained a Successful Platform?', in Elfriede Regelsberger, Philippe de Schoutheete de Tervarent, and Wolfgang Wessels (eds.), *Foreign Policy of the European Union* (Boulder, Colo. and London, 1997), 237–61.

SEDELMAIER, ULRICH, and WALLACE, HELEN, 'Policies towards Central and Eastern Europe', in Helen Wallace and William Wallace (eds.), *Policy-Making in the European Union*, 3rd edn. (Oxford, 1996), 353–87.

SHULTZ, GEORGE P., *Turmoil and Triumph: My Years as Secretary of State* (New York, 1993).

SILBER, LAURA, and LITTLE, ALLAN, *The Death of Yugoslavia* (London, 1995).

SMITH, HAZEL, *European Union Foreign Policy and Central America* (Basingstoke and London, 1995).

SMITH, KAREN E., *The Making of EU Foreign Policy: The Case of Eastern Europe* (Basingstoke and London, 1999).

SPENCE, ARNHILD, and SPENCE, DAVID, 'The CFSP from Maastricht to Amsterdam', in Kjell A. Eliassen (ed.), *Foreign and Security Policy in the European Union* (London and New Delhi, 1998), 43–58.

SPENCE, DAVID, *Enlargement without Accession: The EC's Response to German Unification*, RIIA Discussion Paper No. 36 (London, 1991). (A shorter version appears as 'Die Verhandlungen der Europäischen Gemeinschaft', in Wolfgang Heisenberg (ed.), *Die Vereinigung Deutschlands in Europäischer Perspektive* (Baden-Baden, 1992), 29–51.)

SZABO, STEPHEN F., *The Diplomacy of German Unification* (New York, 1992).

TELTSCHIK, HORST, *329 Tage: Innenansichten der Einigung* (Berlin, 1991).

THATCHER, MARGARET, *The Downing Street Years* (London, 1993).

—— *The Collected Speeches*, ed. Robin Harris (London, 1997).

TORREBLANCA PAYÁ, JOSÉ IGNACIO, *The European Community and Central Eastern Europe (1989–1993): Foreign Policy and Decision-Making* (Madrid, 1997).

TREVERTON, GREGORY F., *America, Germany, and the Future of Europe* (Princeton, NJ, 1992).

TRIFUNOVSKA, SNEŽANA, *Yugoslavia through Documents: From its Creation to its Dissolution* (Dordrecht, 1994).

UETA, TAKAKO, 'The Stability Pact: From the Balladur Initiative to the EU Joint Action', in Martin Holland (ed.), *Common Foreign and Security Policy* (London and Washington, DC, 1997), 92–104.

URBAN, GEORGE R., *Diplomacy and Disillusion at the Court of Margaret Thatcher: An Insider's View* (London and New York, 1996).

VAN DEN BROEK, HANS, 'CFSP: The View of the European Commission', in Spyros A. Pappas and Sophie Vanhoonacker (eds.), *The European Union's Common Foreign and Security Policy: The Challenges of the Future* (Maastricht, 1996), 23–30.

VAN EEKELEN, WILLEM, *Debating European Security* (The Hague, 1998).

VAN HAM, PETER, *The EC, Eastern Europe and European Unity* (London and New York, 1993).

VAN WIJNBERGEN, CHRISTA, 'Germany and European Political Union', in Finn Laursen and Sophie Vanhoonacker (eds.), *The Intergovernmental Conference on Political Union* (Maastricht, 1992), 49–61.

—— 'Ireland and the Ratification of the Maastricht Treaty', in Finn Laursen and Sophie Vanhoonacker (eds.), *The Ratification of the Maastricht Treaty* (Dordrecht, 1994), 181–93.

VÉDRINE, HUBERT, *Les Mondes de François Mitterrand* (Paris, 1996).

WALLANDER, CELESTE E., and PROKOP, JANE E., 'Soviet Security Strategies towards Europe: After the Wall, with their Backs Up Against It', in Robert O. Keohane, Joseph S. Nye, and Stanley Hoffmann (eds.), *After the Cold War* (Cambridge, Mass. and London, 1993), 63–103.

WESTER, ROBERT, 'The Netherlands and European Political Union', in Finn Laursen and Sophie Vanhoonacker (eds.), *The Intergovernmental Conference on Political Union* (Maastricht, 1992), 163–76.

WESTLAKE, MARTIN, *The Passage through the Community's Legislative System of Emergency Measures related to German Unification*, EUI Working Paper EPU No. 92/14 (San Domenico, 1992).

—— *The Council of the European Union* (London, 1995).

WOODWARD, SUSAN L., *Balkan Tragedy* (Washington, DC, 1995).

WYNAENDTS, HENRY, *L'Engrenage: chroniques yougoslaves juillet 1991–août 1992* (Paris, 1993).

YOUNG, HUGO, *This Blessed Plot* (London, 1998).

ZELIKOW, PHILIP, and RICE, CONDOLEEZZA, *Germany Unified and Europe Transformed: A Study in Statecraft*, 1st paperback edn. (Cambridge, Mass. and London, 1997).

INDEX